RESEARCH IN
THE SOCIOLOGY
OF WORK

WORK AND FAMILY

Series Editor: RANDY HODSON
Department of Sociology
The Ohio State University

Volume Editor: TOBY L. PARCEL
Department of Sociology
The Ohio State University

VOLUME 7 • 1999

JAI PRESS INC.
Stamford, Connecticut

ISBN: 0-7623-0605-X
ISSN: 0277-2833

Transferred to Digital Printing 2006

RESEARCH IN THE SOCIOLOGY OF WORK

Volume 7 • 1999

WORK AND FAMILY

CONTENTS

LIST OF CONTRIBUTORS

Pamela Aronson   Department of Sociology
Indiana University

George Cave   Child Trends
Washington, DC

Ann C. Crouter   Department of Human
Development and Family Studies
The Pennsylvania State University

Heather Helms-Erikson   Department of Human
Development and Family Studies
The Pennsylvania State University

Erin L. Kelly   Department of Sociology
Princeton University

Michele Kozimor-King   Department of Sociology
The Pennsylvania State University

Kevin T. Leicht   Department of Sociology
The University of Iowa

Carrie T. Mariner   Child Trends
Washington, DC

Mary C. Maquire   Department of Human
Development and Family Studies
The Pennsylvania State University

Susan M. McHale   Department of Human
Development and Family Studies
The Pennsylvania State University

Sharon M. McGroder   Child Trends
Washington, DC

Phyllis Moen   Cornell Employment and Family
Careers Institute
Cornell University

Toby L. Parcel   Department of Sociology
                                     The Ohio State University

Mary Ann Powell   Department of Sociology
                                     The Ohio State University

Stacy J. Rogers   Department of Sociology
                                     University of Nebraska-Lincoln

Joanne C. Sandberg   Department of Sociology
                                     Vanderbilt University

Kristine M. Witkowski   Institute for Women's Policy
                                         Research
                                     Washington, DC

Yan Tu   Department of Anthropology and
                                         Sociology
                                     Grand Valley State University

Martha Zaslow   Child Trends
                                     Washington, DC

INTRODUCTION
WORK AND FAMILY

Toby L. Parcel

The nexus of work and family continues to generate strong interest among researchers as well as policymakers and citizens. Such interest is motivated by important questions regarding the challenges and opportunities families and societies face in meeting the needs of these two institutions. Changes in the our attitudes regarding adult roles have combined with changing choices by family members for combining paid work and family life. For many families, the result is a "balancing act" that brings rewards as well as concerns. Employers and governments struggle with whether and how to assist in achieving balance. Researchers attempt to understand these changes, and to determine the conditions under which the needs of both institutions can be met.

It is a privilege to contribute to this ongoing conversation by bringing to the academic audience the most current research regarding work and family. In this volume, ten chapters treat various facets of the work-family nexus. In addition, each chapter conveys something about social policy as it affects the connections between these two critical institutions. Taken together, the papers represent current thinking regarding advantages and challenges of combining work and family, and suggest directions for social policies that might make the "juggling act" easier.

The first paper "Parental Work, Family Size and Social Capital Effects on Early Adolescent Educational Outcomes: The United States and Great Britain Compared," by Mary Ann Powell and Toby L. Parcel, relies on a classic finding as a basis for innovation. They use the negative relationship between family size and educational outcomes as a point of departure. They then ask whether the effects of both maternal and paternal work moderate the relationships between family size and student math and reading achievement, and whether dimensions of social capital not tapped by parental work play an analogous role. They further pose these questions across two societies, the United States and Great Britain, thus allowing us to consider the extent to which societal context can affect key findings. They use data from two large national surveys: *The National Educational Longitudinal Study of 1988* (NELS 88) for the United States, and the British child data from the 1991 wave of the National Child Development Survey. Their findings suggest that, regarding social capital, parental aspirations for the child to obtain higher levels of education and the child's own reading for enjoyment are strong predictors of higher math and reading assessment scores in both countries. The authors find that both sibsize and work/family variables are more important to the educational outcomes in the United States than in Great Britain. They speculate that the more developed welfare state in Great Britain may provide supports that mitigate against some of the negative effects of single parent families and larger family sizes that we find in the United States. A well developed welfare state may render less important the role of family social capital or family financial resources in predicting student achievement. This hypothesis deserves replication with data from other countries as a vehicle for policy formulations and further understanding the relationships among parental work, family size and student achievement.

Ann Crouter, Mary Maguire, Heather Helms-Erikson and Susan McHale, in the second paper, "Parental Work in Middle Childhood: Links between Employment and the Division of Household, Parent-Child Activities and Parental Monitoring," identify the crucial role that parental monitoring plays in working parents' fulfilling their responsibilities towards children aged 6-11 years. Their paper reports a piece of a larger research project looking at parents' work-related temporal availability, relative resources, and the division of labor in the home. As children leave early childhood behind, parental time spent in monitoring their physical well-being and providing direct physical care declines. Instead, parents are required to spend more time in monitoring children's activities to assure that these activities are promoting, rather than hindering, parental values, and in supervising children from a distance. The authors' data base consists of 203 two-parent, primarily dual earner families with eldest children in the fourth and fifth grades coming from 16 school districts in central Pennsylvania. Data are longitudinal over three years, with interviews from both parents and children. The authors find that mothers' work hours are a significant factor in determining their relative share of parental monitoring; longer work hours are associated with lower proportional shares of maternal monitoring. Additional analyses reveal that his pattern holds for sons, but not for daughters. Their findings inform policies and practices at the micro level of family interaction. Parents should be aware of the importance of parental monitoring, and recognize that there may be a trade-off between parental work time and time needed for monitoring children. The findings suggest that this relationship is significant for working mothers' monitoring of sons but not daughters. Boys may require additional attention from working mothers that daughters do not; this finding is also worthy of replication.

In the third paper, Pamela Aronson's "The Balancing Act: Young Women's Expectations and Experiences of Work and Family" directs attention to what young women expect regarding their future balancing of work of family obligations, compared to what those who had become mothers are actually experiencing. The data come from the Youth Development Study survey data, itself a longitudinal study, later followed up with interviews with 42 female respondents from the original survey. The findings suggest that rosy expectations are not matched by the realities the mothers actually experience. The study suggests that historical changes in the life course have created difficult issues for contemporary young women on the threshold of adulthood. The respondents take a wide variety of approaches to balancing work and family. Aronson acknowledges that the two groups of women might be inherently different. Those who had postponed motherhood might have well-developed orientations towards planning, which might allow them to more easily balance work and family obligations in the future. However, it is still likely that even these women hold unrealistic expectations regarding the ease with which these obligations can be balanced. Class background differences might also contribute to these findings. Policy implications from these findings include the advisability of supporting young people so that they can complete their schooling. With schooling completed, young adults should be in a better position to balance work and family demands.

Michele Kozimor-King and Kevin Leicht study long term attitude change regarding work and family in the fourth paper, "Sources of Convergence and Divergence in Attitudes About Work and Family Roles among Women." We already know that gender role attitudes are changing in support of women in the paid labor force. This paper examines changes in women's attitudes towards work and family roles using data from the General Social Survey between 1977 and 1994. Thus, their data source is longitudinal, consisting of successive, representative cross sections of survey respondents across those years. They expand on previous studies by focussing on age, life course and occupational differences in attitude change. Although they find a liberalizing trend in almost all subsamples, attitude change is especially large among older women, married women, and women in non-traditional occupations. Education and age exert the largest effects on attitude change, and younger women's attitudes change less with marriage and changes in income and education. Their results suggest that significant attitude change accompanies the adoption of non-traditional occupational roles. The findings also suggest that there are growing subgroups of women whose attitudes toward gender roles are moving in the same direction, albeit at different speeds and from different points of departure. These findings provide greater foundation for inferring what policy changes the public is likely to support in the years ahead. Burstein and Wierzbicki (1999) argue that congressional legislation regarding gender, work and family is heavily influenced by public opinion regarding work and family roles. Kozimor-King and Leicht's findings suggest that such legislation might move in the direction of providing support for adults struggling with work and family balance, provided that these results for women are also mirrored, at least to some extent, by similar changes among men.

In the fifth paper, Phyllis Moen and Yan Yu take an optimistic approach to the challenges involved in adults meeting work and family obligations simultaneously in "Having It All: Overall Work/Life Success in Two Earner Families." They develop models to predict the odds of working couples managing well both at home and at work. They use survey data from the *National Study of the Changing Workforce*, as well as qualitative data from focus groups and interviews from respondents participating in the Cornell Couples and Careers Study. The analysis focuses on dual earner couples; models predicting success in both domains are supplemented by analyses regarding how these couples define successfulness subjectively. They find that stage of the life cycle is an important predictor of feeling successful for both men and women; specifically, those with preschoolers are least likely to report success in managing both work and family. Having a supportive supervisor, having some job security, and having both spouses work normal hours also predicted success. When one spouse consistently worked overtime hours, neither spouse reported feeling successful. Factors traditionally assumed to reduce work/life conflict including job demands, job autonomy, and work schedule flexibility were unrelated to overall work/life success. Both men and women perceive that personal satisfaction defines success at work, while having good relationships at home and spending time with family were key to perceiving success in home life. Variations in the frequency these themes were mentioned by gender and by life stage help to refine the overall conclusions. These findings suggest that job arrangements involving long work hours, lack of job security, and unsupportive supervisors are likely to cause dual earning couples to perceive that they are not managing both work and family well. Changes within thousands of individual firms would be needed to effect change on these dimensions. Combinations of employers' policies as well as attitudes of supervisors could be helpful in promoting feelings of work/life success among dual earner couples.

Stacy Rogers is also concerned with satisfaction among working adults in "The Nexus of Job Satisfaction, Marital Satisfaction and Individual Well-Being: Does Marriage Order Matter?" Her key contribution to this conversation is to consider whether marriage order is a conditioning factor in influencing adult well-being. Specifically, Rogers examines the direct and interactive effects of job satisfaction and marital satisfaction on the well-being of adults in both first marriages and remarriages. The data come from a four-wave panel survey of marital quality and family life, the *Marital Instability Over the Life Course Study* begun in 1980, with follow up interviews in 1983, 1988 and 1992. A sample of 1,122 individuals from the 1983 wave of the study was used in analyses. The results indicate that both marital satisfaction and job satisfaction are significant predictors of adult well-being among both first-married and remarried individuals. Job satisfaction is more important among men than women, although marital satisfaction is more strongly associated with well-being for both men and women, particularly among remarried individuals. Key interactive findings include the fact that greater satisfaction in one domain acts as a buffer against the negative effects of lower satisfaction in the other domain. These findings should be useful to family life educators and counselors in advising individuals and families regarding strategies to promote adult well-being. Employers might use this information to promote employee assistance programs that focus on employee counseling regarding these issues.

The following two papers direct our attention to the formation of family policies in work establishments. In the seventh, Erin Kelly provides a rich account of the conditions that lead firms to adopt family friendly policies in "Theorizing Corporate Family Policies: How Advocates Built 'The Business Case' for 'Family-Friendly' Programs." She poses three questions: Which actors have promoted corporate family policies? What arguments have these advocates invoked to legitimate change? How successful have these advocates and arguments been in effecting policy change? She uses multiple methods to address these questions including analysis of work and family articles from *The New York Times* and *The Wall Street Journal*, analysis of reports written by work-family advocates, interviews with human resource managers in the Northeast, and results from a survey of United States employers focussing on corporate family policies. Her findings suggest that work family specialists, business leaders and government officials have developed a business case for a variety of corporate family policies. The business case argues that these programs help firms attract, retain and manage a productive workforce. Although these arguments attempt to legitimate supportive family policies, advocates have only been moderately successful in having such policies be implemented among firms. Such "theorization" may be effective only when the advocates are powerful professionals or corporate coalitions. This may be particularly true because the business case ignores widely held beliefs regarding the privacy of family life and the primacy of work careers. Widespread attitude change may be necessary before such corporate family policies are more widely adopted.

"Becoming Family Friendly: Work-Family Program Innovation Among the Largest U.S. Corporations," written by Kristine Witkowski, continues this theme by examining work-family program innovation among the largest corporations in the United States. Using data collected from a sample of 188 of the top ranking Fortune 1000 companies, she investigates how boundary-spanning units, organizational approaches to problem-solving, and the organizational life-cycle affect the institutionalization of work-family programs. Information from archives as well as a mail survey supplement data collected from *The Corporate Reference Guide to Work-Family Programs* survey. Discrete-time event history analyses show how these factors affect innovation between 1974 and 1995. Findings suggest that the innovative effects of integrative problem-solving consistently influence various dimensions of work-family programs. Program innovation is more likely when there is female-representation on corporate governing boards and where women are present in key management and human resource occupations. Similarly, total quality management, communication programs and matrix management structures promote innovation. Taken together, these two chapters suggest a number of structural conditions that are likely to facilitate firm innovation regarding family-friendly work policies. In addition, each makes contributions to the organizational literature by studying the conditions under which organizations adopt innovations.

In the next paper we turn to studying the relationship between a single family-support program and child well-being. In "Maternal Employment and Child Outcomes Among Families with Some History of Welfare Receipt," Martha Zaslow, Sharon McGroder, George Cave and Carrie Mariner are motivated by the 1996 Personal Responsibility and Work Opportunity Reconciliation Act to wonder whether moving many families off of welfare will have deleterious effects on child outcomes. They use the Child Outcomes Study of the *National Evaluation of Welfare-to-Work Strategies* (NEWWS). Families in one research site, Atlanta, Georgia, were selected for the analyses reported here; further, the studied respondents were in a control group of a larger study investigating the effects of the JOBS program and were all African American. This sample includes 386 families, each with a preschool age child at the time of the first child evaluation, as well as data two years later. Data on the children include measures of cognition as well as behavioral adjustment. The findings suggest that children of the employed mothers have a more favorable developmental profile than the children of unemployed mothers on four of the five outcome measures considered. These children appear stronger in terms of school readiness, behavioral adjustment, and in terms of physical health. Multivariate analyses suggest, however, that pre-existing differences between employed and non-employed mothers on socio-demographic characteristics of the mothers and/or family are responsible for these effects. These findings suggest caution in inferences regarding favorable effects of maternal employment on children among welfare-eligible populations. Children of those mothers who leave welfare voluntarily are likely more advantaged than those who leave because of changes in program eligibility.

In the last paper, "The Effects of Family Obligations and Workplace Resources on Men's and Women's Use of Family Leaves," Joanne Sandberg studies the effects of the *1993 Family and Medical Leave Act* (FLMA) on actual leave taking behavior. Although close to one half of the workforce is eligible for such leaves, we do not know what factors influence the decision to take advantage of this family friendly policy. The study uses the Family and Medical leave Commission's 1995 national survey of employees that over-samples leave-takers and those who need leaves. Multinomial logistic regression of 1,033 men and 1,155 women is used to analyze the effects of family obligations and workplace resources on the odds of employees taking leaves from work. The results indicate that family obligations have significant effects on both men's and women's use of family leaves.

Workplace resources, however, are better predictors of men's use of family leaves than women's use of family leaves. In particular, larger workplace size and being a salaried employee positively affect men's leave taking behavior, with workplace size effects possibly working through lengthier paid vacations and higher numbers of sick days. These findings suggest that firms with greater resources may enable male employees to take family leaves, which, in turn, promote greater work-family balance at home.

Taken together, these papers have provided important new insights into the work-family nexus. Many of them use longitudinal data to derive important inferences regarding attitude change, the relationships among work, family and life satisfaction, and the determinants of child well-being. They all engage in thinking about work-family policy, either in suggesting how policies are created, in what policies' effects might be, or in suggesting specific policy directions and practices for firms and families to consider. I hope that these chapters also provide intellectual inspiration to other researchers interested in the intersection of these two important institutions.

In editing this volume, my job was aided by several colleagues I acknowledge here. I am grateful to Randy Hodson who offered me the opportunity to edit this volume. I have truly benefited from studying a wide variety of literature in the work and family area, and from his wise advice regarding the editorial process. Mikaela Dufur provided skilled editorial and research assistance, while Linda Shannon and Judy Woodall ably assisted with a variety of clerical tasks. I thank all of them for their assistance and support.

REFERENCES

Burstein, P., and S. Wierzbicki. 1999. "Public Opinion and Congressional Action on Work, Family and Gender, 1945-1990." In *Work and Family: Research Informing Policy,* edited by T. L. Parcel and D. B. Cornfield. Thousand Oaks, CA: Sage.

Toby L. Parcel
Volume Editor

PARENTAL WORK, FAMILY SIZE AND SOCIAL CAPITAL EFFECTS ON EARLY ADOLESCENT EDUCATIONAL OUTCOMES:
THE UNITED STATES AND GREAT BRITAIN COMPARED

Mary Ann Powell and Toby L. Parcel

ABSTRACT

It is well known that children from larger families tend to have lower levels of educational attainment. Research in both the United States and Great Britain demonstrates this relationship (Blake 1989; Fogelman 1983). This paper asks whether this relationship is modified by parental work and whether this relationship varies across the two societies. Increasing proportions of mothers in the United States are working full time while their children are young; in Britain,

Research in the Sociology of Work, Volume 7, pages 1-30.

maternal work is largely a part-time phenomenon. The authors hypothesize that, holding father's work constant, relative to mothers who work full time, children of mothers who work part time may show educational advantages even when they come from larger families. The authors develop these ideas using Coleman's arguments regarding family social capital as an explanatory construct. The authors use data from two large, national surveys: the *National Education Longitudinal Study* of 1988 (NELS 1988) for the United States, and the British Child data from the 1991 wave of the *National Child Development Study*. The authors find that both sibsize and work/family variables are more important to the outcomes in the United States than in Great Britain. In Britain, the work/family variables are not significant for either math or reading assessment outcomes, except that children in mother-only families score lower in math than those from two-parent families. Among the social capital variables, parental aspirations for the child to obtain higher levels of education and the child's own reading for enjoyment are strong predictors of higher math and reading assessment scores in both countries. Other social capital and family resource variables are important for these outcomes, as well. By providing a direct and detailed comparison of the attainment processes in Britain and the United States, this study enhances our understanding of the ways in which parental work and family choices affect children's lives, and helps clarify which effects are due to family characteristics and which are influenced by societal context.

INTRODUCTION

Children from smaller families have higher levels of educational attainment in both the United States (Blake 1989) and Great Britain (Fogelman 1983). In modern societies, education is a key resource for social mobility that may provide opportunity or perpetuate inequality. Knowledge about the educational attainment process is critical to understanding inequality. In this paper we ask whether the relationships between family size and achievement test scores, predictive of later educational outcomes, are modified by parental work and whether these relationships vary across the two societies. Fathers in both societies are typically employed when children are young. In contrast, maternal work patterns vary cross-culturally. Specifically, increasing proportions of mothers in the United States are working full time while their children are young; in Britain, maternal work is largely a part-time phenomenon. Will effects of maternal work vary across these societies because of these different work patterns? We also consider the role that several forms of family social capital may have in modifying the traditional relationships, and whether social capital operates similarly in both countries.

FAMILY SIZE, FAMILY STRUCTURE AND SOCIAL CAPITAL

We derive theoretical guidance from several sources. An important literature demonstrates the fundamental relationship between increased family size and weaker educational outcomes. Both Blake (1989) and Downey (1995) show that adolescent achievement test scores are lower when children come from larger families. Blake (1989) also demonstrates a negative relationship between family size and total years of schooling, and Steelman and Powell (1991) show a similar relationship with parental willingness to pay for higher education. Their analyses point to resource dilution as the explanation for the key negative relationship. Family size effects on attainment have been documented in Britain as well as the United States. Fogelman (1983) studied the respondents of the *National Child Development Study* at ages 7, 11, and 16 and found that the children with 2 or more siblings scored lower on both math and reading attainment at ages 7 and 11. He further found that children with 2 or more siblings had relatively lower gains in math and reading scores by age 11 than those from families with 1 or 2 children. By age 16, higher numbers of older children in the household had a stronger negative effect on test scores than higher numbers of younger children.

We are curious to know whether this relationship is modified by maternal work. On the one hand, maternal work brings additional material resources to the household that may facilitate educational attainment of the young. Greater financial resources may enable children to stay in school longer, or to avoid working while in school, thus devoting more time to school work and promoting greater academic achievement. Greater material resources may also allow parents to enrich their home environments to further support children's academic achievement by purchasing books, educational aids, special lessons or personal computers.

At the same time, such employment typically removes mothers from the home, thus reducing the amount of time and attention they can devote to building family and community social capital. Following this argument, James Coleman's analyses of social capital and its role in the socialization process provide a second source of theoretical guidance. Coleman (1988, 1990) notes that family background consists of: (1) financial capital, (2) human capital (parental cognitive skills and educational attainment), and (3) social capital. The first two elements of this trichotomy have long histories of theory and research in economics. The concept of social capital is derived from the work of Coleman and others in sociology (see Portes 1998, for a review). Specifically, social capital inheres in the structure of relations between and among actors. In the context of the family, social capital includes the time and effort that parents actually spend on their children. Stronger bonds between parents and children are a form of social capital that demands both the physical presence of parents and their attention and involvement. Such parental investment is not perfectly related to parents' socioeconomic status, and thus cannot be adequately captured by traditional measures of earnings and parental schooling in models of child outcomes. Coleman argues that unless parents use their economic resources and human capital as resources in their parental roles, child socialization may suffer. Parents with more meager resources themselves may still efficiently use them in the child-rearing process, with attendant positive effects on child outcomes.

Coleman and others worry, however, that maternal labor force participation will limit the social capital needed to effectively transmit norms and behavior patterns across generations (Coleman 1990; Piotrkowski, Rapoport and Rapoport 1987; Voydanoff 1987). Part of the association may be due to reduced time that mothers will have both to establish bonds with children and to use those bonds in conveying appropriate social behaviors and providing support for cognitive attainment. Part of the association may be due to reduced time she spends in the local community, with attendant reductions in contributing to the web of interactions it represents and drawing upon its resources in the interests of her children. Although some researchers provide negative evidence regarding these hypotheses and also raise the issue of how paternal working conditions may be affecting child outcomes (Parcel and Menaghan 1994a, 1994b), the idea that family social capital promotes child well-being is a compelling one. Coleman is less clear on whether such employment will weaken the emotional bonds between mothers and children. Some might argue that when mothers invest in the "purposive" structure of the paid work world, parent-child emotional bonds may suffer, independent of the amount of time the two spend together. This may be the case even if the sheer quantity of parent-child time is the major determinant of the intensity of these relationships.

These two strands of thinking unite nicely in Downey's (1995) work regarding why family size effects on educational outcomes are negative. Downey demonstrates that family social capital and family economic resources contribute importantly to explaining the key relationship. As family size increases, such resources become diffused more thinly across more children. Such reasoning suggests that family capital is key to promoting child educational outcomes. Those families, of whatever size, with greater stores of social and financial capital will have children who score better on standardized tests of achievement, one precursor to educational achievement itself.

It is important to recognize that family structure also has an impact on educational outcomes; again, family structure may affect availability and or effectiveness of social capital, economic resources, or both. Research shows that growing up in a single- versus a two-parent family reduces the resources available to children, with attendant negative effects on both academic and social outcomes (McLanahan and Sandefur 1994). We can expect this effect to be exacerbated for larger families where resources are further diluted.

We expect, then, large family size and non-intact family status will have negative effects on child academic achievement. These effects may be due to reduced material resources, reduced social capital or both. Given that maternal work may increase material resources but reduce family social capital, controlling for maternal work may modify these expected relationships. But how might these processes vary cross-culturally?

GREAT BRITAIN AND THE
UNITED STATES COMPARED

Although comparisons of attainment processes in the United States and Britain are rare, they are logical and important to our understanding of how variations in social institutions affect people's lives. Britain and the United States are similar in many ways, such as levels of industrial development and democratic forms of government. In both societies children begin school around age 5 or 6, and continue schooling through the mid-teen years (Kerckhoff 1990). But key differences in major institutions exist that might modify these relationships. The educational tracking system is more formalized in Britain than in the United States. Although this has changed in recent years, many of today's adults grew up in a system in which students were explicitly tracked into academic ability groups from early ages. Kerchkoff (1990, 1993) uses the *National Child Development Study*, a longitudinal survey of a 1958 birth cohort in Great Britain, to study educational attainment at several ages. He demonstrates that family background was important for ability group placement and this placement affected subsequent achievement. Turner (1960) characterizes the educational tracking system in Great Britain as one of "sponsored mobility," in which elite status is awarded based on some merit criterion and therefore cannot be claimed via effort alone. Once children are on an educational track, they remain relatively advantaged or disadvantaged throughout their educational careers. In contrast, he characterizes the educational system in the United States as one of "contest mobility" where participants achieve based on their own efforts. Although it would be inappropriate to view this distinction as a strict dichotomy, differences in educational institutions across societies may affect the relationship between family size and educational outcomes. The relatively tracked educational system may dilute the effects of family structure on educational attainment in Britain, while the sequential "contests" in the United States may leave children more vulnerable to the effects of family structure and resources.

In addition, there are differences in maternal work across these two societies that might also modify the key relationships we are studying, with part-time work being more common among British mothers than full-time work (Ward, Dale and Joshi 1996). Part-time workers in Britain have some advantages that are not enjoyed by United States part-time workers, including slightly higher wage rates compared to full-time workers and stronger employment protection laws than in the United States. Unlike United States part-time workers, who seldom have health insurance, the British have health care coverage through the National

Health Care system (Houseman 1996). Part-time jobs were created for women in Britain specifically to help solve problems in the interface between work and the family (Joshi 1996). This lends a stability and permanence to the part-time employment situations of women. A comparison between Britain and the United States will clarify whether societal context is important in the trade-off between earning more money through full-time work and giving children more parental time. The prevalence of part-time maternal work may help British children, who may have more access to their mothers' time relative to American children whose mothers are more likely to work longer hours.

Our strategy, then, is to take the well-known, negative empirical relationship between family size and educational achievement and evaluate how it changes when potentially modifying variables are introduced into the models. In this research, we focus on parental work and measure dimensions of maternal and paternal work separately. We also assess the role of other aspects of family social capital. We then evaluate how this new model may vary cross culturally. These variations will suggest how institutional structures that differ between Britain and the United States may have differing implications for children's lives.

DATA AND METHODS

We use data from two large, national surveys: the *National Education Longitudinal Study of 1988* (NELS:88) for the United States, and the British Child data from the 1991 wave of the *National Child Development Study* (NCDS). We use the NELS:88 because it provides a rich and detailed source of variables that indicate family social and economic capital (Downey 1995). We then select variables from the British Child data to capture similar concepts. These two data sets allow comparisons between children in the United States and Britain who are at similar transition points in their educational development at a similar point in time historically.

The NELS:88 is a nationally representative survey of schools and students in the United States. This data set is collected by the National Center for Education Statistics and is designed to assist in the development and examination of federal education policy, with particular interest in the role of parents in their children's education (Ingels et al. 1994). The study used a two-stage stratified probability sampling design that first sampled public and private schools in the United States ($n = 1,052$) and then selected a random set of eighth-grade students from those schools. In the base year (1988), a total of 24,599 students participated. The study collected information from students, their parents, their teachers and their schools and includes detailed accounts of the students' family backgrounds, their relationships with their parents, their parents' work situations, and their performance in school, including math and reading assessments.

In this study, we selected respondents from the base year of the study who have both math and reading assessment scores. In order to determine the effects of parental work hours on school performance, we further select those whose parents or step-parents filled out questionnaires giving their own and their spouse's work status. Because of our interest in family resources, including social capital, available in the home, we limit our sample to students who lived with the parental respondent at least half of the time. These restrictions result in a sample of 21,039 eighth grade students.

For the British sample, we use data on the children of the 1958 cohort of the *National Child Development Study* (NCDS), a nationally representative survey of all of the children born during the week of March 3-9, 1958, in Great Britain. In 1991, the children of the 1958 cohort were administered a child outcomes survey with questions similar to the NELS:88. The original respondents were followed at several time points during their childhood and were assessed in 1991 at age 33. At that time, a random sample of one-third of the original respondents was selected for further study of their family patterns, with information gathered from spouses and partners and a special mother and child component, including all natural or adopted children of this random one-in-three sample of the cohort. This part of the survey was funded by the United States National Institute of Child Health and Development and was carried out by the Social Statistics Research Unit at City University in London. The study collected information from the children and their mothers, as well as math and reading assessments. Because the original respondents have been followed since birth, detailed accounts of the children's family backgrounds and their parents' work situations are available.

In this study, we use a subsample of respondents' children between the ages of 10 and 14. This allows us to study a sample of British children who are nearing or have reached a transition point in their education that is similar to the transition to high school that American students accomplish around age 14. Because some families have more than one child in this age group, we select the oldest child in each family. In order to determine the effects of parental work hours on school performance, we further select those whose parents or step-parents filled out questionnaires giving their own and their spouse's work status. All children in our sample live in the same household with the respondent. These restrictions result in a sample of 647 ten- to fourteen-year-olds.[1]

Variables

Table 1 lists the concepts we represented by specific variables from the two data sets. The dependent variables are not directly comparable across the NCDS and the NELS:88. For the NELS:88, we used scores that are standardized to a mean of 50 with a standard deviation of 10. Item response theory was used to estimate correct answers on test items. The NELS:88 provides these scores to allow compari-

Table 1. Concepts with Measures from the NELS:88 and NCDS

Concept	Variable	NELS:88 Measures	NCDS Measures
Dependent Variables:			
Reading test scores	Reading	Standardized Reading Score	PIAT Reading Recognition Score US Percentile
Math test scores	Math	Standardized Math Score	PIAT Math Score US Percentile
Family Background Variables:			
Number of children in the family	Sibsize	Number of children in the family, child's report, range 1 to 6+	Same as NELS:88
Gender	Female	Sex of student, Coded 1 female, 0 male.	Same as NELS:88.
Race	White, Black, Mexican Hispanic, Other Hispanic, Asian, Native American	Dummy variables for race by categories: White, Black, Mexican Hispanic, Other Hispanic, Asian, Native American. White is contrast category.	
	White, Non-White		Dummy variables for race in two categories: White and non-white. White is the contrast.
Parental education	Less than high school High school Some college College degree Masters degree Doctoral degree	Dummy variable based on parent's report of educational achievement. Represented by the highest level of education achieved by either parent: no high school diploma, high school diploma (contrast category), some college, college degree, master's degree, doctorate.	

Dummy variables of parental report of educational achievement represented by the highest educational attainment of either parent. From 0-5, with 0 representing no qualifications, 1 some qualifications, 2 O levels, 3 A levels, 4 higher education, and 5 degree. The dummy variables are based on five levels of national vocations qualifications (NVQs) and include miriad qualification levels that approximate the levels mentioned above. Spouse education was roughly estimated based on the number of years they remained in school.

No qualifications
Some qualifications
0 level qualifications
A level qualification
Higher education
College degree

Same as NELS:88.

Interactions constructed to capture combinations of Parents' work hours and family structure.

Note:
The NELS:88 defines full time work as 35 hours/week or more.
The NCDS defines full time work as 30 hours/ week or more.

Twoparent DadFtMomFt	Two parent*Dad Ft*Mom Ft work hours
Twoparent DadFtMomPt	Two parent*Dad Ft*Mom Pt work hours (contrast category)
Twoparent DadFtMomNo	Two parent*Dad Ft*Mom no work hours
Twoparent DadLoMomFt	Two parent*Dad lo/no*Mom Ft
Twoparent DadLoMomPt	Two parent*Dad lo/no*Mom Pt
Twoparent DadLoMomNo	Two parent*Dad lo/no*Mom no work hrs
OnlyDadFt	Dad only*Dad full time work hours
OnlyDadLo	Dad only*Dad low or no work hours
OnlyMomFt	Mom only*Mom full time work hours
OnlyMomPt	Mom only*Mom part time work hours
OnlyMomNo	Mom only*Mom no work hours
Missing Work/Family	Missing on family status or work variables
Other Adult	Dummy variable for other adult in household

9

(continued)

Table 1 (Continued)

Concept	Variable	NELS:88 Measures	NCDS Measures
Dependent Variables:			
Reading test scores	Reading	Standardized Reading Score	PIAT Reading Recognition Score US Percentile
Math test scores	Math	Standardized Math Score	PIAT Math Score US Percentile
Parental occupational status	Unemployed, Manual, Nonprofessional, Lower professional, Professional, Missing Occ. Status	Parental report of occupations converted to five status categories including unemployed or unskilled, manual, nonprofessional (secretary, salesperson), lower professional (manager, nurse), professional (physician, lawyer). Family status represents the highest occupational status of either parent.	Same as NELS:88.
Family income	Family income	Parental report of total family income from all sources for 1987. Income given in ranges, coded to the midpoint. Dollars.	Parental report of earnings in 1991. Pounds. Respondent plus partner net earnings.
Family Resources:			
Involvement in school activities and/or planning	Frequency of talk about school	Frequency student has talked to parents about selecting courses, things studied in class, school activities, or mother or father about planning high school program. Range 0-10.	
	# School involvements		Number of school involvements reported by the mother in the last 12 months. Includes parents meeting, school events, discuss child, join in school day, organize activities, fund-raising. Range 0-6.

10

Parental investment in child's education	Money saved for college	Parents' report of the amount of money saved for child's educational future. Dollars.
	Ways parent chose school	The number of reasons parent selected child's school for other than because they had no choice or it was nearby. Range 0-4. Positive reasons include religion, atmosphere/teachers, other children, academic reputation, pupil/teacher ratio.
Parents' educational aspirations for student	Educational aspirations	Parents' educational expectations for student. 0 = will not graduate high school, 1 = high school, 2 = college, 3 = graduate from college, 4 = will attend graduate school.
		Mother's educational expectations for student from 1, leaved at 16 to 2 stay until 18 to 3, stay past 18.
Educational objects in the home	Educational objects	Student report of the following in the home: place to study, daily newspaper, regular magazine, encyclopedia, atlas, dictionary, more than 50 books, pocket calculator. Range 0-8.
		Student report of the following in the home: over 10 books, musical instrument, daily newspaper. Range 0-3.
Child participates in cultural activities	Cultural activities	Parents' report of whether the student has visited art, science or history museums. Range 0 to 3.
		Parents' report of how often the student has visited art or science museums in the past year. Range 0 to 4.0 = never, 1 = once or twice, 2 = several times, 3 = once a month, 4 = once a week.

(continued)

11

Table 1 (Continued)

Concept	Variable	NELS:88 Measures	NCDS Measures
Dependent Variables:			
Reading test scores	Reading	Standardized Reading Score	PIAT Reading Recognition Score US Percentile
Math test scores	Math	Standardized Math Score	PIAT Math Score US Percentile
Child participates in cultural classes	Cultural classes	Parents' report of the number of art, music or dance classes the student attends outside of school. Range 0 to 3.	Dummy variable of parent's report of whether the child takes special lessons, such as music, sports, art, dance, drama, outside of school. 0 no; 1 yes.
Other Resources	Computer	Parent reports child has access to a computer in the home for educational purposes. 1 = yes.	
	Taken to performances		Parents' report of how often the student went to theatrical or musical performance in the past year. Range 0 to 4.
Child's investment in their own learning process	Reads for enjoyment	Child's report of additional reading they do each week on their own. 0 = never to 5 = 6 or more hours per week.	Parents' report of how often the child reads for pleasure. 0 = never, 1 = several times a year, 2 = several times a month, 3 = several times a week, 4 = daily.

12

Parental investment in adult activities concerning child	Parent knows friend's parents	Number of student's friends' parents the parent knows by name. Range 0 - 5.
	Family visits friends	How often does family go out to see relatives or friends? 0 = never to 6 weekly (same categories as above).
Parental knowledge of child's friends	Parent knows child's friends	Number of student's friends the parent knows by name, range 0 to 5.
	Child has friends over	Number of times the child has friends over. 0 = never, 1 = once every 2 or 3 years, 2 = once a year, 3 = 2 or times per year, 4 = once a month, 5 = 2 or 3 times per month, 6 = once a week.

son between the scores of students who took tests of varying difficulties. This was necessary to keep the student tests of a reasonable length and avoid "ceiling" and "floor" effects (Ingels et al. 1994). For the British children, we used *Peabody Individual Achievement Tests* (PIAT) for the math subscale and the reading recognition subscale. These scores are standardized to United States percentiles. The British children were given the PIATs to allow direct comparability with results from the National Longitudinal Survey of Youth. These standardized test scores provide interval level measures of achievement and allow us to compare the relative strength of independent variables on the outcomes studied in Britain and the United States.

Several variables from the NELS:88 and the NCDS data sets are coded in nearly identical ways. Family background variables are similar in both data sets, including number of children in the family (sibsize), gender, and parental occupational status in 5 categories. Parents' educational attainment consists of a set of dummy variables representing the highest credentials obtained by either parent, but types of credentials differ in the United States and Britain. In the United States the categories correspond to levels of schooling completed, from no high school diploma to a doctoral degree. Britain has a complicated system of exams and qualifications. Myriad qualifications have been categorized into five levels of national vocational qualifications (NVQs). The range of these variables is from "no qualifications," "some qualifications," "O level exams," "A level exams," "higher education," and "degree." According to Kerckhoff (1990), when these adults were in school, Britain did not have anything equivalent to United States high school graduation. Instead, students who wanted educational credentials were able to take General Certificate of Education (GCE) examinations. They could take the "O," ordinary exams, or the "A," advanced exams. Students normally took O levels at age 16 (the normal school-leaving age for this cohort of parents), and A levels at age 18. A level exams were a prerequisite for university attendance. The family's economic status was measured using total family income from all sources in the United States (United States dollars) and combined net earnings of both parents in Britain (British pounds).

To measure social capital, we closely replicate the work of Downey (1995) in the selection of social capital variables from the NELS:88 and then select variables from the NCDS that represent similar concepts. For example, Downey uses an indicator of parents' involvement in the student's academic life from the NELS:88. He counts the frequency with which the student has talked to parents about selecting courses, things studied in class, school activities, or to mother or father about planning high school program; the range is 0-10 discussions. We selected a variable from the NCDS that counts the number of times parents were involved with the school as reported by the mother in the last 12 months, including parents' meetings, school events, discussions about the child, joining the school day, organizing school activities, or school fundraising. We believe both of these variables measure parental engagement with the student's academic career. Other variables are quite similar across the data sets. For example, the NELS:88 data include a measure of parent's educational expectation for the student, and the NCDS asks the mother about the age at which she expects the child to leave school. We include a measure of how much the child reads on his/her own that was not included in the analysis by Downey. We believe that independent reading for pleasure is indicative of an enriched household, and that this should have beneficial effects on test scores. Although some of our resources are not perfect matches between the two studies, as a package their presence indicates levels of social capital available to these children.[2] Our analytic strategy uses OLS regression to compare the effects of family size, family structure, parental work hours and family resources on math and reading test scores in Britain and the United States.

RESULTS

Table 2 summarizes the means and standard deviations for the variables in each data set. The NELS:88 math and reading standardized score means were 50.50 for reading and 50.43 for math. The NCDS children scored higher on the United States percentile for the PIAT reading recognition (65.70) than on the PIAT math (58.69). The families in the United States have a mean of 3.2 children, while the British families have a mean of 2.47. The smaller British families may be due to the young age of the parents in the British sample. It is possible that over time the family sizes will converge, as the British parents complete their families. Regarding race, the United States sample is diverse, with respondents who are 73 percent White, 12 percent Black, and 15 percent Asian or Hispanic. The British sample is racially homogeneous, with 98 percent White respondents. Differences between the United States and British educational systems make a direct comparison of parent's education challenging. Using approximate equivalencies, the British parents are somewhat less well-educated than the American parents. For example, approximately 9 percent of the United States sample did not complete high school, and an additional 20 percent completed only high school. Therefore, approximately 29 percent of the United States sample had a high school diploma or below in education. In Britain, 15 percent of the British parents obtained no qualifications, 29 percent had "some qualifications," and 37 percent passed O level exams. We can conservatively compare the 29 percent of the United States parents who had schooling equal to high school graduation or less to 81 percent of the British parents who completed O levels or below. Fewer of the parents in Britain participated in higher education (8%) than those in the United States (26%).

Regarding family structure and parental work statuses, in Britain, most families consist of two parents with the father working full time and the mother working part time (30%). In the United States these families are only 14 percent of the sample. While 34 percent of the United States families have two parents who both work full time, only 20 percent of British families follow this pattern.

Table 2.   Means and Standard Deviations of Variables

Concept	NELS:88 n = 21,039			NCDS n = 647		
	Variable	Mean	S.D.	Variable	Mean	S.D.
Dependent						
	Reading (standardized)	50.50	9.98	PIAT Reading Comprehension	65.70	28.15
	Math (standardized)	50.43	10.01	PIAT Math	58.69	26.12
Family Background						
Number of children in the family	Sibsize	3.20	1.42		2.46	.87
Gender	Female	.50	.50		.51	.50
Race	White	.73	.44	White	.98	.16
	Black	.12	.32	Non-White	.02	.16
	Mexican Hispanic	.06	.23			
	Other Hispanic	.04	.18			
	Asian	.03	.18			
	Native American	.01	.29			
Parental	Less than high school	.09	.29	No qualifications	.15	.36
Education	High school	.20	.40	Some qualifications	.29	.46
	Some college	.44	.50	O levels	.37	.48
	College degree	.14	.35	A levels	.10	.30
	Masters	.08	.28	Higher education	.06	.16
	Doctorate	.04	.20	College degree	.02	.16
Parents' work hours and family structure	Twoparent DadFtMomFt	.34	.48		.20	.40
	Twoparent DadFtMomPt	.14	.35		.30	.46
	Twoparent DadFtMomNo	.21	.41		.23	.42
	Twoparent DadLoMomFt	.04	.20		.02	.11
	Twoparent DadLoMomPt	.01	.12		.03	.18
	Twoparent DadLoMomNo	.04	.19		.09	.28
	OnlyDadFt	.02	.13		.00	.07
	OnlyDadLo	.00	.06		.01	.09
	OnlyMomFt	.11	.31		.03	.16
	OnlyMomPt	.02	.13		.04	.19
	OnlyMomNo	.05	.22		.06	.23

(continued)

Table 2   (Continued)

Concept	NELS:88 n = 21,039			NCDS n = 647		
	Variable	Mean	S.D.	Variable	Mean	S.D.
	Other Adult	.01	.11		.05	.21
Parental	Unemployed	.02	.13		.07	.25
occupational status	Manual	.34	.47		.38	.49
	Nonprofessional	.28	.45		.22	.42
	Low professional	.30	.46		.26	.44
	Professional	.04	.20		.03	.18
Family Income	(Dollars)	$39,608	$34,494	(Pounds)	£12,312	£12,510
Family Resources[1]						
Involvement in school activities and/or planning	Frequency of talk about school	6.67	2.31	# School Involvements	2.37	1.34
Parental investment in child's education	Money saved for college	$2,236	$4,413	Ways parent chose school	.48	.78
Parents' educational aspirations for student	Educational Aspirations	2.66	.95		2.39	.55
Educational objects in the home	Educational objects	6.11	1.41		2.09	.76
Cultural activities	Cultural activities	1.47	1.21		1.06	.82
Cultural classes	Cultural classes	.46	.70		.61	.48
Other resources	Computer	.26	.43	Taken to performances	.75	.73
Child's investment in their own learning process	Reads for enjoyment	2.07	1.97		3.10	.99
Parental investment in adult activities concerning child	Parent knows friend's parents	2.62	1.71	Family visits friends	4.82	1.61
Parental knowledge of child's friends	Parent knows child's friends	3.47	1.76	Child has friends over	5.54	1.10

Notes: [1] The Family Resources cannot be compared between surveys, either because different resources are used to measure the same concepts or because the scales are not equivalent.

Similar proportions of families are "traditional" two parent families with the father working full time and the mother not working (21% in United States; 23% in Britain). In the United States 11 percent of the families have single mothers who work full time, and only 7 percent have single mothers who work part time or do not work. In Britain, 3 percent of the families have single mothers who work full time. Ten percent of the families are headed by single mothers who work part time or do not work.

Higher percentages of the British parents are unemployed or manual workers (45%) than the American parents (36%). The professional categories comprised 34 percent of the United States parents and 29 percent of the British parents. The mean total family income in the United States was $39,608 in 1987. In Britain, the mean net amount of family earnings in 1991 was £12,312. This translates to approximately $18,000 in 1987 United States dollars, but one cannot directly compare the two amounts for several reasons. As mentioned earlier, the figure for the United States includes total family income from all sources and the British amount only includes net earnings. Also, a direct comparison fails to consider differences in the cost of living between the two countries or differences in such things as health care privileges. Differences also may reflect, in part, the younger ages of the British parents and their lower levels of educational attainment.

Because we use different indicators for social capital across the data sets, we will discuss the social capital variables from the two data sets separately. In the NELS:88, the mean for talking to parents about school was 6.67, out of 10. Parents expected their children to complete some college education, on average. Parents knew, on average, 3.47 of their children's friends by name, and 2.62 of their children's friends' parents. The children read for pleasure approximately 2 hours per week, and had just over 6 educational objects in their households. The mean savings for the child's education reported by parents was $2,236. Children averaged .46 cultural classes (out of 3), and participated in 1.47 cultural activities. One fourth of the children had access to a computer in their homes.

The parents of the NCDS children participated in a mean of 2.37 of 6 possible school involvements. On average, they wanted their children to stay beyond the minimum school-leaving age. The parents also had substantial knowledge about their children's friends, reporting that children had friends over almost once a week (5.54 is the mean, 6 is once a week). The families visited with friends and relatives between once a month and 2-3 times a month. On average, the NCDS children read for enjoyment several times a week. They had a mean of 2 out of 3 possible educational objects in their homes, and 61 percent reported taking cultural classes. Students visited an art or science museum an average of once or twice a year, and either did not go or only went once or twice year to a musical or theatrical performance.

Table 3 conveys the final regression predicting Reading and Math using the NELS:88. Reading scores are negatively affected by family size, minority race, low levels of parental education, and unfavorable combinations of family structure and parental work hours. Positive predictors include being female and having higher levels of parental education and occupation. In addition, a variety of family social capital variables positively predict reading achievement including talking with parents about school, parental aspirations for children's achievement, cultural

Table 3. Regression of Reading and Math Scores from the NELS:88
on Family Background, Parental Family/Work
Interactions and Resources $N = 21,039$

	Reading		Math	
	b (s.e.)	β	b (s.e.)	β
Sibsize	−.242** (.043)	−.034	−.053 (.042)	−.008
Female	1.392** (.121)	.070	−.939** (.119)	−.047
Race[a]				
White (Omitted)	—		—	
Black	−5.260** (.194)	−.171	−5.866** (.191)	−.190
Mexican Hispanic	−3.014** (.264)	−.071	−3.031** (.260)	−.071
Other Hispanic	−3.650** (.319)	−.067	−4.067** (.314)	−.075
Asian	−1.331** (.332)	−.024	1.103** (.326)	.020
Native American	−4.378** (.593)	−.043	−4.140** (.583)	−.041
Parental Education:[b]				
Less than High School	−1.279** (.243)	−.037	−.909** (.238)	−.026
High School (omitted)	—		—	
Some College	.311+ (.160)	.015	.166 (.157)	.008
College Degree	1.575** (.226)	.055	1.941** (.222)	.068
Masters	3.067** (.276)	.085	3.711** (.271)	.103
Doctorate	2.808** (.440)	.055	3.524** (.432)	.069
Parents' work hours and family structure[c]				
Twoparent DadFtMomFt	−.720** (.184)	−.034	−.750** (.181)	−.036
Twoparent DadFtMomPt (Omitted)	—		—	
Twoparent DadFtMomNo	−.310 (.201)	−.013	−.468* (.197)	−.019

(continued)

Table 3   (Continued)

	Reading		Math	
	b (s.e.)	β	b (s.e.)	β
Twoparent DadLoMomFt	−.942**	−.019	−.965**	−.020
	(.319)		(.314)	
Twoparent DadLoMomPt	−.187	−.002	−.209	−.002
	(.525)		(.515)	
Twoparent DadLoMomNo	−1.037**	−.020	−1.113**	−.022
	(.339)		(.333)	
OnlyDadFt	−1.178**	−.016	−1.208**	−.016
	(.459)		(.451)	
OnlyDadLo	−2.116*	−.014	−1.552+	−.010
	(.903)		(.887)	
OnlyMomFt	−.310	−.010	−.518*	−.016
	(.244)		(.240)	
OnlyMomPt	−.490	−.006	−.250	−.003
	(.467)		(.458)	
OnlyMomNo	−1.198**	−.026	−.620+	−.013
	(.330)		(.324)	
Missing Work/Family	−1.847**	−.016	−2.615**	−.022
	(.695)		(.683)	
Other Adult	−.049	−.001	−.047	.000
	(.562)		(.552)	
Parental occupational status[d]				
Unemployed	−.622	−.008	−.723	−.009
	(.466)		(.458)	
Manual (omitted)	—		—	
Nonprofessional	.997**	.045	1.002**	.045
	(.158)		(.156)	
Low professional	1.447**	.066	1.098**	.050
	(.174)		(.171)	
Professional	2.299**	.047	2.029**	.041
	(.405)		(.397)	
Missing on Occupational status	−1.290**	−.018	−1.233**	−.018
	(.417)		(.409)	
Family Income	.000	.009	.000	.043
	(.000)		(.000)	
Family Resources:[e]				
Frequency of talk about school	.386**	.090	.383**	.088
	(.027)		(.027)	
Money saved for college	.000+	.012	.000	.003
	(.000)		(.000)	
Educational aspirations	2.451*	.233	2.714**	.257
	(.071)		(.070)	

(continued)

Table 3   (Continued)

	Reading		Math	
	b (s.e.)	β	b (s.e.)	β
Educational objects	−.037	−.005	−.022	−.003
	(.046)		(.046)	
Cultural activities	.226**	.027	.071	.009
	(.052)		(.051)	
Cultural classes	.803**	.056	.810**	.057
	(.093)		(.091)	
Computer	.925**	.040	1.738**	.075
	(.145)		(.142)	
Reads for enjoyment	.620**	.122	.276**	.054
	(.030)		(.029)	
Parent knows	−.061	−.011	.017	.003
friend's parents	(.056)		(.055)	
Parent knows child's	.238**	.042	.218**	.038
friends	(.054)		(.053)	
Constant	38.737**		38.860**	
R^2	.299		.328	
Adjusted R^2	.297		.326	

Notes: [a]Race variables are significant as a group: Reading $F = 168.479$; Math $F = 323.762$.
   [b]Parental education variables are significant as a group: Reading $F = 509.181$; Math $F = 649.171$
   [c]The work/family interaction variables are significant as a group: Reading $F = 8.33$; Math $F = 9.065$.
   [d]Parental occupation variables are significant as a group: Reading $F = 40.395$; Math $F = 45.720$.
   [e]Resource variables are significant as a group: Reading $F = 271.918$; Math $F = 282.360$.
   + $p \leq .05$.
   * $p \leq .025$.
   ** $p \leq .005$.
   One-tailed test.

activities and classes, parents' knowing child's friends and reading for enjoyment. The findings for predicting math achievement are similar, except that the effect of being female is negative.

Table 4 replicates this model for the NCDS data. For reading in Great Britain, the effect of family size is not significant. The effects of parental education are positive for middle level qualifications, but the various combinations of family status and work hours show no significant net effects. In contrast, several social capital variables are significant. Reading achievement is positively affected by maternal aspirations for children's education attainment, by the number of educational objects in the home, and by whether the child reads for enjoyment. Regarding achievement in mathematics, we also see that family size is not significant and that female children score lower than male children. Parental education effects are stronger than for reading achievement, with similar effects of social capital variables.

Table 4.   Regression of Reading and Math Scores from the NCDS on
Family Background, Parental Family/Work
Interactions and Resources $N = 647$

	Reading		Math	
	b (s.e.)	β	b (s.e.)	β
Sibsize	−.135	−.004	.442	.015
	(1.216)		(1.156)	
Female	−.338	−.006	−6.788**	−.130
	(2.060)		(1.957)	
NonWhite	−1.613	−.009	2.810	.017
	(6.512)		(6.189)	
Parental Education:[a]				
No qualifications	.358	.005	−6.232*	−.086
	(3.172)		(3.015)	
Some qualifications (omitted)	—		—	
O levels	8.186**	.140	.409	.008
	(2.544)		(2.418)	
A levels	10.460**	.110	12.627**	.143
	(3.857)		(3.666)	
Higher education	9.089+	.080	9.917*	.094
	(4.645)		(4.415)	
College degree	6.909	.038	11.109+	.066
	(6.880)		(6.539)	
Parents' work hours and family structure[b]				
Twoparent DadFtMomFt	−3.822	−.054	−.659	−.010
	(2.935)		(2.789)	
Twoparent DadFtMomPt (omitted)	—		—	
Twoparent DadFtMomNo	1.619	.024	.507	.008
	(2.798)		(2.659)	
Twoparent DadLoMomFt	−.594	−.002	4.446	.019
	(9.110)		(8.658)	
Twoparent DadLoMomPt	−6.587	−.041	6.572	.045
	(5.862)		(5.571)	
Twoparent DadLoMomNo	−5.086	−.051	−.528	−.006
	(4.019)		(3.819)	
OnlyDadFt	19.601	.047	7.886	.021
	(15.327)		(14.566)	

(continued)

Table 4 (Continued)

	Reading		Math	
	b (s.e.)	β	b (s.e.)	β
OnlyDadLo	−5.718 (11.486)	−.018	−5.238 (10.916)	−.018
OnlyMomFt	7.759 (6.747)	.045	13.758* (6.412)	.087
OnlyMomPt	1.449 (5.641)	.010	.776 (5.361)	.005
OnlyMomNo	−2.571 (4.865)	−.021	−2.876 (4.624)	−.025
Other Adult	−10.861* (5.250)	−.080	−15.190** (4.989)	−.120
Parental Occupational Status[c]				
Unemployed	−2.380 (4.346)	−.021	−4.021 (4.131)	−.038
Manual (omitted)	—		—	
Nonprofessional	2.283 (2.717)	.034	3.051 (2.582)	.049
Low professional	6.566* (2.802)	.102	2.867 (2.663)	.048
Professional	−.353 (6.000)	−.002	−.857 (5.702)	−.006
Family Income	−.000 (.000)	−.052	.000 (.000)	.030
Family Resources[d]				
# School Involvements	−.003 (.825)	−.002	1.043 (.784)	.054
Ways parent chooses school	.008 (1.303)	.002	.853 (1.238)	.026
Educational aspirations	9.880** (1.883)	.194	4.957** (1.789)	.105
Educational objects	6.070** (1.395)	.163	5.030** (1.326)	.146
Cultural activities	−3.408* (1.364)	−.099	−1.512 (1.297)	−.048
Cultural classes	−.376 (2.167)	−.006	4.045* (2.060)	.075
Taken to performances	1.016 (1.502)	.027	−1.296 (1.427)	−.036
Reads for enjoyment	7.893** (1.102)	.278	5.393** (1.047)	.205

(continued)

Table 4 (Continued)

	Reading		Math	
	b (s.e.)	β	b (s.e.)	β
Family visits	−.421	−.024	−.809	−.050
friends	(.626)		(.595)	
Child has	.522	.020	1.565+	.066
friends over	(.914)		(.868)	
Constant	3.665		11.362	
R^2	.274		.239	
Adjusted R^2	.233		.195	

Notes: [a]Parental education variables are significant as a group: $F = 10.716$ Math $F = 14.211$.
     [b]The work/family interaction variables are not significant as a group for either Reading or Math.
     [c]On Reading, Parental occupation variables are significant as a group: Reading: $F = 2.126$
     signif. at .076.
     [d]Resource variables are significant as a group: Reading: $F = 12.706$ Math $F = 8.476$.
     $+p \leq .05$.
     $^*p \leq .025$.
     $^{**}p \leq .005$.
     One-tailed test.

Table 5 summarizes the results of a controlled stepwise entry of sets of variables into predicting reading and math achievement. This analysis enables us to summarize findings regarding when the effects of family size diminish or disappear. Regarding reading achievement, we see that there are negative zero-order effects of family size in the NCDS, but that in Model 3 controlling for work hours-family structure renders the original relationship not significant. The relationship between family size and mathematics achievement is not significant in the zero order. For the NELS:88 data, social capital variables explain away the family size effects for mathematics achievement, although other steps in the model also contribute strongly to explanation. The findings are similar for reading achievement, except that the family size effects, although strongly diminished as compared with the zero order, remain statistically significant in the final equation.

Table 6 compares the two sets of findings regarding the presence of effects for a number of the social capital variables in the models discussed above. We see that there are similar findings across countries regarding the positive effects of parental educational aspirations, the child's participating in cultural classes, whether the child reads for enjoyment, and whether parents' know their child's friends. The presence of educational objects in the home affects both math and reading outcomes in Great Britain, and having a computer in the home affects both math and reading outcomes in the United States. Parental educational aspirations and

Table 5. Comparing the Sibsize Coefficients Across Models of the NELS:88 and the NCDS

	Model 1: Sibsize Alone		Model 2: Model 1 Plus Female, Race, Parent Educ.		Model 3: Model 2 Plus Work/Family Variables		Model 4: Model 3 Plus Parent Occupation and Family Income		Model 5: Model 4 Plus Resources	
	b (s.e.)	β	b (s.e.)	β	b (s.e.)	β	b (s.e.)	β	b (s.e.)	β
READING										
NELS:88	-1.100** (.048)	-.156	-.511** (.045)	-.073	-.479** (.045)	-.068	-.422** (.045)	-.060	-.242** (.043)	-.034
NCDS	-2.517* (1.274)	-.078	-2.060+ (1.227)	-.064	-1.661 (1.290)	-.051	-1.514 (1.292)	-.047	-.135 (1.216)	-.004
MATH										
NELS:88	-.992** (.048)	-.141	-.343** (.044)	-.049	-.309** (.045)	-.044	-.245** (.044)	-.035	-.053 (.042)	-.008
NCDS	-1.676 (1.183)	-.056	-1.183 (1.129)	-.039	-.468 (1.185)	-.016	-.300 (1.192)	-.010	.442 (1.156)	.015

Notes: NELS:88: n = 21,039
NCDS: n = 647
+ $p \leq .05$.
* $p \leq .025$.
** $p \leq .005$.
One-tailed test.

Table 6. Comparison of NELS:88 and NCDS Resource Variables that are Significant in the Final Equation:

Variables	NELS:88 Reading	NCDS Reading	NELS:88 Math	NCDS Math
Resources:				
School involvement: NELS:88: frequency of talk about school NCDS: # of school involvements	pos.**		pos.**	
Parental investment in child's education: NELS:88: Money saved for college NCDS: Ways parent chose school	pos.**			
Educational aspirations	pos.**	pos.**	pos.**	pos.**
Educational objects		pos.**		pos.**
Cultural activities	pos.**	neg.*		
Cultural classes	pos.**		pos.**	pos.*
NELS:88: Computer	pos.**	n.a.	pos.**	n.a.
NCDS: Taken to performance	n.a.		n.a.	
Reads for enjoyment	pos.**	pos.**	pos.**	pos.**
Parental investment in adult activities concerning child: NELS:88: Parent knows friend's parents NCDS: Family visits friends				
Parental knowledge of child's friends: NELS:88: Parent knows child's friends NCDS: Child had friends over	pos.**	pos.+	pos.**	pos.+

Notes: + $p \leq .05$.
* $p \leq .025$.
** $p \leq .005$.

whether the child reads for enjoyment positively affect both measures of achievement in both societies.

DISCUSSION

Our purpose has been to study the effects of family size on student academic achievement in the United States and Great Britain in order to further understand this important relationship, and to suggest how cross-cultural differences in the operation of key institutions might be affecting the work family nexus differently across these societies. We hypothesized a negative effect of family size on educational attainment, and argued that aspects of family social capital might modify or account for the original finding. We also hypothesized that non-intact family status would have a negative effect on educational outcomes; again, access to family social capital and/or family financial resources might explain this relationship. Findings for the United States suggested that there was a negative relationship between family size and both reading and math achievement. In Great Britain, these effects are duplicated for reading achievement but not for math. As we note below, if our British sample had included a broader range of family sizes, perhaps this zero order relationship would have appeared.

Our analytic results suggested that there are both similarities and differences in the operation of key variables explaining family size effects on reading and math achievement across the two societies. When added to the model as a group, family background variables are very important to explaining family size effects in the United States and Great Britain (see Table 5, Model 2). In the United States, for both reading and math, race, parental educational attainment and child gender all contribute significantly to reducing the negative effects of family size. In Great Britain for reading, parental educational attainment and child gender are important to explaining the family size effects (not shown). These are important similarities across the two societies in the operation of key demographic variables predicting achievement outcomes.

In addition, some of the family social capital variables operate in common. When parents have higher aspirations for child educational achievement, children achieve higher reading and math scores in both the United States and Great Britain. Such aspirations, likely known to the child, may promote greater child effort and encourage the behaviors needed for achievement. Also, children reading for pleasure has similar effects. Although it is not surprising that such reading would promote reading achievement, it is less predictable that there would be a similar effect on math. Such reading may promote achievement across several curricular areas; it may also represent a general form of motivation that facilitates academic achievement beyond that detected in reading achievement tests. The more scattered effects across societies and outcomes of cultural classes, parents' knowing their child's friends, and having a home computer are broadly consistent with the notion that family social capital and investment in children pays dividends in child achievement.

There are cross-cultural differences, however, in the strength of the parental work and family structure effects. In the United States, the negative effect of family size on student achievement is partly explained by parental work hours, parental occupation and income, and family structure. In Great Britain, these potentially explanatory factors are largely not significant. It may be that the British welfare state acts to protect children's achievement from the negative effects of non-intact family status that are so clearly present in the United States. The presence of universal health care may be one mechanism that renders variations in family structure of less importance for child achievement in Great Britain than in the United States. A well-developed welfare state may render less important the role of family social capital and/or family financial resources in predicting student achievement. In the United States, where the "safety net" is less well-developed, parental investments associated with intact family status appear to be more important in promoting child achievement.

It is important to note that the absence or relative weakness of family size effects in Great Britain might be due to truncation of family sizes of our British sample. The parents of the children we are studying are age 33, and so may not have completed their families yet. Thus the variance in family size in the British sample may be constrained relative to the United States sample where the children have parents of varying ages. So it is possible that if the British cohort were followed up in ten years when their families were more nearly complete, variation in family size would have increased with perhaps stronger effects of this variable on child achievement. This is an important avenue for future research.

We believe that our strategy of studying a known social relationship across societies is a useful one for comparative research. This approach allows the researcher to learn more about the original relationship, as well as evaluate the extent to which the same processes are operative cross-culturally. What is required, of course, are data sets that are comparable enough in design and measurement of variables to allow researchers to construct similar models that can be compared. We invite other researchers to join us in pursuing this important line of inquiry.

ACKNOWLEDGMENTS

An earlier version of this paper was presented at the 1998 annual meeting of the Society for the Advancement of Socio-Economics in Vienna, Austria, and we thank Kevin Leicht for his helpful comments. We also thank Doug Downey and Mikaela Dufur, for their expertise and assistance. The Center for Human Resource Research at Ohio State provided the revised NCDS Child & Parent Data and documentation. We are grateful for support and documentation provided by the NCDS User Support Group at the Social Statistics Research Unit of City University in London and the ESRC Data Archive at the University of Essex. This research was supported in part by the College of Social and Behavioral Sciences at The Ohio State University.

NOTES

1.   We were concerned about non-comparability of sample sizes between the NELS:88 ($n = $ 21,089) and the NCDS ($n = 647$). We wanted to be certain the sample size differences did not account for differences in results. Therefore, we drew 10 random samples of 647 respondents from the NELS:88. We performed the analyses for both math and reading on the smaller samples to determine if the larger sample size results were robust. The overall results of the smaller sample analyses are similar to the results with the larger sample. In several cases, variables that were significant in the larger

sample are significant in several of the smaller samples, but not all of them. The directions of the relationships are generally the same, except in three instances where the original relationship between the resource and the outcome was rather weak or non-existent. For example, educational objects were non significant in predicting higher reading scores in the NELS:88. In two of the samples, they were significant predictors, but in opposite directions. In cases where effects differ between the British and United States children, we feel confident of our results. For example, in Equation 1 where sibsize was entered alone on math and reading scores, higher numbers of siblings predicted lower math and readings scores in the United States sample, but not in the British sample. In the NELS:88, for math, 9 of the smaller test groups had significant negative coefficients for sibsize; for reading, 8 had significant negative coefficients.

2. Missing data were minimal for most variables in both the NELS:88 and the NCDS. In some cases, we were able to obtain data for missing values from other variables. For example, although there were missing values on the child's report of the number of children in the family, we were able to look at parental reports to determine family size. For remaining missing data, we used mean substitution. For the NELS:88, missing data ranged from 3 missing cases (.0) for child reads for enjoyment and parental knowledge of the child's friends, to 6.7 percent for cultural activities. Typical missing values were in the 2-6 percent missing range. For the NCDS, missing values ranged from none missing for ways parent chose school to 11.3 percent missing on parent's educational aspirations for child and 15 percent on family income. Typical variables had fewer than 5 percent missing values. In both data sets, we tested to determine whether missing data on three key family background variables were problematic for our estimates. We created dichotomous variables for missing data for the parent's work hours/family structure, parent's occupational status and family income. For the NELS:88, the indicators for parent's work hours/family structure and parent's occupational status were significant; those who were missing information about parental work/family structure and/or the parent's occupation scored significantly lower on both math and reading than those in two parent families in which the father worked full time and the mother worked part time. The dichotomous variable indicating missing data on family income was not significant. In the NCDS, we were especially concerned about the high number of missing values on family income. However, none of the three background indicators was significant for either math or reading scores.

REFERENCES

Blake, J. 1989. *Family Size and Achievement*. Los Angeles: University of California Press.

Coleman, J. S. 1988. "Social Capital in the Creation of Human Capital." *American Journal of Sociology* 94: S95-120.

———. 1990. *Foundations of Social Theory*. Cambridge, MA: The Belknap Press of Harvard University.

Downey, D. B. 1995. "When Bigger Is Not Better: Family Size, Parental Resources, and Children's Educational Performance." *American Sociological Review* 60: 746-761.

Fogelman, K. 1983. "Social Class and Family Size." In *Growing Up In Great Britain*, edited by K. Fogelman. London: Macmillan for the National Children's Bureau.

Houseman, S. N. 1995. "Part-time Employment in Europe and Japan." *Journal of Labor Research* 16(3): 249-262.

Ingels, S. J., K. L. Dowd, J. D. Baldridge, J. L. Stipe, V. H. Bartot, and M. R. Frankel. 1994. *NELS:88: Second Follow-Up: Student Component Data File User's Manual*; NCES 94-374.

Joshi, H. 1996. "Combining Employment and Child-Rearing: The Story of British Women's Lives." Chapter 5 in *In Pursuit of the Quality of Life*, edited by A. Offer. Oxford, England: Oxford University Press.

Kerckhoff, A. C. 1990. *Getting Started: Transition to Adulthood in Great Britain*. Boulder, CO: Westview Press.

————. 1993. *Diverging Pathways: Social Structure and Career Deflections*. New York: Cambridge University Press.

McLanahan, S., and G. Sandefur. 1994. *Growing Up with a Single Parent: What Hurts, What Helps*. Cambridge, MA: Harvard University Press.

Parcel, T. L., and E. G. Menaghan. 1994a. "Early Parental Work, Family Social Capital, and Early Childhood Outcomes." *American Journal of Sociology* 99(4): 972-1009.

————. 1994b. *Parents' Jobs and Children's Lives*. New York: De Gruyter.

Piotrkowski, C. S., R. N. Rapoport, and R. Rapoport. 1987. "Families and Work." Pp. 251-283 in *Handbook of Marriage and the Family*, edited by M. B. Sussman and S. K. Steinmetz. New York: Plenum.

Portes, A. 1998. "Social Capital: Its Origins and Applications in Modern Sociology." *Annual Review of Sociology* 24: 1-24.

Steelman, L. C., and B. Powell. 1991. "Sponsoring the Next Generation: Parental Willingness to Pay for Higher Education." *American Journal of Sociology* 96: 1505-1529.

Turner, R. H. 1960. "Sponsored and Contest Mobility and the School System." *American Sociological Review* 25(6): 855-867.

Voydanoff, P. 1987. *Work and Family Life*. Beverly Hills: Sage.

Ward, C., A. Dale, and H. Joshi. 1996. "Participation in the Labor Market." Chapter 4 in *Life at 33: The Fifth Follow-up of the National Child Development Study*, edited by E. Ferri. London: National Children's Bureau.

PARENTAL WORK IN
MIDDLE CHILDHOOD:
LINKS BETWEEN EMPLOYMENT AND
THE DIVISION OF HOUSEWORK,
PARENT-CHILD ACTIVITIES AND
PARENTAL MONITORING

Ann C. Crouter, Mary C. Maguire,
Heather Helms-Erikson, and Susan M. McHale

ABSTRACT

The research examines workplace conditions that may influence how mothers and fathers divide three aspects of family work: housework, involvement in parent-child activities, and parental monitoring of children's daily activities. Mothers, fathers and firstborn and secondborn school-aged children in each of 181 dual-earner families participated in home interviews about work and family life and a series of 7 evening telephone interviews focused on family members' daily activities and parents'

Research in the Sociology of Work, Volume 7, pages 31-54.
Copyright © 1999 by JAI Press Inc.
All rights of reproduction in any form reserved.
ISBN: 0-7623-0605-X

monitoring of their children's experiences. Variables were created to reflect the proportion of the total parental load in each area that was performed by the mother Regression analyses revealed that the division of housework was related to the relative time mothers and fathers spent at work and their relative earnings. The division of parental monitoring (particularly of sons) was related to the relative time parents spent at work, as well as their experiences of pressure on the job. Parents' work conditions were not related to their division of involvement in parent-child activities. The importance of examining both family work and employment from the perspective of the parental dyad is emphasized.

In this paper, we consider some of the ways in which husbands' and wives' job characteristics are linked to the ways they divide family work when they are at a specific point in the family life course: that is, when parents are bringing up school-age children, who are roughly between the ages of 6 and 11 years old. We build on a body of research, primarily in the fields of family sociology and economics, that documents the importance of parents' work-related temporal availability, relative resources, and psychological demands for the way mothers and fathers divide the many tasks that comprise family work. For our purposes here, we conceptualize family work as the division of household tasks, parent-child joint activities, and parental monitoring. Our approach is also influenced by recent research in developmental psychology and behavior genetics which argues for the importance of studying within-in family variability in children's experiences. Most developmental research on parenting identifies a single "target child" in each family, ignoring the messy possibility that there is rich variation in the experiences of children within families that is little understood. We have built comparisons of firstborn versus secondborn siblings into our research design.

From a parent's point of view, child rearing activities shift markedly as children enter and progress through middle childhood (Collins, Harris and Susman 1995). Raising infants, toddlers, and preschoolers often involves considerable physical labor on the parts of mothers and fathers; the daily responsibility for feeding, bathing, dressing, and cleaning up after young children is demanding. When children reach middle childhood, however, they can accomplish many of these activities on their own. At this developmental period, parent-child joint activities take center stage; parents participate in various activities with their school-age children as companions, coaches, or merely chauffeurs. To the extent that parents engage in activities with their children that they too enjoy, parent involvement may take a more recreational and social tone and be less likely to be perceived as work.

In middle childhood, children also become increasingly involved in contexts outside the family such as elementary school, peer groups, and extracurricular activities. This growing independence necessitates that parents take on an important new role, that of "monitor." Because school-aged children are on their own more than they were as preschoolers, parents must become adept at supervising them from a distance, making sure that they know where their children are, what they are doing, and who they are with (Collins et al. 1995). There is a growing literature documenting that low levels of parental monitoring in middle childhood are associated with lower school achievement and higher conduct problems, especially in boys (Crouter, MacDermid, McHale and Perry-Jenkins 1990; Patterson and Stouthamer-Loeber 1984).

Most of the literature on the connections between parents' paid employment and the division of family work focuses on housework, with an emphasis on the conditions under which husbands assume a larger share of those tasks (Coltrane 1996; Pleck 1983; Spitze 1988). Much less is known about the conditions under which parents divide child rearing activities or responsibilities (Coltrane 1992). One reason the division of parenting activities has been overlooked is that developmental researchers have tended to examine mothers and fathers separately. For example, considerable attention has recently been devoted to understanding the correlates of father involvement because fathers have long been neglected in developmental research (for a review, see Parke 1995). Less attention has been paid to the dyadic issue of how mothers and fathers divide child rearing activities and responsibilities between themselves. The few studies that have been conducted in this area have tended either to focus on very young children (i.e., those age five or younger; e.g., Coltrane 1992, 1996) or to blur the lines between early and middle childhood by simply studying "children" (e.g., Peterson and Gerson 1992). Little research has examined the division of parenting when children are in the middle childhood years. This lacuna is surprising, given that it is precisely during this period that children are elaborating their understanding of gender and gender roles (Huston 1983). Indeed, during middle childhood, children may be particularly attentive to how family work is assigned to mothers versus fathers (Crouter, Manke and McHale 1995; Katz and Ksansnak 1994).

Parents with school-aged children confront at least three distinct demands in terms of family work. First, like all couples, they have household tasks to accomplish such as cooking, cleaning, laundry, car maintenance and home repairs. Second, parents generally engage in some activities with their children, including helping them with homework, eating meals together, chauffeuring them to athletic events or club meetings, participating with them in leisure activities, attending religious services together, and the like. Finally, they must monitor their children's activities, whereabouts, and companions from a distance. In this chapter, we examine all three aspects of the division of family work—housework, parent-child involvement in joint activities, and parental monitoring—with an eye to whether and how these family dynamics are related to characteristics of mothers' and fathers' paid employment. In studying the work-relationships between parental work and division of parent-child involvement and parental monitoring in middle childhood, we are breaking new ground. Including the division of household tasks in our analyses enables us to assess how well our sample conforms to patterns that are well known in the literature (e.g., Coltrane 1996). It also provides a yardstick against which to compare the predictors of the division of parent-child involvement and parental monitoring. To the extent, for example, that the determinants of the division of parent-child involvement or parental monitoring resemble the predictors of the division of housework, we may be able to infer how much parents conceptualize parenting as "work."

At the heart of this paper is an interest in how parents' experiences at work and at home are linked, a field of inquiry that has burgeoned in recent decades (Crouter and McHale 1993; Menaghan and Parcel 1990; Parcel and Menaghan 1994). The literature on the conditions under which wives and husbands divide housework more or less equally offers a theoretical basis for thinking about how characteristics of parents' jobs might be linked to their division of parent-child activities and monitoring. Coltrane (1996), building on the work of Peterson and Gerson (1992) and others, argues that social-structural theory is a useful perspective for understanding how husbands and wives divide family work:

> Social-structural theory concentrates on inequitable access to market resources and the unequal institution of marriage. Labor markets are assumed to be structured or stratified to exclude women from higher status jobs, thus rendering their market labor less valuable than men's. This forces women into the unequal bargain of marriage, within which they are expected to care for home and children. Like human capital theory, social-structural theory looks at people's responses to time availability and resources, but it also includes consideration of ideology and starts from a different set of assumptions. According to social-structural theory, various economic, institutional, and ideological forces encourage couples to assume that women will handle most of the child care and housework. In this view, couples depart from a traditional division of domestic labor only when situational constraints in the home or the workplace demand it (1996, p. 153).

TEMPORAL AVAILABILITY

Drawing from the literature on the division of housework (Coltrane 1996; Pleck 1983; Spitze 1988), we have identified three domains of employment characteristics that may be linked to how parents divide family work because they qualify, in Coltrane's terms, as "situational constraints." They are: (1) temporal availability; (2) relative resources; and, (3) psychological demands. There is considerable evidence pointing to the importance of temporal availability. Studies of the division of housework have generally indicated that, as women's hours in the workplace increase, the proportion of time they spend on housework, relative to their spouse, declines. The decline, however, is primarily attributable to women reducing the time they spend on housework—by becoming more efficient or lowering their standards of quality—rather than men increasing their time (Geerken and Gove 1983; Pleck 1979).

Scholars interested in father involvement have noted that men have been more likely to respond to maternal employment by participating in child care than by participating in housework (Parke 1995; Coltrane 1996). Little is known, however, about how mothers' and fathers' work hours are linked to the way they divide parenting. In a study of the conditions under which men and women take responsibility for making child care arrangements, Peterson and Gerson (1992) found that when women worked longer hours, they took less responsibility for making child care arrangements and their husbands took more. As Peterson and Gerson (1992) explained, "Husbands' involvement in paid work and relatively low participation in household work appear to be the path of least resistance; only when a wife's long hours on the job begin to reduce her involvement in household labor significantly does her husband raise his level of responsibility" (p. 532). In contrast, as Peterson and Gerson had predicted, husbands' work hours were not related to either spouse assuming responsibility, presumably because "men do not trade off between home and market work in the same way that women do" (Peterson and Gerson 1992, p. 532). In an earlier study, we found that among dual-earner families, child-oriented activities were divided in a more egalitarian way when mothers' and fathers' work hours were more similar (McHale, Crouter and Bartko 1992). In keeping with Peterson and Gerson's findings, we predicted that mothers' work hours will be negatively related to the proportion of family work that they perform relative to their spouses, while fathers' work hours will not be related to the division of family work. We also expected that the more time wives devote to paid employment, relative to the time contributed by their spouse, the less time wives will contribute, proportionally, to family work.

RELATIVE RESOURCES

Resource and social exchange theory suggest that husbands will perform more family work when their wives' relative income or occupational prestige is higher. This hypothesis, which has received some empirical support in the literature (e.g., Brayfield 1992; Brines 1994; Kamo 1988; McHale and Crouter 1992; Ross 1987), assumes that income translates into marital power and that husbands and wives use their resources to bargain for greater assistance from the partner. For example, Brayfield (1992), using a national Canadian sample, found that the greater the income gap favoring husbands, the fewer feminine-typed household tasks (e.g., cooking, cleaning) husbands performed. Men were particularly likely to "buy out" of feminine-typed tasks when they were at the lower end of the income distribution, presumably because men in this social stratum are more conservative in gender role ideology than are men with higher status and earnings. In our earlier work, we found that in families where wives' incomes were more similar to their husbands', the division of child care responsibilities was more equal (McHale et al. 1992), and the role of wives' incomes was particularly important in negotiating an egalitarian division of child care for families with daughters (Updegraff, McHale and Crouter 1996). Extending this line of research, we hypothesized that the more wives earn and the greater their occupational prestige, relative to their husbands', the less they will contribute proportionally to family work. We also explored whether children's sex moderates the relationship between parents' work characteristics and the division of family work.

PSYCHOLOGICAL DEMANDS OF WORK

Recently, research studies have gone beyond the structural dimensions of parents' jobs, such as work hours and income, to consider the impact of occupational stress and overloads (Bolger, DeLongis, Kessler and Wethington 1989; Repetti 1989, 1994) on family life. Few studies, however, have linked the psychological demands posed by parents' jobs to the division of family work. Using longitudinal daily diary data on dual-earner couples, Bolger and his colleagues found that "overloads" at work on specific days (i.e., having to do a lot of work) were linked to how much family work was performed during the evening. On days when husbands experienced overloads at work, they subsequently performed less domestic work at home. On these stressful days, their wives stepped in and performed more work at home. The parallel pattern did not occur, however. When wives experienced overloads at work, they too performed less work at home, but their husbands did not compensate by performing more. Given this finding, we hypothesized that both parents' reports of work pressure should be correlated with the division of family work, and that the relationship will be stronger for husbands than for wives because a husband's stress presumably not only reduces his involvement but increases his wife's.

We are also interested in the extent to which mothers and fathers are emotionally involved or absorbed in their jobs. Kanter (1977) identified work absorption as a central dimension of work that has implications for employees' lives off the job. There is no empirical literature on the implications of mothers' and fathers' emotional involvement in work for the way they divide family work. It is conceivable, however, that emotional involvement operates much like temporal involvement. Because there is virtually no literature on the implications of mothers' and fathers' emotional absorption in their jobs, we offer no formal hypotheses and treat those analyses as exploratory in an effort to widen the repertoire of work characteristics that are examined in research on work and family linkages.

WITHIN-FAMILY COMPARISONS

In considering the ways in which parents divide parent-child activities and parental monitoring, it is important to consider variations within families. Parents do not necessarily treat their children alike; indeed, in the field of child development there is considerable current interest in what behavior geneticists have called "the family as a nonshared environment" (Plomin and Daniels 1987; Dunn and Plomin

1990; Hetherington, Reiss and Plomin 1994). Researchers pioneering this new direction of work typically build the comparison of two or more siblings into their research designs in order to compare family experiences across siblings. To our knowledge, we are breaking new ground in considering the division of family work from this angle.

In our research, we have studied both the firstborn and secondborn siblings in each family, and both siblings are in middle childhood. We are interested in comparing how consistent parents are in the way they divide parent-child involvement and parental monitoring vis a vis their older and younger children, as well as in comparing the correlates of the division of parent-child activities and monitoring for older versus younger siblings. To the extent that secondborns are younger and possibly less independent or more demanding than their older siblings, for example, we may find stronger work correlates for secondborn as opposed to firstborn children. Of course, with cross-sectional data, we cannot disentangle whether it is children's age or birth order that is responsible for any effects we observe. These ideas are in keeping with the notion that children, by virtue of their characteristics and behavior, have an impact on how their parents treat them.

In this paper, we consider whether the patterns of work-related correlates for older and younger children vary as a function of children's sex. Like others, we have found that parent-child involvement and, to a lesser extent, parental monitoring, are sex-typed family processes, with mothers paying special attention to daughters and fathers to sons, regardless of birth order (Crouter et al. 1995; Crouter, Helms-Erikson, Updegraff and McHale 1999; McHale, Crouter and Tucker in press). To the extent that involvement with a child of the other sex is perceived as optional, mothers' involvement with sons and fathers' involvement with daughters may be more vulnerable to work demands. Sex may also be a marker for personal characteristics. In a classic article calling for attention to "child effects," Bell (1968) argued that, early in development, male infants are more irritable than females, a sex difference that sets into motion different patterns of mother-child interaction for boys and girls. To the extent that males are more irritable, difficult or demanding, it is possible that parents' work-related characteristics are related to the division of parenting for sons more so than for daughters because parents may choose to use their work circumstances to lower their share of involvement with more difficult children. These thoughts are highly speculative, but intriguing.

METHODS AND PROCEDURES

Participants

The data were drawn from the first phase of a new longitudinal study that explores the interconnections between parents' work circumstances, family dynamics, and the psychosocial functioning of school-aged siblings. The 203 two-parent, predominantly dual-earner families were recruited via letters sent home to the families of fourth and fifth grade students in each of 16 school districts in central Pennsylvania. The sample was divided into two cohorts. In 1995, 100 families were recruited to cohort 1; in 1996, 103 families were recruited to cohort 2. The letter to families described the research effort in general terms, indicated that families would receive a $100 honorarium for each phase of participation in the three-year longitudinal study, listed the criteria for participation, and asked families to return a self-addressed, stamped postcard to the project if interested in participating. The criteria were as follows: (1) the family had to be maritally intact; (2) the eldest child in the family had to be in the fourth or fifth grade; and (3) there had to be at least one additional sibling 1 to 4 years younger. We also sought to include as many families as possible in which both parents were employed at least part-time because we were interested in parental work as an influence on family dynamics, including the division of family work. Of the 203 families in the sample, we omitted 17 from these analyses because the mother was not employed, one additional family because, despite our screening efforts, they included children older than the targets of our study, and 4 families who had missing data on family work. Thus, the sample on which these analyses are based included 181 families. Sample sizes in some analyses change slightly, however, due to missing data on work characteristics and earnings. With the exception of two adopted Asian-American children, all participants were White. They resided primarily in small cities, towns, and rural areas. Occupations for fathers included business owner, teacher, lawyer, forklift operator, and sales representative. Mothers' occupations included teacher, secretary, factory worker, and judge.

Procedures

Family members participated in two distinct types of data collection. First, family members were interviewed individually in their homes about themselves, their relationships with other family members, and, for parents, their work experiences. After the home interview, families were telephoned on seven different evenings (5 week nights, 2 weekends) about an hour before the children's bedtime. Three of the calls included the father and both children; three were directed to the mother and both children; the seventh call included all four family members. These structured interviews focused on the parents' and children's activities on those specific days. In addition, we asked parents and children separately a different set of questions each evening designed to tap parental monitoring, that is, how knowledgeable the parent was about each child's experiences that particular day.

Home Interview Measures

The home interviews were the source of information about mothers' and fathers' work experiences. The measures utilized in the analyses presented here include:

Total Work Hours

Parents each reported the total number of hours spent on the job, and working on work-related matters at home. These two figures were summed to create an index of total work hours.

Earnings

Mothers and fathers were each asked to report their annual pre-tax income.

Occupational Prestige

Parents' occupations were coded using the NORC occupational prestige codes (Nakao and Treas 1990).

Work Pressure

Parents completed the work pressure sub-scale from the Work Environment Scale (Moos 1986), a 9-item scale tapping the extent to which work overloads, deadlines, and time pressure characterize the respondent's job (those working more than one job completed this measure about their primary job). Using a 4-point scale, parents responded to such items as "It is very hard to keep up with your workload." Cronbach's alphas were .79 for mothers' and .72 for fathers' reports.

Emotional Involvement

Mothers' and fathers' emotional involvement and absorption in their jobs were assessed with Lodahl and Kejner's (1965) 20-item measure tapping the individual's commitment to and investment in his or her job. Using a 4-point Likert-type scale, parents responded to items such as "I'll stay overtime to finish a job, even if I'm not paid for it." Cronbach's alphas were .79 for mothers' and .76 for fathers' reports.

Education

Mothers' and fathers' levels of education are included in the bivariate analyses because education is an antecedent of work placement and is often used as a control variable in studies of the connections between work and family. We asked mothers and fathers how far they went in school.

Telephone Interview Measures

Measures Based on Daily Activities

The seven telephone interviews were our source of information about the ways in which mothers and fathers divided housework and parent-child activities, a modified version of a daily diary. This approach has several strengths (Huston and Robins 1982). First, it enables the researcher to collect data on a larger number of activities and over a longer period of time than would be feasible for observational research. Second, data are collected at the level of the activity, a strategy which minimizes memory distortion and errors in mental arithmetic. For example, parents are not asked to estimate how they usually divide housework. Rather, parents simply report each night on what household tasks they performed each day, and the researcher subsequently aggregates those data across days and computes the percentages of husbands' and wives' involvement.

Feminine-Typed Household Tasks

Each night we asked parents to report whether they had performed any of 12 household tasks and, for each instance, how much time they had spent in the activity. In these analyses, we focus on the four tasks that are traditionally assigned to women (i.e., cooking, cleaning, laundry, washing dishes), with the rationale that these routine, repetitive activities are the tasks that are most likely to elicit bargaining and negotiation on the part of spouses (Brayfield 1992). We computed the sum of the duration of time mothers spent in all feminine-typed tasks, across all days, and divided that figure by the sum of both parents' duration of time spent on these tasks to obtain an index of the division of feminine-typed tasks. A higher percentage means that the mother performed a larger share of housework. (See Table 1 for means, standard deviations, and ranges for the division of family work variables.)

Division of Parent-Child Activities

We used children's reports of time spent with mothers and fathers in joint activities to measure parent involvement because we had 7 daily reports from children, as compared to 4 from each parent. We summed the duration of time spent in any of the 53 activities about which we inquired (see Table 2 for examples) in which

Table 1. Means, Rangers, and Standard Deviations for Division of Family Work Variables[1] ($n = 181$)

Variable	Mean	Range	S.D.
Division Feminine Household Tasks	.79	.16-1	.17
Division Involvement w/Firstborns	.54	.12-.97	.15
Division Involvement w/Secondborns	.56	.18-.89	.15
Division Monitoring of Firstborns	.53	.42-.79	.05
Division Monitoring of Secondborns	.53	.36-.72	.05

Note: [1]Mother's involvement is the numerator, and the sum of mother's and father's involvement is the denominator. Scores indicate the percentage of family work performed by the mother.

Table 2. Examples of Activities from Children's Telephone Interviews (53 Activities in All)

Household Tasks
- Do Dishes
- Prepare a meal or snack (cook, set table)

Home and Personal Activities
- Homework
- Read books or magazines

Athletic Activities
- Sports (baseball, football, etc.)
- Dance

Toy and Games
- Computer or video games
- Play with blocks, legos, construction sets

Outdoor Activities
- Outdoor play (swings, jungle gym, tag, etc.)

Hobbies
- Draw, paint, color, or clay
- Attend club (4H, Scouts, etc.)

Entertainment
- Watch educational programs on TV (news, PBS, etc.)

Sibling Care

the parent had participated with the child in question. (We used a measure of "inclusive time," meaning that other people could have participated in the activities as well). As was the case for household work, we divided the total duration of time that mother spent in activities with a given child by the total time both parents spent with that child to obtain the index of the division of parent-child activities.

Table 3.   Correlations of Family Members' Report of
Joint Activities (Inclusive Time in Minutes)
($n = 181$)

Mothers and Fathers (Household Tasks Only)	.73
Mothers and Firstborns	.65
Fathers and Firstborns	.65
Mothers and Secondborns	.58
Fathers and Secondborns	.53
Firstborns and Secondborns	.55

Using our data from multiple family members regarding their joint activities, we have examined the associations between family members' reports of joint activities as an index of "inter-rater reliability." Table 3 summarizes inter-rater reliability for the total amount of time that individuals reported doing any activity with the partner. Note that family members were not trained to do this the way observers would be in a more traditional developmental study. The correlations are reasonable for parents and older siblings. The correlations involving secondborns are rather low. Another strategy we have used is to ask respondents the same questions twice, at the beginning and end of their interviews (a measure of test-retest reliability); we have consistently found test-retest correlations in the high .90's (McHale et al. 1992).

Division of Monitoring

At the end of each telephone interview, we asked parents and children an additional set of specific questions about each child's day designed to tap "parental monitoring." We define parental monitoring as the extent to which the parent is knowledgeable about the child's daily activities, whereabouts, and companions on a daily basis. To measure monitoring, we adapted the procedure developed by Crouter et al. (1990) which in turn was adapted from Patterson and Stouthamer-Loeber (1984) to create an index of monitoring. Each evening we asked parents and children (separately) a series of questions about the child's day that the parent presumably could only answer correctly if he or she had monitored the child. Parents were asked the questions twice: once about the firstborn and once about the secondborn. Questions were not repeated across a parent's calls, and mothers and fathers were asked questions in different sequences so that they could not prepare ahead for them. The analyses here focus on the 18 items which were asked of mothers and fathers on week nights (see Table 4). We omitted the weekend data here because we were interested in how parental employment was related to the division of monitoring and therefore selected days in which monitoring was more likely to be constrained by parents' work.

Table 4. Examples of Parental Monitoring Items
from Telephone Interviews

- Did (you/child) have any special academic successes in school today, like receiving a good grade on homework, a test, a paper, or a project?
  - If yes, in what subject(s) did that happen?
- Did (you/child) do anything fun with his/her friends today?
  - If yes, what did he/she do?
- Did (child) break any family rules today?
  - If so, what did he/she do?
- Were you (Was the child) outside of the home at 4 p.m. today?
  - If yes, where was he/she?

Questions were coded from 0 to 2, on the basis of the extent to which the parent's answer matched that of the child. Each question included a follow-up probe for details. Parents received full credit if the entire answer matched the child's, partial credit if the initial answer matched but the probe did not, and no credit if there was no initial match or the parent indicated not knowing the answer. Total monitoring scores were calculated as the percent of matching answers. The division of monitoring was calculated by dividing the mother's score by the sum of both parents' scores.

RESULTS

Preliminary Analyses

Table 5 summarizes the characteristics of the sample. While there was considerable variability in the sample, on average parents had completed 14.7 years of school, meaning they had completed some college. The mean occupational prestige code for fathers was 49.7; jobs at that level include office manager and computer operator. The mean level for mothers was 48.3, roughly the level of real estate agent or wholesale sales representative.

We next examined the intercorrelations among the work variables and the division of family work variables (see Table 6). Our first interest was in the interrelationships among the indicators of parents' division of family work. The division of feminine-typed household tasks was related to the division of involvement ($r = .19, p < .05$) and monitoring of the firstborn ($r = .15, p < .05$), but not to the division of family work with the secondborn. The indicators of the division of parenting were intercorrelated: the division of involvement with the older child was positively correlated with the division of involvement with the younger child ($r =$

Table 5.   Means and Standard Deviations of
Sample Background Characteristics

Variable	n	Range	Mean	Standard Deviation
Fathers' Education	181	10-20	14.7	2.39
Mothers' Education	181	12-20	14.7	2.12
Fathers' Total Work Hours	181	10-106	50.7	12.0
Mothers' Total Work Hours	181	1-70	33.3	14.8
Fathers' Occupational Prestige	181	22.33-74.77	49.7	12.6
Mothers' Occupational Prestige	177	22.3-74.77	48.3	13.2
Fathers' Earnings1	175	0-175,000	40,051	23,451
Mothers' Earnings1	177	0-93,000	19,526	14,750
Family Size	181	4-7	4.6	.76
Fathers' Age	181	29-66	39.0	5.0
Mothers' Age	181	29-66	36.8	3.7
Firstborns' Age	181	9.5-12.5	10.4	.55
Secondborns' Age	181	6.0-10.3	8.2	.92

Note: [1]Four respondents reported 0 income including three full-time students and 1 self-employed business owner.

.39, $p < .01$), and the division of monitoring of firstborn was positively correlated with the division of monitoring of the secondborn ($r = .57$, $p < .01$). These correlations, while significant, leave plenty of room for within-family variability in siblings' experiences. Note also that the division of involvement and monitoring were linked; when a mother spent proportionally more time with a child, relative to the father, she knew relatively more about that child's daily experiences ($r = .27$, $p < .01$; $r = .29$, $p < .01$, for firstborns and secondborns, respectively).

Bivariate Associations Between Mothers' and Fathers' Work Characteristics and the Division of Family Work

We next examined the associations between parents' work characteristics and the indicators of the division of family work (see Table 6). Fathers' individual work characteristics were generally unrelated to the indicators of the division of family work, with a few exceptions. The more hours fathers devoted to work, the more mothers contributed proportionally to feminine-typed household tasks and to monitoring the younger child. In addition, fathers who were more emotionally involved in their jobs performed less housework, and they contributed proportionally less to the monitoring of their firstborn children when they experienced

Table 6. Bivariate Correlations Between Indicators of the Division of Family Work and Characteristics of Mothers' and Fathers' Work[1]

	1	2	3	4	5	6	7	8	9	10	11	12	13	14	15	16	17
Div. Feminine Housework	—	.19*	.13	.15*	.13	.19*	.04	-.03	.04	.15*	-.12	-.36**	-.45**	-.17*	-.18*	-.14	-.30*
Div. Involvement w/Firstborn		—	.39**	.27**	.20**	.03	.11	.09	.05	-.01	.10	-.14	-.01	-.02	-.16*	-.02	.11
Div. Involvement w/Secondborn			—	.15*	.29**	.06	.01	.02	-.10	-.05	.03	-.02	-.10	-.01	-.18*	-.07	.03
Div. Monitoring of Firstborn				—	.57**	.14	.08	-.01	.17	.01	-.05	-.23**	-.13	-.09	-.02	-.12	-.02
Div. Monitoring of Secondborn					—	.19**	.12	.08	.14	.09	.05	.20**	-.15*	.00	-.11	-.07	.04
Father's Total Work Hours						—	.04	.16*	.30**	.39**	.09	-.06	-.11	.01	.03	-.04	.05
Father's Earnings							—	.37**	.09	.07	.40**	-.22**	-.11	.09	.01	.06	.19
Father's Job Prestige								—	.15*	.17*	.67**	-.15*	.04	.25**	.03	.05	.34**
Father's Work Pressure									—	.30**	.04	-.11	-.05	-.01	-.01	-.03	.0
Father's Work Involvement										—	.09	.05	.05	.02	.01	.11	.04
Father's Education											—	-.04	.20**	.31**	.11	.08	.59**
Mother's Total Work Hours												—	.59**	.24**	.37**	.28**	.19**
Mother's Earnings													—	.55**	.35**	.22**	.47**
Mother's Job Prestige														—	.27**	.23**	.56**
Mother's Work Pressure															—	.12	.22**
Mother's Work Involvement																—	.23**
Mother's Education																	—

Notes: * $p < .05$.
** $p < .01$.
[1]Due to occasional missing data on parents' work characteristics, sample sizes for individual correlation coefficients ranged from 171-181.

45

greater work pressure. This scant pattern is consistent with Peterson and Gerson's (1992) point that men generally do not "buy out" of family work in the way that women do.

There was a stronger pattern of correlations for mothers' individual work characteristics, although the pattern was more consistent for the division of housework than for the division of involvement and monitoring of children. Mothers spent proportionally less time on feminine-typed household tasks when they worked more hours, earned more, had greater occupational prestige, and reported more pressure on the job. In contrast, the division of involvement with children was linked only to work pressure; when mothers experienced more pressure, they were relatively less involved with both of their children. The division of monitoring was related to mothers' work hours; the more mothers worked, the less monitoring they performed, relative to their spouses. In addition, the more earnings mothers produced, the less monitoring they performed vis á vis the secondborn, relative to their husbands.

Bivariate Associations Between Dyadic Indicators of Couples' Work Circumstances and the Division of Family Work

Examining mothers' and fathers' work characteristics separately does not take into account the fact that parents operate as a team (Crouter and Helms-Erikson 1997). A parent's ability to negotiate a lighter share of housework, for example, depends not only on his or her individual work circumstances but also on how those circumstances compare to the spouse's work situation. We next created dyadic indicators. For work hours and income, the dyadic indicators were the proportion of total parental work time—or income—contributed by mother. For occupational prestige, work pressure, and work involvement, we followed Brayfield's (1992) lead, calculating difference scores (mother minus father) to indicate the gap in parents' experiences.

The dyadic variables reflecting the combination of spouses' work characteristics presented a stronger and more consistent picture than did the individual characteristics, although the pattern was still more pronounced for housework than for parenting (see Table 7). Mothers performed proportionally fewer feminine-typed household tasks when they contributed a larger share of work time and earnings, when they experienced more work pressure than their partner, and when they were more emotionally invested in work than their partner. Similarly, mothers monitored their offspring less, relative to the father, when they contributed a larger share of work time and earnings. In addition, mothers performed proportionally less monitoring of the younger child when they experienced more pressure at work as compared to their partner. In contrast, with only one exception, there were no significant dyadic correlates of involvement in activities with either firstborn or secondborn children. These dyadic analyses suggest that, to some extent, the

Table 7. Correlations Between Dyadic Work Variables and
Indicators of the Division of Family Work

	Div. Fem. Housework	Div. Involvement w/FB	Div. Involvement w/SB	Div. Monitoring of FB	Div. Monitoring of SB
Proportion of Hours Worked by Mother (n =181)	−.43**	−.14	−.06	−.26**	−.27**
Proportion of Earnings Earned by Mother (n = 171)	−.40**	−.07	−.11	−.15*	−.18*
Difference in Prestige[1] (n = 177)	−.11	−.01	−.01	−.10	−.13
Difference in Pressure (n = 177)	−.16*	−.16*	−.07	−.11	−.17*
Difference in Emotional Involvement (n = 178)	−.22*	−.01	−.01	−.10	−.13
Difference in Education (n = 181)	−.17*	.00	−.00	.04	−.02

Notes: * $p < .05$.
   ** $p < .01$.
[1] Difference scores were computed by subtracting fathers' scores from mothers' scores.

division of parental monitoring resembles the division of housework in its relationship to parents' work lives, but the division of parent-child activities does not.

Putting it All Together

In her analysis of the predictors of involvement in feminine-typed tasks, Brayfield (1992) examined the cumulative predictive power of individual work characteristics, relative (dyadic) work characteristics, and the interactions between the two. The interactions are interesting because they can reveal, for example, that the time a mother devotes to work, relative to the time devoted by her spouse, has different implications for the division of family work depending upon the absolute level of time she spends at work. We followed Brayfield's lead, choosing three variables to include in ordinary least squares regression analyses: work time, income, and pressure. These variables: (a) represented the three substantive domains of interest: temporal availability, relative resources, and occupational demands; and (b) tended to be significantly associated with the division of family work at the individual or dyadic level. The regressions included mothers' work hours, earnings, and pressure, the dyadic variables, which reflected mothers' level relative to fathers' on these three constructs, and the interaction terms involving the absolute and relative scores. We conducted separate regressions for each of the five indicators of the division of family work.

Table 8.   OLS Unstandardized Regression Coefficients for
Equations Predicting Division of Family Work[1,2]

Predictors	Div. Feminine Housework	Div. Monitoring Firstborn	Div. Monitoring Secondborn
M's Earnings	−.024	.002	.003
	(.000)	(.000)	(.000)
M's Work Hours	22.40	−5.74	6.52
	(.002)	(.001)	(.001)
M's Pressure	−27.77	23.77[+]	2.42
	(.004)	(.001)	(.001)
Dyadic Earnings	129.13	−30.95	−184.53
	(.202)	(.07)	(.037)
Dyadic Hours	−.6821.75**	−.228.74	−1074.16[+]
	(.202)	(.07)	(.066)
Dyadic Pressure	23.73	−19.29[+]	−12.74
	(.003)	(.001)	(.001)
M's Inc. x Dyadic Earnings	−.084*	−.015	−.012
	(.000)	(.000)	(.000)
M's Hrs. x Dyadic Hrs.	−89.40	28.89	49.48**
	(.006)	(.002)	(.002)
M's Pressure x Dyadic Pressure	2.60	−1.40	−1.10
	(.000)	(.000)	(.000)
n	168	168	168
R^2	.30	.09	.11
F	7.63**	1.65[+]	2.11*

Notes: [+]$p < .10.$
*$p < .05.$
**$p < .01.$
[1] Standards errors of estimates are in parentheses.
[2] Regression coefficients multiplied by 10,000.

The model predicting the division of feminine-typed tasks revealed that the dyadic measure of work hours is a significant predictor, controlling for other variables (see Table 8); the more mothers worked, relative to their spouses, the less they contributed proportionally in terms of housework. The significant interaction between mothers' earnings and the dyadic earnings measure indicates that the effect of mothers' earning more relative to their partners was more strongly related to the division of feminine-typed tasks at higher levels of mothers' absolute earnings. In other words, the slope of the regression line is steeper at higher levels of mothers' earnings. Mothers are more likely to use their relative resources to "buy out" if they are earning more overall, a finding that makes sense when conceptualized in terms of marital power. Not surprisingly, given the lack of significant correlations at the bivariate level for the division of parent-child activities with firstborns and secondborns, those models were not significant in the regression analyses and are not labled here. Turning to the regression analyses on parental monitoring, none of the predictors of the division of monitoring of the firstborn achieved conventional levels of significance, although there were several nonsignificant trends. The only significant predictor of the division of monitoring of the secondborn was the mothers' work time X dyadic work time interaction. When mothers devoted more time to work at an absolute level, their relative involvement in work was more strongly related to the division of monitoring than was the case when mothers worked fewer hours.

Do the Connections Between Work and Parenting Vary as a Function of Children's Sex?

We made the point earlier that parents may approach the division of parenting differently when they have sons versus daughters. If parenting boys is more demanding and challenging, for example, parents may use work-related resources to "buy out" of monitoring sons but not daughters; alternatively, social norms or initiations from their children may mean that fathers maintain a higher level of involvement with sons in the face of forces emanating from the workplace. To explore whether there was a different pattern of work-related correlates for the division of parent-child involvement and monitoring with sons versus daughters, we re-ran the regressions separately for boys and girls. Again, the models for the division of parent-child involvement were not significant for older sons, older daughters, younger sons, or younger daughters. Parents appear to divide time in joint activities with children along same-sex lines, but not as a function of the particular work circumstances examined here.

The findings for the division of monitoring tell a different story. The regression models for firstborn and secondborn girls were not significant (and, to save space, are not tabled here). In contrast, the work variables accounted for 19 and 24 percent of the variance in the division of monitoring of older and younger boys, respectively (see Table 9). For older sons, controlling for other variables in the model, the only significant predictor was the mothers' work hours X dyadic work hours interaction. The more hours mothers worked, at an absolute level, the stronger the relationship was between their relative involvement at work and the division of monitoring. For younger sons, the difference in mothers' and fathers' work pressure was a significant predictor of the division of parents' monitoring. The more pressure mothers experienced relative to fathers, the less mothers contributed proportionally to the division of monitoring. These results suggest that the significant regressions pertaining to monitoring for the sample as a whole were primarily attributable to the pattern of correlates for sons, but not for daughters. They also reveal the interrelatedness among the work variables; these variables shared a considerable amount of the variance and hence frequently did not emerge as significant predictors. Perhaps most interesting, however, the regressions

Table 9.   OLS Unstandardized Regression Coefficients for Equations Predicting Division of Monitoring for Sons[1,2]

Predictors	Firstborns	Secondborns
M's Earnings	.008	.002
	(.000)	(.000)
M's Work Hours	−5.62	8.03
	(.001)	(.001)
M's Pressure	16.85	29.49
	(.002)	(.002)
Dyadic Earnings	31.89	−684.94
	(.05)	(.045)
Dyadic Hours	−436.97	−907.01
	(.074)	(.088)
Dyadic Pressure	−8.40	−39.83[**]
	(.001)	(.001)
M's Inc. x Dyadic Earnings	−.034[+]	.002
	(.000)	(.000)
M's Hrs. x Dyadic Hrs.	54.25[*]	40.80
	(.002)	(.003)
M's Pressure x Dyadic Pressure	3.09	.537
	(.000)	(.000)
n	79	8
R^2	.19	.24
F	1.77[+]	2.71[**]

Notes: [+] $p < .10$.
[*] $p < .05$.
[**] $p < .01$.
[1] Standard errors of estimates are in parentheses.
[2] Regression coefficients multiplied by 10,000.

revealed the utility of considering individual work characteristics and dyadic measures of the same constructs in combination.

DISCUSSION

Our analyses highlight several important issues in the study of the work-family interface. The first has to do with the multidimensional nature of family work during the middle childhood years. This idea is evident in the different patterns of predictors of the division of housework and parent-oriented activities. Although parents appear to use work related demands and resources to negotiate a more egalitarian division of household work, we found virtually no links between parents' work experiences and their division of involvement in parent-child activities. By middle childhood parents may be thinking of their joint activities with their children as something other than work. We did find some evidence, however, that the division of parental monitoring is linked to mothers' and fathers' work characteristics. Why might this be the case? Monitoring children may require considerable energy. Parents have to observe their children and ask them questions about their day; to the extent that children are not forthcoming about their daily experiences, parents may need to keep a special eye on their activities or obtain information from other sources (e.g., the other parent, a sibling, a teacher, or coach). Our regression analyses suggest that the division of monitoring depends upon both parents' work hours, as well as their experience of pressure on the job, especially when they are monitoring the daily experiences of young boys.

Why did we find work-related predictors of the division parental monitoring for families with sons but not daughters? One possibility is that school-age boys are more active and demanding than girls and therefore are harder to monitor. Moreover, girls may be more forthcoming about their daily experiences, making it easier for parents to be knowledgeable about daughters' experiences without having to go to great lengths to monitor them. To the extent that monitoring sons takes deliberate effort and concentration by parents, parents' performance may depend in part upon their work situations.

The second theme that our findings underscore is the utility of investigating spouses' work and family experiences at the level of the dyad. In the past, much of the work and family literature focused on the links between mothers' employment and the way they raised their children. In our work, however, we adopted a dyadic perspective. This perspective: (1) emphasizes how the world of work, like the domain of family life, is stratified by gender, (2) highlights the differences in the circumstances of husbands and wives, and, (3) by definition pays equal attention to the family roles and activities of mothers and fathers (Crouter and Helms-Erikson 1997). Studied dyadically, each partner's work and family experiences serve as the context for the other's. Seen in context, men's and women's work—in and out of the home—becomes invested with meaning that often has to do with power and status. In our analyses, the clearest picture of the connections between parents' work characteristics and the division of family work emerged when the analyses combined individual and dyadic indicators of parental work.

What are the policy implications of our findings? One of the ironies of the literature on work and family is that patterns of inequality in one context are usually attributed to inequality in the other, a vicious circle that poses a challenge to policymakers. Inequality in the division of housework and child care, for example, holds women back from aspiring to and attaining the kinds of jobs that will put them on a par with men. Similarly, inequality in earnings and work hours holds women back from negotiating for greater participation in housework and child care on the part of their husbands. Our findings suggest that pushing for equal opportunities for women in the workplace may lead to more involvement in the family on the part of husbands and fathers, at least in the areas of housework and monitoring. We favor Coltrane's (1996) optimistic view that greater family involvement on the part of fathers in the long run will not only benefit mothers, but will also enhance the development of fathers themselves, as well as their children.

In addition, parents of school-aged children may benefit from parent education programs that highlight the connections between their work and their family lives. Frequently parenting education is seen as important for couples making the transition to parenthood but is overlooked at later points in the life course when it might be quite beneficial. Parents need to know, for example, about the developmental significance of parental monitoring. Parenting education should also stress the importance of attending to both husbands' and wives' work experiences and the ways in which couples balance the demands of work and family. For example, parents need to understand that mothers may not be able to monitor their children effectively when they are working long hours and experiencing considerable pressure on the job and that fathers need to be keeping an eye on their children's daily activities as well. A potential avenue for dissemenating this information to parents of school-aged children is through corporate-sponsored educational seminars in the workplace. such seminars, begun by a number of companies in the 1980s, feature topics related to balancing work and family demands (Galinsky 1990). The findings presented here suggest that these topical seminars would better serve parents by incorporating developmental and dyadic perspectives.

Our findings in this chapter have focused on one (cross-sectional) slice of time during middle childhood. Ultimately, we will have three waves of longitudinal data on these families. These data will enable us to examine whether and how the division of family work changes as mothers' and fathers' work situations change over time. Do fathers take on a greater share of monitoring when their wives increase their work hours or experience new work pressures? Does the division of parent-child involvement in joint activities remain unconnected to mothers' and fathers' work characteristics throughout the transition from middle childhood to adolescence, or does this relationship change? As children move into the teenage years, does it become harder to monitor girls, and, if so, does the division of monitoring daughters become connected to parents' work demands? The agenda for future research in this area is a rich and potentially fruitful one.

REFERENCES

Bell, R. Q. 1968. "Reinterpretation of the Direction of Effects in Studies of Socialization." *Psychology Review* 75: 81-95.

Bolger, N., A. DeLongis, R. C. Kessler, and E. Wethington. 1989. "The Contagion of Stress Across Multiple Roles." *Journal of Marriage and the Family* 51: 175-183.

Brayfield, A. A. 1992. "Employment Resources and Housework in Canada." *Journal of Marriage and the Family* 54: 19-30.

Brines, J. 1994. "Economic Dependency, Gender, and the Division of Labor at Home." *American Journal of Sociology* 100(3): 652-688.

Collins, W. A., M. L. Harris, and A. Susman. 1995. "Parenting During Middle Childhood." In *Handbook of Parenting*, Vol. 1, edited by M. Bornstein. Mahwah, NJ: Lawrence Erlbaum.

Coltrane, S. 1992. "Predicting the Sharing of Household Labor: Are Parenting and Housework Distinct?" *Sociological Perspectives* 35: 629-648.

Coltrane, S. 1996. *Family Man: Fatherhood, Housework, and Gender Equity.* New York: Oxford University Press.

Crouter, A. C., and H. Helms-Erikson. 1997. "Work and Family From a Dyadic Perspective: Variations in Inequality." Pp. 487-503 in *Handbook of Personal Relationships*, edited by S. Duck. New York: John Wiley.

Crouter, A. C., H. Helms-Erikson, K. Updegraff, and S. M. McHale. 1999. "Conditions Underlying Parents' Knowledge About Children's Daily Lives in Middle Childhood: Between- and Within Family Comparison. *Child Development* 70: 246-259.

Crouter, A. C., S. M. MacDermid, S. M. McHale, and M. Perry-Jenkins, M. 1990. "Parental Monitoring and Perceptions of Children's School Performance and Conduct in Dual-Earner and Single-Earner Families." *Developmental Psychology* 26: 649-657.

Crouter, A. C., B. Manke, and S. M. McHale. 1995. "The Family Context of Gender Intensification in Early Adolescence." *Child Development* 66: 317-329.

Crouter, A. C., and S. M. McHale. 1993. "The Long Arm of the Job: Influences of Parental Work on Childrearing." In *Parenting: An Ecological Perspective*, edited by T. Luster and L. Okagaki. New York: Lawrence Erlbaum.

Dunn, J., and R. Plomin. 1990. *Separate Lives: Why Siblings are so Different.* New York: Basic Books.

Galinsky, E. 1990. "Strategies for Integrating the Family Needs of Works into Human Resource Planning." Pp. 152-170 in *The Human Side of Corporate Competitiveness*. Newbury Park, CA: Sage.

Geerken, M., and W. Gove. 1983. *At Home and at Work: The Family's Allocation of Labor.* Beverly Hills, CA: Sage.

Hetherington, E. M., D. Reiss, and R. Plomin. 1994. *Separate Social Worlds of Siblings: The Impact of Nonshared Environment on Development.* Hillsdale, NJ: Lawrence Erlbaum.

Huston, A. C. 1983. Sex-Typing. In *Handbook of Child Psychology: Socialization, Personality, and Social Development*, Vol. 4, edited by P. Mussen. New York: Wiley.

Huston, T. L., and E. Robins. 1982. "Conceptual and Methodological Issues in Studying Close Relationships." *Journal of Marriage and the Family* 44: 901-925.

Kamo, Y. 1988. "Determinants of Household Division of Labor: Resources, Power, and Ideology." *Journal of Family Issues* 9: 177-200.

Kanter, R. M. 1977. *Work and Family in the United States: A Critical Review and Agenda for Research and Policy.* New York: Russell Sage.

Katz, P. A., and K. R. Ksansnak. 1994. "Developmental Aspects of Gender Role Flexibility and Traditionality in Middle Childhood and Adolescence." *Developmental Psychology* 30(2): 272-282.

Lodahl, T., and M. Kejner. 1965. "The Definition and Measurement of Job Involvement." *Journal of Applied Psychology* 49: 24-33.

McHale, S. M., and A. C. Crouter. 1992. "You Can't Always get What you Want: Incongruence Between Sex-role Attitudes and Family Work Roles and its Implications for Marriage." *Journal of Marriage and the Family* 54: 537-547.

McHale, S. M., A. C. Crouter, and W. T. Bartko. 1992. "Traditional and Egalitarian Patterns of Parental Involvement: Antecedents, Consequences, and Temporal Rhythms." In *Life-Span Development and Behavior*, Vol. 11. New York: Lawrence Erlbaum.

McHale, S. M., A. C. Crouter and C. J. Tucker. in press. *Gender Role Socialization in Middle Childhood: Comparisons Within and Between Families Child Development.*

Menaghan, E. G., and T. L. Parcel. 1990. "Parental Employment and Family Life: Research in the 1980's." *Journal of Marriage and the Family* 52: 1079-1098.

Moos, R. H. 1986. *Work Environment Scale Manual*, 2nd edition. Palo Alto, CA: Consulting Psychologists Press, Inc.

Nakao, K., and J. Treas. 1990. "Computing 1989 Occupational Prestige Scores." *General Social Survey Methodological report Number 70*.

Parcel, T. L., and E. G. Menaghan. 1994. *Parents' Jobs and Children's Lives*. New York: Aldine de Gruyter.

Parke, R. D. 1995. "Fathers and Families." In *Handbook of Parenting*, edited by M. Bornstein. Mahwah, NJ: Lawrence Erlbaum.

Patterson, G. R., and M. Stouthamer-Loeber. 1984. "The Correlation of Family Management Practices and Delinquency." *Child Development* 55: 1299-1307.

Peterson, R. R., and K. Gerson. 1992. "Determinants of Responsibility for Child Care Arrangements Among Dual-Earner Couples." *Journal of Marriage and the Family* 54: 527-536.

Pleck, J. H. 1979. "Men's Family Work: Three Perspectives and Some New Data." *Family Coordinator* 29: 94-101.

———. 1983. "Husbands' Paid Work and Family Roles: Current Research Issues." In *Research in the Interweave of Social Roles: Families and Jobs*, Vol. 3. Greenwich, CT: JAI Press.

Plomin, R., and D. Daniels. 1987. "Why are Children in the Same Family so Different From Each Other?" *The Behavioral and Brain Sciences* 10: 1-16.

Repetti, R. 1989. "Effects of Daily Workload on Subsequent Behavior During Marital Interaction: The Roles of Social Withdrawal and Spouse Support." *Journal of Personality and Social Psychology* 52: 710-720.

———. 1994. "Short-Term and Long-Term Processes Linking Job Stressors to Father-Child Interaction." *Social Development* 3: 1-15.

Ross, C. E. 1987. "The Division of Labor at Home." *Social Forces* 65: 816-833.

Spitze, G. 1988. "Women's Employment and Family Relations." *Journal of Marriage and the Family* 50: 595-618.

Updegraff, K. A., S. M. McHale, and A. C. Crouter. 1996. "Gender Roles in Marriage: What Do They Mean for School Achievement?" *Journal of Youth and Adolescence* 25: 73-88.

THE BALANCING ACT:
YOUNG WOMEN'S EXPECTATIONS
AND EXPERIENCES OF WORK AND FAMILY

Pamela Aronson

ABSTRACT

This paper examines the dilemmas of young women as they initiate their work and family life trajectories. Based on *Youth Development Study* survey data and interviews with forty-two of the female respondents, this paper compares the expectations of young women who had not yet become mothers to the actual experiences of those who were already mothers. Their concerns are situated in the context of three related historical trends: changes in women's employment, marriage and motherhood; the increasingly individualized life course; and the so-called "postfeminist" era. Most of the women who were not yet mothers were optimistic about how they would balance work and motherhood, while those who were already mothers experienced much difficulty balancing these often conflicting demands. This study suggests that historical changes in the life course have created difficult issues for contemporary young women on the threshold of adulthood. Consistent with the "destandardized," "postfeminist" era, the young women in this study took

Research in the Sociology of Work, Volume 7, pages 55-83.
Copyright © 1999 by JAI Press Inc.
All rights of reproduction in any form reserved.
ISBN: 0-7623-0605-X

a wide range of approaches to balancing work and family, suggesting an individualistic way of crafting of work and family strategies to suit their own goals and
interests.

INTRODUCTION

How do young mothers balance work and family? How do young women who are
not yet mothers anticipate their future in terms of work and family? How are these
realities and expectations shaped by the social context? Negotiating the often conflicting demands of work and family is a balancing act that nearly all women face
during their lifetimes. However, work and family issues vary dramatically at different points in the life course, and differ as a result of the changing historical context. For contemporary young women poised on the threshold of adulthood,
decisions about work and family produce particular challenges and dilemmas as a
result of the convergence of several related forces in the contemporary social context: historical changes in women's lives, particularly in the areas of employment,
marriage, and motherhood (Evans 1989; Harris 1995; Forest, Moen and McClain
1995; McLaughlin et al. 1988; Modell 1989); an increasingly "destandardized"
life course (Buchmann 1989); and the so-called "postfeminist" era (Stacey 1991).
This study examines young women's expectations and experiences of work and
family in this contemporary context.

Prior research on work and family has focused on two major concerns. First,
studies of adult women have examined the dilemmas and strategies used to juggle
work and family demands. Second, researchers have studied the future plans of
adolescents and young adults—namely, how they anticipate combining work and
family roles. However, prior research has not examined how young women actually negotiate the demands of work and family as they make the transition to
adulthood and begin to move into these roles for the first time.

As a result of the so-called "postfeminist" (Stacey 1991) era and the increasingly "individualized" life course (Buchmann 1989), contemporary young women
face a wide range of options and opportunities when deciding how to live and
structure their lives. However, these same options have produced confusion and
ambivalence for young women who are in the process of moving into roles which
are often contradictory. Young women who are first entering the worlds of both
work and family anticipate how they will prioritize these responsibilities. However, expectations about these roles may differ tremendously from the realities
these women subsequently experience. This paper examines the expectations of
young women who have not yet become mothers, and contrasts them with the
dilemmas and compromises which young mothers face when trying to meet the
demands of both work and family.

Historical Changes in Women's Life Courses

Life course research emphasizes the interaction of biography with the historical context; the life course unfolds in sequences and is marked by transitions within particular historical circumstances (Elder and O'Rand 1995; Elder 1974, 1985). Women's life course patterns have changed dramatically over the last thirty years. There has been an increase of women in the labor force, particularly married women with children under age six (Gerson 1985; U.S. Department of Labor 1980), and women's employment has become normative (Evans 1989). The movement of women into the labor force coincided with a decline in the birthrate (Gerson 1985; U.S. Department of Labor 1980, p. 3; Moen 1992; McLaughlin et al. 1988), a rise in the average age at marriage, and a greater number of women choosing to remain unmarried (McLaughlin et al. 1988; Moen 1992; Evans 1989; U.S. Bureau of the Census 1985).

The women's movement of the late-1960s and 1970s helped to produce these dramatic changes in many women's lives (Evans 1979, 1989; Freeman 1975; Ryan 1992; Taylor and Whittier 1992). New conceptions of being a woman emerged, and these challenged women's previous roles (Evans 1979, 1989). However, with the decline of the women's movement, the contemporary period is sometimes characterized as "postfeminist" (Stacey 1991). Despite some women's hostility towards feminism, Stacey (1991, p. 262) argues that many women have "semiconsciously incorporated feminist principles into their gender and kinship expectations and practices." For young women, this means assuming women's work opportunities, sexual freedom, and male participation in domestic work and child rearing (Stacey 1991).

Along with dramatic changes in women's life courses and identities, there have been historical changes in the transition from adolescence to adulthood. In the 1970s and 1980s, lengthened schooling delayed entry into the full-time labor market (Modell 1989; Peters, Guit and Rooijen 1992). Family formation has also occurred at later ages, resulting in the extension of adolescence (Modell 1989; Elder and O'Rand 1995; Stevens 1990). Additionally, the variance in school completion has steadily increased during the past century (Arnett and Taber 1994; Modell et al. 1976), and the variance in age at marriage and becoming a parent also increased between 1960 and 1980 (Arnett and Taber 1994; Model 1989). Parenthood has become less tied to marriage than in the past (Furstenberg et al. 1987), and almost one-third of all births in the United States are to single mothers (National Center for Health Statistics 1995).

These changes are tied to technological changes in the economy (the movement from a manufacturing economy to a service and information based economy), and rising levels of income for human capital investment (Hogan and Mochizuki 1988). Arnett and Taber (1994) argue that in such a complex economy, it takes longer for adolescents to learn useful skills. In fact, some scholars argue that advanced industrial capitalism has resulted in young people being "forced to remain in school longer" despite a situation where they are unable "to make a meaningful contribution to the economy," even after completing postsecondary education (Cote and Allahar 1994).

With all of these historical changes, the life course has become "destandardized," with a larger diversity of possible pathways, and a greater diversity among individuals (Buchmann 1989). As a result, the transition to adulthood is "a more extended, diversified, and increasingly individualized period" (Buchmann 1989, p. 187). Because consensus on appropriate ages for particular transitions has decreased (Arnett and Taber 1994), the life course more frequently changes in mid-stream (Gerson 1985; Furstenberg et al. 1987; Buchmann 1989) and youth face greater subjective choice in the "biographical field of options" (Peters, Guit and Rooijen 1992, p. 333). In fact, Modell (1989, p. 326) argues that young adults "have increasingly taken control of the construction of the youthful life course." In this context, "one's own identity has come to matter correspondingly more" (Modell 1989, p. 331). However, flexibility in the life course makes it more difficult to predict one's future from one's current circumstances (Buchmann 1989). This reduces the possibility that young adults will develop long-term, stable expectations about their life paths and results in the "internalization of diffuse expectations and aspirations" (Buchmann 1989, p. 77).

Combining Work and Family

Historical changes in women's life courses have brought about profound changes in work and family arrangements. However, women's employment often fails to alter the traditional wife and mother responsibilities that typically characterize family life (Moen 1992; Hochschild 1989). As a result, women experience more conflict and disjuncture than men between these spheres (Moen 1992; Mortimer and London 1984; Mortimer and Sorensen 1984; Maines and Hardesty 1987; McLaughlin et al. 1988), and women's biographies reflect the difficulties of reconciling work and family (Becker-Schmidt 1991). Women have different commitment levels to work and family: some are "captives," engaged in one role primarily when they actually prefer the other; some are "conflicted," with ambivalence about work and family roles; others are "copers," who successfully manage work with young children; still others are "committed" to both work and family realms (Moen 1992). Women's initial work and family orientations often remain the same over the life course (some women maintain domestic paths, while others maintain career-focused paths), although other women experience particular "triggering events" which push them to alter their initial work and family orientations (Gerson 1985).

Within the last twenty years, there has been a convergence in contemporary adolescent boys' and girls' achievement and employment aspirations (Stevens, Puchtell, Ryu and Mortimer 1992; Dennehy and Mortimer 1994; Danzinger 1983; Farmer 1983; Crowley and Shapiro 1982; Herzog 1982; Shapiro and Crowley

1982; Bush Simmons, Hutchinson and Blyth 1978). Although almost all girls coming of age today expect to have a job, they differ in how they plan to combine their work with motherhood (Peters, Guit and Rooijen 1992). While young men anticipate uninterrupted work trajectories, women's plans for achievement are often contingent upon family demands (Maines and Hardesty 1987). For example, girls' future plans are more family-focused than boys': they are more likely to see marriage and parenthood as important, to plan to marry and to have children, and to expect career interruptions to care for their children (Dennehy and Mortimer 1994). While "undergraduate men are moving full-steam ahead," with respect to occupational aspirations, the women "are talking career but thinking job": they have less specific career expectations than young men, and expect to interrupt work for child rearing (Machung 1989, pp. 52-53).

Most contemporary young women orient themselves toward a "double life concept" (Geissler and Kruger 1992) or "have it all" approach to work and family (Sidel 1990; Erwin 1995, 1996). Rather than viewing work and family as alternatives to each other, they anticipated combining these spheres, often in the form of uninterrupted involvement in both work and family. Despite structural impediments, many expected to be able to make individual arrangements to realize their goals (Geissler and Kruger 1992). Sidel (1990) labeled these women "New American Dreamers," because they believed that they needed to achieve their goals on their own. Rather than seeing themselves as supporting the achievements of others, these women defined their lives in terms of their own self-realization and independence.

Contemporary young women at the threshold of adulthood face a unique historical juncture and a particular life course stage as they begin to move into work and family roles. This study compares the expectations of young women who have not yet become mothers to the experiences of young mothers. Women who did not yet have children had many ideas about how they would deal with these demands, but they had not been forced to confront these realities in their own lives. For these women, idealized visions of combining work and family were prevalent, often with little idea about how these visions would in fact be implemented. In contrast, most of the women who were already mothers spoke of juggling and conflicting demands, and little support from male partners.

METHODS

This project combines in-depth interviews with survey data from the *Youth Development Study*, an ongoing longitudinal study of adolescent development and the transition to adulthood. The *Youth Development Study* panel was studied from the ninth grade to four years beyond high school. The sample ($N = 1,000$) was randomly chosen from a list of enrolled ninth grade students in St. Paul, Minnesota in 1988. Respondents completed surveys annually, with the eighth year in 1995. In

Table 1.   Youth Development Study

					Administration			
						Mail Survey		
		In School: Full Survey						Full Survey
Grade level	9	10	11	12				
Age	14-15	15-16	16-17	17-18	18-19	19-20	20-21	21-22
Year	1988	1989	1990	1991	1992	1993	1994	1995
No. adolescent respondents	1,000[a]	964	957	933	816	782	799	780
% Retention rate	—	96.2	95.4	92.8	81.3	77.7	79.6	77.6
No. mothers responding	924	—	—	690	—	—	—	
No. fathers responding	649	—	—	440	—	—	—	
% Respondents with at least one parent responding	95.9	—	—	79.1	—	—	—	

Note: [a] 1,010 consented to participate in Fall 1987.

wave four (twelfth grade), the retention rate was 92.8 percent; in wave eight (age 21-22), it was 77.6 percent (see Table 1). That is, of the original 1,000 panel members who took part in the first year of data collection, the *Youth Development Study* has retained 78 percent over an eight-year period. In the eighth year, there were 448 female respondents and 332 male respondents.

Based on the survey data, I initially identified young women with divergent patterns of experience with regard to careers, education, and parenthood. Following Glaser and Strauss' (1967) suggestions for theoretical sampling, interviewees were chosen to represent different trajectories, as well as to obtain class and racial diversity. As Glaser and Strauss (1967) propose, comparing groups allows for the continued development of emerging theory.

By mail, the Principal Investigator of the *Youth Development Study* invited women to be interviewed; they consented by returning a postcard indicating their interest. Once a positive response was received, I called the respondent to schedule the interview. In order to obtain an appropriate number of interviewees, but to not accrue too many affirmative responses, I sent out three separate mailouts. In all, I invited 138 women to be interviewed. Forty-two women agreed and were interviewed between November, 1996 and March, 1997. This represents a 30.4 percent affirmative response rate. Consequently, 9.4 percent of the 448 Youth Development Study women who responded in the eighth year of the study were interviewed. The women were aged 23-24 at the time of the interviews.

The first group from which I drew my interview sample (28.6% of the Y.D.S. sample overall) were those whose primary involvement was post-secondary education in the four years following high school (see Table 2). Typically, these women had attended a four-year college or university for at least eight months annually, in three of the four years following high school. The second group (30.6% of the Y.D.S. sample) had become mothers by the eighth year of the study. As the interviews revealed, most of these women had become mothers in their teenage years. The third group (40.8%) were those who did not have an extensive school trajectory (i.e., they did not meet the first criterion), nor had they become mothers. These women typically were in the full-time labor force or moved back and forth between post-secondary school and work after high school. Although many of the women in this group had attended four-year colleges or universities, community colleges, or vocational school, their primary focus and identity appeared to be work, since they typically worked full time in the fifth through eighth years of the study. This distinction was based on survey questions, as well as life history calendar data collected during the fifth through eighth years of the study. On the life history calendar, respondents check the months they spent in different school, work, and living arrangements. In general, I sought to obtain a sample with roughly equal numbers of women in each group, a strategy which led to slight differences between the percent of respondents in the *Youth Development Study* sample and the interview sub-sample (see Table 2). Whereas the distinctions among these trajectories are important for other parts of this study, in this analysis the "school" group and "other" group are combined to highlight the distinction between the mothers and the other young women. Thus the comparison here will be made between the those who had already become mothers and those who were not yet mothers.

The interviewees were diverse; thirty-three percent were women of color, and they had a wide range of socioeconomic backgrounds (see Tables 3 and 4). Social class background was based on parents' income and education as reported in the parent surveys in the first year of the study (1988). Approximately thirty-one percent of the interview sample fell into the working class (this included those whose parents had less than a bachelor's degree and earned less than $30,000 per year in 1988). The majority of the sample, nearly forty-eight percent, came from middle class backgrounds. This included four sub-groups: parents who had high

Table 2.   Transition Patterns of Youth Development Study Women and Interviewees

Group	% in YDS Sample	N Interviewed	Percent of Interviewees in Each Group
In School	28.6%	15	35.7%
Parents	30.6%	14	33.3%
Other	40.8%	13	31%
Total	100%	42	100%

Table 3.   Class Background of Interviewees and Y.D.S. Sample

Class Background	N Interviewed	% of Interviewees	N in YDS Sample	% of YDS Sample
Working	13	31%	384	38%
Middle	20	47.6	470	46.5
Upper-Middle	9	21.4	86	8.5
Unknown	0	0	70	6.9
Total	42	100	1010	100

educational attainment (at least a bachelor's degree) and low income (less than $30,000 per year in 1988); low educational attainment (less than a bachelor's degree) but high income (at least $50,000 per year in 1988); high education (at least a bachelor's degree) and middle income (between $30,000 and $50,000 per year in 1988); and low education (less than a bachelor's degree) and middle income. Twenty one percent were classified as upper-middle class because their parents had high educational attainment (at least a bachelor's degree) and earned a middle to high income (over $50,000 per year in 1988).

Table 3 compares the class backgrounds of the interview sub-sample with the *Youth Development Study* sample as a whole. This comparison suggests that the interview sub-sample contained quite similar proportions of working and middle class respondents as the overall sample. However, the interview sample consisted of a larger proportion of upper-middle class respondents and fewer unknown cases, resulting in a slightly more advantaged sub-sample than the sample overall. In Table 4, the same comparisons are made with regard to racial background. We see that the interview sub-sample was composed of a greater proportion of minority respondents than existed in the *Youth Development Study* sample as a whole. Thus, although some differences exist, the interview sub-sample is quite comparable to the Youth Development Study overall.

I conducted interviews face-to-face, in a place chosen by each participant. Typically, the location was interviewees' homes, although some were conducted in coffee shops. These interviews were tape recorded and transcribed. I followed an interview guide, which covered a range of themes related to education, work, and family (see Appendix). The interviews ranged from forty-five minutes to three hours, although most lasted one and one-half hours. The interviews consisted of "structured conversations" (Taylor and Rupp 1991, p. 126), and allowed space for participants to bring up the issues they found most important.

After each interview, I wrote field notes, including the main themes of the interview, my reflections on the interview, and emerging research questions. Transcriptions were analyzed according to Glaser and Strauss' (1967) inductive principles for constructing grounded theory. In the analysis, I utilized a qualitative data

Table 4.   Racial Background of Interviewees and Y.D.S. Sample

Race	N Interviewed	% of Interviewees	N in YDS Sample	% of YDS Sample
White	28	66.7%	721	71.4%
African American	5	11.9	98	9.7
Hispanic	1	2.4	45	4.5
Asian	4	9.5	38	3.8
Mixed Race	4	9.5	59	5.8
Native American	0	0	9	.9
Other	0	0	9	.9
Unknown	0	0	31	3.1
Total	42	100	1010	100

analysis program (Q.S.R. N.U.D.I.S.T 1996) to assist with the identification and organization of themes which emerged from the interviews.

EXPECTATIONS OF THE NON-MOTHERS

Choosing Career or Family

Only a handful of the non-parents I interviewed thought that they would choose either work or family as a future solution to conflicts between these spheres. In fact, only one woman thought she would choose career over family, and she was in prison at the time of the interview (see Table 5 for a breakdown on the interviewees' approaches to balancing work and family). In contrast, four women who were not yet parents planned to focus on family and veer away from work and careers once they had children (see Table 5). Several factors operated as a pull toward domesticity (also see Gerson 1985). First, three of these women were already married, while the fourth wanted to get married soon, despite her lack of a serious romantic relationship. Second, all were employed in traditionally female occupations: clerical work, day care and retail sales aimed at mothers. Third, they all saw their preference for a family focus as a choice which fit their ideal conceptions of family.

For Paige,[1] a married middle class white woman who was pregnant at the time of the interview, a lack of opportunity in her field served to reinforce her focus. Her ideal vision of family life in high school was linked to the Cleavers on the T.V. show *Leave it to Beaver.* She said: "one of my goals [in high school] was to be like June CLEAVER[2] . . .. She had the perfect HUSBAND, the perfect KIDS, and she wore her pearls everyday . . . and her little dress or whatever. [laugh] . . . I guess

Table 5.   Interviewees' Approaches to Balancing Work and Family

			Have It All		
	Career over Family	Family over Career	Concurrently	Sequencing	Decide Later
Non-Parents	1	4	3	6	14
Parents	2	6	6	0	0

that's the kind of family I'd like to have." Paige's career path had not proceeded as she had desired, and it appears that this led her to move toward the world of motherhood (also see Gerson 1985). Although she had graduated from college, she was unable to secure a position in her field, and worked as a secretary part time despite her dislike of her job. She said:

> I'm NOT too hip about working full time, just because I see other people do it and I know it's difficult. . . . I WOULD work full-time if I found like this spectacular JOB that would make me very HAPPY, but . . . that pretty much would have to fall in my lap to do that. . . . So [my husband has] got a really good job and job security. He makes good money. And so I'm . . . the one who's . . . left to take care of the kids.

This discussion of Paige's choices was quite similar to the other three women who planned to focus on domesticity, with the exception that Paige was the only woman who had experienced dissatisfaction with her job prospects, although the others were also in traditionally female, low-paying jobs. This suggests that several forces pulled them toward domesticity: marriage (or strong desire for marriage), employment in female dominated occupations, strong ideal conceptions of their future families, and, for one woman, dissatisfaction with her job prospects.

Having it All

Unlike those who thought they would choose family over career, the majority (twenty three) of the non-parents I interviewed hoped to "have it all" (see Table 5). Only a few wanted to "have it all" by focusing on work and motherhood at the same time. Some planned to sequence a work and family focus, and others felt unsure about how this balancing would occur. An example of someone who wanted to focus on work and motherhood concurrently is Linda, a middle class white woman. Linda had a boyfriend she had been seeing since high school and she worked in the field of accounting. She told me that in the future she wanted to be the C.E.O. of her company, as well as have a family with her boyfriend, whom she hoped to marry. When I asked how she saw her future, she said that she envisioned:

> Doing it all. That's what I want. I want to have it all. I want to be a real strong pro-
> fessional woman and I want also the family. And I want them both to be number one.
> I don't want either one or the other to have to suffer. And I KNOW that with [my boy-
> friend] I'd have a real supportive partner. So . . . in five years I'd like to be married
> and have some kids, that's my main goal. By the time I'm thirty I'd like to have my
> [accounting] exams done.

Here, Linda suggests that she has specific goals for herself in the areas of both work and family. She does not see these goals in conflict with each other, but instead expects that her partner will serve as a support system which will help her accomplish her goals. He planned to be a teacher, and she thought this would help: "That's why I want my husband to be a teacher, so HE can stay home." She also planned to rely on her company, which she said is "family oriented." As she put it,

> I think you have to have a husband who's willing to take the kids for three hours at
> night when I go to the library and study. Who's . . . willing to watch the kids when I
> go on business trips. And then of course I'd do the same for him. . . . On the other end
> of the scale, a work, a company that lets you take off early for conferences, and . . .
> when your kid's sick, you can leave, and lets you leave at reasonable hours, and
> doesn't expect a lot of overtime. . . . My company is real family orientated and [. . .
> keeps] an individual well-rounded. So I think that's the two most important things, is
> company and your spouse.

This young woman, like others who expect to "have it all," felt that she had found a supportive partner and employer to be able to maintain the balancing act.

In contrast to planning to simultaneously focus on both work and motherhood, six of the non-mothers planned to be committed to both parenthood and their professional lives by sequencing these demands one after the other (see Table 5). This approach to "having it all" attempted to conquer the demands of both parenthood and working by scheduling them so that they were not simultaneously overwhelming. Three key expectations were common in this group. First, they expected that they would work part-time while their children were young and resume their careers later in their lives. Second, they expected to have flexible jobs. Third, similar to Linda quoted above, these women expected that their male partners would be equally involved in parenting, thus lessening their own burden. A consequence of having increased flexibility and individualized scheduling of the life course, these strategies represent individual solutions.

For Hillary, an engaged working class Korean American woman, wanting to "have it all" went along with knowing that these goals might be somewhat difficult to achieve. For her, the solutions were flexible work and equal participation from her fiancee. She wanted to find a job "that I like, that I can do, that I'm good at, but that ALSO allows me room to raise my family and to be there for my kids and be a responsible parent." As she put it,

I would like to do something that allows me to [be there for my kids] but at the same time my whole life . . . I've had people tell me that I'm bright and talented . . . and I'd like to be able to do something with that too. So I'm grappling with the nineties-woman's dilemma of how do you have it all.

As this quote suggests, Hillary realized that it might be difficult to be both committed to her children and her career. One of her solutions was to think about flexible career options. She was considering getting a Ph.D. to allow her to teach at the college level, which she saw as having a large amount of flexibility. She contrasted this with her fiancee's profession, medicine, which might not allow for such flexibility. However, her vision of this solution appears to be somewhat unrealistic, since she mentioned being able to cancel class when her children were sick and having her summers off. She also thought that her fiancee would participate in child rearing equally. She said: "I also don't think [child rearing is] just the woman's job, obviously. The husband should participate in everything equally."

Others agreed that part-time work was a feasible way of balancing the demands of work and motherhood. For Felicia, a middle class white woman, "having it all" meant taking time off to have children, but returning to her work or working part time. Although she also expressed a negative viewpoint about day care, she was concerned about her children making her "crazy," and planned to pursue her own self-fulfillment as well. She said:

I REALLY DO want the little family thing, the perfect little thing, the husband and kids, and I want to be a mom. And I want to take care of my kids when they're infants, . . . not work at least for a SHORT time. [But . . .] you could go crazy staying with the kids ALL the time. . . . I mean at least working somewhat, you know? Ideally NOT full time, I think, but then I don't know how crazy my kids would drive me either, so [I may] go to work.

Although some women may want to take time off to care for their children, they often see part-time work as an option which will help them maintain their own identities and provide some type of activity beyond child rearing.

Most of these women did not give much thought to how they would resume their careers after raising children for several years. Some were aware of the difficulties of accomplishing this goal, yet planned to try to do so in spite of the obstacles. Although this might be more of a possibility for those who are in traditionally female occupations, it might be difficult for others. As several woman suggested, it might be that less demanding professions were chosen for their flexibility— either consciously or unconsciously.

Fully one-third of the total interview sample planned to delay their decision about precisely how they would "have it all" (see Table 5). These women did not have children, and planned similar types of approaches to "having it all" as the women described above. However, their strategies for balancing work and family were less specified and more vague. They planned to decide how to handle these conflicting demands after facing them directly, and most felt optimistic about handling this balancing act. These women seemed to have made less progress in the transition to adulthood; their career plans were still in flux and they were not involved in established committed relationships. Many were still in school or considering returning to school, which contributed to uncertainty about their future career paths and how this might connect with motherhood.

This uncertainty is linked to the increasingly individualized life course of the contemporary era. Since the transition to adulthood has become more extended and diverse, many young women have vague expectations about how their lives will proceed. In contrast to normatively ordered events and pathways, the greater flexibility has led many young women to delay thinking about how they will structure their lives. Consequently, many expect that an exploration of their own identities will lead them to these needed work and family decisions at later times in their lives.

For example, Esther is a working class white woman who graduated from college. She was involved in theater but had not yet embarked on her career path. She was also considering a move across the country. When I asked her how she thought she might balance work and family, she told me: "I haven't really thought about how I would work it out. I kind of figure I'll cross that bridge when I come to it." Echoing this uncertainty about her future in terms of work and family is Whitney, a middle class Korean American woman. At the time of the interview, she was working full time and just beginning to pursue her undergraduate degree. For Whitney, not having plans about work and family was linked to feeling that she was not yet "grown up." As she put it, "I don't really have a mapped out plan of WHEN I grow up what I want to DO. . . . I don't really know what I want to do. . . . I just never think that far." The unestablished nature of life pathways and the uncertainty about future trajectories delay future work and family plans. These tendencies, at the level of the individual, reflect the "destandardization" (Buchmann 1989) of the life course.

Despite this uncertainty about their precise future career paths, one strategy, also mentioned above, was to expect their male partners to contribute to finding a solution to the demands of both parenting and work. Hoa, a middle class Vietnamese American woman who was in law school at the time of the interview, expressed uncertainty about balancing work and family yet had faith that her male partner would provide assistance. For her, having both a family and a career was important in the future, yet she had not "thought about it TOO much." She was more certain about her expectation that her male partner would assist equally with domestic tasks, thus lessening her own burden. As she put it,

> I think I would like to have kids, but I think part of that is also the reason why I'm not worried about that or think of it as a problem is because I think that whoever I would have as a partner, would be somebody [who] would make it EASIER for me, where . . . I won't HAVE to be a superwoman. . . . I'm not going to be the one

to make dinner because I can't cook. . . . We're both going to take a cooking class together. [laugh] So, I think for ME it's not that much of a strain. . . . It depends on WHO you're with, I think, and WHAT you want to do. . . . So for me it's not, a scary thing, what can I do?

Gabrielle, a middle class biracial (African American and white) woman, put it this way: "I would definitely need a husband who was participating 50 percent, if not more. DEFINITELY! [laughs]."

In summary, of the twenty-eight non-parents I interviewed, most expected that they would be heavily involved in both work and family in their future lives. Only a few of these women expected to simultaneously focus on both work and family. Six women expected to be committed to both motherhood and careers by sequencing these demands one after the other. This plan was associated with three specific anticipated strategies for balancing work and family: pursuing part-time work while their children were young and returning to their careers once their children entered school, choosing flexible jobs and professions, and expecting that their male partners would contribute equally to the demands of parenting. However, occupational flexibility of this degree is often difficult to obtain. Many employers make it difficult to move back and forth between a part-time and full-time career trajectory, and may penalize those who do not fully invest in their careers. Additionally, as the mothers revealed in their interviews, the assistance of a male partner is often difficult to obtain.

The majority of non-mothers expressed a delayed decision approach to how they would balance work and family demands. Most of these women were less established in their adult lives than those who had identified specific strategies. In contrast to the majority of those who had more specific plans (who had graduated from college), many of the women with a delayed-decision approach were still in school or were considering returning to school. As a result, their careers were not as stable as those who had more specific plans with regard to balancing work and family. Additionally, most of these women were not involved in long-term committed relationships.

This uncertainty about their future paths in general, a feature of the individualized life course, contributed to an uncertainty about how they would approach juggling work and family. Since the transition to adulthood has become more extended and diverse, and since many women feel that options which were previously closed to them are now open, many young women have vague expectations about how their lives will proceed. In contrast to normatively ordered events and pathways, the greater flexibility has lead many young women to delay thinking about how they will structure their lives. Additionally, the extension of adolescence has created a longer life course period of uncertainty and exploration. Consequently, many expect that an exploration of their own identities will lead them to these needed work and family decisions at later times in their lives. However, it should be pointed out that these types of anticipated strategies are individual in nature. Although some recognized that other women also experienced the same difficulties, they thought that they themselves would be able to transcend such problems.

Additionally, race and class structure young women's approach to their life plans. The women who were not yet mothers were disproportionately white, middle and upper-middle class in background, and college educated. In contrast, the mothers were disproportionately women of color, working class, and had not pursued a college education. These features of the lives of the non-mothers may provide more of an opportunity to reflect on their hopes and desires, whereas the mothers, whose lives are fraught with more intense daily struggle, have little time or room in their lives for such flexibility.

EXPERIENCES OF THE MOTHERS

In contrast to the women who did not yet have children, the fourteen mothers I interviewed were struggling directly with questions of balancing work, motherhood, and sometimes school, in their everyday lives. Since the majority (9 out of 14) were single mothers who got pregnant during their teens, they faced added demands associated with a lack of support from their children's fathers. However, even among those who were married or involved in serious committed relationships, support from male partners was often inadequate. These interviews with young mothers reveal that parenthood, particularly single parenthood, is a life pathway which leads to difficulty balancing work and motherhood.

Accommodating Work to Family or Family to Work

Six of the mothers chose strategies which involved a greater commitment to motherhood than to work to address these conflicting demands on their time and energy (see Table 5). These strategies included remaining out of the labor force, or pursuing part-time work. In contrast, two women focused on work rather than motherhood by having shared custody of their children (see Table 5). These choices were often very difficult and involved direct experiences with the costs of trying to balance both work and family.

One strategy, which was not very feasible for most of the interviewees, was to stay out of the labor force. Because of financial difficulties, this was typically seen as a temporary solution. Rita, a working class white woman who did not work outside the home, felt comfortable raising her child and her two step-sons while her husband worked. She said: "I always knew I would have children, and I always knew that when I had my child or children that I would be a full-time mother and a full-time wife, and I would revolve around them until pre-school, kindergarten, and then first grade they're independent."

Similarly, Shonda, a working class African American woman, left a night shift job so that she could focus on finishing her associate's degree. For her, the costs of trying to balance life with her two children, full-time work and school were too demanding, and she needed to compromise somewhere, rather than "trying to catch up, catch up, catch up all the time." Although her job paid well, it was classified as temporary, and she did not receive benefits that permanent workers received, including medical benefits for her children. She had a history of "anxiety attacks" for which she sought professional help. The stress of balancing work, school and family which Shonda faced as a single mother illustrates the costs of the "destandardized" life course and the lack of social supports for young women during the transition to adulthood (Buchmann 1989). Because she tried to balance roles which in the historical past were more likely to be taken on consecutively rather than concurrently, she felt overwhelmed. She describes her difficulty balancing her family, work and school, and her solution, as follows:

> But I had to let [the job] go so I could go to school and have time for my kids. I just didn't want to step aside and not be a part of the household. I didn't want to neglect my kids. . . . And so I just sat home and [thought] "okay, I've got to stop." So I took a break, and I guess that's what I needed. Time to say "okay stop, you've got to rest," because I was overworking myself really bad. I got about four hours sleep, if that, a DAY. So and I was always on the go. It's just [that] so many people depend on me.

Instead, she decided to go on AFDC to be able to focus on her children and completing her education, which she felt would help her more in the long run. She said of this decision, "I'm better off doing what I'm doing now. I might STRUGGLE a little bit more, but hey, I don't mind struggling. You've got to crawl before you walk."

Other women chose part-time work as a balancing strategy. For example, Gail and Sherri, both married upper-middle class white woman, worked part time in an attempt to reconcile the difficulties balancing employment and motherhood. For Sherri, "FAMILY is the MOST important thing" and her lack of desire to work full time was linked to several factors: enjoying being at home with her two children, financial support from her husband, not wanting to put her children in day care because of her belief that she should be home with them, and difficulty juggling full time work with motherhood. Although she did not mention it directly, it should be noted that, in contrast to those women who needed to work to provide for their families, Sherri could rely on the financial support of her husband. However, she decided to work part time because she enjoyed working and needed the financial assistance which her job provided. When I asked her about her decision to work part time, she told me:

> Well, daycare for one, we didn't want to put them in . . . daycare. I just think it's important for the MOM to be home with the KIDS, to be there for them. . . . But I

want to have my job too. I like my job and I don't want to quit, you know? And plus I'm the insurance provider, so that's REALLY important for us. So I guess insurance is one of the biggest reasons why I went back to work.

For two of the women, part-time parenting made balancing easier. Rochelle, a middle class African American woman, let her parents raise her daughter because she was not ready for the responsibility of teenage motherhood. Because of this arrangement, she was able to go to college, work full time, and achieve residential independence from her parents. Her daughter lived with her parents, yet saw Rochelle frequently. Similarly, Wendy, a working class white woman, shared joint custody of her son with her ex-fiancee. As a result, they each cared for their son for half of the week. Although this arrangement did assist with conflicting demands, Wendy was critical of the schedule because it meant that she never was able to go out on the weekends.

These women's experiences suggest that the choices were often difficult, but that it was possible to accommodate work to their family demands or family to their work demands (Moen 1992). However, it is important to note that most of their solutions, such as staying out of the labor force or working part time, were individual strategies for easing what they saw as individual dilemmas. The greater diversity in young women's options has produced not only new opportunities, but also strain and difficulty balancing work and motherhood.

Doing It All

In contrast to those women who chose to accommodate work to motherhood or were part time parents, the remaining six women (14% of the interview sample) attempted to be equally committed to work and motherhood (see Table 5). Many were faced with difficult compromises because they were simply unable to do everything. Typically employed full time, their stories of juggling work and family illustrate the difficulty many women face in the "individualized" (Buchmann 1989), "postfeminist" (Stacey 1991) era.

Many women mentioned the difference between what they had anticipated their lives would be, and what they were in actuality. When articulating their previous visions, they often mentioned that these visions were "fantasy," suggesting that they blamed themselves for having unrealistic expectations. However, these difficulties may be particularly acute because of the sole responsibility most of these women had for supporting themselves financially and caring for their children. Teenage motherhood poses special burdens for resolving work and family conflicts because of the discrepancy between the expected and realized life path. As I will discuss later, some received support for this balancing act through the assistance of their children's father, the option many non-parents saw as a primary way to resolve such conflicts, although this was not always easily forthcoming.

According to Moen's (1992) categorization of working mothers, "captives" include those who are in the labor force reluctantly. Among my interviewees, Victoria, a working class white woman, was a "captive" as a single parent and sole breadwinner. Victoria worked full time in a job she did not find satisfying and was considering returning to school to get training in a field in which she could work out of her home. She would have preferred not to work, but worked out of financial necessity. As she put it: "I'd love to stay home EVERY DAY and not have to work. . . . I would like to stay home and be able to work out of my home and be there for my son if I have to pick him up from school or take him to school." For her, being a single parent involved a lot of juggling: "the hardest part of it though, being a single parent, is just having enough time for everything and everyone."

Other interviewees also expressed conflict and ambivalence about their roles as both a mother and a worker. For Darlene, a white working class woman, both work and motherhood came with a price: she frequently felt conflicted and guilty. At the time of the interview, Darlene had just received her associate's degree, was working full time (and had done so while in school as well), and was in the process of looking for a new job in nursing. Her demands as a student, worker, wife and mother were very difficult to juggle and left her feeling guilty about her inability to handle them all. As she put it,

> It's hard because of my son. He's five now, but he was just, "Mommy, why don't you stay with me?" "Mommy, why do you have to study?" "Mommy, can't we go play?" "Mommy, don't go to school." And when he was sick I felt horrible, because my husband . . . [is] an excellent father, but he isn't a MOMMY, you know? My son . . . would want me to hold him when he was sick. He wanted ME to stay with him. And it was really hard, . . . just breaking my heart because, a lot of times I did have to call in sick to work, or to school . . . to stay home with HIM.

This difficulty balancing multiple demands was far different than she had originally expected. When she was in high school, she thought she would be economically well off, yet her actual situation was far different: "those dreams HELPED, because they make you want to set goals but in reality, it's all fantasy."

Many of the women found solutions or strategies to lessen the conflicts. As Moen (1992) suggests, these women often choose jobs with flexibility to accommodate family demands. This was the case for both Betsy and Jill. Betsy, a middle class, white single parent, worked full time, yet she was also committed to spending time with her son. When she was in high school, she did not expect to work outside the home after having children, yet she saw this as a fantasy compared to the reality of her financial situation:

> I don't know what I thought about . . . this kind of stuff. . . . [It] was kind of DREAM-like in ninth grade, . . . like "yeah, I'll be here, and I'll have kids." And so I probably didn't think I'd HAVE TO go back to work until I wanted to.

When Betsy felt conflicts between work and family, she requested to switch her work schedule, which made the situation considerably easier. She described her employer's flexibility in terms of not only allowing her to switch her hours, but being "very understanding" that "if I need to go, if he's sick, I go." She said: "I'm not explaining myself all the time to them."

This type of job flexibility was also important for Jill, a middle class, white single mother with two children and two jobs. For Jill, needing to work full time was different than she had always expected. Although she works "with what I got now," she told me that she had expected to "be married and have kids and not have to worry too much about a job." She said about her expectations during high school: "I was a DREAMER, I guess. Eighteen, you get married, you get pregnant, and that's it. You get a part-time job and the man's supposed to take care of everything. And that's not it."

Similarly, Ann, a married working class white woman, had to make compromises about her work-related responsibilities. When I asked her if she saw any potential conflicts between her job as a teacher and her family, she told me:

> The potential's there. It's there. It's easy, I think, to get wrapped up in your work. I want to be the GREATEST . . . I can be. But . . . that requires taking some time away from being at home. . . . I like going to work. I like being a teacher. I don't mind staying after school, but then I want to come home and I want to be a MOM. And I still want to be a mom on the weekends. And so there is a potential for that to just to get TOO wrapped up.

One example of a way Ann accommodated her work responsibilities to her family was to decline an additional coaching job she was offered.

In summary, eight of the parents I interviewed were attempting to juggle full-time work and/or school with the demands of motherhood. Those mothers who accommodated work to family left the labor force or worked part time, although they typically saw their situations as temporary. Those who accommodated family to work shared custody of their children. Still others sought to "do it all" simultaneously. Although the balancing act was quite difficult for all of the women in some way, most were able to cope with such conflicting demands. These women drew on a number of strategies, including working for flexible employers, choosing their priorities for a given day, and giving up optional work responsibilities. Additionally, many of these women had given up on their "fantasies" and accepted the realities of their lives: rather than having the financial ability to stay home with their children, they needed to work. Accepting this reality may have made it easier for them to face the actualities of balancing which was in front of them.

Support for the Balancing Act

A major potential form of support for balancing work and motherhood comes from either women's male partners or the fathers of their children. For most of the mothers I interviewed, support from these sources did not solve balancing dilemmas. This stands in contrast to the wishes of many of the women who did not yet have children, since many planned to "have it all" by depending on the support of their male partners. I will begin with mothers who were married or involved in committed relationships, and then I will turn to those who were single mothers.

Only three of the women were married to the fathers of their children. Although these women received some support from their husbands, they often took on a "second shift" (Hochschild 1989) in the area of family and domestic responsibilities. For example, Sherri, who was balancing part-time work, school, and raising two children, described her domestic responsibilities in terms of the second shift demands which her husband did not have:

> I feel that I have the pressure that I have to do EVERYTHING. . . . I'm working, I have to clean the house and do the laundry, . . . make sure the kids are fed . . .. Where I don't think my husband, I mean, maybe that's just us too, but . . . I was thinking about that [in . . .] my [sociology of the family textbook], that when women work they're expected to do EVERYTHING and not necessarily share responsibilities . . . . But I think WOMEN feel that they have to do everything, especially if they work. . . . I think that women have more expectations on them than men do, because men go to work, come home and we're supposed to have dinner waiting for them and things like that.

Sherri's experiences suggest that while part-time work may lessen the difficulty women have juggling work and family, it is not necessarily a solution because women still face the burden of the second shift.

Four of the women I interviewed were involved in committed relationships with men who were not the fathers of their children, yet many of these men took on responsibilities for the children. Moesha, a middle class African American woman whose first two children had a different father than her third child, had no contact with the father of the older two. This inequity in child rearing responsibilities angered her. She said:

> I . . . just decided that that . . . wasn't a good thing for my CHILDREN to be AROUND, because he was a father when he WANTED to be a father. And if he didn't TODAY, then he just DIDN'T today, and that was supposed to be accepted and I didn't BELIEVE in that. . . . I COULDN'T just say that one day I don't want to be a mother today and go off and do what I WANTED, because I think that's, . . . something that you just SHOULDN'T do. If you decide to HAVE them, then they're yours EVERYDAY ALL DAY LONG.

Once the father of her two children realized that she was romantically involved with another man, he stopped pursuing his relationship with her and their children. Her boyfriend at the time of the interview (and father of her third child) took on some child rearing responsibility for all three children. She said that "not only did my older children gain the father that they never really knew in the first place, but now it's kind of like that didn't even matter, because he's their father to them, and he sees them as his children." However, they maintained separate households, suggesting that Moesha herself took on the majority of the domestic labor. Despite this situation, this suggests that women who had additional children with another man were often able to receive support for all of their children.

Three of the women I interviewed shared custody of their children with the children's fathers. Although she believed that "nobody holds fathers accountable," Ann, who was married to a different man, felt satisfied with her arrangement with her daughter's father. He was also married, and had regular visitation with their daughter. Additionally, Ann's husband took on major responsibilities for her daughter, including making spending time as a family a priority in his life. For example, he decided not to continue college courses because he felt that it took too much time away from their family life.

In contrast to the women who were married, were involved in serious relationships, or shared custody with their children's fathers, five of the women were essentially on their own with their children. Although these women themselves felt a great amount of responsibility for their unplanned pregnancies and their children, most saw their children's fathers as extremely irresponsible in terms of parental responsibilities. The effect of this irresponsibility was to make these single mothers feel as if they had complete responsibility for their children.

In addition to Moesha quoted above, Betsy describes her son's father as follows: "He's a zero. He's what I don't want my son to grow up to be. Takes advantage of people, and he thinks the world owes him something. And he smokes weed and doesn't do anything. Can't hold a job, won't pay child support." Because she knew about his unreliable nature before she got pregnant, she felt guilty over her choice to have a child with him. She said: "so, in my own way, I made a choice to have [my son] be hurt."

In summary, it appears that the women who were married, involved in serious relationships with men, or shared child custody with their children's fathers, received some support for the demands of parenting. However, this support was not extensive and many of these women took on "second shift" responsibilities. The women who received no such support faced child rearing on their own, and often were quite angry about these additional responsibilities.

CONCLUSIONS

This paper has compared the expectations of young women who had not yet become mothers to the actual experiences of those who were already mothers. I found that most of the women who were not yet mothers were optimistic about combining work and motherhood, while those who were already mothers experienced great difficulty balancing these often conflicting demands. This suggests that balancing work and motherhood poses difficult issues for young women at the time in which they are moving into adult roles. Consistent with the "destandardized," "postfeminist" era, the young women in this study took a wide range of approaches to balancing work and family, suggesting an individualistic way of crafting of work and family strategies to suit their own goals and interests.

Although prior research in this area has focused on either work and family linkages among adult women, or future plans among adolescents and young women, this study suggests that the transition to adulthood represents a unique phase in the life course for resolving work and motherhood conflicts. During the transition to adulthood, there are many important developmental issues at hand, including completing school, establishing a career, achieving financial independence, forming committed relationships, and having children. Because the mothers in this study faced nearly all of these issues simultaneously, the pressures and conflicts were significant. Since most were single mothers, they lacked the support of a male partner. Because many were still in the process of completing school, they had not yet established themselves financially or in the workplace. As a result, they faced financial strain, as well as difficulty balancing not only work and motherhood, but school as well.

There are two alternative interpretations for the discrepancies between the expectations of non-parents and the actual experiences of parents found here. The first interpretation is that many women who have not yet become parents have unrealistic views about the ease with which they will balance work and family in the future. As the experiences of the mothers suggest, juggling parenting with work is often much more difficult than one expects prior to becoming a parent. It might be thought that when the non-mothers become mothers themselves, they will experience problems that are similar to the mothers in the sample. Lending evidence to this conclusion are statements made by the mothers which suggest that before they had children, they thought that balancing work and motherhood would not be very difficult. Once they faced the actual demands of motherhood, some labeled their previous visions "fantasy."

Alternatively, it might be argued that the women in this study represent distinctly different groups. That is, the non-parents might be more oriented toward planning, as suggested by their delay of parenthood. As Clausen (1993) asserts, this type of "planful competence" can have implications for the rest of the life course. This interpretation suggests that the young women who are currently non-parents might pursue careers which could lessen work and family conflicts, marry men who could contribute to child rearing, and delay child bearing until it fit well with their career demands. In contrast, it might be argued that the young mothers I interviewed had less of planning orientation, which might have resulted in increased difficulties balancing work and motherhood.

However, it is probably more accurate that both of these interpretations partially explain the differences observed here. Although the non-mothers may be better planners than the mothers, it is probably also the case that the non-mothers are somewhat unrealistic about the ease with which they will be able to juggle work and motherhood in their future lives. A longitudinal interview design could provide evidence about the life circumstances of the non-mothers once they do indeed have children.

It is also possible that the differences in the groups might be related to differences in class background. The mothers I interviewed came from less advantaged backgrounds than the non-mothers; half of the mothers were from working class families while only twenty percent of the non-mothers were from similar backgrounds. It might be that when the non-mothers do indeed become parents, they are able to draw on more financial resources, thus lessening their need to work full time. For those who are already mothers, it might be the case that the influence of class background and difficult life circumstances (i.e., early parenthood) results in a greater necessity for work, and feelings of strain balancing work and motherhood. Additionally, class background itself may be intertwined with planning orientation. That is, planning itself is fostered by resources, since those with more resources will be more confident in their ability to follow through on their goals and objectives.

Despite the commonality of difficulties women have in balancing work and motherhood, both the mothers and non-mothers in this study focused on individual solutions. Characteristic of the destandardized life course and the depoliticized nature of the so-called "postfeminist" (Stacey 1991) era, these women viewed balancing work and motherhood as an individual problem, rather than a difficulty which most women face. As a consequence, these women felt responsible for resolving these dilemmas themselves, in their own lives. For the non-mothers, this often meant thinking that they themselves would be able to resolve the conflicts which other women have encountered. For the mothers, this meant skillfully juggling conflicting demands on a daily basis by relying on the generosity of flexible employers or the financial resources of male partners.

Public policies aimed at lessening these burdens could assist young people during this critical period of the life course. Some policies, such as job sharing, flexible hours, and affordable day care, would be beneficial to balancing work and family at many stages of the life course. However, to address the unique difficulties of contemporary young people, public policies should also focus on this particular phase of the life course. For example, youth who are in the midst of completing their education and are not yet established in their careers often struggle with the added demands of expected financial independence. Providing more public financial support for the completion of college or vocational education might allow young people to reduce the pressure to support themselves economically at this critical point in their development. Additionally, since child care expenses greatly contribute to the economic difficulties of young women, affordable child care alternatives are critical. With their financial burdens lessened, young people would have more freedom to gain important training, and might experience less difficulty balancing the conflicting demands of school, work, and family. Since early motherhood coincides with a period of expected educational advancement and career development, unstigmatized, non-means tested financial assistance could lessen the balancing demands which many young mothers face.

The stigma which receiving public assistance now connotes in the United States has created an environment where many young women feel that they alone must bear the responsibilities of single motherhood. Given that current "welfare reform" will lessen the availability of public support for many economically-pressed young women, economic supports that are granted across the board become all the more important. Therefore, public policy should be aimed specifically at the young adult stage of the life course to facilitate a smoother transition to adulthood.

APPENDIX

Interview Guide

1. Current Situation
   *What are you doing now (working, school, family)?
2. Work/Career
   *feelings about how this area of life has gone so far
   *what has been important or discouraging about work experiences?
   *if full time in labor force, feelings about starting work
3. Education
   *feelings about how this area of life has gone so far
   *why started school?
   *something particularly important or discouraging about experiences?
   *feelings about graduating
4. Family/Relationships
   *feelings about how this area of life has gone so far
   *in romantic relationship?
   *something particularly important or discouraging about the relationship?
   *ideal relationship
   *if married or cohabiting, decision process
   *if a parent, feelings about having baby/decision process and motivations
5. Goals, Plans for the Future (work/career, education, family/relationships)

6. Obstacles to Achieving Goals
    *4 years after high school (1995)
    —one-third of the YDS women expected that lack of money to complete their education would influence their future career plans; one-third said it interfered already
    *has this been a concern for you?
    *what are some obstacles you have thought about your life in the future?

7. Life Paths Overall
    *potential conflicts between different roles (work, school, family)
    *what are the major turning points in your life?
    *differences between the current paths and the paths expected when in high school (school, work, family)? Why did things turn out differently and thoughts about that?
    *feelings about different parts of life—what parts happy about? Disappointed about? Proud of? Insecure about?
    *anything else important in forming who you are today?

8. Views about Others
    *who do you want/don't you want to end up like?
    *who is the woman who you most admire? What about her?
    *how does your life compare with the lives of your friends from high school, especially those whose lives are different from yours?

9. YDS Results

First Table (Presented to interviewees)
In 1988 (9th Grade) Youth Development Study women said:

Expected Age at Marriage	**Average** 25 years old				
Expected Number of Children	**Average** 2 children				
Expect to Work After Having Have Children	**Yes** 88%	**No** 6%	**Do Not Plan to Have Children** 6%		
Will Return to Work When Child is:	**< 1 Year Old** 15%	**1 or 2 Years Old** 37%	**In Nursery School** 22%	**In Kindergarten** 13%	**Older than in Kindergarten** 13%

*do you remember what you thought in 9th grade?
*how does your life now compare with what you thought would happen when you were in high school?

Second Table (Presented to interviewees)
In 1995 Youth Development Study women said:

Racial or Ethnic Discrimination—worried about the future	9%
Racial or Ethnic Discrimination—already experienced	3%
Gender Discrimination—worried about the future	20%
Gender Discrimination—already experienced	4%

    *have these issues been a concern for you?

10. Views about the Contemporary Context
    *what obstacles and opportunities do young women face today?
    *how do these compare with those of your mother or her generation? Why changed?
    *do women in general have the same opportunities as men?
    *how have you experienced this in your own life (same opportunities as men you know?)

11. Views about Feminism
    *thoughts about feminism/women's rights
    *if a feminist, what influenced this? Did something change your views? What issues are important to you?
    *if not, what do you think of feminists?
    *political issues or event in the news which are important to you?
    is there anything else you'd like me to know?

ACKNOWLEDGMENTS

This research was supported by a National Research Service Award from the National Institute of Mental Health (Training Program in Identity, Self, Role, and Mental Health—PHST 32 MH 14588), the National Institute of Mental Health (MH 42843, Jeylan T. Mortimer, Principal Investigator), the Personal Narratives Award from the Center for Advanced Feminist Studies, University of Minnesota, and a Graduate School Block Grant Stipend Award from the Department of Sociology, University of Minnesota. The author would like to thank Jeylan T. Mortimer and Toby Parcel for comments on previous versions of this paper.

NOTES

1. All names and identifying characteristics have been changed to maintain confidentiality.
2. Words quoted in capital letters signify the emphasis which interviewees gave to particular words during the interview.

REFERENCES

Arnett, J. J., and S. Taber. 1994. "Adolescence Terminable and Interminable: When does Adolescence End?" *Journal of Youth and Adolescence* 23(5): 517-537.

Becker-Schmidt, R. 1991. "Continuity and Discontinuity in Women's Life Courses." In *Theoretical Advances in Life Course Research: Status Passages and the Life Course,* Volume 1, edited by W. Heinz. Deutscher Studien Verlag: Weinheim.

Buchmann, M. 1989. *The Script of Life in Modern Society.* Chicago: University of Chicago Press.

Bush, D. E., R. G. Simmons, B. Hutchinson, and D. A. Blyth. 1978. "Adolescent Perception of Sex-Roles in 1986 and 1975." *Public Opinion Quarterly* 41: 459-474.

Clausen, J. A. 1993. *American Lives: Looking Back at the Children of the Great Depression.* New York: The Free Press.

Cote, J. E., and A. L. Allahar. 1994. *Generation on Hold: Coming of Age in the Late Twentieth Century.* New York: New York University Press.

Crowley, J. E., and D. Shapiro. 1982. "Aspirations and Expectations of Youth in the United States, Part 1: Education and Fertility." *Youth and Society* 13: 391-422.

Danzinger, N. 1983. "Sex-Related Differences in the Aspirations of High School Students." *Sex Roles* 9(6): 683-695.

Dennehy, K., and J. T. Mortimer. 1994. "Work and Family Orientations of Contemporary Adolescent Boys and Girls in a Context of Social Change." Pp. 87-107 in *Work, Family, and Masculinities,* edited by J. Hood. New York: Sage.

Elder, G., Jr. 1985. "Perspectives on the Life Course." Pp. 23-49 in *Life Course Dynamics: Trajectories and Transitions, 1965-1980,* edited by Glen Elder, Jr. Ithaca: Cornell University Press.

———. 1974. *Children of the Great Depression: Social Change in Life Experience.* Chicago: University of Chicago Press.

Elder, G. Jr., and A. O'Rand. 1995. "Adult Lives in a Changing Society." In *Sociological Perspectives on Social Psychology,* edited by K. Cook, G. Fine and J. House. Boston: Allyn and Bacon.

Erwin, L. 1995. "'Having it All' in the Nineties: The Work and Family Aspirations of Women Undergraduates." Paper presented at the National Research and Policy Symposium on Research on Youth in Transition to Adulthood, Kananakis, Alberta, Canada: April 25-29.

———. 1996. "Constructing Social and Career Identities: Undergraduate Women and Cultural Politics." Paper presented at the National Women's Studies Association annual conference, Skidmore College, June 12-16.

Evans, S. 1989. *Born For Liberty: A History of Women in America.* New York: Free Press.

———. 1979. *Personal Politics: The Roots of Women's Liberation in the Civil Rights Movement and the New Left.* New York: Vintage Books.

Farmer, H. S. 1983. "Career and Homemaking Plans for High School Youth." *Journal of Counseling Psychology* 30(1): 40-45.

Forest, K., P. Moen, and D. Dempster-McClain. 1995. "Cohort Differences in the Transition to Motherhood: The Variable Effects of Education and Employment Before Marriage." *Sociological Quarterly* 36(2): 315-336.

Freeman, J. 1975. *The Politics of Women's Liberation.* New York: Longman.

Furstenberg, F., Jr., J. Brooks-Gunn, and S. P. Morgan, 1987. *Adolescent Mothers in Later Life: Human Development in Cultural and Historical Contexts.* New York: Cambridge University Press.

Geissler, B., and H. Kruger. 1992. "Balancing the Life Course in Response to Institutional Requirements." Pp. 151-167 in *Institutions and Gatekeeping in the Life Course: Status Passages and the Life Course,* Volume 3, edited by W. R. Heinz. Weinheim: Deutscher Studien Verlag.

Gerson, K. 1985. *Hard Choices: How Women Decide about Work, Career, and Motherhood.* Berkeley: University of California Press.

Glaser, B., and A. Strauss. 1967. *The Discovery of Grounded Theory.* Chicago: Aldine.

Harris, A. 1995. *Broken Patterns: Professional Women and the Quest for a New Feminine Identity.* Detroit: Wayne State University Press.

Herzog, A. R. 1982. "High School Seniors' Occupational Plans and Values: Trends in Sex Differences 1976 Through 1980." *Sociology of Education* 55: 1-13.

Hochschild, A. (with A. Machung). 1989. *The Second Shift.* New York: Avon Books.

Hogan, D., and T. Mochizuki. 1988. "Demographic Transitions and the Life Course: Lessons from Japanese and American Comparisons." *Journal of Family History* 13(3): 291-305.

Maines, D. R., and M. Hardesty, 1987. "Temporality and Gender: Young Adults' Career and Family Plans." *Social Forces* 66: 102-120.

Machung, A. 1989. "Talking Career, Thinking Job: Gender Differences in Career and Family Expectations of Berkeley Seniors." *Feminist Studies* 15: 35-39.

McLaughlin, S. D., B. D. Melber, J.O.G. Billy, D. M. Zimmerle, L. D. Winges, and T. R. Johnson. 1988. *The Changing Lives of American Women.* Chapel Hill: University of North Carolina Press.

Modell, J. 1989. *Into One's Own: From Youth to Adulthood in the United States 1920-1975.* Berkeley: University of California Press.

Modell, J., F. Furstenberg, Jr., and T. Hershberg. 1976. "Social Change and Transitions to Adulthood in Historical Perspective." *Journal of Family History* 1: 7-31.

Moen, P. 1992. *Women's Two Roles: A Contemporary Dilemma.* Westport, CT: Auburn House.

Mortimer, J. T., and J. London. 1984. "The Varying Linkages of Work and Family." Pp. 20-35 in *Work and Family: Changing Roles of Men and Women,* edited by P. Voydanoff. Palo Alto: Mayfield Publishing Co.

Mortimer, J. T., and G. Sorensen. 1984. "Men, Women, Work, and Family." Pp. 139-167 in *Women in the Workplace: The Effects on Families,* edited by D. Quarm, Kathryn Borman, and S. Gideonse. Norwood, NJ: Ablex.

National Center for Health Statistics. 1995. *Report to Congress on Out-of Wedlock Childbearing: Executive Summary.* Hayttsville, Md: U.S. Department of Health and Human Services, Public Health Service, Centers for Disease Control and Prevention, National Center for Health Statistics.

Peters, E., H. Guit, and E. van Rooijen. 1992. "Changing Patterns? A Comparison of the Transition to Adulthood of Two Generations of Girls." Pp. 331-352 in *Adolescence, Careers, and Cultures,* edited by W. Meeus, M. de Goede, W. Kox and K. Hurrleman. Berlin: Walter de Gruyter.

Q.S.R. N.U.D.I.S.T. 1996. Australia: Qualitative Solutions and Research Pty. Ltd.

Ryan, B. 1992. *Feminism and the Women's Movement: Dynamics of Change in Social Movement Ideology and Activism.* New York: Routledge.

Shapiro, D., and J. E. Crowley. 1982. "Aspirations and Expectations of Youth in the United States, Part 2: Employment Activity." *Youth and Society* 14: 33-58.

Sidel, R. 1990. *On Her Own: Growing Up in the Shadow of the American Dream.* New York: Viking.

Smith, D. 1990. *The Conceptual Practices of Power: A Feminist Sociology of Knowledge.* Boston: Northeastern University Press.

Stacey, J. 1991. *Brave New Families: Stories of Domestic Upheaval in Late Twentieth Century America.* New York: Basic Books.

Stevens, C. J., L. A. Puchtell, S. Ryu, and J. T. Mortimer. 1992. "Adolescent Work and Boys' and Girls' Orientations to the Future." *The Sociological Quarterly* 33(2): 153-169.

Stevens, D. 1990. "New Evidence on Timing of Early Life Course Transitions: United States: 1900-1980." *Journal of Family History* 15(2): 163-178.

Taylor, V., and L. Rupp. 1991. "Researching the Women's Movement: We Make Our Own History, But Not Just As We Please." In *Beyond Methodology: Feminist Scholarship as Lived Research.* Bloomington: Indiana University Press.

Taylor, V., and N. Whittier. 1992 "Collective Identity in Social Movement Communities: Lesbian Feminist Mobilization." In *Frontiers in Social Movement Theory.* New Haven: Yale University Press.

U.S. Bureau of the Census. 1985. *Current Population Reports, Series P-20, No. 399, Table A.* Washington, DC: U.S. Government Printing Office.

U.S. Department of Labor. 1980. *Perspectives on Working Women: A Databook.* Bulletin 2080. Washington, DC: U.S. Government Printing Office.

SOURCES OF CONVERGENCE AND DIVERGENCE IN ATTITUDES ABOUT WORK AND FAMILY ROLES AMONG WOMEN

Michele Kozimor-King and Kevin T. Leicht

ABSTRACT

Numerous studies have examined trends in gender role attitudes in the United States. Most of these studies have found that gender role attitudes are changing in support of women in the paid labor force. Researchers have spent less time focusing on variation in attitude change, especially among women themselves. Our study examines changes in women's attitudes toward work and family roles using data from the *General Social Survey* (1977-1994), focusing on age, lifecourse, and occupational differences in attitude change. Although we find a liberalizing trend in almost all our subsamples, attitude change is especially large among older women, married women, and women in non-traditional occupations. Education and age still exert the largest effects on attitude change, and younger women's attitudes change less with marriage and changes in income and education. Our results suggest that significant

Research in the Sociology of Work, Volume 7, pages 85-108.
Copyright © 1999 by JAI Press Inc.
All rights of reproduction in any form reserved.
ISBN: 0-7623-0605-X

attitude change accompanies the adoption of non-traditional occupational roles. Our results also suggest that there is a growing "supporting cast" of women whose attitudes toward gender roles are moving in the same direction, albeit at different speeds and from different starting points.

INTRODUCTION

Since the 1970s, there has been a significant increase in women who combine traditional family roles with paid employment in the labor force. Women in the United States are seeking out paid employment for diverse reasons. While some women enter the labor force to fulfill financial needs, others work to increase their independence and self-esteem.

The domains of women's work have become as diverse as their reasons for entering the paid labor force. Though women are still clustered in clerical and low-level service occupations (Fox and Hesse-Biber 1984; Foss and Slaney 1986; Greenfeld, Greiner and Wood 1980; Lyson 1984; Walshok 1981) women's work has diversified considerably (cf. Reskin and Roos 1990). The implications of widening work opportunities remain unclear, and many researchers (especially Reskin and Roos 1990) present an ambivalent picture of women's inroads into traditionally male-dominated occupations.

Research on the consequences of rising opportunities is complicated by cohort differences in the experiences and expectations of these opportunities, and differences in lifecourse circumstances. Studies by Gerson (1985) and others suggest that adaptations to changing opportunities are grounded in the concrete life circumstances of women. These differences have important implications for gender roles, especially those reflecting the interface between home and work.[1]

Our research addresses the following questions regarding differences in attitudes toward home and work:

1. Have conceptions of work and family changed over time and (if so) how have they changed?
2. What are the relative contributions of age, period, occupation, and lifecourse circumstances toward explaining evolving differences and similarities in work-family attitudes?
3. Are there significant differences within as well as between age groups in the effects of occupation and lifecourse circumstance on work-family attitudes?

We think that a systematic analysis of change in attitudes among different groups of women will shed light on the evolution of work-family attitudes from the late 1970s to the early 1990s.

ATTITUDE CHANGE

Numerous studies have examined trends in gender role attitudes in the United States. Most of these studies have found some degree of attitude change. Research by Cherlin and Walters (1981) suggests that women have displayed increasing support for non-traditional gender roles from the early 1960s to the early 1970s. Thornton, Alwin and Camburn (1983) also found a trend toward more egalitarian attitudes toward women's work and family roles from the 1970s to the 1980s. Mason and Lu (1988) refute the claim that a backlash against feminism may have caused a slowdown in support for women in the paid labor force. Using *General Social Survey* data, they find a significant increase in profeminist views of women's gender roles between 1977 and 1985. More of this change occurred within cohorts than through cohort succession.

Many studies that address change in gender role attitudes have focused on key variables that affect these outcomes. Like other studies, Firebaugh (1992) finds that there have been changes in gender role attitudes in the United States between the years 1972 and 1988, and examines the source of attitude change. Firebaugh finds that changes in gender role attitudes are a product of individual opinion changes, population turnover, and a combination of both individual differences and population turnover.

Our study attempts to further previous research by studying changes in work-family attitudes through 1990 and (subsequently) through 1994. We attempt to identify the role that age, occupation, and life course circumstance play in producing aggregate change in work-family attitudes among women.

WORK AND PERSONALITY

Many studies have suggested that the structure and conditions of work in the paid labor force have a profound psychological affect on people's views of social reality (Kohn 1969, 1977, 1990; Kohn and Schooler 1983; Mortimer, Lorence and Kumka 1986). In his classic work, Class and Conformity (1969), Kohn finds that relatively privileged occupational positions are consistently related to flexible social orientations and values. While all occupational characteristics have some impact on personality, Kohn identifies certain conditions that are the most crucial. Opportunity for self-direction and the substantive complexity of work are two such conditions that have a particularly strong causal effect on values and orientation. Job conditions that offer opportunities for occupational self-direction (the absence of close supervision and nonroutinized flow of work) and substantively complex work are related to favorable self-conceptions, flexible social orientations, and effective intellectual functioning. Workers in these types of jobs are more open-minded in their views of what is socially acceptable, more receptive to change, tend to emphasize intrinsic aspects of the job, and have positive evaluations of the self. Those job conditions that are closely supervised, contain large amounts of routinized work, and include intense pressure or uncertainty are related to less favorable self-conceptions, more rigid social orientations, resistance to change, the need for conformity, and less effective intellectual functioning (Kohn 1969, 1977; Kohn and Schooler 1983; Mortimer, Lorence and Kumka 1986). Although the relationship between work and personality may have reciprocal effects, Kohn states that "the substantive complexity of work affects each of these facets of psychological functioning more—in most cases, much more—than that facet of psychological functioning affects the substantive complexity of work" (1977, p. xl).

Although Kohn's early work focused only on the relationship between occupational conditions and psychological functioning of men, his later research (Kohn and Schooler 1983) examines how day-to-day job experiences relate to women's self-perceptions, intellectual functioning, and social orientations. There are several reasons why conclusions about the relationship of work conditions and psychological functioning may be substantively different for women. Women have distinctly different sets of normative expectations surrounding their work and family roles. As Hochschild (1989, 1997) and others (McHale and Crouter 1992; Oppenheimer 1994; Presser 1994; Thompson 1991; Crouter and Helms-Erikson 1997) have suggested, women frequently carry dual responsibilities for home and job, becoming fatigued and stressed by the role strain. There are also structural constraints that differentiate women's job experiences from that of men. Many women face sex-segregation, discrimination, and employment interruption.

Although women's experiences of work in the paid labor force are substantively different from those of men, Kohn and Schooler (1983) found that the impact of job conditions on psychological functioning is nearly identical to that of men. Job conditions that encourage self-direction were conducive to effective intellectual functioning and to an open orientation to change in oneself and others. Constraints on self-direction and less complex work was linked to less effective intellectual functioning, a more rigid social orientation, and unfavorable evaluations of self for women. Despite the traditionally emphasized family roles of women and structural constraints on their work careers, the personality development of women is directly affected by their current occupational conditions (Kohn and Schooler 1983).

These results are very important for our study of women's changing attitudes toward work-family roles. Women who work in nontraditional occupations experience substantively different work environments and job conditions than women working in traditional occupations. Male-dominated occupations contain higher levels of substantively complex work and more opportunity for self-direction than traditionally female-dominated occupations. Overall, nontraditional occupations often contain the most economically and socially rewarding jobs and resources (Anderson and Tomaskovic-Devey 1995; Bianchi 1995; Felmlee 1982; Wallace 1982). Based on the previous discussion of the effect of job conditions on personality, we hypothesize that women in nontraditional occupations will exhibit a more open orientation and be more receptive to the changing gender roles of both themselves and other women. Women in more traditional occupations will have more conservative attitudes, exhibit resistance to change, and demonstrate the need to conform to traditional normative expectations.

Based on the learning transfer and generalization thesis of Kohn and Mortimer and Lorence and Kumka, women in nontraditional occupations and women in traditional occupations should have different attitudes toward the relationship between work and family. One study by Moore and Rickel found that women who function in nontraditional roles were likely to differ from women who occupy traditional jobs on attitudinal factors toward the family and domestic tasks (1980). Almquist and Angrist (1970) and Rossi (1967) have found that women in nontraditional male-dominated occupations are more likely to marry later, have fewer children, and return to work earlier after the children are born than their traditional counterparts.

EXPECTATIONS AND HYPOTHESES

Our first goal is to determine if work-family attitudes have become more supportive of women in the paid labor force between 1977 and 1994. More specifically, we are interested in whether the support for women's work roles has steadily increased through the late 1980s into the 1990s.

Our second goal is to determine if there are significant differences in the work-family attitudes of women in traditional and nontraditional occupations from 1977 to 1990. We expect that women who work in nontraditional occupations will demonstrate less conformity to traditional work-family roles and will be more receptive to innovation and change. Women in traditional occupations should have more conservative attitudes toward work and family. We expect women who are currently out of the labor force to have the most traditional attitudes toward work and family.

Our third goal is to determine the source of attitude change. By studying ten-year age groupings of women, we will examine whether changes in attitudes toward work and family are a product of individual opinion change, a cohort replacement effect, or a combination of both individual changes in attitudes and population turnover. Today's younger adults may hold more egalitarian or liberal work-family attitudes than their elders. As younger adults with more egalitarian attitudes replace older cohorts of women, the overall change in work-family attitudes may result from cohort replacement and not individual attitude change (see Firebaugh 1992).

DATA, VARIABLES, AND STATISTICAL METHODS

Data

The data for this study are taken from the *General Social Survey* (GSS) furnished by the National Opinion Research Center (NORC) of the University of Chicago from 1977 through 1994. About 1,500 adults are surveyed each year. The surveys were conducted annually (except 1979, 1981, and 1991) in the months of February, March and April of most years. The method of survey consists of 90 minute face-to-face interviews of individuals. Each yearly survey is conducted with an independently drawn sample of English speaking persons, at least 18 years of age, living in noninstitutional arrangements, and occupying a residence in the United States. This analysis is restricted to those 5,792 women who worked full-time, part-time, or were out of the labor force, and answered questions pertaining to women's work and family roles.

WORK-FAMILY ATTITUDE MEASURES

To measure work-family attitudes we use five of the most frequently asked *General Social Survey* questions. The exact wording of the questions is provided below:

1. "Do you agree or disagree with this statement? Women should take care of running their homes and leave running the country up to men." (1 = disagree; 0 = agree)
2. "Do you agree or disagree with this statement? A preschool child is likely to suffer if his/her mother works?" (3 = strongly agree; 0 = strongly disagree)
3. "Do you approve or disapprove of a married woman earning money in business or industry if she has a husband who is capable of supporting her?" (1 = approve; 0 = disapprove)
4. "Do you agree or disagree with this statement? It is much better for everyone involved if the man is the achiever outside the home and the woman takes care of the home and family." (3 = strongly agree; 0 = strongly disagree)
5. "Do you agree or disagree with this statement? It is more important for a wife to help her husband's career than to have one herself?" (3 = strongly agree; 0 = strongly disagree)

The first two items pertain to the domesticity dimension while the next three questions pertain to the issue of women in the paid labor force.

Since two of the work-family variables are dichotomous and three of the variables are categorical (with four possible responses) the variables are standardized with a mean of zero and a standard deviation of one. An unweighted principal components factor analysis suggests that there is one factor underlying the associations among these work-family items (results not shown but available from the authors). Based on the factor analysis we created a scale of work-family attitudes for use in the multivariate analyses. The scale is created by summing the standardized responses on the five work-family variables so that a liberal or nontraditional response produces a positive score and a traditional or conservative response produces a negative score. The scale ranges from −9.87 to 5.99. The mean of the work-family scale was 0.215 with a standard deviation of 3.66. Reliability (alpha) for the work-family attitudes scale is .76.

Work-Family Attitudes—Differences by Age

To highlight differences and discontinuities in the effects of age on work-family attitudes, we construct five, ten-year birth cohorts from the GSS to capture decade discontinuities in age effects. Respondents are categorized into one of five birth cohorts; 20-30 years old; 31-40; 41-50; 51-60 and over 61 (the omitted category in our analysis). We expect work-family attitudes to become steadily more liberal among younger cohorts, net of controls for period effects (i.e., the year of the survey).

Occupational Gender Composition

Occupations will be considered "nontraditional" if the proportion of female workers in the occupation is 25 percent or less (cf. Perry et al. 1994; Reskin and Roos 1990; Leicht and Marx, 1997). Occupations with a proportion of female workers equal to or above 75 percent will be labeled "traditional." Occupations having a proportion of women falling above 25 percent but below 75 percent are labeled "mixed." Occupational category is obtained by using the three-digit classification codes used by the 1980 U.S. census and the GSS survey and calculating the percentage of women in each of the 984 occupations of respondents.[2] Students, women working in unpaid domestic labor at home, and retired women are treated as currently out of the paid labor force.

Lifecourse Circumstances

Numerous studies have suggested that the background characteristics of women holding nontraditional occupations differ considerably from women in traditional occupations (Almquist and Angrist 1970; Auster and Auster 1981; Greenfield, Greiner and Wood 1980; Lunneborg 1982; Lyson 1984; Moore and Rickel 1980; Walshok 1981). These studies have found that women in nontraditional careers are from higher SES backgrounds, have more education, have mothers with nontraditional careers, have husbands with either professional or high-paying jobs, and have fewer children of their own in the family. Powell and Steelman (1982) examined the relationship between a mother's work status and her offspring's attitudes toward women in the paid labor force. Using 1977 GSS data, they found that maternal status characteristics have more impact on work-family attitudes of male offspring than on females. Since these background variables influence attitudes toward work and family, we should control for these factors in our models. In our analysis, *education* (measured in years), *children at home*, *marital status*, and *respondent's income* will be used to measure lifecourse circumstance.

Our preliminary inspection suggested that there was substantial missing data on measures of respondent's income, so we used mean substitution for respondents missing information on income. Further, the GSS does not provide detailed occupational information after 1990, so we use the years 1977-1990 in our descriptive analysis of changes in work-family attitudes across occupation types and use the 1990 distribution of women across occupations for 1991, 1993 and 1994 in the regression analysis.[3] Respondents with missing data on any other measures in this analysis are excluded from the sample.

We first plot trends over time in work-family attitudes for our age groups, for women in different occupational groups, and different life course circumstances. Our analysis then examines the independent effects of age, occupational groups, and lifecourse circumstances on work-family attitudes, exploring interaction terms to reveal differences within age groups and across occupational groups and lifecourse circumstances. We then conduct some elementary regression simulations that provide some insights on the relative effect of age, occupations and lifecourse circumstance on work-family attitudes.

RESULTS

Figure 1 plots the trend in work-family attitudes for the total sample and for each age group. There is a secular trend toward more liberal work-family attitudes across years. There is also a narrowing of opinions regarding work-family roles across cohorts with the greatest changes occurring among the oldest women (61 years and older). This suggests that one source of the secular trend toward more liberal work-family attitudes involves relatively large changes in the attitudes of the oldest women. But the figure also suggests that work-family attitudes of the youngest age group peaks relatively early in the study period (1985) and there is little change in attitudes after that. While differences between groups remain statistically significant over the entire period, the gap between the most liberal and most conservative group narrowed from 3.66 in 1977 to 2.19 in 1994.[4]

Figure 2 plots the trend in work-family attitudes by occupational type. This figure reveals two trends that can account for changes in work-family attitudes. First, changes in work-family attitudes from 1977-1990 are as large for women in traditional occupations (3.17) as they are for women in nontraditional occupations (3.06). However, there is considerable change in work-family attitudes among

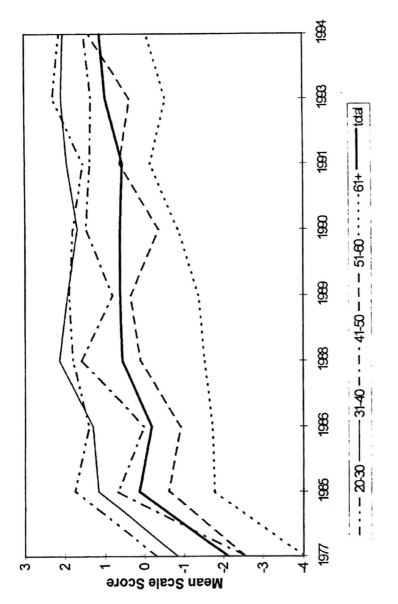

Figure 1. Change in Work-Family Attitudes by Age

20-30 ——— 31-40 -·-· 41-50 --- 51-60 ······ 61+ ······ total ———

93

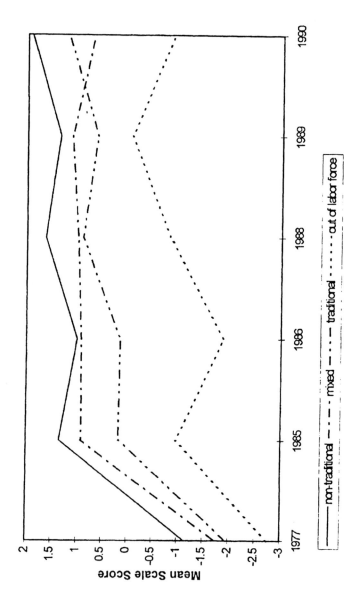

Figure 2. Change in Work-Family Attitudes by Occupational Category

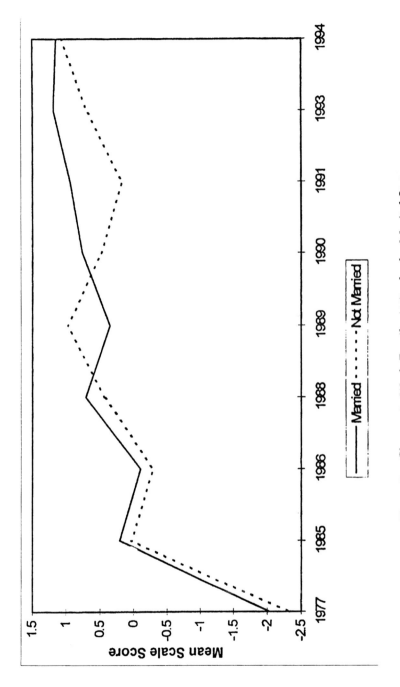

Figure 3. Change in Work-Family Attitudes by Marital Status

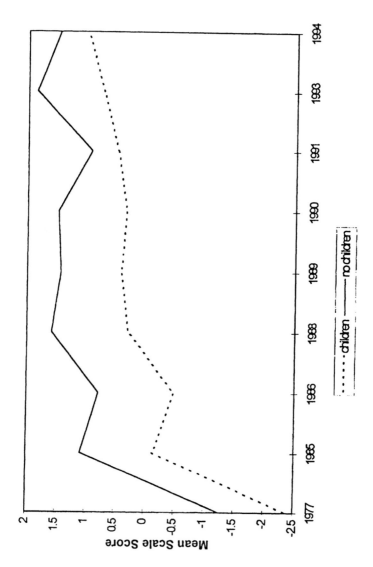

Figure 4. Change in Work-Family Attitudes by the Presence of Children

other groups, including those out of the labor force. Overall, occupational group attitudes have diverged slightly over time. The gap between the most and least conservative occupational group is 1.61 on the work-family scale in 1977. By 1990, all occupational groups have more liberal general role attitudes, but the gap between women in non-traditional occupations and those out of the labor force has widened to 2.82.

Figures 3 through 5 assess the effects of different lifecourse circumstances on work-family attitudes. Figure 3 suggests that there is a secular liberal trend in work-family attitudes among married and unmarried women. Although married and unmarried women change positions on the scale in 1989 and 1990, marriage does not appear to be the source of significant divergence in work-family attitudes. In fact, the mean difference between married and unmarried women on work-family attitudes is statistically significant only in 1989 and 1991. Further analysis suggests that the overall slope predicting change in work-family attitudes by year is not significantly different for married and unmarried women (results not shown but available from the authors).

Figure 4 suggests that women with children are consistently more conservative than those without children, though the trends seem to be converging from the bottom as women with children become more liberal in their attitudes over time. The overall slope for women with children differs significantly from the slope for women without children (results not shown but available from the authors). The gap between women with children and childless women is statistically significant in every year except 1991(results also available from the authors). The gap is widest in 1988 and narrows due to changes in the attitudes of women with children.

Figure 5 portrays combinations of marriage and parenthood to examine trends for women in a variety of lifecourse and family circumstances. Unmarried women with children are consistently the most conservative. Married women with children are slightly more conservative than married childless women. The effects of marriage without children vary wildly across years, though the trend converges with the trend for single childless women by 1990. This graph supports several interesting conclusions that would be hidden in an aggregate analysis of trends:

1. the trend toward more liberal work-family attitudes among unmarried, childless women peaks in 1989 and declines slightly after that.
2. Women with children are generally more conservative than women without children, and only the attitudes of unmarried women with children differ statistically from the other three groups after 1990 (results not shown but available from the authors).
3. The overall change in work-family attitudes is greatest for the most conservative group; unmarried women with children.

These results point to a liberalizing trend that is being propelled by "convergence from the bottom"—relatively conservative groups have become more

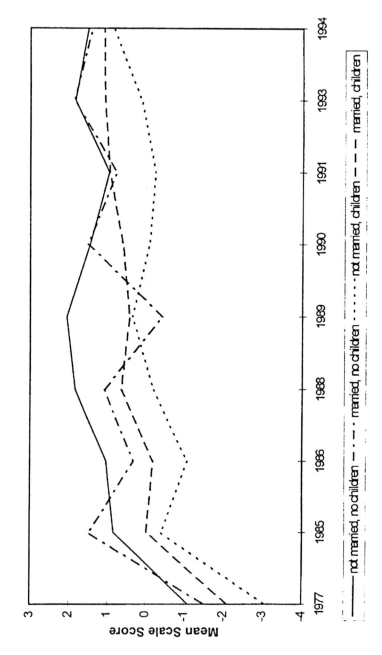

Figure 5. Change in Work-Family Attitudes by Marital Status and the Presence of Children

Table 1. The Additive Effects of Period, Age, and Occupational
Group on Work-Family Attitudes, 1970-1994
(ordinary least squares, N=5792)

	(1)	(2)	(3)	(4)
PERIOD AGE[a]	.18**[c]	.18**	.18**	.18**
20-30 yrs. old	–	3.92**	–	3.80**
31-40 yrs. old	–	3.75**	–	3.60**
41-50 yrs. old	–	2.92**	–	2.76**
51-60 yrs. old	–	2.14**	–	2.00**
OCCUPATIONAL GROUPS[b]				
Non-traditional	–	–	2.36**	.92**
Mixed	–	–	2.04**	.73**
Traditional	–	–	1.68**	.40**
CONSTANT	−15.8	−18.3	−17.4	−18.6
R-SQUARE	.07	.24	.09	.25

Notes: [a] respondents 61 and over are the reference category.
[b] respondents out of the labor force are the reference category.
[c] unstandardized regression coefficients
* $p \leq .05$;
** $p \leq .01$.

liberal at the same time as relatively liberal groups are staying in place. The changes in attitudes among women with children, in particular, points to the growing salience of children as a public policy issue.

Since the overall trend is work-family attitudes is toward greater liberalization, we turn to regression models to examine whose attitudes are changing and how much. We then use regression simulations to highlight convergence and divergence in work-family attitudes across occupation, age, and lifecourse groups.

REGRESSION ANALYSIS

Table 1 examines the additive effects of period, age, and occupational type on work-family attitudes. Equation 1 simply documents the secular trend toward more liberal work-family attitudes. Equation 2 shows that, net of this secular trend, successive age groups are becoming more liberal in their attitudes toward women's labor market roles. The coefficients suggest that the two older groups are more conservative concerning issues of work and family and the two younger groups are more liberal. Equation 3 shows that women in non-traditional occupations are most liberal in their work-family attitudes, followed by women in mixed-gender occupations and women in traditional occupations. Finally, Equation 4 shows that each of these trends remains when period, age group, and occupational type are included in the model together.[5]

Table 2. The Additive Effects of Period, Age, Marriage,
Children,Education, and Respondent's Income on
Work-Family Attitudes,1970-1994
(ordinary least squares, $N = 5792$)

	(1)	(2)	(3)	(4)
PERIOD AGE[a]	.18[**][c]	.13[**]	.13[**]	.13[**]
20-30 yrs. old	–	–	–	3.35[**]
31-40 yrs. old	–	–	–	3.04[**]
41-50 yrs. old	–	–	–	2.27[**]
51-60 yrs. old	–	–	–	1.74[**]
LIFECOURSE[b]				
Marriage	–.28	–	–.28	–.30
Children	–1.49[**]	–	–.57[**]	.12
Marriage* Children	.92[**]	–	.52[*]	–.01
Education	.45[**]	–	.43[**]	.31[**]
R Income	.09[**]	–	.09[**]	.10[**]
CONSTANT	–15.2	.17.4	–17.0	–19.6
R-SQUARE	.09	.20	.20	.31

Notes: [a] respondents 61 and over are the reference category.
　　　　[b] single respondents are the reference category.
　　　　[c] unstandardized regression coefficients
　　　　[*] $p \leq .05$;
　　　　[**] $p \leq .01$.

Table 3. Interactions Between Age, Marriage, Children, Education,
and Respondents' Income, 1977-1994 (ordinary least squares, $N = 5792$)

LIFECOURSE	20-30 yrs. old	31-40 yrs. old	41-50 yrs. old	51-60 yrs.[a] old
Marriage	–.49[*]	–.18	–.18	–.24
Children	–.18	–.35	.11	.41
Education	–.13[**]	–.06	.08[*]	–.01
Income	–.12[**]	.04	.05	.07

Notes: [a] respondents 61 and over are the reference category.
　　　　[b] unstandardized regression coefficients
　　　　[*] $p \leq .05$;
　　　　[**] $p \leq .01$.

Table 2 examines the effects of lifecourse circumstances on work-family attitudes. The major findings in this table are that most of the effects of marriage and children on work-family attitudes are mediated and accounted for by age differences. The presence of children produces more conservative attitudes. However,

Table 4. The Additive Effects of Period, Age, Occupational Group and Lifecourse Circumstance on Work-Family Attitudes, 1970-1994 (ordinary least squares, $N = 5792$)

	Work-Family Attitudes
PERIOD AGE[a]	.14**[c]
20-30 yrs. old	3.27**
31-40 yrs. old	2.95**
41-50 yrs. old	2.17**
51-60 yrs. old	1.65**
OCCUPATIONAL GROUPS[b]	
Non-traditional	.69**
Mixed	.48**
Traditional	.30**
LIFECOURSE	
Marriage	−.35**
Children	.10
Marriage Children*	.02
Education	.31**
R Income	.10**
CONSTANT	−18.8
R-SQUARE	.31

Notes: [a] respondents 61 and over are the reference category.
     [b] respondents out of the labor force are the reference category.
     [c] unstandardized regression coefficients
     * $p \leq .05$;
     ** $p \leq .01$.

this effect is partially offset through the interaction of marriage and children. Education and income both produce more liberal work-family attitudes net of lifecourse and age effects.

Table 3 examines interactions between age groups and lifecourse circumstances, controlling for the additive effects of age and life-course variables (the full set of controls is listed in Table 4). Almost all of the significant departures in this table occur for the youngest respondents. Those in the youngest age group who are married, have more education and higher incomes are significantly more conservative on work-family attitudes than their counterparts.

Finally, Table 4 presents a complete additive picture of the effects of age, period, occupation and lifecourse circumstance on work-family attitudes. Women in non-traditional occupations are consistently more liberal in their attitudes than their counterparts in other occupational groups or those out of the labor force. Of the lifecourse measures only marriage exerts a statistically significant effect on work-family attitudes. The effects of children and the interaction between marriage and children are accounted for by the other measures in the equation. Finally, income and education continue to produce large liberalizing effects on work-family attitudes. Overall, these results suggest that age, occupation and life-course circumstance exert distinctive effects on work-family attitudes.

So far, our results support several conclusions about changing attitudes toward home and work. The overall liberalizing trend in work-family attitudes is produced by movement among the most conservative groups; older women, women in traditional occupations, and women with children. While the youngest age group has the most liberal work-family attitudes, their attitudes change less with changes in marriage, education and income than the other cohorts. But what characteristics would change the observed differences across age groups, occupations, and life course circumstances?

What Accounts for Differences? Regression Simulations

In order to assess the contributions of each factor to changes in work-family attitudes, we performed some basic regression simulations. These simulations substitute values for different groups in the sample for the values on variables in the models and then assess changes in predicted work-family attitudes that result. Using the results from Table 4, we examined changes in the predicted work-family attitudes that would result if we replaced the total sample means with means for specific subgroups.[6]

These simulations reveal the constellations of characteristics that produce change in work-family attitudes at different times, locations, and stages of the life-course. The overall predicted work-family attitude score using the means of the predictors for the total sample is .32. But substituting characteristics of subgroups into the prediction equations changes the prediction considerably. Specifically;

1. The highest predicted work-family attitude score occurs using the characteristics of single women (1.73). The lowest predicted score occurs from using the characteristics of women who are out of the labor force (−2.19).
2. A comparison of the sample characteristics using the first and last year of our data (1977 and 1994) suggests that changes in women's lives from 1977 and 1994 are responsible for considerable change in work-family attitudes. The predicted mean work-family attitude score using women's characteristics in 1977 is −1.63. The predicted mean work-family attitude score using women's characteristics in 1994 is 1.49.
3. Comparing predicted scores across lifecourse groups suggests that most of the difference produced by lifecourse circumstances are accounted for by differences in education and the age distribution across lifecourse groups. Specifically, giving single childless women (the most liberal group) the age distribution of single women with children (the most conservative group) reduces the predicted score for single, childless women from 1.24

to .352. If we substitute the mean education of single women with children for education levels of single, childless women the predicted score declines to −.268, almost exactly what the mean score for single women with children (−.28).

4. There are considerable differences in predicted scores across occupational groups as well. However, the biggest changes occur when comparing predictions for women out of the labor force (−2.19) with women in nontraditional occupations (.74). Most of this difference (63%) can be accounted for by differences in the age distributions of the two groups and (to a lesser extent) differences in education (15%, the remainder is accounted for by differences in the intercepts). Overall, these results suggest that differences in the age and educational distributions for women in different circumstances account for large differences in work-family attitudes. These differences occur over time in a context of general liberalizing trends in work-family attitudes that are sparked by relatively large changes among the most conservative subgroups of women.

CONCLUSION

Our study began as an attempt to flesh out the divergent patterns in work-family attitudes by age, occupations, and lifecourse groups. Our results point to education and age as major producers of differences in work-family attitudes. These effects are occurring in a context of the overall liberalization of work-family attitudes marked by significant changes in the attitudes of those thought to be most traditional in their orientations.

Taken together, our results support several conclusions:

1. work-family attitudes have become more liberal because of changes in the attitudes of traditionally less liberal groups, older women and married women.

2. The major exception to this trend occurs for occupational groups. There the greatest changes have occurred among women in both non-traditional and traditional occupations. Women out of the labor force have developed more liberal attitudes over time, but their attitudes have changed the least overall.

3. Younger women's attitudes change less with marriage and increases in education and income relative to their older counterparts. This could be taken as a backlash against feminist ideas. However, younger women are not more conservative than older women. Instead, their attitudes are the most liberal and are less responsive to changes in education and income.

4. Overall, most of the attitude change in our analysis is fueled by changes in levels of education, age differences, and differences within age, occupational groups, and lifecourse circumstances. Most importantly, differences

in characteristics within subgroups produce changes in work-family attitudes that are at least as great as differences between subgroups. Changes in
education and age distributions, either alone or in combination with
changes in lifecourse circumstances change predicted work-family attitudes substantially. Generally complex interactions between education,
age, lifecourse circumstance, and occupational location are necessary to
explain variation in work-family attitudes.

Our analysis supports not so much a "generalization" hypothesis (cf.
Mortimer, Lorence and Kumba 1986) as much as an "integration" hypothesis
(cf. Gerson 1985). Attitudes forged in the workplace do seem to carry over into
other spheres of life for women. However, other significant life events affect
work-family attitudes (like differences in education, age, and lifecourse circumstance) within similar occupational settings. Further, differences in characteristics among single women, married women and women with children produce
differences that are as great or greater than differences caused by lifecourse circumstance alone. If anything, our results suggest that many of the effects
attributable to occupational experience or different lifecourse circumstances are
due to the constraints, opportunities and selection mechanisms that operate to
place women in these structural positions.

Our results also provide a broader context for interpreting Kohn's findings
regarding the role of substantively complex work in the production of attitude
flexibility. Women in less traditional occupations do express the most flexibility with regard to work-family attitudes, but there are significant differences in
lifecourse circumstances that affect attitudes within traditional and non-traditional occupational groups and there are substantial changes in attitudes among
those who are not in the labor force as well. In sum, we find support for
Kohn's thesis in a context where there are overall secular trends in work-family attitudes that transcend the substantive complexity of jobs among working
women.

Most importantly, a general liberalizing of work-family attitudes should not be
confused with convergence. There is little evidence in our analysis that work-family attitudes are becoming more similar, with the exception of the reduced effects
of income and education for the youngest women. However, there is also little evidence that work-family attitudes are diverging either. Further, the greatest changes
in work-family attitudes come from those who were least liberal at the beginning
of the study. This is perhaps the greatest sign of the attitudinal acceptance of
changing roles for women in American society.

Our results also have larger policy implications. Organizations and government
agencies that are interested in adopting laws and policies in support of better work/
family accommodations will be deceived if they limit their perceptions to divergence among women based on occupation and lifecourse circumstance at a single
time point. Instead we would point to the general broadening of support for work/

family accommodations among all women both in and out of the labor force as an indication that new and innovative initiatives would be welcomed by a broad spectrum of women in the United States. The declining effects of marriage and education among younger cohorts, in particular, suggests that overall support for work/family accommodations in the workplace is gaining momentum as a general societal trend that will continue as younger cohorts of women replace older cohorts. The attitudes of younger women will be reinforced further as trends toward greater labor force participation and declines in occupational segregation place them in (historically) non-traditional work roles.

Obviously, a complete picture of changes in work-family attitudes must document changes in the attitudes of men as well (cf. Reskin 1988). In particular, we would be interested in seeing if the views of men and women have polarized, or if different "pockets of dissent" exist among men that do not exist among women and (if so) what the exact form of this "resistance" takes. Also, we think more research is needed on retrospective accounts of work-family attitudes over time among the same individuals. To date, we still have little understanding of how attitudes about work and family, or gender roles more broadly, evolve through one's lifetime and what events, if any, change those attitudes. Research like ours really does not address this question, but it is all the more necessary in a time of great economic and cultural uncertainty.

ACKNOWLEDGMENT

A prior version of this paper was presented at the 1996 meetings of the Eastern Sociological Society, Boston, Massachusetts. We thank Glenn Firebaugh, Richard Bord and Toby Parcel for comments on prior versions of this paper, the Obermann Center for Advanced Study for research support, and the Population Research Institute at The Pennsylvania State University for computational assistance.

NOTES

1. We refer to these studies as studies of gender role attitudes even though we will refer to our own work as a study of "work-family attitudes." We label our research in this way because our measures of gender roles are all related to issues of the interface between work and family. We think that our label more specifically locates our research as a study of gender role attitudes even though we focus on only a subset of all possible gender role attitude dimensions.

2. The breakdown of occupational categories in the GSS uses the three-digit 1980 Census occupation codes. For further information about this measure consult the GSS codebook, Appendix F.

3. The conclusions reached from our analysis are not substantially altered by using only the years 1977-1990.

4. Means for individual subgroups by year are available from the authors on request. Differences in the trajectory of work-family attitudes in Figure 1 can also be seen by looking at the effect of survey

year on work-family attitudes for each age cohort. This analysis contrasts the trend in work-family attitudes of the first four cohorts with the oldest cohort (age 61+). These year slopes are presented below:

$$20\text{-}30 \text{ years old} \quad -.058^{**}$$
$$31\text{-}40 \text{ years old} \quad -.022$$
$$41\text{-}50 \text{ years old} \quad .048^{**}$$
$$51\text{-}60 \text{ years old} \quad .045^{**}$$
$$^{**}p \le .01$$

These results add additional credence to the idea that the biggest changes in the direction of more liberal work-family attitudes are occurring among older women.

    5.   Results using Firebaugh's (1992) method for desegregating age, period, and cohort effects pro-
duces similar results to those presented here (results available on request). We decided to go with
ten-year age cohorts to make the graphics more intelligible, and because cohorts are often defined by
the decades of their birth (the "50's generation," "60's generation," etc.).

    6.   The regression simulation calculations are not shown in tables but are available from the authors
on request. The 1991, 1993, and 1994 waves of the GSS use the gender occupational breakdowns from
the 1990 GSS wave.

REFERENCES

Almquist, E.M., and S.S. Angrist. 1970. "Career Salience and Typicality of Occupational Choice
    Among College Women." *Journal of Marriage and Family* 32: 242-249.
Anderson, C.D., and D. Tomaskovic-Devey. 1995. "Patriarchal Pressures: An Exploration of Organiza-
    tional Processes that Exacerbate and Erode Gender Earnings Inequality." *Work and
    Occupations* 22: 328-356.
Auster, C.J., and D. Auster. 1981. "Factors Influencing Women's Choice of Nontraditional Careers:
    The Role of Family, Peers, and Counselors." *Vocational Guidance Quarterly* 29: 253-263.
Beller, A. H. 1985. "Changes in the Sex Composition of U.S. Occupation, 1960- 1981." The Journal of
    Human Resources 20: 235-250.
Bianchi, S. M. 1995. "Changing Economic Roles of Women and Men." Pp. 107-154 in *State of the
    Union: America in the 1990's*, Volume 1, edited by R. Farley. New York: Russell Sage
    Foundation.
Chatterjee, J., and M. McCarrey. 1989. "Sex Role Attitudes of Self and Those Inferred of Peers, Per-
    formance, and Career Opportunities as Reported by Women in Nontraditional vs. Traditional
    Training Programs." *Sex Roles* 21: 653-669.
Cherlin, A., and P. Barnhouse Walters. 1981. "Trends in United States Men's and Women's Sex-Role
    Attitudes: 1972 to 1978." *American Sociological Review* 46: 453-460.
Crawford, J. D. 1978. "Career Development and Career Choice in Pioneer and Traditional Women."
    Journal of Vocational Behavior 12: 129-139.
Crouter, A. C., and H. Helms-Erikson. 1997. "Work and Family from a Dyadic Perspective: Variations
    in Inequality." Chapter 21 in *Handbook of Personal Relationships*, 2nd ed., edited by S. Duck.
    New York: John Wiley and Sons Ltd.
Davis, J.A., and T.W. Smith. 1993. *General Social Surveys, 1972-1994 (MRDF)*. Chicago: NORC
    (Distributed by Roper Public Opinion Research Center, New Haven, Connecticut).
Ely, R. 1995. "The Power in Demography: Women's Social Constructions of Gender Identity at Work."
    The Academy of Management Journal 38: 589-634.
Felmlee, D. H. 1982. "Women's Job Mobility Processes Within and Between Employers." *American
    Sociological Review* 47: 142-151.

Firebaugh, G. 1989. "Methods for Estimating Cohort Replacement Effects." Pp. 243-62 in *Sociological Methodology*, edited by C. Clogg. Oxford: Basil Blackwell.

———. 1992. "Where Does Social Change Come From?" *Population Research and Policy Review* 11: 1-20.

Firebaugh, G., and B. Harley. 1995. "Trends in Job Satisfaction in the United States by Race, Gender, and Type of Occupation." In *Research in the Sociology of Work*. Greenwich, CT: JAI Press.

Foss, C. J., and R. B. Slaney. 1986. "Increasing Nontraditional Career Choices in Women: Relation of Attitudes Toward Women and Responses to a Career Intervention." *Journal of Vocational Behavior* 28: 191-202.

Fox, M. F., and S. Hesse-Biber. 1984. *Women at Work*. New York: Mayfield Publishing Company.

Greenfield, S., L. Greiner, and M. M. Wood. 1980. "The 'Feminine Mystique' in Male-Dominated Jobs: A Comparison of Attitudes and Background Factors of Women in Male-Dominated versus Female- Dominated Jobs." *Journal of Vocational Behavior* 17: 291-309.

Harlan, S. L., and B. O'Farrell. 1982. "After the Pioneers Prospects For Women in Nontraditional Blue-Collar Jobs." *Work and Occupations* 9: 363-386.

Holder, B. H. 1983. "Nontraditional Workers Move into the Real World." *Personnel Journal* 62: 34-36.

Hochschild, A. 1989. *The Second Shift*. New York: Viking.

———. 1997. *The Time Bind: When Work Becomes Home and Home Becomes Work*. New York: Metropolitan Books.

Kanter, R. M. 1977. *Men and Women of the Corporation*. New York: Basic Books, Inc.

Kohn, M. L. 1969. *Class and Conformity: A Study in Values*. Homewood: Dorsey.

———. 1977. *Class and Conformity: A Study in Values*, 2nd edition. Chicago: University of Chicago Press.

———. 1990. "Unresolved issues in the relationship between work and personality." In *The Nature of Work: Sociological Perspectives*. New Haven: Yale University Press.

Kohn, M. L., and C. Schooler. 1983. *Work and Personality: An Inquiry into the Impact of Social Stratification*. Norwood, NJ: Ablex Publishing Corporation.

Leicht, K. T., and J. Marx. 1997. "The Consequences of Informal Job Finding for Men and Women." *Academy of Management Journal* 40: 967-987.

Lunneborg, P. W. 1982. "Role Model Influencers of Nontraditional Professional Women." *Journal of Vocational Behavior* 20: 276-281.

Lyson, T. A. 1984. "Sex Differences in the Choice of a Male or Female Career Line: An Anaylsis of Background Characteistics and Work Values." *Work and Occupations* 11: 131-146.

Mason, K. O., and L. Yu-Hsia. 1988. "Attitudes Toward Women's Familial Roles: Changes in the United States 1977-1985." *Gender and Society* 2: 39-57.

Moore, L. M., and A. U. Rickel. 1980. "Characteristics of Women in Traditional and Nontraditional Managerial Roles." *Personnel Psychology* 33: 317-332.

McHale, S.M., and A.C. Crouter. 1992. "You Can't Always Get What You Want: Incongruence Between Sex-Role Attitudes and Family Work Roles and Its Implications for Marriage." *Journal of Marriage and the Family* 54: 537-547.

Mortimer, J. T., J. Lorence, and D.S. Kumka. 1986. *Work, Family, and Personality: Transition to Adulthood*. Norwood, NJ: Ablex Publishing Corporation.

McIlwee, J. S. 1982. "Work Satisfaction Among Women in Nontraditional Occupations." *Work and Occupations* 9: 299-335.

Oppenheimer, V. K. 1994. "Women's Rising Employment and the Future of Family in Industrial Societies." *Population and Development Review* 20: 293-342.

Perry, E.L., A. Davis-Blake, and C. Kulic. 1994. "Explaining Gender-Based Selection Decisions: A Synthesis of Contextual and Cognitive Approaches." *Academy of Management Review* 19: 786-820.

Powell, B., and L. C. Steelman. 1982. "Testing an Undertested Comparison: Maternal Effects on Sons' and Daughters' Attitudes Toward Women in the Labor Force." *Journal of Marriage and Family* 43: 349-355.

Presser, H. B. 1994. "Employment Schedules Among Dual-Earner Spouses and the Division of Household Labor by Gender." *American Sociological Review* 59: 348-364.

Reskin, B., and P. Roos. 1990. *Job Queues, Gender Queues: Explaining Women's Inroads into Male Occupations.* Philadelphia, PA: Temple University Press.

Rossi, A.S. 1967. "The Working Wife: How Does She Live? What Does She Want?" *Management Review* April: 9-13.

Stewart, H. R. 1989. "Job Satisfaction of Women in Nontraditional Occupations." *Journal of Employment Counseling* 26: 26-34.

Thompson, L. 1991. "Family Work: Women's Sense of Fairness." *Journal of Family Issues* 12: 181-196.

Thornton, A., D. Alwin, and D. Camburn. 1983. "Causes and Consequences of Sex-Role Attitudes and Attitude Change." *American Sociological Review* 48: 211-227.

Wallace, P. A. 1982. *Women in the Workplace.* Boston: Auburn House Publishing Company.

Walshok, M. L. 1981. *Blue-Collar Women: Pioneers on the Male Front.* Garden City: Anchor Books.

HAVING IT ALL:
OVERALL WORK/LIFE SUCCESS
IN TWO-EARNER FAMILIES

Phyllis Moen and Yan Yu

ABSTRACT

The paper draws on statistical data from a national sample as well as in-depth interviews of married workers in two-earner arrangements to investigate the odds of overall work/life success, that is, of working couples managing well on both fronts—at work and at home, as well as balancing the two. Specifically, the authors model the factors in work and family environments most predictive of perceived success across work and family domains. The authors find that life stage matters considerably for both men and women in dual-earner couples, with those with preschoolers the least likely to report successfully managing their work/life obligations, even net of their hours on the job. Three work-related factors stand out in predicting overall work/life success: a supportive supervisor, the absence of job insecurity, and both spouses working "regular" hours. Most apt to experience work/life success are those where both spouses are working 39-45 hours a week. When one spouse (typically the husband) puts in over 45 hours a week, both husbands and wives are less likely to report

Research in the Sociology of Work, Volume 7, pages 109-139.
Copyright © 1999 by JAI Press Inc.
All rights of reproduction in any form reserved.
ISBN: 0-7623-0605-X

work/life success. Wanting to work fewer hours is negatively tied to women's overall success. Nonprofessional men whose wives are professionals or managers have a low likelihood of overall work/life success. Surprisingly, the factors traditionally assumed to promote or reduce work/life conflict or strain—job demands, job autonomy, the ability to compress work hours or work at home, working a reduced schedule—are unrelated to perceived overall work/life success. While these factors may well be related to overload and conflict, we are examining the perception of actually succeeding on both work and family fronts and in balancing the two—no easy feat!

INTRODUCTION

The popular literature frequently portrays the conflicting nature of work and family obligations. For example, a recent cover of *Fortune magazine* (March 17, 1997) posed the question: "Is Your Family Wrecking Your Career?" The case examples in the *Fortune* article (Morris 1997) suggested the answer was definitely "yes." This is not surprising, given that work and family are what Coser (1974) described as "greedy" institutions, requiring high amounts of time, energy, and emotional investment. The fact that both can be simultaneously demanding and "absorptive" (Kanter 1977) points to their obvious intersections.

Considerable research evidence has shown that time conflicts and overloads in managing work and family obligations are without doubt a major challenge for working mothers and fathers (Gerson 1985; Hertz 1986; Higgins, Duxbury and Irving 1992; Hochschild 1989; Ladewig and White 1984; Moen 1989, 1992; Parasuraman et al. 1989; Williams and Alliger 1994). This leads to the common assumption that success in one domain may well come at the expense of the other (and vice versa). But the literature also suggests the possibility of positive and/or negative spillover. Having a satisfactory family life can facilitate perceived career achievement (Gattiker and Larwood 1986, 1988, 1990) while employees with problems at home report role conflict and stress at work (Frone and Rice 1987).

In this paper we investigate the odds of overall work/life success, of working couples managing well on both fronts—at work and at home, as well as balancing the two. Specifically, we draw on data from a national sample of workers, selecting a subsample of married workers in two-earner arrangements to model the factors in work and family environments most predictive of perceived success across work and family domains. We supplement this quantitative analysis with illustrative data drawn from in-depth and focus group interviews with members of working couple families. First, we consider the evidence regarding success across work and family domains. Second, we locate overall success in three ecological niches: gender, occupation, and life stage. Third, we report on our empirical findings. We conclude with implications for contemporary working families, for theory and research, and for policy and practice.

THE EXISTING EVIDENCE:
THE NATURE OF SUCCESS

"Success" is typically defined and measured by social scientists in terms of economic and/or occupational attainment (e.g., Blau and Duncan 1967; Breiger 1995; Mortimer 1996). But occupational success is as much subjective as it is objective (Barley 1989; Brim 1992; Weiss 1990); those who are objectively successful in terms of job status and income may or may not **perceive** themselves as successful. And only a subset of those who are successful in their jobs will also see themselves as successful in their families and at balancing both roles.

Two studies have thus far examined the subjective, interpretational aspects of occupational success. Gattiker and Larwood (1990) investigated individual perceptions of career achievement among 215 employees in major corporations in California (84% of the participants had families and 61% of the men and 57% of the women were married). They found that feeling successful at work conflicted with a successful family life. Respondents who perceived themselves to be higher up in the corporate hierarchy felt that their career had taken time away from their families and that their family responsibilities made career achievement more difficult.

A second study by Swiss and Walker (1993) examined how professional women defined success, drawing on data from 902 women graduates of Harvard's professional schools. They found that these women's concepts of success were not defined exclusively in terms of income and job position, but included the home front as well. Swiss and Walker drew on life history data to provide useful insights into how the women in their sample fought against traditional characterizations of success, seeking to create new notions of success that gave room to both career and family life: "many women are pursuing a new and powerful agenda: they want to succeed in their work, but on their own terms. They are determined to create a work culture that has room for professional success and a sane life-style" (p. 126).

The Spillover of Success

Perceived overall success in the various domains of one's life probably reflects general satisfaction at home and at work, as well as manageable, if not low, levels of work/family conflict and strain. The concept of spillover is often used to explain how performing a job influences family life or vice versa, with researchers distinguishing between positive and negative spillover (Evans and Bartolome 1984). Positive spillover, for example, is seen in Williams and Alliger's (1994) study of the ways that satisfaction and stimulation at work are correlated with high levels of energy and satisfaction at home. Negative spillover typically focuses on how problems and conflict at work drain and preoccupy the individual, making it difficult to achieve a successful or satisfactory family life (Higgins, Duxbury and Irving 1992; Parasuraman et al. 1989).

In their study of full-time employed two-earner couples in two communities in the greater Boston area, Barnett and Rivers (1996) found that men's and women's work and family lives were "like a spider's interconnected web: a tug that occurs at one section of the web sends vibrations throughout it" (p. 53). For both men and women in their study, what happened at home affected what happened at work, and vice versa, what they term "dynamic interaction." They found boundaries between work and family have become blurred and have integrated with each other.

Another study of 220 men and women in dual-professional couples (both working full time with children living at home) revealed spillover in conflict, with the more conflict the professionals experienced at work, the more conflict they had at home (Higgins, Duxbury and Irving 1992).

Williams and Alliger (1994) investigated[1] mood spillover, finding that spillover of unpleasant mood occurs both from work to family settings and from family to work, whereas the spillover of pleasant moods was weak. In other words, people who felt depressed at work tended to feel depressed at home and vice versa. This negative spillover was stronger for women than for men, which makes sense given that employed mothers are likely to have greater combined work and family work loads than are employed fathers (Pleck 1985) with correspondingly less opportunity to recover from the stress of either their work or their family roles.

Parasuraman and colleagues (1989) found that work role overload was a significant source of work/family conflict for both spouses. However, job involvement was not significantly related to time-based conflict for husbands, but significantly and positively related to the time-based conflict of wives.[2]

To conclude, there is evidence for both spillover and conflict models of the work/family interface. But the absence of work/family conflict or strain may mean one is simply "getting by"; no studies have considered work/life effectiveness in terms of subjective success in both the public and the private aspects of life. Moreover no research has contextualized this interface in terms of life stage, occupation, and gender.

THE EMBEDDEDNESS OF OVERALL SUCCESS

The Significance of Gender

Role theory suggests that gender as a "master status" (Merton 1968; Ridgeway and Walker 1994) shapes both the opportunity for, and the experience of, success in various domains. This is especially true in the case of work and family roles. In the middle of the twentieth century the "solution" to potential work/family conflicts was, for those who could afford it, one spouse (typically the wife) serving as a full-time homemaker. This freed the other spouse (typically the husband) to concentrate on becoming successful at work. In fact, advanced industrial societies have traditionally operated on the premise that wives and mothers would do the domestic labor of society in order to free husbands and fathers to work (and achieve success) in the paid economy (Moen 1992). Today, however, most married workers, regardless of gender, have an employed spouse. This means that both husbands and wives are increasingly having to cope with the demands of their jobs and their families, given the constraints of their spouses' job demands as well.

With the traditional mold broken (i.e., with no full-time homemaker available to both facilitate a successful family life and enable others in the family to be successful at work), contemporary working couples are having to devise new strategies to achieve success in their jobs and personal lives. But the traditional gendered division of labor persists even when both spouses work outside the home, with women still responsible for most domestic chores and timetables (Apter 1993; Barnett and Rivers 1996; Gerson 1985; Hertz 1986; Hochschild 1989). We would anticipate, therefore, that women in two-earner couples would be less successful—or at least perceive themselves as less successful—at effectively managing both their work and their family obligations. Men, on the other hand, frequently continue in their traditional role as primary breadwinner (Corrigall 1997), wherein their role obligations as provider at home and as dedicated worker on the job are synergistic rather than conflictual, possibly facilitating their perceptions of work/life effectiveness. This may especially be the case for men in prestigious and well-paying jobs; success at work translates into status and purchasing power for the household. Employed men may also be more highly committed to the work role than are employed women, given the salience of their work/career identities (Simon 1992), and may see success at work intertwined with success at home. By contrast, due to their location in frequently less rewarding "female" occupations (Reskin and Padevic 1994), and the fact that they continue to invest more of themselves in their families, employed women may be especially vulnerable to the overloads and strains of competing role obligations (cf. Goode 1960).

Achieving **both** a successful career and a successful family life requires time and energy investments. However, given the way work is structured (along the male breadwinner model), contemporary workers often have to choose between the competing demands of either their jobs or their personal lives (Goode 1960). How men and women respond to these competing demands is influenced by ingrained gender role attitudes (Corrigall 1997), with men typically socialized and rewarded for their role as providers, and women typically taking responsibility for childrearing. For men, we hypothesize that feeling successful at work will "spill over" into their sense of success in their private lives, promoting a sense of overall effectiveness. By contrast, we expect that women achieve and interpret success at work as at the expense of their success in their family role (or vice versa), making it more difficult for women in two-earner families to feel they have the best of both worlds.

The Significance of Occupation

The life course of individuals is socially structured by their attachment to the work force. For most adults, paid work is a major, if not the principal source of purposive activity, social relations, identity, and self-respect. As Riesman (1958) pointed out in the 1950s, many people work, not in order to have leisure time, but instead use leisure to be better prepared to work. In other words, they work not in order to be able to live, but live in order to work. Employment is a central role in American society; it is virtually isomorphic with contemporary notions of productivity and achievement. Institutional arrangements in the work place (in the form of internal labor markets and career lines) shape the potential for, and pathways to, objective occupational success in the form of income and status (Althauser 1989; Breiger 1990). Occupational level typically serves an index of objective attainment; occupation also shapes individuals' identities, interpretations, and dispositions, including their subjective assessments of their career success (Barley 1989).

Occupation is therefore also a "master status" coloring virtually every aspect of contemporary life, private as well as public. Sewell (1992) points out that "structure" the noun always implies "structuring" the verb. Location in the occupational hierarchy structures not only resources and opportunities but also habits, expectations, and everyday life experiences (Bourdieu 1990; Breiger 1995). Those in different occupations can be expected to hold different interpretations of their success in their personal lives as well as at work. Concretely, this means that individuals who are managers or professionals should be better off, not only objectively (in terms of income and other resources) but also subjectively, tending to see themselves as successful both at home and at work. By contrast, those in service or clerical work might feel less effective in all domains. The organization and culture of work also "structures" the rhythm, flexibility, and hours of the day, often in ways that are incompatible with the tasks and goals of childrearing (Moen 1989, 1992); thus active engagement in childrearing may be incompatible with the tasks and goals associated with occupational attainment. Nevertheless, given the primacy of work in contemporary society and the household as a unit of consumption, economic achievement in the workplace promotes the viability of the family economy. This suggests that objective success at work may invariably translate into effectiveness or "success" at managing work and family role obligations. In other words, occupational success (such as holding a high level job) may spill over to feelings of effectively juggling both private and public roles, promoting a sense of overall success.

The Significance of Life Stage

A life course focus raises the issue of continuity and change over time (Elder, George and Shanahan 1996; Moen 1996). How do men and women at various life stages evaluate their success on and off the job? Are employed men apt to feel more successful than employed women at both family and work roles, regardless of their ages or the ages of their children? Are women more likely to feel successful both at work and home at particular points in their lives?

Given that role demands change over the life course (Aldous 1996; Hill 1970; Ishii-Kuntz and Coltrane 1992; Shelton 1992; Riley 1987; Wilensky 1961), we anticipate similar shifts in overall success. Specifically, we expect that workers raising young children will be the least apt to feel they are effectively managing their work and family roles. This should be especially the case for working mothers, given their disproportionate child care and other domestic responsibilities.

The difficulty with much of the existing literature concerning successfulness, spillover, and conflict in work or personal life is that scholars do not consider potential differences across various life stages. Both conflicts between and spillover across the two domains may shift in intensity over the life course, in tandem with shifts in demands and resources.

Individuals in different life stages experience different demands in both their work and personal lives; they also have different expectations as well as different amounts of rewards and resources. Consequently, they may well interpret their achievements (or "success") in their work and family roles differently. For example, Wilensky (1961) suggested that low morale would be especially prevalent among workers with preschoolers. While Wilensky was referring to male workers, women in this launching stage, traditionally shouldering the additional time demands and tasks accompanying having young children at home while trying to meet the expectations of and frequently inflexible hours on the job, can be expected to be the least apt to report high levels of success at work, at home, and at balancing.

RESEARCH DESIGN

We employ survey data from the 1992 National Study of the Changing Workforce, as well as illustrative qualitative data from focus groups and in-depth interviews conducted as part of the Cornell Couples and Careers Study, to investigate the circumstances related to the perceived overall success at managing both work and family roles over various life course stages. We focus specifically on workers in dual-earner arrangements. After describing similarities and differences between dual-earner men and women, we document variations in their perceived overall success. We then draw on logistic regression techniques to model the factors related to overall success in both work and family roles and their balance. Finally, we consider the subjective meanings of successfulness in work and family/personal life to see whether men and women at different life stages define "success" differently.

Sample

The quantitative data for this study come from a national survey of a sample of 3,381 American workers (working ten or more hours a week), the 1992 *National Study of the Changing Workforce* (NSCW 1992). We use the 1992 NSCW because it contains information on different aspects of respondents' work lives as well as couples' joint work arrangements. The descriptive data were weighted to reflect the characteristics of the U.S. labor force as estimated by the March 1992 *Current Population Survey* (Galinsky, Bond and Friedman 1993). We draw on a subsample of workers who are members of two-earner families. Weighted to represent the national population of workers in dual-earner arrangements, this produces a sample of 1670 respondents.

Measures

Overall work/life success is measured by respondents' perceptions of feeling successful (above average) in three areas: their work life, their personal or family life, and their balancing of work and family/personal life. This is dichotomized as overall success (above average on all three measures), versus the absence of overall success (below average on one or more).

Independent variables (described in Table 1) consist of measures of couples' family life, couples' work arrangements, and other individual work characteristics. Though workers in dual-earner couples are on average in their late 30s and early 40s, "average age" masks the considerable heterogeneity in family and occupational "careers." To clarify the potential importance of temporal location we construct ideal types, dividing the individuals in working couples (employed and married to a spouse who is employed) into six life-course stages. We see the six life-course stages as reflecting both family and occupational career circumstances; however, they are operationalized on the basis of age of respondent and presence and age of (youngest) child. The stages are *anticipatory* (ages 20-29, no children, just beginning work career); *non-parents* (ages 30-49, married and in the career launching and building years but with no children); *launching* (ages 25-39, married with children younger than 6 and launching or building their work careers); *late-launching* (ages 40-61, married with children younger than 6, older than most parents of young children); *establishment* (ages 35-54, married with children ages 6 to 18 and typically established in the world of work); and *shifting gears* (ages 50-64, married with no children living at home and beginning to consider (or already) changing careers or cutting back on work involvement).

A number of variables capture both the respondents' and their spouses' work circumstances: couples' occupational status, couples' work hour arrangements, couples' employment sector, couples' multiple job arrangements, and perceptions of job priority of members of working couples. Couples' occupational status considers each spouses' status in tandem and is coded into four categories: (1) both are

Table 1. Variable Definitions

Variable	Definition
Success (Self Perceptions)	
Overall Success at Work, at Home, and at Balancing Both	Above the mean on the following: "How successful do you feel in your work life?"; "How successful do you feel in your family or personal life?"; "How successful do you feel in balancing work and family/personal life?": 1 "Not successful at all," 2 "somewhat not successful," 3 "somewhat successful," 4 "very successful."
Life Course Stage	
Stages	
Anticipatory	Ages 20 to 29, no children;
Non-parents	Ages 30 to 49, no children;
Launching	Ages 25 to 39, with children younger than 6;
Late launching	Ages 40 or older, with children younger than 6;
Establishment	Ages 35 to 54, with children ages 6 to 18;
Shifting gears	Ages 50 to 64, no children living at home.
Family	
Number of Children	Total number of children under 18 1) child under one year old; 2) child aged 2 to 5; 3) child aged 6 to 10;
Age of the Youngest Child	4) child aged 11 to 13; and 5) child aged 14 to 18.
Caregiving	A dummy variable with "1" indicating that respondents provide special care or attention to a friend or family member because of a handicap, illness, or old age.
Individual's Work Life	
Size of Organization	A dummy variable with 1 referring to 25 or more people and 0 to less than 25 people.
Occupational Level	A dummy variable with 1 referring to managerial/professional jobs and 0 to non-professional jobs such as technical, sales, administrative, services, and manual.
Employment Sector	Three categories: 1) respondent self employed; 2) respondent employed in private sector; and 3) respondent employed in public sector. A similar variable was constructed for the spouse's employment sector.
Actual Work Hours	Respondent's estimate of weekly hours put in on all paid jobs.

(continued)

Table 1. Variable Definitions

Variable	Definition
Work Hour Preference	Three categories: 1) prefer to work less (actual hours exceed desired hours; the time difference > 0); 2) satisfied with hours (no difference between actual and desired hours; the time difference = 0); and 3) prefer to work more (ideal hours exceed actual hours; the time difference < 0).
Job Shift	Three categories: 1) regular shift; 2) variable shift; and 3) evening, night, rotating, or split shift.
Job Demands	"My job requires working very fast"; "my job requires working very hard"; "I am asked to do an excessive amount of work"; "I have enough time to get the job done"; and "I have deadlines that are difficult to meet" (alpha = .696).
Job Autonomy	"I have a lot to say about what happens on my job"; "I am given a lot of freedom to decide how to do my work." (alpha = .69)
Job Insecurity	"How likely do you think it is that you will be temporarily laid off from your job in the next year?" "How likely do you think it is that you will lose your current job during the next year and have to look for a new one?" We reversed the response categories so that a higher score indicates greater insecurity (alpha = .809).
Job Ethic	"I don't care how well I do my job, I just want to finish it"; "I always try to get my job done well, no matter what it takes"; "When my job requires it, I work very hard." 1 "strongly disagree" 2 "disagree" 3 "agree" 4 "strongly agree" (alpha = .672).
Supervisor Support	"My supervisor is fair and doesn't show favoritism in responding to employees' personal or family needs"; "My supervisor accommodates me when I have family or personal business to take care of for example, medical appointments, meeting with child's teach, etc."; "My supervisor is understanding when I talk about personal or family issues that affect my work"; and "I feel comfortable brining up personal or family issues to my supervisor"; "My supervisor keeps me informed of the things I need to know to do my job well"; "My supervisor has expectations of my performance on the job that are realistic"; "My supervisor recognizes when I do a good job"; "My supervisor is supportive when I have a work problem"; and "My supervisor values difference in culture and background among the people who work for him/her" (alpha = .913).
Able to Compress Time	"Are you allowed to work additional hours on some days in order to take time off on other days?".
Able to Work at Home	"Are you allowed to do some of your work at home on a regular basis?"

Couple's Work Interface

Couple's Occupational Status

Four categories: 1) both professional (or managers); 2) husband is professional, wife nonprofessional; 3) wife is professional, husband nonprofessional; and 4) both spouses are in nonprofessional occupations.

Couple's Work Hour Arrangement

Four categories: 1) one or both spouses work less than 39 hours per week; 2) both spouses work between 39 hours and 45 hours per week; 3) one works over 45 hours per week; and 4) both spouses work over 45 hours per week.

Couple's Job Arrangement

Three categories: 1) both spouses hold one job; 2) respondent (only) holds more than one job; and 3) spouse holds more than one job.

Couple's Job Priority

Three levels: 1) spouse's job is more important; 2) respondent's job is more important; and 3) both equally important.

Source: National Study of the Changing Workforce, 1992

119

professionals (or managers); (2) husband is professional, wife nonprofessional; (3) wife is professional, husband nonprofessional; and (4) both spouses are in nonprofessional occupations. Couples' work hour arrangements are also grouped into four categories: (1) one or both spouses work less than 39 hours per week (this is almost always the wife); (2) both spouses work between 39 hours and 45 hours per week; (3) one (either respondent or spouse) works over 45 hours per week (this is almost always the husband); and (4) both spouses work over 45 hours per week.

We first created a couples' employment sector variable, but because of low numbers of cases in some cells, we reverted back to including this variable separately for each spouse. Employment sector is created on the basis of a question "Is your main job with a private company or organization, a local, county, state or federal government agency, or are you self-employed?" This variable has three categories: (1) respondent self-employed; (2) respondent employed in private sector; (3) respondent employed in public sector, with category 2 as the reference group in the multivariate analysis. A similar variable was constructed for the spouses' employment sector.

Couples' multiple job arrangements consist of three categories: (1) both spouses hold one job; (2) respondent (only) holds more than one job; and (3) spouse holds more than one job (this also includes the few cases where both spouses hold more than one job).

Couples' job priority is measured by the question "How do you compare your job with the job that your spouse has?" Three levels were created: (1) spouse's job is more important; (2) respondent's job is more important; and (3) both equally important.

FINDINGS

Table 2 lists the percents, means and standard deviations of the variables used in the analysis. It provides an overview of the NSCW sample of respondents in two-earner families by gender. Not surprisingly, wives in dual-earner arrangements tend to earn less, work fewer hours, and are more apt to be self-employed. They are also more likely to want to work fewer hours than men in two-earner households. On average, women in dual-earner couples see the ideal work week as consisting of 32.4 hours. Men in dual-earner arrangements would like to work a typical work week; they tend to see 40.2 hours a week as ideal. But both men and women are apt to want to work fewer hours than they actually do, although some would like to put in more hours. There is a small gender difference in work hour preference, with more men than women in dual-earner couples wanting to work less than they do. There's also a gender difference in how workers assess their own and their spouses' jobs. Wives tend to see their husbands' jobs as more important than their own, while few husbands see their wives jobs as more important than theirs.

Table 2. Selected Characteristics of Workers in
Two-Earner Families, by Gender, 1992

Characteristics	Men	Women	Significance
Sample (weighted)	831	848	
Family Life			
Age (std.dev.)	40.5 (9.8)	39.4 (9.6)	*
Years with Spouse (std. dev.)	14.1 (10.2)	15.6 (10.6)	**
Number of Marriages (%)			
First time marriage	73.1%	75.1%	
More than one	26.9%	24.9%	
Caregiving (%)	6.9%	10.4%	**
No. of Children < 18 (%)			
No children	39.6%	38.2%	
One child	25.3%	24.7%	
Two children	23.2%	22.4%	
More than two	11.8%	14.7%	
Life Stage (%)			
Anticipatory	9.2%	8.6%	
Nonparents	18.9%	20.3%	
Launching	19.1%	23.3%	
Late Launching	6.1%	3.9%	
Establishment	32.5%	31.0%	
Shifting Gears	14.1%	13.0%	
Individual's Work Life			
Size of Organization (%)			
Under 25	40.5%	42.3%	
25 or more	59.5%57.7%		
Total Number of Jobs (%)			
One job	90.5%	91.9%	
More than one	9.5%	8.1%	
Income, 1991 (std.dev.)	$35114.4 (23173)	$21533 (13754)	***
Actual Work Hours (std.dev.)	48 (11.7)	39.5 (12.6)	***
Ideal Work Hours (std.dev.)	40.2 (11.6)	32.4 (11.5)	***
Work Hours Preference (%)			*
Want less hours	55.2%	49.9%	
Satisfied with hours	31.7%	38.1%	
Want more hours	13.0%	12.0%	
Occupational Status (%)			*
Professional	40.8%	35.9%	
Non-professional	59.2%	64.1%	

(continued)

Table 2   (Continued)

Characteristics	Men	Women	Significance
R's Employment Sector (%)			
Self-employed	15.8%	13.1%	
Private	64.5%	65.1%	
Public	19.7%	21.8%	
SP's Employment Sector (%)			***
Self-employed	6.2%	13.2%	
Private	68.1%	65.9%	
Public	25.7%	20.9%	
Job Shift (%)			
Regular	74.2%	74.5%	
Variable	12.6%	11.7%	
Night/rotating	13.2%	13.8%	
Job Demands (std. dev.)	2.57 (.51)	2.61 (.51)	
Job Autonomy (std. dev.)	3.07 (.67)	2.96 (.66)	***
Job Demands/Autonomy (%)			***
Both high	20.0%	14.1%	
High demand, low autonomy	30.1%	40.4%	
Low demand, high autonomy	15.0%	15.2%	
Both low	34.8%	30.3%	
Job Insecurity (std.dev.)	1.49 (.80)	1.50 (.78)	
Job Ethic (std.dev.)	3.56 (.44)	3.59 (.44)	
Supervisor Support (std.dev.)	3.08 (.58)	3.13 (.57)	
Able to Compress Time (%)	44.6%	48.7%	
Able to Work at Home (%)	30.9%	29.5%	
Couple's Work Interface			
Couple's Occupational Status (%)			
Both professional	18.3%	20.6%	
Husband professional, wife nonprofessional	22.4%	20.9%	
Wife professional, husband nonprofessional	16.0%	13.4%	
Both nonprofessional	43.3%	45.0%	
Couple's Work Hour Arrangements (%)			
One or both under 39 hours	24.4%	28.0%	
One over 45 hours	41.4%	40.0%	
Both over 45 hours	25.8%	22.8%	
Both 39-45 hours	8.5%	9.2%	

(continued)

Table 2 (Continued)

Characteristics	Men	Women	Significance
Couple's Job Arrangements (%)			
Both one job	85.5%	84.2%	
R more than 1 job	7.4%	6.8%	
SP more than 1 job	7.1%	9.1%	
Couple's Job Priority (%)			***
SP's job more important	11.7%	39.2%	
R's job more important	29.2%	9.3%	
Equally important	59.1%	51.5%	
Work/Life Success (%)	18.2%	17.3%	

Notes: $^*p < .05;$
$^{**}p < .01;$
$^{***}p < .001$

Source: National Study of the Changing Workforce, 1992 ($N = 1670$)

We find a striking depiction of life course differences in family and occupational circumstances, from years married (and number of marriages) to income and work hours.[3] For example, job demands are greatest for workers with young children and lowest for those in the *shifting gears* phase (data not shown, a table of differences by life stage available from the authors).

While there is no gender difference in the proportion of workers in dual-earner couples reporting overall work/life success, both gender and life stage combined shape the likelihood of dual-earner workers reporting overall work/life success. The highest proportion of overall work/life success is reported by women in the *shifting gears* phase (see Figure 1). And men in dual-earner arrangements in their 20s (without children) are more apt than women at this stage to see themselves as successful overall. Clearly it is having children in the home, not age, that is most related to work/life success, especially for men in two-earner households. Over one in four young men (in their 20s) and older men (in their 50s) with no children (at home) report overall work/life success, as do over one in five men without children who are in their 30s and 40s. The least apt to report work/life success are men and women with young preschoolers (*launching* stage). Note, however, that those having preschoolers at a later age (*late launching*) are slightly more apt to report work/life success. Women seem to successfully manage the various strands of their lives only in their later work years, but do so better than the men in the *shifting gears* stage.

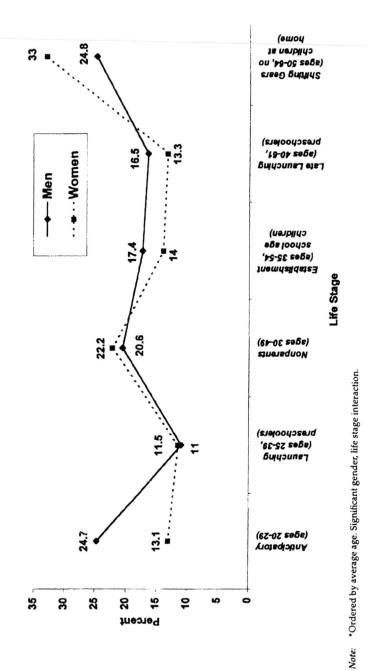

Figure 1. Proportion of Workers in Two-Earner Families Reporting High Overall Work/Life Success (at Work, at Home and at Balancing) by Gender and Life Stage, 1992*

Note: *Ordered by average age. Significant gender, life stage interaction.

124

Table 3. Estimating Successful Work/Lives in Terms of Work and Family Characteristics by Gender, Members of Two-Earner Families, 1992

Variables	Model 1 Work/Life Success		Model 2 Work/Life Success	
	Men	Women	Men	Women
Life Stage				
Anticipatory	.124	−.881*	−.059	−1.01*
Nonparents	−.086	−.196	−.005	−.252
Launching	−.751*	−.998***	−.608+	−.662+
Late launching	−.302	−.765	−.347	−.494
Establishment	−.273	−.747**	−.253	−.532+
Shifting gears (reference)				
Caregiving	—	—	.239	−.246
Number of Children	—	—	.015	−.200
Couple's Work Interface				
Couple's Occupational Status				
Both professionals	−.165	.483+	−.515	.256
Husband professional, wife nonprofessional	.091	.462+	−.121	.325
Wife professional, husband nonprofessional	−.742*	.524*	−.868*	.315
Neither professional (reference)				
Couple's Work Time				
One or both under 39 hours	−.611*	−.432+	−.618**	−.405
One over 45 hours	−.592**	−.548*	−.526*	−.443+
Both over 45 hours	−.570	−.603	−.283	−.202
Both 39-45 hours (reference)				
Couple's Employment Sector				
Respondent self employed	—	—	−.313	.593
Respondent in public sector	—	—	−.234	−.207
Respondent in private sector (reference)				
Spouse self employed	—	—	.863	−.562
Spouse in public sector	—	—	.340	−.363
Spouse in private sector (reference)				
Couple's Job Arrangements				
R more than one job	—	—	.747*	.215
SP more than one job	—	—	1.091*	−.392
Both one job (reference)				

(continued)

Table 3   (Continued)

Variables	Model 1 Work/Life Success		Model 2 Work/Life Success	
	Men	Women	Men	Women
Other Work Characteristics				
Size of Organization	—	—	.194	.413[+]
Job Shift				
Night/rotating	—	—	.300	−.059
Variable	—	.—	.051	−.228
Regular (reference)				
Job Demands	—	—	.240	−.293
Job Autonomy	—	—	.174	.039
Able to Work at Home	—	—	.178	.168
Able to Compress Work Hours	—	—	−.149	−.088
Job Insecurity	—	—	.444**	−.401*
Job Ethic	—	—	.835***	−.159
Supervisor Support	—	—	.481*	.594**
Gap between Actual and Ideal				
Work Hours				
Want less hours	—	—	.246	−.799***
Want more hours	—	—	.313	−.573
Satisfied (reference)				
Constant	−.795***	−.989***	−4.47***	−.211
2 Log Likelihood	795.6	746.4	701.0	679.0
Model Chi-Square	24.0**	28.6**	82.5***	96.0***
N (unweighted)	831	848	831	848

Notes: [+]$p < .1$;
  $p < .05$;
  $p < .01$;
  $p < .001$

Source: National Study of Changing Workforce (1992).

Multivariate Models

To examine the links between couple and individual characteristics and the odds of overall success we estimate a series of multivariate models separately by gender, using logistic regression techniques. We begin with life stage, couples' occupational status and couples' work hour arrangements (Model 1, Table 3).

We see (in Model 1) that, for women in dual-earner couples, even net of occupational status and the hours both couples work, life stage matters considerably. As we saw in Figure 1, it is not until the *shifting gears* phase that women in dual-earner arrangements are likely to report overall success, with those in the launching stage the least apt to feel successful in their work/lives. Similarly, for men in dual-earner couples, those in the launching stage are the least likely to report successfully managing their work/life obligations, even net of their hours on the job.

Not surprisingly, couple work hour arrangements matter. Most apt to experience work/life success are those where both spouses are working "regular" (39-45 hours) hours. Men in arrangements where one spouse (typically their wives) is part time or where one spouse (typically themselves) puts in over 45 hours a week are less likely to report work/life success than in circumstances where both spouses put in a regular work week. (There are a few respondents where both spouses work over 45 hours a week; and this coefficient, while not statistically significant, is also negatively related to men's overall work/life success.) For women also, when one spouse (typically their husbands) puts in long hours, they themselves are less likely to report overall work/life success. There is a trend for women working less than full time to also be unlikely to report successful work/life.

Net of life stage and couples' work time, the couples' joint occupational status is related to the odds of both men's and women's work/life success. Nonprofessional men whose wives are professionals or managers have a low likelihood of overall work/life success. By contrast, in those same circumstances, women professionals or managers are more likely (than where both are nonprofessionals) to report overall work/life success. And there are trends for women in couples where anyone holds a professional level job—themselves, their husbands, or both—to report overall success in their work/lives. Including other family and work characteristics (Model 2, Table 3) produces little difference in the distribution of work/life success by life stage. In other words, it is not their family and work environments that account for the life stage differences in women successfully managing their work and family roles. However, wanting to work fewer hours is negatively tied to women's overall success. Note also that work time continues to predict work/life success even net of work-hour preferences and other family and work circumstances. Having a spouse in a job seen as the most important is negatively related to women's overall work/life success. Holding an insecure job is negatively linked to work/life success for both men and women in two-earner households. Positively related to both men's and women's overall work/life success is supervisor support.

For men in non-professional jobs, having a wife who is in a professional or managerial occupation continues to be predictive of low work/life success (compare coefficients in Models 1 and 2, Table 3) once specific aspects of the job and family are included. Net of other factors included in the model, non-professional men married to professionals or managers continue to be less likely than those with wives in non-professional jobs to feel they are successfully managing their work/life obligations and goals. There is as well a continuing trend for those dual-earner men with young children (*launching* stage) to be less apt to report work/life success. Couples' combined work hours continue to matter, even net of other aspects of work and home circumstances. Having both spouses work regular full time hours seems to be the most predictive of men's work/life success. Both men putting in long hours (whose wives work at least full time) and men in arrangements where one spouse (typically the wife) works part time are less likely to report overall work/life success. And there remains a trend for women who have at least one spouse working long hours (typically their husbands) to be less apt to see themselves as successful overall.

Surprisingly, men working more than one job see themselves as successful in their overall work/life, but not when their *wives* hold more than one job. Having a highly demanding job is not related to overall success in managing work and family roles, for either men or women in dual-earner families. But both women and men having an understanding, supportive supervisor are more apt to report overall work/life success, while those whose jobs are insecure are less likely to do so. A strong work ethic is also positively related to men's overall work/life success.

Meanings of Success

In this study we are considering employees' interpretations of their successfulness, that is, success not as gauged by any objective yardstick but as perceived by individuals. But "being successful" at work and in one's family/personal life may mean different things to men and women at different life stages. In the following analyses we examine the subjective meanings of success—in terms of the language workers use to describe what it means to be successful in work and family life. We look for similarities and differences by gender and selected life stages, as well as by whether employees rate themselves as high (above average) in success. (Recall that employees are placed in the high level of success if their scores in work/family/personal life and balancing are all above the mean and in the low level of success if any score is below the mean.)

Neither those interviewed in depth in the *Cornell Couples and Careers Study* nor the respondents to the *National Study of the Changing Workforce* offered any one dominant view of what it means to be successful. We now examine the factors respondents equated with success in each domain.

Success at Work

Most working men and women believe that personal satisfaction is key to being successful at work (see Table 4), but this varies by life stage and by gender. Fully 70 percent of women in the *shifting gears* stage define personal satisfaction as essential to being successful at work, compared to only 43.7 percent of the men in this life stage. There is a life stage difference in women's equating work success with personal satisfaction, with only 47 percent of young working

Table 4. Meanings of Successfulness at Work and Family, by Gender and Four Life Stages, 1992

	Anticipatory		Launching		Establishment		Shifting Gears		Total %		Diff.	Diff. (p²)	
	Men	Women	Men	Women	Men	Women	Men	Women	Men	Women	p¹	Men	Women
Success at Work (%)													
Coworker Recognition	26.1	26.4	37.1	35.1	26.8	36.7	26.9	22.1	29.1	28.3	.751	.238	.144
Advancement[3]	32.4	37.7	21.9	24.4	19.2	9.7	27.2	13.7	21.9	19.0	.203	.128	.000
Personal Satisfaction[4]	42.2	47.4	52.7	49.0	50.2	60.3	43.7	70.2	50.0	54.1	.150	.376	.021
Good Income[5]	32.3	19.0	29.2	24.5	29.8	12.5	28.7	9.0	29.4	19.3	.000	.951	.058
Feeling Work is Important	9.8	13.2	14.5	13.6	2.6	18.2	7.9	4.4	9.1	13.2	.021	.016	.079
Control over Schedule[6]	4.4	3.9	1.4	8.8	9.7	7.7	1.6	2.8	5.1	6.6	.260	.008	.349
Personal Success (%)													
Good Relationships[7]	36.1	51.4	56.5	50.3	53.5	61.8	56.6	57.0	48.1	50.8	.352	.012	.384
Time with Family[8]	25.6	20.3	54.0	57.4	42.5	35.9	20.6	29.2	33.4	36.1	.329	.000	.000
Afford Things[9]	33.9	20.5	29.2	13.5	43.6	11.7	24.2	18.6	31.8	19.9	.000	.343	.002
Time to Do Things	30.6	25.5	12.1	33.0	17.8	13.5	11.5	17.7	20.1	19.8	.889	.001	.015
No Stress with Family	13.6	10.1	12.0	22.2	8.9	27.1	4.9	7.3	10.9	14.9	.037	.207	.002

Notes: [1] Chi-square differences by gender;
[2] Chi-square differences by life stage, for men and women;
[3] Chi-square differences by life stages, for men (p = .046) and for women (p = .001) who report being successful at work;
[4] Chi-square differences by life stages for men (p = .000) and for women (p = .094) who report being successful at work;
[5] Chi-square differences by life stages for women (p = .002) who report being successful at work;
[6] Chi-square differences by life stages for men (p = .014) who report being successful at work;
[7] Chi-square differences by life stages for men (p = .014) who report being successfulness in their personal/family life;
[8] Chi-square differences by life stages for men (p = .000) and for women (p = .028) who report being successful in their personal/family life;
[9] Chi-square differences by life stages for men (p = .014) who report being successful in their personal/family life.

Source: National Study of Changing Workforce (1992).

129

women in the *anticipatory* phase doing so. Still, personal satisfaction is the most commonly mentioned aspect of feeling successful at work in every life stage. In our in-depth interviews, one working mother in the *establishment* stage who directs a day care center and has two young children illustrates the common theme of personal satisfaction:

> I think success is a lot about perception. It has to do with how you feel about it. You can be someone who hasn't checked off a lot on the list and still feel successful.

While occupational advancement is a typical objective indicator of success at work, this was mentioned as important to their feelings of success by only about one in four working men and about one in five working women in the NSCW survey. Advancement was more likely to be cited by younger women (*anticipatory* phase = 37.7%; *launching* phase = 24.4%) than by those *established* in their careers and families (9.7%) or in the *shifting gears* phase (13.7%).

Another objective aspect of occupational success is economic return, with having a good income cited by about three in ten (32.3%) men in the NSCW survey (no significant life stage difference). Clearly this is an important component of success at work for a significant minority of working men. In our in-depth interviews, one man, an engineer in the shifting gears stage working for a major (Fortune 100) corporation, pointed out that, for him,

> salaries and promotions are more important in terms of whether you are successful or not. You will not feel very successful if you don't have a reasonable salary.

Fewer (16.3%) women mention this tangible aspect of occupational success, but this varies by life stage, with one in four (24.5%) women in the *launching* phase mentioning income as key, compared to less than one in ten (9%) women in the *shifting gears* phase.

Whether respondents equate success with "feeling one's work is important" also varies by life stage and by gender, though few mention this. Almost one in five (18.2%) women in the *establishment* phase say that success is related to doing important work; even fewer (14.5%) men in the *launching* phase mention this factor. Note that very few workers describe control of their work and their work schedule as key to feeling successful at work. For men, however, this varies by stage, with men in the *establishment* phase most apt to mention this (9.7%).

We also looked at whether actually feeling successful at work was related to items mentioned as fundamental components of success (data not shown). We found that men in the NSCW survey who felt more successful at work in the *launching* (69.4%) and *establishment* (78.8%) stages were more apt to use language related to personal satisfaction as a significant factor in being successful at work. By contrast, more men in the *anticipatory* stage who felt less successful perceived personal satisfaction as an important measure of success at work.

Advancement was more apt to be mentioned by both men and women in the *launching* phase who did not feel successful at work. Income was more frequently cited by women in the *establishment* and *shifting gears* stages who felt less successful at work.

Overall, these findings suggest that men and women tend to define success at work more internally (or subjectively) rather than externally (or objectively, see Mortimer 1996). But conceptions of what it means to be successful on the job are related to both life stage and gender, with women and older workers tending to weight personal satisfaction heavily. Those men in the *launching* and *establishment* phases who equated job success with personal satisfaction are the ones in these stages most apt to feel successful at work.

Success in Family/Personal Life

Having good relationships at home is mentioned by over half the working men and women in our sample as key to feeling successful in their family/personal lives. This varies by stage of the life course for men but not women, with fewer young men in the *anticipatory* phase (36.1%) saying good relationships are key, compared to those further along in their careers and their lives (see Table 4).

Spending time with family is also important for a sense of success in one's private life, especially for mothers and fathers in the *launching* phase. Over half the men (54.0%) and women (57.4%) in the *launching* stage put an emphasis on time with family as key to personal and family success. In an in-depth interview, one manager who is also the mother of two young children related family success with

> taking time to see if your family is working, are you spending time with them, do you feel good about them.

More men than women in all life stages believe that being able to afford things is an important factor in achieving a successful family/personal life, with men in the *establishment* phase especially likely to mention this (43.6%). This suggests persisting differences in gender roles, with a number of men still viewing their role as financial providers as key to a successful family life. For them, being the family breadwinner, able to earn a good income and provide sufficient goods for their families, remains important to their feeling successful both at work and on the home front.

Women, by contrast, were more apt to mention "no stress in the family" as key to their success at home. This varies by life stage for women (but not men), with women in the *launching* and *establishment* stages most likely to cite no stress as important for their sense of family/personal success (see Table 4). Women with young preschoolers in the *launching* phase (33.0%) were most likely to mention "time to do things" as an important component of their personal/family success as were young men in the *anticipatory* stage (30.6%).

There are few differences in criteria for family/personal success by whether respondents felt successful themselves (data not shown). However, fathers in the *establishment* phase who felt successful in their family/personal lives are less apt to cite "time with family" as key to success, compared to fathers in the *launching* stage. And young women in their 20s (*anticipatory* stage) who felt personally successful were more apt to mention "good relationships" and less apt to mention "time to do things" as aspects of success.

DISCUSSION

Success in contemporary America has typically been equated with occupational achievement, and especially with upward mobility on a career ladder (cf. Barley 1989; Breiger 1995; Mortimer 1996). But while objective social position on that ladder shapes both individuals' sense of what is possible as well as their self-image (Bourdieu 1990), position in terms of career clocks and family clocks also color individuals' overall work/life success. In this paper we have broadened the concept of success to consider feelings of successfulness in both public (work) and private (personal/family) domains and in the balancing of the two for men and women in dual-earner families. We drew on a life course perspective to better contextualize success, assessing how overall work/life success in work and personal domains (and in balancing the two) varies by life stage and gender. To do so we constructed "ideal type" stages that roughly correspond to life course changes in both the occupational career and the family "career." We found identifiable patterns based on both life stage and gender.

As expected, but nevertheless intriguing is the fact that men and women in the *launching* stage are the least apt to report work/life success. Men in two-earner families, of all ages, are apt to feel successful across the public and private domains of their lives when there are no children in the home. Women in dual-earner families are most apt to report overall work/life success in the *shifting gears* phase, once they are in their 50s and 60s and their children have left home. These variations by life stage point to the plight of two-earner families with young children, where both partners are just starting their occupations and families. Family and work roles converge to render working couples with preschoolers particularly vulnerable. Only one in ten at this life stage reported overall success in both work and family domains. But women with school-aged children are similarly unlikely to feel successful in their overall work/lives, as are young women who do not have children.

The evidence from the analysis reported in this chapter also suggests the importance of **work hours** for work/life success. Qualitative analysis confirms that having enough time with one's family is equated by many with success on the home front. Our multivariate analysis of NSCW survey data reveals that workers in dual-earner families whose work hours are more evenly divided (both working

39-45 hours a week) are the most apt to report overall work/life success. Long hours for one spouse (typically the husband) is negatively related to feeling successful across work and family domains. Additionally, preferences matter, especially for women. For women, preferring to work fewer hours negatively predicts work/life success.

Insights from our in-depth interviews in the *Cornell Couples and Careers Study* reinforce the importance of work hours as related to overall success. One woman, who at fifty was in her second marriage and had a young daughter, valued the involvement with her child that her teaching career allowed. She noted that an ideal part of her own work life was the fact that she had time to contribute to raising her child. Getting home from work early and having summers allowed her to spend quality time raising her daughter and save money that would have been spent on childcare. Another woman we interviewed, who at twenty-eight is partnered and planning for both a career and children describes as ideal:

> ...jobs that you can depend on income-wise and give you self-worth but also to be able to provide a good environment for kids. And flexibility has to be a part of that.

Our statistical analysis of the NSCW data shows that actual work hours matter for overall work/life success—even net of preferred work hours. Regular work week (39-45 hours) **for both spouses** is the most predictive of success. Men who are in couples with a reduced work arrangement are typically married to wives who work part time. Neither this arrangement nor arrangements where one spouse puts in long hours are conduce to having the best of both worlds. When one spouse puts in long hours it is usually the husband. Men who report this arrangement work an average of 55.7 hours per week. Women in this arrangement work only an average 40-hour work week, underscoring that it is their husbands who are putting in the long hours. In an in-depth interview, a forty-two year old man reinforced the importance of "sane" hours on the job, describing the most important aspects of an ideal career are:

> both enjoying your job and the opportunity to spend time with family.

Knowing couples' joint occupational status doesn't improve the odds of predicting overall work/life success, net of work hours and other work and family considerations, with one important exception. Men in non-professional jobs married to professionals are the least likely to report overall work/life success. The fact that wives who are professionals or managers married to nonprofessionals are more apt to report overall success can be explained by other factors (compare Model 1 to Model 2 in Table 3). Much of the story of occupational level is confounded with couples' hours on the job. Husbands who are professionals or managers married to wives in non-professional jobs put in the most hours at work (mean = 52); wives in these circumstances put in the least (mean = 35). When the wives are professionals or managers and their husbands are not, they both tend to put in the same hours per week (mean = 44). This is the highest hours for women and the lowest for men in our dual-earner sample.

Surprisingly, the factors traditionally assumed to promote or reduce work/life conflict or strain—job demands, job autonomy, the ability to compress work hours or work at home, working a reduced schedule—are unrelated to perceived overall work/life success. While these factors may well, in fact, be related to role overload and conflict, we are examining the perception of actually succeeding on both work and family fronts and in balancing the two—no easy feat! Three work-related factors stand out in predicting overall work/life success: a supportive supervisor, the absence of job insecurity, and both spouses working "regular" hours.

The theme of both spouses' circumstances as critical to success emerges in our qualitative data as well. A case in point is a man who said:

> Frankly, my ideal family life is to have everyone happy, which means my wife has to continue and be happy with her career, because that makes her happy.

IMPLICATIONS FOR THEORY AND RESEARCH

A life course approach to work/life success is useful because it captures the **temporality of lives**, the way work and family responsibilities and resources change with age. Feelings of overall success at work, at home, and at balancing the two increase with age, seniority, and occupational achievement, but are also related to hours put in on the job, for both working men and working women in dual-earner families. And employment remains gendered for members of two-earner couples both within and across life stages. The *launching* life stage, a time of high family and work demands, is negatively linked to overall success for both women and men in two-earner households. But it continues to be a distinctively gendered experience: men in dual-earner couples with young children at home are working on average 49.4 hours a week, while women at this stage are working an average of 38.1 hours a week.[4] However, both men and women are likely to report lower levels of overall work/life success at this stage, and this remains the case even net of other work and family circumstances.

Also useful is focusing on **couple level** variables. Multivariate analyses (reported in Table 3) reveal that spouses' occupation does matter. We have shown that workers' interpretations of their overall work/life success are contingent on both spouses' work hours. Moreover, husbands in non-professional jobs married to professionals or managers tend to feel less successful overall. And wives who see their husbands' jobs as more important than their own are less apt to report high overall success.

These results suggest the importance of considering the combination of both spouses' jobs. This whole issue of couples' joint occupational status points to the complexity of contemporary occupational and family "careers," with couples strategizing about his job, her job, and their family (Moen and Wethington 1992). Unfortunately, the data from the National Study of the Changing Workforce do not permit an analysis of the joint overall work/life success between spouses. But qualitative data suggest that a husband's occupational success may come at the expense of that of his wife's and (more rarely) vice versa. Many in our qualitative analysis reported that one spouse had a "job" while the other pursued a "career." How two-earner couples strategize their lives affects their occupational and family environments. Couples' conjoint choices of working hours, occupation, and particular work environments, as well as the timing and number of children, may well be part of the story of contemporary pathways to effectively managing work/life obligations.

While our use of a life course approach to this cross-sectional data aimed to tease out temporal aspects of working couples' lifestyles, the fact is that coping and strategies of adaptation are processes that unfold both over time and over the life course (Lazarus and Folkman 1984; Moen and Wethington 1992). Longitudinal research, following couples over a period of time, is required to examine their strategies as they emerge over time, and the long term consequences of various strategies for earnings, job security and advancement, as well as for family and personal well-being. For example, qualitative research findings suggest that some couples adopt a "trading off" strategy, giving primacy to each spouse's career at different points in time (Becker and Moen 1999). How does this play out over the life course, and with what consequences? What is the role of anticipated and unanticipated events and transitions in fostering one set of strategies over another? How do couples manage when their careers are moving at similar, or different, speeds? The gendered nature of couples' strategies and the implications for women's career paths also need to be fleshed out (Han and Moen 1999).

Implications for Policy and Practice

A fundamental concern for contemporary men and women in working couples is the issue of **time** (see also Hochschild 1997; Moen 1992). Women who feel squeezed, who would like to work less are unlikely to report overall success in both their work and family domains. Men and women in families where one spouse is putting in long hours are unlikely to feel successful at work, at home, and in their interface.

The fact that couples' time spent at work is negatively related to both men's and women's overall work/life success underscores the constraints of time as jobs are currently structured. Wage and hour laws as well as prevailing corporate policies emphasize **time at work** over work performance. Work hours are seen as a tangible manifestation of individuals' dedication to their jobs. Working long hours is part of societal and employers' definition of working hard (a strong work ethic) signaling commitment to the job and the employer. This reflects American society's value of individual accomplishment through hard work and a corporate culture equating work time with productivity (cf. Hochschild 1997). It also helps to explain why few employees are likely to take advantage of reduced work hours or other alternative work arrangements. These options are not incorporated into the organization of work. They remain "options," not institutionalized patterns, and as such are interpreted as antithetical to occupational success. The way time is socially constructed by the bureaucracies of the state and the market remains a fundamental issue in considering strategies to facilitate success both at work and at home.

Our evidence also underscores the vulnerability of working couples with young children. Policies and practices that can ease the demands and enhance the resources of working parents of preschoolers, who are simultaneously experiencing heavy family and occupational obligations, would permit them to successfully negotiate the multiple facets of their lives. Child care policies are only part of the solution; also required are flexible work hour policies and the lengthening of career ladders.

Having supportive supervisors promotes the overall work/life success of both men and women in dual-earner families. The policy issue is how to provide such supportiveness. We believe it goes beyond simply "training" supervisors to creating a certain discretionary flexibility in work arrangements that would be built in to jobs, with supervisors fully aware of, and endorsing, all options.

Another policy concern that is less tractable is the issue of job security. In a restructuring and downsizing environment, workers will be less likely to be able to obtain or retain "secure" employment. Policy strategies are required to empower workers to manage their own careers rather than rely on past employer/employee contracts (trading commitment for security) that are growing increasingly rare.

The occupational career as a social institution, an individual trajectory, and a focus of study is being transformed as boundaries between home and work become more permeable and contingent, and firms and employees move away from the contract implied by the notion of "career" jobs. What we are experiencing, what we are in the midst of, are changes in the culture of occupational careers, from an individual, male, lock-step model to a variety of patchwork arrangements. The problem is that policies and practices are grounded on the standardized model of work, and the breadwinner/homemaker model of work and family.

Increasing numbers of contemporary workers are in dual-earner families. But jobs remain structured as if all workers have a spouse to facilitate their focus on their work. This "structural lag" (Riley and Riley 1994; Moen 1994) between policies and practices on the one hand and contemporary realities on the other will require more than simple band-aid solutions. What is required are new visions of careers, new measures of commitment (beyond hours on the job), and new templates of success (Moen 1998) that permit men and women to "have it all" at home and at work.

ACKNOWLEDGMENT

Support for the research reported here was provided by a grant from the Alfred P. Sloan Foundation (grant #96-6-9) and grants from the National Institute on Aging (grants #IT50 AG11711 and #P50AG1171106).

NOTES

1. Through the use of daily reports from forty-one full-time employed men and women in the Albany, New York area.
2. Looking at both time-based conflict and strain-based conflict in their study of a random sample of 119 couples (both spouses highly educated and largely employed full-time in a wide variety of business and professional career fields measuring overload with four items such as "There is a great deal to be done on my job" and in measuring job involvement by four items from Lodahl and Kejner's job involvement scale, for example, "The most important things that happen to me involve my job").
3. Data separated by life stage available from the authors.
4. Similar differences in work hours exist for the late launchers (those in their 40s and 50s with preschoolers), with men working an average of 47.5 and women 37.2 hours a week.

REFERENCES

Aldous, J. 1996. *Family Careers: Rethinking the Developmental Perspective.* Thousand Oaks, CA: Sage Publications.

Althauser, R. P. 1989. "Job Histories, Career Lines and Firm Internal Labor Markets: An Analysis of Job Shifts." *Research in Social Stratification and Mobility* 8: 177-200.

Apter, T. 1993. *Working Women Don't have Wives: Professional Success in the 1990s.* New York: St. Martin's Press.

Barley, S. R. 1989. "Careers, Identities, and Institutions: The Legacy of the Chicago School of Sociology." Pp. 41-65 in *Handbook of Career Theory.* New York: Cambridge University Press.

Barnett, R. C., and C. Rivers. 1996. *She Works/He Works: How Two-Income Families are Happier, Healthier, and Better-Off.* New York: Harper Collins Publishers, Inc.

Becker, P. E., and P. Moen. 1999. "Scaling Back: Dual Career Couples' Work-Family Strategies." *Journal of Marriage and the Family* 6: 4.

Blau, P. M., and O. D. Duncan. 1967. *The American Occupational Structure.* New York: Wiley.

Bourdieu, P. 1990. *The Logic of Practice.* Stanford, CA: Stanford University Press.

Breiger, R. 1990. *Social Mobility and Social Structure.* Cambridge: Cambridge University Press.

_____. 1995. "Social Structure and the Phenomenology of Attainment." *Annual Review of Sociology* 58: 703-722.

Brim, G. 1992. *Ambition: How We Manage Success and Failure Throughout our Lives.* New York: Basic.

Corrigall, E. 1997. *Work-Family Interface: Investments in Tending the Hearth and Bringing Home the Bacon.* Internet URL: <http://blue.temple.edu/~eastern/corrigal.html>.

Coser, L. 1974. Greedy Institutions: Patterns of Undivided Commitment. New York: Free Press.

Elder, G. H., Jr., L. K. George, and M. J. Shanahan. 1996. "Psychosocial Stress Over the Life Course." In *Psychosocial Stress: Perspectives on Structure, Theory, Life Course, and Methods.* Orlando, FL: Academic Press.

Evans, P., and F. Bartolome. 1984. "The Changing Picture of the Relationship Between Career and the Family." *Journal of Occupational Behavior* 5: 9-21.

Frone, M. R., and R. W. 1987. "Work-Family Conflict: The Effect of Job and Family Involvement." *Journal of Occupational Behavior* 8: 45-53.

Galinsky, E., J. T. Bond, and D. E. Friedman. 1993. *The Changing Workforce: Highlights of the National Study.* New York: Families and Work Institute.

Gattiker, U. E., and L. Larwood. 1986. "Subjective Career Success: A Study of Managers and Support Personnel." *Journal of Business and Psychology* 1: 78-94.

_____. 1988. "Predictors for Managers' Career Mobility, Success, and Satisfaction." *Human Relations* 41: 569-591.

_____. 1990. "Predictors for Career Achievement in the Corporate Hierarchy." *Human Relations* 43: 703-726.

Gerson, K. 1985. *Hard Choices: How Women Decide about Work, Career, and Motherhood.* Berkley, CA: University of California Press.

Goode, W. I. 1960. "A Theory of Role Strain." *American Sociological Review* 25: 483-496.

Han, S.-K., and P. Moen. 1999. "Clocking Out: Temporol Pattering of Retirement." *American Journal of Sociology* 105: 1.

Hertz, R. 1986. *More Equal Than Others: Women and Men in Dual-Career Marriages.* Berkley, CA: University of California Press.

Higgins, C. A., Duxbury, L. E., and R.H. Irving. 1992. "Work-Family Conflict in the Dual-Career Family." *Organizational Behavior and Human Decision Processes* 51: 51-75.

Hill, R. 1970. *Family Development in Three Generations.* Cambridge, MA: Schenkman Publishing Company.

Hochschild, A. 1989. *The Second Shift.* New York: Avon Books.

_____. 1997. *The Time Bind: When Work Becomes Home and Home Becomes Work.* New York: Metropolitan Books.

Ishii-Kuntz, M., and S. Coltrane. 1992. "Predicting the Sharing of Household Labor: Are Parenting and Housework Distinct?" *Sociological Perspectives* 35: 629-647.

Kanter, R. M. 1977. *Work and Family in the United States: A Critical Review and Agenda for Research and Policy.* New York: Russell Sage.

Ladewig, B. H., and P. N. White. 1984. "Dual-Earner Marriages: The Family Social Environment and Dyadic Adjustment." *Journal of Family Issues* 5: 343-362.

Lazarus, R. S., and S. Folkman. 1984. *Stress, Appraisal, and Coping.* New York: Springer.

Merton, R. K. 1968. *Social Theory and Social Structure.* New York: Free Press.

Moen, P. 1989. *Working Parents: Transformations in Gender Roles and Public Policies in Sweden.* Madison, WI: University of Wisconsin Press.

_____. 1992. *Women's Two Roles: A Contemporary Dilemma.* Westport, CT: Greenwood Publishing Group, Inc.

_____. 1994. "Women, Work, and Family: A Sociological Perspective on Changing Roles." In *Age and Structural Lag: The Mismatch Between People's Lives and Opportunities in Work, Family, and Leisure.* New York: John Wiley & Sons.

_____. 1996. "Gender, Age, and the Life Course." In *Handbook of Aging and the Social Sciences.* New York: Academic Press.

_____. 1998. "Recasting Careers: Changing Reference Groups, Risks, and Realities." *Generations* 22: 40-45.

Moen, P., and E. Wethington. 1992. "The Concept of Family Adaptive Strategies." *Annual Review of Sociology* 18: 233-251.

Morris, B. 1997. "Is Your Family Wrecking Your Career?" *Fortune*, March 17, 71-90.

Mortimer, J. T. 1996. "Social Psychological Aspects of Achievement." In *Generating Social Stratification: Toward a New Generation of Research.* Boulder, CO: Westview.

Parasuraman, S., C. S. Granrose, S. Rabinowitz, and N. J.N. Blutell. 1989. "Sources of Work-Family Conflict Among Two-Career Couples." *Journal of Vocational Behavior* 34: 133-153.

Pleck, J. H. 1985. *Working Wives/Working Husbands.* Beverly Hills, CA: Sage Publications.

Reskin, B. F., and I. Padevic. 1994. *Women and Men at Work.* Thousand Oaks, CA: Pine Forge Press.

Ridgeway, C. L., and H. Walker. 1994. "Status Structures." In *Sociological Perspectives on Social Psychology.* Boston, MA: Allyn & Bacon.

Riesman, D. 1958. "Work and Leisure in Post-Industrial Society." In *Mass Leisure.* Glencoe, IL: Free Press.

Riley, M. W. 1987. "On the Significance of Age in Sociology." *American Sociological Review* 52: 1-14.

Riley, M. W., and J. W. Riley. 1994. "Structural Lag: Past and Future." In *Age and Structural Lag: Society's Failure to Provide Meaningful Opportunities in Work, Family, and Leisure.* New York: Wiley and Sons.

Sewell, W. H. 1992. "A Theory of Structure: Duality, Agency, and Transformations." *American Journal of Sociology* 98: 1-29.

Shelton, B. A. 1992. *Women, Men and Time: Gender Differences in Paid Work, Housework, and Leisure.* New York: Greenwood Press.

Simon, R. W. 1992. "Parental Role Strains, Salience of Parental Identity and Gender Differences in Psychological Distress." *Journal of Health and Social Behavior* 33: 25-35.

Swiss, D. J., and J. Walker. 1993. *Women and the Work/Family Dilemma: How Today's Professional Women are Finding Solutions.* New York: John Wiley & Sons, Inc.

Weiss, R. S. 1990. *Staying the Course.* New York: Free Press.

Wilensky, H. L. 1961. "Orderly Careers and Social Participation." *Annual Review of Sociology* 26: 521-539.

Williams, K. J., and G. M. Alliger. 1994. "Role Stressors, Mood Spillover, and Perceptions of Work-Family Conflict in Employed Parents." *Academy of Management Journal* 37: 837-868.

THE NEXUS OF JOB SATISFACTION, MARITAL SATISFACTION AND INDIVIDUAL WELL-BEING:
DOES MARRIAGE ORDER MATTER?

Stacy J. Rogers

ABSTRACT

This research investigates the direct and interactive effects of job satisfaction and marital satisfaction on the well-being of 1,122 employed adults in first marriages and remarriages. Data are taken from a nationally representative sample of married individuals. The results indicate that both marital satisfaction and job satisfaction are significantly associated with individual well-being, regardless of marriage order. However, job satisfaction is more strongly associated with the well-being of men compared to women. Compared with job satisfaction, marital satisfaction is more strongly associated with well-being for both women and men, and is particularly important for remarried individuals. Further, greater satisfaction in one domain acts as a buffer against the negative effects of low satisfaction in the other domain.

Research in the Sociology of Work, Volume 7, pages 141-167.
Copyright © 1999 by JAI Press Inc.
ISBN: 0-7623-0605-X

141

INTRODUCTION

Work and marital roles are among the most salient of the life course (Thoits 1992). A substantial body of research attests to the importance of these roles for individuals' physical health (Ross, Mirowsky and Goldsteen 1990; Rushing, Ritter and Burton 1992; Wickrama et al. 1997) and various dimensions of emotional well-being (Greenberg and Grunberg 1995; Martin and Roman 1996; Ross 1995; Umberson et al. 1996; see Glenn 1990 for a review). Previous research also attests to the complexity of the relationship between work and marital roles and adult outcomes. For example, the effects of work roles and marital roles on individuals are determined in part by factors such as role demands and the spillover of multiple roles (Lennon 1994; Glass and Fugimoto 1994; Voydanoff 1988, 1989), the capacities that the individual brings to the role (Wethington and Kessler, 1989), and the subjective meanings that individuals attach to their roles (Simon 1995).

The impact of work and marital roles is also influenced by role satisfaction. This acts as a link between role occupancy and individual outcomes (Coverman 1989; Greenberg and Grunberg 1995). Indeed, subjective experience in a role is argued to be a more accurate predictor of psychological distress than simple role occupancy (Ross 1995; Thoits 1992; Wickrama et al. 1997). That is, 'good' marriages or 'good' jobs can enhance the well-being of individuals only if they are also satisfying to some degree.

Previous studies of work and marital roles and their effects for individuals have considered numerous dimensions of the family context within which these roles are performed including spouses' gender role attitudes (Greenstein 1996; Simon 1995), the balance of power and division of household labor (Lennon 1994; Lennon and Rosenfield 1992; Ross, Mirowsky and Huber 1983), and the presence and ages of children (Belsky and Rovine 1990; Lennon and Rosenfield 1992; McLanahan and Adams 1987). However, most previous research does not address marriage order—whether the marriage is a first marriage or a remarriage—as an important context for understanding the interplay between work and marital roles (but see Rogers 1996 for an exception). This is an important aspect of the family context given that remarriage is a common experience. Only about 40 percent of recent marriages will continue to widowhood and of those individuals experiencing divorce, three-quarters will eventually remarry (Bumpass, Sweet and Martin 1990). Further, Bumpass and colleagues (1990) note that remarriage is now as common as first marriage, with one half of all recent marriages involving at least one previously married partner. In addition, studies of remarriage suggest that marriage order may be associated with important differences in work and marital roles, satisfaction with these roles, and their effects for individual well-being (Booth and Edwards 1992; Furstenberg and Spanier 1984; Rogers 1996; Thomson 1994).

In the research presented here, I investigate the effects of job satisfaction and marital satisfaction on individual well-being within the context of marriage order by comparing a group of individuals in first marriages and in remarriages. Three broad questions form the focus of this research. First, how important are job satisfaction and marital satisfaction for individual well-being? Second, to what extent do the effects of marital satisfaction and job satisfaction differ depending on marriage order? Finally, is there a compensatory relationship between job satisfaction and marital satisfaction? That is, do high levels of satisfaction in one domain compensate for the effects of low satisfaction in the other domain? For example, high marital satisfaction may be particularly important for the well-being of individuals with very low job satisfaction, or alternatively, high job satisfaction may be particularly important when individuals have low marital satisfaction.

I use data from a nationally representative sample of married men and women (not couples) from the early 1980s to investigate these questions. The 1980s can be viewed as the beginning of a period of relative equilibrium in family-related attitudes and behavior following the important changes of the 1960s and 1970s (Cherlin 1992; Thornton 1989). The present research attempts to provide insights into the interrelationship between marriage and work, their effects for individuals, and the role of the marital context, in a particular historical moment. Because both job satisfaction and marital satisfaction are the focus of this research, the research sample is limited to those women and men who are married, either in a first marriage or a remarriage, and employed.

MARRIAGE, JOBS AND MARRIAGE ORDER

As noted above, numerous previous studies support the importance of both job satisfaction and marital satisfaction for individual well-being among both women and men (Greenberg and Grunberg 1995; Martin and Roman 1996; Ross 1995; Repetti, Matthews and Waldron 1989; Wickrama et al. 1997; see Glenn 1990; Spitze 1990 for reviews). However, recent research by Hochschild (1997) raises the possibility that, regardless of marriage order, job satisfaction may be particularly important for the well-being of both women and men as marital commitments are perceived as more tenuous and difficult.

Changes in the Centrality of Marriage

There can be no doubt that satisfying marital relationships have significant beneficial effects for individual well-being (Ross 1995; Umberson et al. 1996; Coverman 1989). However, attitudes and behavior regarding marriage and other family-related issues have changed considerably in recent decades. Thornton (1989) notes that changes in attitudes and behavior were most dramatic during the 1960s and 1970s. During the early 1980s, change continued, but at a less dramatic pace (Thornton 1989). In the wake of such rapid social change, marriage appears to be a less mandatory social status for adults (Thornton 1989) and a less central feature of the adult life course (Bumpass, Sweet and Martin 1990; U.S. Bureau of the Census 1992). One consequence of this may be that, by the early 1980s, marital satisfaction is less important for the well-being of both women and men, than is job satisfaction.

Public opinion data and demographic information support the declining centrality of marriage. Public attitudes reflect more positive evaluations of permanent singlehood and more negative attitudes toward marriage with greater emphasis on the restrictive nature of marital bonds (Thornton 1989). In addition, Thornton (1989) notes that there was a significant increase in the age at which young adults expected to marry between 1960 and 1980. This is supported by trends in the median age at first marriage. Between 1960 and 1980, the median age at first marriage increased approximately 2 years for both women and men to approximately 22 and 24 years, respectively. This figure has continued to increase and by 1990 had reached turn-of-the-century levels for men (26.1 years) and an historic high for women (23.9 years) (U.S. Bureau of the Census 1992). The most dramatic increase in public acceptance of divorce also occurred during the 1960s and 1970s (Thornton, 1989) which is consistent with demographic data showing that the divorce rate doubled during the 1970s and leveled off early in the 1980s (Cherlin 1992). Declining rates of remarriage in favor of cohabitation (Bumpass, Sweet and Cherlin 1991) also support the notion that marriage may be a less central part of individuals' lives, or at least, a less permanent part.

At the same time, some observers suggest that marital relationships may be more difficult today than in previous decades. Glenn (1991) reports that, despite high divorce rates that should eliminate unhappy marriages from the pool of married individuals, the percentage of people reporting that their marriages are "very happy" declined gradually from 1973 to 1988. Rogers and Amato (1997) used data from a national probability sample of two cohorts of individuals married between 1969-1980 and 1981-1992 to investigate potential declines in marital quality across cohorts. They found significantly lower marital quality among the members of the more recent marriage cohort. Both women and men in this cohort reported less marital interaction, more marital conflict, and more problems in their marriages. Interestingly, compared to the older cohort, the more recent cohort reported no differences in the stability of their marriages despite the differences in marital quality and satisfaction.

The Growing Importance of Jobs

While marriage is an increasingly optional and often transitory part of the adult life course, employment for both women and men is a normative and persistent feature of adult life regardless of marital status, or the presence of children (Spain and Bianchi 1996). Both women and men show strong attachment to the labor force, have similar levels of job satisfaction, and similar work values (Hodson 1989, 1996; Mannheim 1983; Rowe and Snizek 1995). Using data from the U.S.

Bureau of Labor Statistics, Spain and Bianchi (1996) indicate that by 1980, women had begun to demonstrate a pattern of continuous labor force participation over the life course, even during the prime childbearing years (approximately 25 to 34), that was similar to men's. This is in contrast to the patterns evident in 1960 and in 1970 which show distinct declines in women's labor force participation during the prime childbearing years (Spain and Bianchi 1996). In 1990, 75 percent of women and 68 percent of married mothers with children under age 6 had some employment in the previous year and 28 percent were employed full time, year round (Spain and Bianchi 1996). Employment rates for men continued to be high in 1990 at 93 percent; however this rate is one point in a trend of declines in men's labor force participation rates in the decades since 1950 (Spain and Bianchi 1996).

The employment of both spouses is necessary for the economic well-being of families. Though women's earnings are consistently lower than those of men, married women's earnings are essential in maintaining their families' standard of living. Their earnings substantially decrease the likelihood that their families will be in poverty (Hernandez 1993). On average, working wives contributed 30 percent of their families' income by 1990. If they worked full-time, year round, their average contribution increased to approximately 40 percent (Spain and Bianchi 1996; U.S. Bureau of the Census 1992). The necessity of wives' (as well as husbands') economic contributions, the importance of employment for the personal well-being of both women and men (Blumstein and Schwartz 1983; Hood 1983), and the evidence that employed women and men share work values that favor greater pay and advancement opportunities (Rowe and Snizek 1995) lends support to Hochschild's (1997) arguments about the centrality of work in adults' lives.

In sum, both marital satisfaction and job satisfaction are important for individual well-being, but changes in the domains of marriage and work during the 1960s and 1970s suggest that by the early 1980s, marriage may have been less central and jobs more central in peoples' lives. Thus, job satisfaction may be a stronger predictor of well-being than marital satisfaction.

Marriage Order

Most of the research addressing the interrelationship of work roles, marital roles, and individual outcomes has focused on first marriages. However, as a context within which work and marital roles are performed, remarriage differs in important ways from first marriage (Booth and Edwards 1992; Furstenberg and Spanier 1984; Rogers 1996). Previous research on remarriage suggests that marital roles may be less important, and work roles may be more important predictors of well-being for those in remarriages. This may mean that job satisfaction is a particularly important predictor of well-being among the remarried.

Marital Satisfaction and Remarriage

Comparisons of first marriages and remarriages indicate that overall levels of marital quality tend to be similar for these groups (Booth and Edwards 1992; Vemer, Coleman, Ganong and Cooper 1989). However, the risk of dissolution is greater, and the median time to divorce is shorter in remarriage (Bumpass, Sweet and Martin 1990; Cherlin and Furstenberg 1994), especially when stepchildren are present (White and Booth 1985). In addition, attitudes toward and beliefs about marriage appear to vary systematically depending on marriage order.

Beginning in 1977, Furstenberg and Spanier (Furstenberg 1982) followed a group of recently separated and divorced individuals through the transition from divorce to remarriage. Using a combination of structured interviews and in-depth personal interviews, this work provides a unique source of detailed information about the subjective experience of 'conjugal succession' and how second marriages differ from first marriages. Furstenberg (1982) argues that remarried individuals' beliefs and behavior regarding marriage are most strongly influenced by their previous experiences of marital disillusionment and divorce. For example, many of the respondents indicated that, having already experienced a divorce, they were reluctant to remarry. Many also expressed the conviction that they had entered into the first marriage impulsively, or as a result of social pressure, and that they had not chosen their first spouses with enough care. Interestingly, Furstenberg (1982) notes that these beliefs were not significantly related to the likelihood of remarriage or the speed of remarriage as many of those with the strongest objections had remarried within 2 and one half years. In addition, remarried individuals report more pragmatic attitudes toward, and behavior in, the courtship process and marriage. They actively acknowledge the flaws in dating partners and expose their own. Furstenberg's respondents reported doing this to facilitate an environment that dispels romantic illusions and where threats to the marriage are anticipated and addressed (Furstenberg 1982). In addition, divorced and remarried individuals report emphasizing characteristics such as communication and ability to compromise that they hope will facilitate marital success, rather than factors such as attractiveness or prestige (Furstenberg 1982; Furstenberg and Spanier 1984).

Perhaps most important for the present study, individuals in remarriage claim to have fewer emotional expectations from marriage, and to be more willing to leave an unhappy marriage than those in first marriages (Booth and Edwards 1992; Furstenberg 1982; Furstenberg and Spanier 1984). Furstenberg (1982) notes that remarried individuals are simultaneously willing to leave an unhappy marriage, and highly committed to working for successful, happy marriage. This group, more than those in first marriages, seems to view marriage as a conditional contract fraught with both risks and rewards. Further, individuals in remarriage may be more likely to view marriage as only one of the many important roles that they perform. Thus, marital satisfaction may be a weaker predictor of individual well-being in the lives of remarried individuals than is the case for first married individuals.

Job Satisfaction and Remarriage

Previous research has not addressed the role of job satisfaction in the lives of remarried individuals. However, Hochschild's (1997) suggestions regarding the relative importance of work and marriage, and previous evidence regarding attitudes toward marriage and divorce among remarried individuals (Furstenberg and Spanier 1994), suggest that job satisfaction may be more influential for the well-being of remarried individuals than for those in first marriages. Further, this effect may be stronger for remarried women because they report highly valuing employment and economic independence.

Remarried women report highly valuing economic independence (Furstenberg and Spanier 1984), and are more likely to be employed full time than first married women (Thomson 1994). Employment and shared breadwinning appear to be a more integral part of remarried women's family roles than is the case for women in first marriages (Rogers 1996; Thomson 1994). If they have children, their employment increases the likelihood that women will remarry at all (Cherlin and Furstenberg 1994) and working more hours per week contributes to improved marital quality when they have more children (Rogers 1996). Remarried women's income may form a more significant portion of the family's resources given that remarried families have, on average, fewer economic resources than first married families (Thomson 1994) but potentially greater demands on those resources (Seltzer 1994).

COMPENSATORY ROLES

Given that work and marital roles are often enacted simultaneously, it is important to consider not only their additive effects for individual well-being, but also the extent to which they have interactive or compensatory effects on well-being. Thus far, this research has focused on the separate, additive effects of marital satisfaction and job satisfaction on well-being. However, interactive effects of these two dimensions are also likely. That is, high levels of job satisfaction may ameliorate some of the negative effects of low marital satisfaction. Alternatively, individuals with low job satisfaction may reap particular benefits from a satisfying marital relationship.

This conceptualization also is similar to that found in interactive stress-buffering models (Wheaton 1985). According to Wheaton's (1985) discussion of these models, a resource that moderates the effects of stress is a condition (such as social support, individual coping resources, or perhaps role satisfaction) under which stress has substantially less impact on individuals' level of distress. For the moderating effect to be present, the impact of stress on individuals must be significantly reduced under higher levels of the resource. In the present study, low levels of satisfaction with job or with marriage may act as a source of stress, and high levels of satisfaction in the other role may be an important resource for individuals.

HYPOTHESES

In sum, previous research suggests that attitudes and behavior regarding marriage and jobs changed considerably prior to the 1980s and that marriage order is an important aspect of the family context within which work and marital roles are performed. Based on these arguments, I test four central hypotheses which correspond to the three broad research questions discussed above. The first hypothesis corresponds to the first research question, and addresses the direct effects of job and marital satisfaction. The first hypothesis states that,

> **Hypothesis 1.**   Both job satisfaction and marital satisfaction will have positive effects on individual well-being.

I expect this to be true for both women and men and regardless of marriage order. Given that attitudes and behavior have become less marriage-oriented in recent decades (Hochschild 1997; Thornton 1989) and the growing convergence in men's and women's economic roles (Spain and Bianchi 1996), the relative importance of marital satisfaction and job satisfaction will be of particular interest in these results.

The second and third hypotheses correspond to the second broad research question regarding the extent to which marriage order moderates the effects of job satisfaction, and of marital satisfaction. Given evidence that remarried individuals have more cautious and pragmatic attitudes toward marriage, and appear to view marriage as only one of the important dimensions of adult life (Booth and Edwards 1992; Furstenberg 1982), the second hypothesis states that,

> **Hypothesis 2.**   The positive effect of job satisfaction on individual well-being will be stronger for those in remarriages compared to individuals in first marriages.

In other words, marriage order is expected to interact with job satisfaction in predicting individual well-being. Further, this effect is expected to be stronger for remarried women than for remarried men, given the importance they place on economic resources and independence (Furstenberg and Spanier 1984). This will be represented by a three-way interaction between job satisfaction, marriage order, and gender. To consider whether marriage order moderates the effects of marital satisfaction on individual well-being, the third hypothesis states that,

> **Hypothesis 3.** The positive effect of marital satisfaction on individual well-being will be stronger for individuals in first marriages compared to those in remarriages.

This hypothesis specifies that marriage order will interact with marital satisfaction in predicting individual well-being.

The fourth hypothesis corresponds to the final research question regarding the presence of a compensatory relationship between job satisfaction and marital satisfaction. The fourth hypothesis states that,

> **Hypothesis 4.** There will be an interactive relationship between job satisfaction and marital satisfaction in predicting individual well-being.

Moderators

Other characteristics of individuals, of work, and of family may moderate the effects of job satisfaction or marital satisfaction on individual well-being. The present research takes into account several characteristics of individuals including, age (Mottaz 1987), education, (Glenn and Weaver 1982) race, gender (Hodson 1989; Mannheim 1983), and gender role attitudes. Job characteristics include weekly work hours, schedule demands, and whether the individuals have experienced spells of unemployment. Highly demanding jobs may weaken the positive effects of job satisfaction for individual well-being. Alternatively, high levels of job satisfaction may be particularly important for the well-being of individuals with highly demanding jobs. Family characteristics include the presence of step-children in remarriages, the ages of children living in the household, and family income. Family demands, such as the presence of an adolescent or preschool-aged child in the household, or low family income may weaken the positive effects of job and marital satisfaction on well-being. Alternatively, satisfaction with job or marriage may be particularly important for individuals facing high levels of family demands. Finally, job satisfaction may be particularly important for the well-being of women with nontraditional gender role attitudes, and of men with more traditional gender role attitudes.

SAMPLE AND METHODS

These hypotheses were tested using data from the Marital Instability Over the Life Course Study (Booth, Amato, Johnson and Edwards 1991). This is a 4-wave panel study of marital quality and family life begun in 1980 when telephone interviews were conducted with a random sample of 2,034 married individuals (not couples) under age 55 selected through a clustered random-digit dialing procedure. The completion rate for the initial survey was 65 percent, with 18 percent refusing and 17 percent unreachable after 10 or more callbacks. Comparison with Census data showed that respondents were similar to the national population of married individuals on age, race, region, household size, presence of children, and home ownership. Attempts were made to reinterview these respondents in 1983, 1988, and 1992. Sample attrition was greatest between the first and second waves, with successful reinterviews being achieved with 78 percent, 66 percent, and 58 percent of the original sample in the second, third, and fourth waves. Due to selective attrition, the 1,189 respondents in the fourth wave slightly underrepresent those who were younger, renters, without a college education, African American, or Hispanic in 1980.

To minimize the effects of sample attrition, data from the second (1983) wave of the study were used in this research. The first wave of data from 1980 did not contain all the variables required by the present study. The research sample consisted of 213 individuals in remarriages and 909 individuals in first marriages.

Analytic Strategy

The present research focuses on the effects of job and marital satisfaction for individual well-being, and the ways in which marriage order and other characteristics of work and family roles may moderate these effects. In the first phase of the analysis, I test an additive model of the effects of job satisfaction and marital satisfaction on individual well-being. This analysis is followed by tests of interactive models that consider the extent to which these relationships are moderated by marriage order, selected characteristics of the respondents' and the spouses' jobs, and selected family characteristics.

Measures

Individual Well-Being

The dependent variable in this research is a twenty-item measure of individual well-being. The measurement of this variable and of the independent variables is summarized in Table 1. As the selected items in Table 1 indicate, the measure of individual well-being taps respondents' attitudes and as well as their experience of physical symptoms. Each of the individual items is coded on a 1-3 metric. The composite measure of well-being also ranges from 1 to 3 and is obtained by taking the mean of the total items answered by a respondent. For example, if a respondent reports a '3' on each of the 20 items, they receive a value of 3 for the overall measure of well-being. Higher values on the overall scale indicate higher levels of well-being. This measure has a Cronbach's alpha of .80. Descriptive statistics for

Table 1. Measurement of Independent and Dependent Variables

Individual Well-Being

20 items tapping attitudes toward life and presence of physical symptoms. Higher scale score indicates greater well-being.

  Things seem better than I thought they would be

  I have gotten more breaks than most people

  This is the dreariest time of my life

  These are the best years of my life

  Bothered by acid or sour stomach

  Bothered by cold sweats

  Felt restless, nervous

  Felt isolated among friends

Marriage Order

'1' if current marriage is remarriage for either respondent or spouse, '0' if current marriage is first marriage for both respondent and spouse.

Job Satisfaction

'On the whole, how satisfied are you with this job?' '1' very dissatisfied to '4' very satisfied.

Marital Satisfaction

'Taking all things together, how would you describe your marriage?' '1' not too happy to '4' very happy.

Job Characteristics:

  Weekly Work Hours

  Continuous measure of hours worked by respondent in the average work week.

  Demanding Schedule

  4 items coded '1' yes '0' no. Higher scale score indicates greater schedule demands. 'Does your job involve: irregular hours? shift work? evening meetings? overnight trips?'

  Spells of Unemployment

  1 item coded '1' yes '0' no. 'In the last 3 years were you unemployed for a month or longer?'

Family Characteristics:

Age of children in household

  3 dichotomous variables.

  Preschool Aged Child (0-4 years) '1' yes '0' no

  Primary Aged Child (5-12 years) '1' yes '0' no

  Adolescent Aged Child (13-18 years) '1' yes '0' no

  Stepchild present in household

  '1' yes '0' no

  Family income

  Measured continuously.

(continued)

Table 1   (Continued)

Individual Background Characteristics:

Gender

'1' male '0' female

Race

'1' white '0' non-white

Age

Measured continuously.

Years of Education

Measured continuously.

Gender Role Attitudes

7 items coded '1' strongly agree to '4' strongly disagree. Higher scale score indicates more traditional gender role attitudes.

  A husband should earn a larger salary than his wife

  It should not bother a husband if his wife travels overnight for business

  A woman whose husband can support her should not work

  Even if the wife is employed, the husband should be the main breadwinner, and the wife should have the responsibility for the home and children.

---

well-being are presented in Table 2 for those in first marriages and in remarriages. The table indicates that, on average, individuals in both first marriages and remarriages report high levels of well-being. However, the average level of well-being is significantly lower for remarried individuals.

Marriage Order

As Table 1 indicates, marriage order is measured with a dummy variable that is coded 1 if respondents are in a remarriage and 0 if respondents are in a first marriage.

Job and Marital Satisfaction

The measurement of job satisfaction and of marital satisfaction are described in Table 1. An important limitation of these data is that they do not provide information on whether or not the respondent is employed at more than one job. Users of the data must assume that, if respondents have multiple jobs, that they are referring to their 'primary' job when they respond. Table 2 indicates that, on average, individuals in this sample report high levels of job satisfaction. Job satisfaction does not differ significantly for those in first marriages compared to remarriages. Regarding marital satisfaction, Table 2 indicates that on average, individuals in both first marriages and remarriages report high levels of marital satisfaction.

Table 2. Descriptive Statistics for Research Sample of Adults in
Continuous, First Marriages, and in Remarriages

	First Marriages		Remarriages	
	Mean	SD	Mean	SD
Well-Being	2.64	.22	2.59	.25*
Job Satisfaction	3.30	.75	3.31	.78
Marital Satisfaction	2.56	.56	2.39	.61*
Job Characteristics:				
Weekly work hours	44.33	15.43	46.04	15.33
Schedule demands	.23	.27	.27	.29
Spell of unemployment in last 3 years (1 = yes)	.21	.41	.25	.44
Family Characteristics:				
Preschool-aged child in household (1 = yes)	.26	.44	.26	.44
Primary-aged child in household (1 = yes)	.38	.49	.44	.50
Adolescent-aged child in household (1 = yes)	.33	.47	.33	.47
Respondent has stepchild in household (1 = yes)	-.-	-.-	.15	.35
Family income in 1983 (in 10,000)	3.47	1.44	3.71	1.52*
Income not reported (1 = yes)	.01	.11	.01	.12
Background Characteristics:				
Gender (1 = male)	.50	.50	.47	.50
Age (in years)	38.99	9.05	39.33	8.22
Education (in years)	14.12	2.79	13.57	2.72*
Race (1 = white)	.92	.27	.87	.34*
Traditional gender role attitudes	15.65	2.92	15.16	2.97*

Notes: N = 213 remarriages and 909 first marriages.
*Means are significantly different at $p < .05$ for first marriages and remarriages, two-tailed test.

However, the mean levels of satisfaction are significantly lower for individuals in remarriages.

Job Characteristics

The present research also considers three job characteristics that may have direct effects on well-being or may moderate the relationship between job satisfaction and well-being. The items used to assess respondents' weekly work hours, schedule demands, and spells of unemployment are summarized in Table 1. Tests for non-linear relationships using categorical measures failed to show significant direct effects or moderating effects. As a result, the simplest measure of respondent work hours was retained in the analysis. Table 2 indicates that, on average, first married and remarried respondents work 44 to 46 hours per week, respectively. This does not differ significantly for those in first marriages or remarriages. The extent to which respondents' jobs have demanding schedules is measured by the proportion of 'yes' responses to the four items shown in Table 1. Table 2 indicates that individuals in both first marriages and remarriages reported that their jobs have few unusual schedule demands. Table 2 also indicates that on average, only 21 percent of first married respondents and 25 percent of remarried respondents had experienced a spell of unemployment in the three years prior to the interview. This difference is not statistically significant.

Family Characteristics

Selected family characteristics may have direct or interactive effects for both role satisfaction and individual well-being. Table 1 presents the items used to assess the ages of children, the presence of stepchildren in the household, and family income. It is important to note that the dichotomies measuring child ages are not used as a set with a reference group. Instead, they simply indicate the effect on well-being of having a child in that particular age category. Regarding the presence of stepchildren in the household, Table 2 indicates that, of those in remarriages, 15 percent ($N = 31$) are living with stepchildren. Family income is reported in $10,000s. Table 2 indicates that, among those who reported their income, the average was $34,700 for those in first marriages and $37,100 for those in remarriages, and that this is a statistically significant difference. Approximately 1% did not report their family's income. To retain these cases in the analysis, their income was coded to the mean, and a dichotomous variable was added to all analyses to indicate income nonresponse.

Individual Background Characteristics

As Table 1 indicates, respondents' gender and race were measured with dichotomous variables. Table 2 shows that approximately 50 percent of the sample is male, and that the sample is primarily White. A smaller proportion of the remarried sample is White, and this is a statistically significant difference. Table 2 also indicates that remarried individuals reported significantly lower levels of education, on average, than those in first marriages. Selected items used to measure gender role attitudes are shown in Table 1. Items were scored in the direction of traditional attitudes, and the mean response served as the scale score (alpha = .65). Table 2 indicates that, on average, the individuals in this sample score in the mid-range on traditionalism. However, remarried individuals are, on average, significantly less likely to report traditional gender role attitudes than those in first marriages.

FINDINGS

Additive Results

Table 3 presents the results for the additive model testing the direct effects of role satisfaction, marriage order, and selected job, family and individual background characteristics on individual well-being. Consistent with previous research, and with the first hypothesis, these results indicate that higher levels of job satisfaction and higher levels of marital satisfaction are both significantly associated with reports of greater well-being. Marriage order appears to negatively affect individual well-being but only for remarried individuals who are living with stepchildren. This clarifies the mean comparisons in Table 2. Further, as Table 3 indicates, this difference is only marginally significant ($p < .10$) in the multivariate model. Remarried individuals who are not living with stepchildren do not report significantly different levels of well-being in comparison to first married individuals.

Job characteristics have direct estimated effects on individual well-being. Working more hours per week and having experienced a spell of unemployment in the last three years are both significantly associated with lower well-being. The only family characteristic that influences individual well-being is income. Higher family income is positively associated with individual well-being. Interestingly, well-being is not significantly associated with the ages of children in the household. Gender and race also significantly influence well-being with men and Whites indicating higher well-being than women, or non-Whites, respectively. Finally, holding more traditional gender role attitudes is significantly associated with lower levels of well-being.

Comparison of the standardized coefficients presented in Table 3 indicates that, of the variables in this model, job satisfaction and marital satisfaction have the strongest associations with individual well-being. Further comparison of these coefficients provides evidence relevant to previous arguments about the declining importance of marriage and the increasing emphasis on work. The results shown in Table 3 do not provide support for the notion that job satisfaction is a stronger predictor of well-being than marital satisfaction. The standardized coefficients indicate that marital satisfaction has a stronger relationship to individual well-being than does job satisfaction. Further evidence comes from an examination of the sr^2 coefficients in Table 3. The sr^2 refers to the increments in explained variation uniquely attributable to the respective sets of variables included in the analyses. The sr^2 for job satisfaction is .08 compared to the sr^2 for marital satisfaction of .12. In contrast to the hypothesized relationship, marital satisfaction explains a greater proportion of the variance in individual well-being than does job satisfaction.

Table 3.   Regression Models Predicting Well-Being for
Continuously Married and Remarried Individuals

	B	beta	sr^2
Job Satisfaction	.09**	.28	.08**
Marital Satisfaction	.14**	.35	.12**
Marriage Order:			.00
Remarried, R has no stepchild in household	−.01	−.02	
Remarried, R has stepchildren in household	−.06#	−.04	
Continuous, first marriage[a]	−.−	−.−	
Job Characteristics:			.01**
Weekly work hours	−.13**	−.09	
Schedule demands	−.03	−.03	
Spell of unemployment in last 3 years (1 = yes)	−.03*	−.06	
Family Characteristics:			.01
Preschool-aged child in household (1 = yes)	−.00	−.00	
Primary-aged child in household (1 = yes)	−.00	−.01	
Adolescent-aged child in household (1 = yes)	.00	.01	
Family income in 1983 (in 10,000)	1.29**	.08	
Income not reported (1 = yes)	.00	.00	
Background Characteristics:			.02**
Gender (1 = male)	.05**	.11	
Age (in years)	−.00	−.04	
Education (in years)	.00	.04	
Race (1=white)	.04*	.05	
Traditional gender role attitudes	−.84**	−.11	
Constant			2.09
R^2		.28	

Notes: # $p < .10$
    * $p < .05$
    ** $p < .01$, two-tailed test.
    $N = 1122$,
    [a] = Reference category.

Interactive Results

The next set of analyses focused on the second and third research questions and
their corresponding hypotheses. Recall that the second research question asks
whether marriage order moderates the main effects of job satisfaction or of marital
satisfaction. The corresponding hypotheses, numbers two and three, state that the
effects of job satisfaction will be stronger for remarried individuals, and that the
effects of marital satisfaction will be stronger for first married individuals,

Table 4. Interactive Regression Models Predicting Well-Being for Continuously Married and Remarried Individuals

	Model 1 B	Model 2 B
Job Satisfaction	.08**	.14**
Marital Satisfaction	.14**	.22**
Marriage Order:		
Remarried (1 = yes)	−.02	−.21**
Job Characteristics:		
Weekly work hours	−.13**	−.13**
Schedule demands	−.03	−.03
Spell of unemployment in last 3 years (1 = yes)	−.03*	−.03*
Family Characteristics:		
Preschool-aged child in household (1 = yes)	−.00	−.00
Primary-aged child in household (1 = yes)	−.00	−.00
Adolescent-aged child in household (1 = yes)	.00	−.00
Family income in 1983 (in 10,000)	1.28**	1.24**
Income not reported (1 = yes)	.00	.01
Background Characteristics:		
Gender (1 = male)	.05**	−.06
Age (in years)	−.00	−.00
Education (in years)	.00	.00
Race (1 = white)	.04*	.04#
Traditional gender role attitudes	−.82**	−.82**
Interaction Effects:		
Gender * Job satisfaction		.03*
Remarried * Marital satisfaction		.08**
Job satisfaction * Marital satisfaction		−.03*
Constant	2.09	1.96
R^2	.28	.29

Notes: # $p < .10$
 $p < .05$
 $p < .01$
 $N = 1122$

respectively. The third research question asks whether job and marital satisfaction interact in affecting well-being. In the corresponding hypothesis, number four, interactive effects of these two dimensions are hypothesized.

In this stage of the analysis, I also investigated the moderating effects of other individual, job and marital characteristics. To accomplish this, I conducted a series of analyses for each of the moderating variables (individual, job, and family characteristics). I tested the effects of two-way interactions by marriage order and gender, as well as appropriate three-way interactions by adding them, in appropriate sets, to separate tests of the additive model. Significant terms were then tested together and if still significant, they were retained in the final model. The unstandardized coefficients from these analyses are presented in Table 4.

Model 1 in Table 4 presents the results for the additive model. Note that the marriage order variable no longer distinguishes remarried individuals by the presence of stepchildren. It was necessary to combine all remarried individuals for the tests of interactive effects due to the small number of remarried individuals living with stepchildren ($N = 31$). The marriage order variable used in these analyses contrasts individuals in remarriages with those in first marriages.

Model 2 in Table 4 shows the results when the significant interaction terms were included in the additive model. Although not shown in the table, it is interesting to note that characteristics of individuals, of jobs, and of families did not have significant moderating effects on the relationships of interest in this research. Only three interaction terms were statistically significant. The significant Gender * Job Satisfaction term provides additional evidence with regard to the first hypothesis. Recall that the hypothesized positive effect of job satisfaction was expected to be similar for both women and men. The results in Table 4 do not provide support for this idea. The positive estimated effect of job satisfaction on well-being is significantly stronger for men than for women. This relationship is shown in more detail in Figure 1. To facilitate the interpretation, well-being scores have been transformed into standardized scores. This figure indicates that husbands and wives are equally disadvantaged when job satisfaction is low, with estimated levels of well-being at 1.28 and 1.39 standard deviations below the mean for wives and husbands, respectively. Similarly, when job satisfaction is high, both husbands and wives benefit. However, high job satisfaction has a stronger positive effect on husbands' well-being than on wives'. High job satisfaction raises the well-being of husbands to .89 standard deviations above the mean, and the wives' to .56 standard deviations above the mean. This is a statistically significant difference in slopes.

The second and third hypotheses addressed the importance of marriage order. The second hypothesis stated that the positive effect of job satisfaction would be stronger for remarried individuals. However, analyses (not shown) did not provide support for this hypothesis. The estimated effect of job satisfaction was not significantly stronger for those in remarriages, or for remarried women.

The third hypothesis stated that the positive effect of marital satisfaction would be stronger among first married individuals than those in remarriages. The significant Remarried * Marital Satisfaction term shown in Model 2 fails to support this hypothesis. Unexpectedly, the positive estimated effect of marital satisfaction on well-being is stronger for those in remarriages than for those in first marriages. This relationship is shown in Figure 2. This figure indicates that when marital satisfaction is high, marriage order is not influential—both first married and remarried individuals experience greater well-being when they are satisfied with their

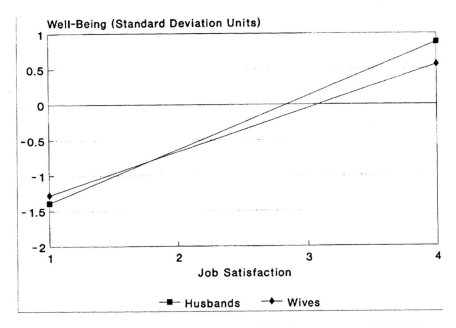

Figure 1.   The Interaction of Gender and Job Satisfaction on Well-Being

marriage. Estimated levels of well-being for the first married and remarried individuals with high marital satisfaction are .71 and .81 standard deviation units
above the mean, respectively. However, when marital satisfaction is low, the
well-being of remarried individuals is significantly lower than for first married
individuals. Well-being among those in the remarried group is 1.78 standard deviation units below the mean when marital satisfaction is low, while the well-being
of first married individuals with low marital satisfaction is 1.19 standard deviations below the mean.

The significant Job Satisfaction * Marital Satisfaction interaction term shown in
Model 2 of Table 4 addresses the third research question and the corresponding
fourth hypothesis. This significant term provides support for the fourth hypothesis
and indicates that in addition to additive estimated effects, job satisfaction and
marital satisfaction also have interactive effects on individual well-being. Regardless of marriage order, the positive estimated effects of job satisfaction are stronger for individuals with low marital satisfaction. The converse is also true, the
positive estimated effects of marital satisfaction are stronger when individuals
have low job satisfaction.

This relationship is illustrated in Figure 3 which presents the estimated effects
of job satisfaction on well-being for individuals at the three levels of marital satisfaction. This figure indicates first, that at all levels of marital satisfaction,

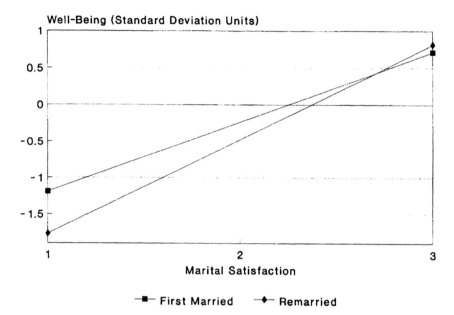

Figure 2.   The Interaction of Marriage Order and
Marital Satisfaction on Well-Being

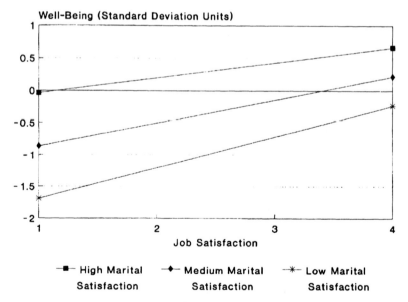

Figure 3.   The Interaction of Job Satisfaction and
Marital Satisfaction on Well-Being

individual well-being is lowest when job satisfaction is low. Second, regardless of the level of job satisfaction, individuals with high marital satisfaction have higher levels of well-being than those with moderate or low marital satisfaction. The level of well-being is highest when both marital satisfaction and job satisfaction are high. Third, when marital satisfaction is low and job satisfaction is also low, individuals have the lowest level of well-being at 1.69 standard deviations below the mean. However, high job satisfaction increases the well-being of this group to .23 standard deviations below the mean. This is an increase of 1.46 standard deviation units. Having high job satisfaction provides less dramatic gains in well-being for those with moderate levels of marital satisfaction (increase of .65 standard deviation units) and for those with high levels of marital satisfaction (increase of .63 standard deviation units). These findings provide support for the notion that greater satisfaction in one domain may compensate individuals for lower satisfaction in the other.

DISCUSSION

This research focused on three questions. The first question was whether, given the changes in marriage-related attitudes and behavior (Thornton 1989; Cherlin 1992), and in men's and women's economic roles (Spain and Bianchi 1996) during the 1960s and 1970s, marital satisfaction would be a weak predictor of individual well-being and job satisfaction would be a more important predictor of well-being in the early 1980s. The results indicate that both marital satisfaction and job satisfaction are significant predictors of individual well-being. This is true for both wives and husbands. Further, when standardized coefficients and sr^2 coefficients are compared, it is marital satisfaction, rather than job satisfaction, that exerts the strongest effect on well-being.

The importance of marital satisfaction is consistent with previous work which attests to the unique ability of marriage to provide essential experiences of social integration and social support (Waite 1995). It is also consistent with the work of Ross (1995) who emphasizes that social integration alone is not enough to confer benefits on individuals, but that the relationship must be positive and satisfying as well.

In addition, contrary to expectations, job satisfaction is still particularly important for the well-being of husbands. Previous research supports this finding. Traditional expectations within marriage, especially regarding the responsibility for breadwinning (Blumstein and Schwartz 1983; Thompson and Walker 1989) are highly resilient. Most married men, even those with employed wives, retain responsibility for breadwinning and view it as a central part of their family role (Blumstein and Schwartz 1983; Hood 1983; Simon 1995). When families face economic hardship, men exhibit the strongest negative effects (Conger et al. 1990).

The second question guiding this research was whether marriage order, as a dimension of the family context, moderates the relationship between role satisfaction and individual well-being. The results suggest that this is true, though not in the expected ways. Based on previous research, job satisfaction was expected to have a stronger effect on the well-being of remarried individuals. However, this is not supported by the results. Instead, marital satisfaction is particularly important for the well-being of individuals in remarriage. This is true for both husbands and wives in remarriages. The strong influence of marital satisfaction for those in remarriage may reflect the fact that they are somewhat older, and have already experienced one divorce and perhaps the difficulty of finding a new partner. Previously married individuals may be especially invested in their current marriages knowing the psychological and economic costs of marital disruption. This is consistent with Furstenberg's (1982) findings that remarried individuals, although unwilling to remain in an unsatisfying marriage, were strongly committed to anticipating and trying to address potential threats to the marital relationship.

Considering the greater difficulty that women experience (compared to men) in finding remarriage partners (Cherlin and Furstenberg 1994), it would be consistent with this argument to find that marital satisfaction was particularly important for remarried women. However, this is not the case. Marital satisfaction is equally important for the well-being of both women and men in remarriage. This finding further supports the early arguments that by divorcing, individuals are not expressing dissatisfaction with marriage, but with a particular partner (Furstenberg 1982). There may be less support for this interpretation today as fewer divorced individuals remarry, choosing instead to cohabit (Bumpass, Sweet and Martin 1990). However, the findings of the present research suggest that the marital relationship continues to be highly influential for the well-being of people who do enter remarriage as well as for those in first marriages.

The third question this research addressed is whether there are interactive or compensatory effects of job and marital satisfaction on well-being. That is, whether high levels of satisfaction in one domain could compensate for low satisfaction in another domain. The findings indicate that this is the case. Although all individuals benefit from higher job satisfaction, the benefits are greatest among those with low levels of marital satisfaction. Similarly, although all individuals benefit from greater marital satisfaction, the benefits are greatest among those with low levels of job satisfaction. This attests to the possible 'stress-buffering' effects of role satisfaction (Wheaton 1985). Greater role satisfaction may act as an important buffering mechanism facilitating well-being when one role is particularly unsatisfying.

The importance of marital satisfaction for well-being, and its ability to protect individuals from the negative effects of dissatisfying jobs suggests that, in contrast to Hochschild's (1997) notion, work does not seem to be replacing marriage as a source of satisfaction and integration. Hochschild (1997) raises the possibility that job satisfaction may be particularly important for the well-being of both women and men as marital commitments are perceived as more tenuous and difficult. However, the results presented here indicate that work is not supplanting marriage—indeed, marital satisfaction is somewhat more influential for adult well-being than job satisfaction. Further, being more satisfied in either work or marriage helps protect individuals from the negative effects of dissatisfaction in the other domain. This finding is consistent with stress buffering arguments.

The current findings are also interesting given the economic trends since 1973 which have probably decreased job satisfaction among a substantial proportion of adults. In a recent book, Farley (1996) details several important economic trends and their effects. Among the most important are the growing gap between the top and bottom of the income distribution, industrial restructuring, and the stagnation in men's wages (Farley 1996). One important outcome of the economic changes since 1973 has been their differential effects on individual workers; those with technical skills and advanced education have found higher pay rates, and more job opportunities while those with few technical skills and less than a high school education have found lower pay rates, fewer good blue-collar jobs, and fewer opportunities for full-time employment (Farley 1996). Given this economic environment, satisfying marital relationships are not likely to become obsolete. Indeed, it is likely that they will continue to provide an essential source of integration and support for most individuals.

Though this paper does not have an applied focus, the conclusions suggest some steps that might be taken to improve the well-being of individual workers and potentially their effectiveness in, and loyalty to the businesses for which they work. Fundamentally, the research presented here illustrates the direct, positive effects of marital satisfaction for all adults, and its particular importance as a resource for those in less satisfying jobs. Family life educators and family counselors may be able to use this information to communicate the important stress-buffering potential of satisfying marital relationships. Individuals can be encouraged to view strong marital relationships not only a goal in themselves, but as potential resources that can protect against some of the negative effects of other life stressors. Within the corporate community, this research provides further support for the notion that work and family are overlapping spheres that affect individuals' lives, and that employer contributions to the 'family sphere' may have real benefits for business productivity. Employers could ensure that marital enrichment or counseling programs are part of the employee assistance programs that they make available to their staff. Further, corporations may want to consider the linkages between all 'family-friendly' policies and their employees' marital relationships. Services such as on-site day care, adequate maternity and paternity leaves, flexible scheduling, and middle management support of such programs make an important contribution to the well-being of workers and the success of business (Hochschild 1997).

There are important limitations to the research presented here. First, the conclusions of this study are limited by the relatively small number of remarriages in the sample. Although the total number of remarriages is adequate, it affords limited ability to address potentially important variations among remarriages. The presence of stepchildren is an important example. Thirty one individuals are living with stepchildren at the time of this study, and, consistent with the work of White and Booth (1985), this group reports significantly lower levels of well-being than individuals in first marriages. However, the small size of this group prohibits any further investigation of the ways in which the presence of stepchildren might moderate the effects of marital satisfaction on individual well-being.

This research investigates the relationship between work and marriage during the early 1980s when many family-related changes of the 1960s and 1970s had reached a new equilibrium. The results suggest that both jobs and marriage are important predictors of well-being, that they interact in their effects, and that marriage order is an important contextual dimension that must be taken into account in future work. However, additional research with a similar cross-section of married individuals from the 1990s is necessary to consider whether these patterns of relationships persist or continue to change. Future work along these lines is in progress.

The cultural imperative to marry has weakened (Thornton 1989), the economic gains to marriage have lessened, and large scale social change has made marriage more difficult in some ways (Hochschild 1997; Rogers and Amato 1997). However, this research suggests that marriage continues to make essential contributions to the well-being of adults. First, marital satisfaction predicts well-being better than job satisfaction. Second, it is more important in second marriages than in first marriages. This is particularly important given that one half of all recent marriages are remarriages and involve at least one previously married partner (Bumpass, Sweet and Martin 1990). Finally, marital satisfaction is especially important when people are dissatisfied with their jobs. In an era of economic uncertainty and polarization, satisfying marital relationships are likely to become increasingly important to individual well-being.

ACKNOWLEDGMENT

This research was supported in part by a Faculty Summer Research Fellowship from the University of Nebraska Research Council. I thank Paul Amato for helpful comments on earlier versions of this paper.

REFERENCES

Belsky, J., and M. Rovine. 1990. "Patterns of Marital Change Across the Transition to Parenthood: Pregnancy to Three Years Postpartum." *Journal of Marriage and the F~~ily* 52: 5-19.

Blumstein, P., and P. Schwartz. 1983. *American Couples: Money, Work, Sex.* New York: William Morrow and Company.

Booth, A., and J. N. Edwards. 1992. "Starting Over: Why Remarriages are More Unstable." *Journal of Family Issues* 13: 179-194.

Booth, A., P.R. Amato, D. Johnson, and J. Edwards. 1991. *Marital Instability Over the Life Course: Methodology Report for Fourth Wave.* Lincoln, NE: University of Nebraska Bureau of Sociological Research.

Bumpass, L. L., J. A. Sweet, & T. Martin. 1990. "Changing Patterns of Remarriage." *Journal of Marriage and the Family* 52: 747-756.

Bumpass, L. L., J. A. Sweet, and A. Cherlin. 1991. "The Role of Cohabitation in Declining Rates of Marriage." *Journal of Marriage and the Family* 53: 913-927.

Cherlin, A. 1992. Marriage, Divorce, Remarriage, Rev. ed. Cambridge, MA: Harvard University Press.

Cherlin, A. J., and F. F. Furstenberg. 1994. "Stepfamilies in the United States: A Reconsideration." *Annual Review of Sociology* 20: 359-381.

Conger, R. D., G. H. Elder, Jr., F. O. Lorenz, K. J. Conger, R. L. Simons, L. B. Whitbeck, S. Huck, & J. N. Melby. 1990. "Linking Economic Hardship to Marital Quality and Stability." *Journal of Marriage and the Family* 52: 643-656.

Coverman, S. 1989. "Role Overload, Role Conflict, and Stress: Addressing Consequences of Multiple Role Demands. *Social Forces* 67: 965-982.

Farley, R. 1996. *The New American Reality.* New York: Russell Sage Foundation.

Furstenberg, Jr., F. F. 1982. "Conjugal Succession: Reentering Marriage after Divorce." Pp. 107-146 in *Life Span Development and Behavior.* Academic Press.

Furstenberg, Jr., F. F., and G. Spanier. 1984. *Recycling the Family: Remarriage after Divorce.* Newbury Park, CA: Sage.

Glass, J., and T. Fujimoto. 1994. "Housework, Paid Work, and Depression Among Husbands and Wives." *Journal of Health and Social Behavior* 35: 179-191.

Glenn, N., and C. N. Weaver. 1982. "Further Evidence on Education and Job Satisfaction." *Social Forces* 61: 46-55.

Glenn, N. 1990. "Quantitative Research on Marital Quality in the 1980s: A Critical Review." In *Contemporary Families: Looking Forward, Looking Back.* Minneapolis, MN: National Council on Family Relations.

_____. 1991. "The Recent Trends in Marital Success in the United States." *Journal of Marriage and the Family* 53: 261-270.

Greenberg, E., and L. Grunberg. 1995. "Work Alienation and Problem Drinking Behavior." *Journal of Health and Social Behavior* 36: 83-102.

Greenstein, T. N. 1996. "Gender Ideology and Perceptions of the Fairness of the Division of Household Labor: Effects on Marital Quality." *Social Forces* 74: 1029-1042.

Hernandez, D. J. 1993. *America's Children: Resources from Family, Government, and the Economy.* New York, NY: Russell Sage Foundation.

Hochschild, A. R. 1997. *The Time Bind.* New York: Holt.

Hodson, R. 1989. "Gender Differences in Job Satisfaction: Why Aren't Women More Dissatisfied?" *Sociological Quarterly* 30: 385-399.

Hodson, R. 1996. "Women and Job Satisfaction." In *Women and Work: A Handbook.* New York: Garland.

Hood, J. C. 1983. *Becoming a Two-Job Family.* New York: Praeger.

Lennon, M. C. 1994. "Women, Work, and Well-Being: The Importance of Work Conditions." *Journal of Health and Social Behavior* 35: 235-247.

Lennon, M. C., and S. Rosenfield. 1992. "Women and Mental Health: The Interaction of Job and Family Conditions." *Journal of Health and Social Behavior* 33: 316-327.

Mannheim, B. 1983. "Male and Female Industrial Workers: Job Satisfaction, Work Role Centrality, and Workplace Preference." *Sociology of Work and Occupations* 10: 413-436.

Martin, J. K., and P. Roman. 1996. "Job Satisfaction, Job Reward Characteristics and Employees' Problem Drinking Behaviors." *Sociology of Work and Occupations* 23: 4-25.

McLanahan, S., and J. Adams. 1987. "Parenthood and Psychological well-being." *Annual Review of Sociology* 13: 237-257.

Mottaz, C. J. 1987. "Age and Work Satisfaction." *Sociology of Work and Occupations* 14: 387-409.

Repetti, R. L., K. Matthews, and I. Waldron. 1989. "Effects of Paid Employment on Women's Mental and Physical Health." *American Psychologist* 44: 1394-1401.

Rogers, S. J. 1996. "Mothers' Work Hours and Marital Quality: Variations by Family Structure and Family Size. *Journal of Marriage and the Family* 58: 606-617.

Rogers, S. J., and P. R. Amato. 1997. "Is Marital Quality Declining? Evidence from Two Generations." *Social Forces* 75: 1089-1100.

Ross, C. 1995. "Reconceptualizing Marital Status as a Continuum of Attachment." *Journal of Marriage and the Family* 57: 129-140.

Ross, C. E., J. Mirowsky, and J. Huber. 1983. "Dividing Work, Sharing Work, and In-Between: Marriage Patterns and Depression." *American Sociological Review* 48: 809-823.

Ross, C. E., J. Mirowsky, and K. Goldsteen. 1990. "The Impact of the Family on Health: The Decade in Review." In *Contemporary Families: Looking Forward, Looking Back.* Minneapolis, MN: National Council on Family Relations.

Rushing, B., C. Ritter, and R. P. D. Burton. 1992. "Race Differences in the Effects of Multiple Roles on Health: Longitudinal Evidence From a National Sample of Older Men." *Journal of Health and Social Behavior* 33: 126-139.

Rowe, R., and W. E. Snizek. 1995. "Gender Differences in Work Values: Perpetuating the Myth." *Sociology of Work and Occupations* 22: 215-229.

Seltzer, J. 1994. "Intergenerational Ties in Adulthood and Childhood Experience." In *Stepfamilies: Who Benefits? Who Does Not?* Hillsdale, NJ: Lawrence Erlbaum Associates.

Simon, R. 1995. "Gender, Multiple Roles, Role Meaning, and Mental Health." *Journal of Health and Social Behavior* 36: 182-194.

Spain, D., and S. Bianchi. 1996. *Balancing Act: Motherhood, Marriage, and Employment Among American Women.* New York: Russell Sage Foundation.

Spitze, G. 1991. "Women's Employment and Family Relations: A Review." In *Contemporary Families: Looking Forward, Looking Back.* Minneapolis, MN: National Council on Family Relations.

Thoits, P. A. 1992. "Identity Structures and Psychological Well-Being: Gender and Marital Status Comparisons." *Social Psychology Quarterly* 55: 236-256.

Thompson, L., and A. J. Walker. 1989. "Gender in Families: Women and Men in Marriage, Work, and Parenthood." *Journal of Marriage and the Family* 51: 845-871.

Thomson, E. 1994. "'Settings' and 'Development' From a Demographic Point of View." In *Stepfamilies: Who Benefits? Who Does Not?* Hillsdale, NJ: Lawrence Erlbaum Associates.

Thornton, A. 1989. "Changing Attitudes Toward Family Issues in the United States." *Journal of Marriage and the Family* 51: 873-893.

Umberson, D., M. D. Chen, J. S. House, K. Hopkins, and E. Slaten. 1996. "The Effect of Social Relationships on Psychological Well-Being: Are Men and Women Really so Different?" *American Sociological Review* 61: 837-857.

U.S. Bureau of the Census. 1992. "Households, Families, and Children: A Thirty Year Perspective." (Current Population Reports, Series P23, No. 181). Washington, DC: U.S. Government Printing Office.

Vemer, E., M. Coleman, L. H. Ganong, and H. Cooper. 1989. "Marital Satisfaction in Remarriage: A Meta-Analysis." *Journal of Marriage and the Family* 51: 713-725.

Voydanoff, P. 1988. "Work Role Characteristics, Family Structure Demands, and Work/Family Conflict." *Journal of Marriage and the Family* 50: 749-761.

_____. 1989. "Work and Family: A Review and Expanded Conceptualization." In *Work and Family: Theory, Research and Applications.* Newbury Park, CA: Sage.

Waite, L. 1995. "Does Marriage Matter?" *Demography* 32: 483-507.

Wethington, E., and R. C. Kessler. 1989. "Employment, Parental Responsibility, and Psychological Distress: A Longitudinal Study of Married Women." *Journal of Family Issues* 10: 527-546.

Wheaton, B. 1985. "Models for the Stress-Buffering Functions of Coping Resources." *Journal of Health and Social Behavior* 26: 352-364.

Wickrama, K. A. S., F. O. Lorenz, R. D. Conger, and G. H. Elder. 1997. "Marital Quality and Physical Illness: A Latent Growth Curve Analysis." *Journal of Marriage and the Family* 59: 143-155.

White, L. K., and A. Booth. 1985. "The Quality and Stability of Remarriages: The Role of Stepchildren." *American Sociological Review* 50: 689-698.

THEORIZING CORPORATE
FAMILY POLICIES:
HOW ADVOCATES BUILT "THE BUSINESS CASE"
FOR "FAMILY-FRIENDLY" PROGRAMS

Erin L. Kelly

ABSTRACT

This paper focuses on the cultural work of constructing and promoting "family-friendly policies" or corporate family policies. Drawing on a neo-institutionalist perspective, the author examines this cultural work, or theorization, by asking three questions. Who has promoted corporate family policies? What arguments have these advocates used to legitimate the new practices? And how successful have advocates been in institutionalizing corporate family policies? Work-family specialists, business leaders, and government officials have developed and presented a business case for a variety of corporate family policies. The business case argues that these programs will help organizations attract, retain, and manage a productive work force. These arguments try to legitimate the new programs as reasonable actions for employers to take, but advocates have been only moderately successfully in

Research in the Sociology of Work, Volume 7, pages 169-202.

promoting and implementing these programs. The author argues that theorization may only be effective when the theorists are powerful professionals, state actors, or corporate coalitions. Also, the business case ignores some important, deeply ingrained assumptions about the privacy of family life and the primacy of careers. Further work on de-institutionalizing these assumptions and structures may be necessary before corporate family policies are widely adopted and effective in changing workers' family lives and work experiences.

INTRODUCTION

In the last twenty years, a new set of employer benefits, "family-friendly" policies, has emerged on the American business scene. Organizations that adopt these new programs are touted in the business and mainstream press as "family-friendly" companies. The idea that employers should be involved in helping their workers deal with family care-giving is a new one, which stands in contrast to the idea that work and family are separate and largely unrelated spheres of life (Kanter 1977).[1] In recent years, mainstream press sources have paid more attention to the intersection of work and family, and prominent figures, from Presidents to CEOs, have supported the idea that employers should respond to family caregiving needs (Devroy 1990; Shellenbarger 1994a; Morgan and Tucker 1991). Formal corporate responses include maternity leaves, paternity leaves, and broader family leaves; flex-time; job-sharing; work-at-home arrangements; child care centers sponsored by employers; information and referral services to help employees find care for children and elderly relatives; tax-free spending accounts for dependent care expenses; and work-family workshops. Many American employers now provide at least one or two of these programs, often family leave, dependent care spending accounts, and flex-time (Galinsky et al. 1991; Glass and Estes 1997; Osterman 1995).

I focus on the cultural work of constructing and promoting corporate family policies, and ask how these programs became reasonable and legitimate actions for employers to take. In particular, I ask who has promoted corporate family policies and how they have developed arguments for these new programs. I call this cultural work the theorization of corporate family policies (Strang and Meyer 1993). I use the term corporate family policies, rather than the popular term "family-friendly" policies, because the former term brackets the question of whether these programs successfully help workers and their families. The term corporate family policies also stresses that these programs are a private form of social welfare provision, which parallels and substitutes for public programs to assist working families.

My discussion of the theorization of corporate family policies relies on several data sources. To survey the arguments found in discussions of corporate family policies and other work-family topics, I analyzed two hundred articles that were randomly selected from the population of work and family articles in *The New York Times, The Wall Street Journal*, and *HRMagazine*, a human resources management journal. I also examined over thirty reports created by work-family advocates and conducted interviews with eighteen human resources managers in the Northeast. In addition, I discuss results from a new survey of American employers that focused on corporate family policies. For more information, see the Appendix.

In the following sections, I describe the neo-institutionalist perspective on organizational change and quickly review the prevalence of various corporate family policies in U.S. organizations. Then I discuss who has promoted these corporate family policies, introducing the new work-family specialists, highlighting executives' and managers' involvement, and elaborating the role of the federal government. Next I outline the business case—the claim that employers provide family programs because these programs meet employers' needs for increased productivity and lower recruitment and turnover costs. Despite the efforts of many advocates and increased press attention over the past twenty years, many employers have made only small changes in the way they handle workers' family responsibilities. In the last section, I consider some limitations to the current theorization and implementation of corporate family policies.

THEORETICAL PERSPECTIVE

This paper builds on neo-institutionalist studies of organizational change. Neo-institutionalists claim that organizations adopt policies to signal their legitimacy within an organizational field, but note that employers almost always claim they are motivated by concerns with efficiency and effectiveness (Meyer and Rowan 1977; DiMaggio and Powell 1991; Dobbin 1994). Organizations often do not test whether the practice is efficient or effective for their particular situation. Instead, organizations adopt practices because powerful actors—peer organizations, professionals, or the state—push new practices as legitimate (and sometimes required) actions. In other words, organizations talk about new structures and practices as practical improvements adopted to meet organizational needs. But neo-institutionalist studies suggest that organizations often adopt new practices and structures to demonstrate their conformity with new norms about what organizations should do and how they should be structured (DiMaggio and Powell 1983; Dobbin et al. 1993; Edelman 1992; Fligstein 1990). In this paper, I examine the construction of new norms about how organizations should respond to workers' family needs.

I focus on the process by which corporate family policies have been socially constructed as rational and reasonable actions. I trace the cultural work done by advocates, to show that the rationality of corporate family policies has been carefully and consciously constructed over the past twenty years. This is not to say that organizations are acting irrationally when they adopt corporate family policies, but to point out that their decisions have been guided by carefully constructed claims about the rationality of corporate family policies as solutions to certain common business problems. Rational business decisions are not divorced from advocacy.

The case of corporate family policies is a useful one for highlighting the strategies used by advocates and business agents as they promote new practices and try to create new standards for what responsible employers should do. Often, neo-institutionalist scholarship examines practices that are institutionalized, or so well established as to be "taken-for-granted" (DiMaggio and Powell 1991). Because institutionalized structures and practices are already accepted and entrenched in a group's or society's view of the way things are, it is often difficult to see the actors who helped accomplish this institutionalization (DiMaggio 1988; Jepperson 1991; Colomy 1998). With corporate family policies, advocates are still working towards possible institutionalization and so their actions and agency are easier to document. In particular, we can see how advocates of new practices point out particular organizational problems and present the new practices as solutions to these problems (Cole 1989).

What is theorization, in practical terms? Advocates theorize new practices when they create concepts, develop arguments, and present claims that new practices are reasonable and valuable additions to current practices. Theorization helps people make sense of new practices and presents convincing arguments about how those practices fit into actions and systems that are already in place, thereby encouraging decision makers to adopt the new practices (Strang and Meyer 1993, p. 487). For example, work-family experts, public officials, executives, and writers at key business journals have discussed work and family as interrelated spheres. This is a crucial concept for the promotion of corporate family policies. Advocates have also claimed that these policies are similar enough to be discussed as a group of "family-friendly" programs, that employers should strive to be known as a "family-friendly" company, and that there are legitimate business reasons for these programs. Importantly, it is not necessary that every organization have a manager who goes through the process of theorizing, or developing the concepts and arguments. Instead, legitimated theorists use already accepted models and accounts to link the new practice to older practices (Strang and Meyer 1993, p. 494).

After quickly reviewing the current prevalence of various corporate family policies, I introduce the actors who have been involved in promoting corporate family policies and discuss the main arguments used to advocate corporate family policies. Despite the cultural work performed by advocates, many of the policies and programs are still quite rare. This leads me to ask what conditions are required for new practices to become institutionalized. I argue that theorization may only be effective when the theorists are powerful professionals, state actors, or corporate coalitions. Also, theorization may need to challenge some common management practices and beliefs before changes can occur. The business case ignores some important, deeply ingrained assumptions about the privacy of family life and the primacy of careers. Further work on de-institutionalizing these assumptions and structures may be necessary before corporate family policies are widely adopted and effective in changing workers' family lives and work experiences.

PREVALENCE OF PARTICULAR POLICIES

In the arguments detailed below, advocates often discuss these practices as a set of "family-friendly" policies. Yet employers have adopted some policies and programs much more often than others. Table 1 shows the prevalence of various unpaid leaves, which the *Family and Medical Leave Act of 1993* mandates for employers of this size. Following leaves, tax-free spending accounts are the most popular program. Flextime, a practice that allows workers to set their own starting and stopping times within given parameters, is offered by over one-third of the employers in this survey. About one-fourth of the organizations provide information and referral services for workers who need to find child care or elder care. Other programs, including paid leaves and child care centers, are still relatively rare.

Now I turn to the question of how these programs became acceptable, if not always common, actions for employers to take.

PROFILING THE ADVOCATES

Work-Family Specialists

In the past twenty years, a new set of work-family specialists has appeared. These specialists have created both non-profit and for-profit organizations that research, advocate for, and provide services for working families. Some of the early, and most prominent, work-family organizations include the non-profit Families and Work Institute, New Ways to Work, and Catalyst. In the past fifteen years, a small, for-profit industry of work-family specialists has also appeared. These specialists include independent consultants, service providers, and work-family managers employed by large organizations.

Work-family specialists include both children's advocates and human resources specialists, and many individuals try to fill both roles at once. Many advocates believe that corporate family policies are good for business, but they are primarily (or were initially) motivated by a concern for children and working parents (Rose 1997). These dual concerns for the well-being of families and the profitability of corporations sometimes place work-family specialists in an awkward position. Hochschild (1997, p. 22) describes these advocates as "the social workers of the corporate world" and notes that "Like many social workers, they [are] both part of the system and idealistically critical of it."

Table 1.   Percentage of Organizations with Corporate Family
Policies and Programs, 1997

Policy or Program	Percent
Maternity leave[1]	96
Paternity leave[2]	86
Leave to care for ill family	86
Tax-free spending accounts—dependent care	56
Flex-time policy	35
Child care info & referral service	25
Elder care info & referral service	20
Work-family workshops	18
Paid maternity leave[3]	15
Child care center (on- or near-site)	13
Job-sharing policy	13
Work-at-home policy	10
Paid paternity leave[4]	7
Full-time work-family staff	7

Notes: N = 389 organizations. National, stratified random sample of establishments with
50+ workers from the following industries: food manufacturing, chemicals manufacturing, transportation equipment manufacturing, computer equipment manufacturing, trucking and transport services, wholesale trade, banks, business services,
non-profit social services, and local government agencies. Survey funded by the
Alfred P. Sloan Foundation (Frank Dobbin, principal investigator) and conducted by
the University of Maryland Survey Research Center.

[1] Question asked about leave policy covering women giving birth, to capture leaves
called family leave, parental leave, or maternity leave. These figures include those
establishments with a written policy and those establishments that regularly allow
leaves in this situation.

[2] Question asked about leave policy covering new fathers, to capture leaves called
family leave, parental leave, or paternity leave. These figures include those establishments with a written policy and those establishments that regularly allow leaves in
this situation.

[3] Question asked about pay beyond vacation days, sick days, or disability insurance
for mothers on leave.

[4] Question asked about pay beyond vacation days, sick days for fathers on leave.

Because many of the first work-family experts had backgrounds in child development and education, they initially focused on introducing child care programs
that would be subsidized and sponsored by employers (Friedman 1983; Pleck
1992). As Dana Friedman, a researcher and consultant, described the situation in
the early 1980s: "Armed with briefcases and business cards, a new army of consultants has emerged, knocking on company doors in the hopes of selling, in most
cases, day care centers. Their shortsightedness in not offering a range of options
results in very few contracts" (Friedman 1983, p. 82). A few companies, notably
Bright Horizons and Corporate Family Solutions, did succeed as vendors and

managers of on-site child care centers; these two firms currently have over two hundred centers operating nationwide (Lawson 1991; Jordano and Oates 1998). For the most part, however, consultants did not succeed in establishing many on-site child care centers.

Work-family specialists soon added a variety of services—including less costly options, such as workshops, how-to books, and needs assessments—to their portfolios. One of the most successful innovations has been the information and referral service, which provides workers with details on local child care and elder care providers. For example, *Work/Family Directions* began in 1984 when IBM decided to provide child care referral services to its employees nationwide (Morgan and Tucker 1991, pp. 93-100). Work/Family Directions created a network of local referral agencies to provide information to IBM employees in many locations. Work/Family Directions is now called WFD, to reflect its expanded consulting business, and had over one hundred Fortune 500 clients and over five hundred employees by 1997.

Today work-family specialists promote corporate family policies in three major ways. First, they try to keep family issues in the public eye and on management's agenda. Researchers in non-profit advocacy organizations share their findings with the popular media, public officials, and business leaders. When consultants and vendors market their services, they are also keeping human resources managers and executives apprised of the options for corporate involvement in family issues. Second, work-family specialists create demand for their programs and services. Advocates and consultants often show organizations their options for less costly initiatives that mark employers' "family-friendliness." These options include short work-family seminars, information centers and lending libraries (now Internet resources), and training for managers on work-family issues. Third, work-family experts also provide research and discourse that helps interested managers or workers sell these programs to their bosses. As I will detail below, work-family specialists have tried to legitimate their policies and programs by "making the business case," in the hopes of convincing managers and executives to lend their support.

Management Support

Work-family advocates regularly state that "top management buy-in" is critical for the adoption and implementation of corporate family policies (Galinsky et al. 1991; Morgan and Tucker 1991). Support from top executives is important because these executives can often make independent decisions to add family programs and services. For example, the co-owner of Patagonia, Malinda Choinard, first supported employees' family needs with informal arrangements in the 1970s and early 1980s:

Our children started in the box method. We all kept our babies under our desks—in cardboard boxes with blankets in them—or on our backs. There weren't very many of us, but we all did it that way and we had no trouble at all . . .And then we got an employee who had a screaming baby . . . it was a logistical nightmare (Morgan and Tucker 1991, pp. 150-151).

Choinard responded to these difficulties by having Patagonia build an on-site child care center, thereby replacing the firm's informal family-friendliness with a generous corporate child care program. In addition to direct decision making power, executives can help convince other organizations to adopt corporate family policies. Work-family organizations collect testimonials from prominent CEOs and executives, which they use to suggest that other organizations change their own practices (e.g., Miranda and Murphy 1993; Peters et al. 1990; WFD 1998). Many managers now believe that their top executives support corporate family policies. In my recent survey of 389 organizations, about half of the respondents reported that the CEO or top executive of their organization fully supported corporate involvement with work and family issues.

Besides top executives, human resources managers are important potential advocates of corporate family policies. Human resources specialists may lobby their superiors to adopt certain programs and policies, thereby helping to create "top management buy-in." Human resources managers also try to translate corporate family policies into management practice by publicizing the programs and by training supervisors to manage the new arrangements. Many articles in human resources journals focus on case studies that show managers how to implement corporate family policies in their own organizations.

Yet some human resources managers resist changing organizational practices, especially working hours, to allow workers to deal with family needs. In several interviews, human resources managers explained that they chose not to formalize flextime or job-sharing policies because they worried about having to allow all workers to use the new arrangements (cf. Rapoport and Bailyn 1996). Several managers brought up the problematic case of the receptionist—"What if the receptionist wanted to use flextime? Who would answer the phones when she was not in?"—and used this worry to explain their ad hoc decisions about non-traditional schedules.

Human resources professional organizations have also been a locus of resistance to or ambivalence about some corporate family policies. Articles in *HRMagazine*, the journal of one national professional association, criticized the proposed family leave laws (e.g., Freeman and Etzkorn 1987; *Personnel Administrator* 1987; Overman 1989). After the family leave law passed, this national professional association joined the "Fix the FMLA" coalition, a lobby group that proclaimed its support for family leaves but wanted to "tweak the law" in certain ways. Association representatives and human resources executives argued in public hearings that the FMLA defined serious illness too broadly and created administrative headaches with its provision for intermittent leave (Martinez 1995).

Management support both legitimates corporate family policies and translates those policies into helpful practices. However, managers, including the human resources specialists who might seem to be natural proponents of corporate family policies, can also oppose these new practices and stall their diffusion or implementation.

Federal Coercion and Cheerleading

The federal government has few social policies to aid workers with family responsibilities, as compared to other industrialized states and especially Western Europe (e.g., Frank and Lipner 1988; Kamerman and Kahn 1991). The gap in U.S. social policies for families is clear, but the story is not just about what the federal government has not done.

Instead, the federal government has actively encouraged employers to create corporate family policies, hoping employers will make up for the lack of public responses to changing work and family conditions. The state has mandated some corporate family policies, notably leaves, in direct ways (i.e., *the Family and Medical Leave Act of 1993*) and indirect ways (i.e., EEOC Guidelines on pregnancy discrimination and the *Pregnancy Discrimination Act of 1978*; Kelly and Dobbin 1999). Federal benefits and tax laws have also created new practices, which some employers then offer as family benefits. Tax reforms in 1973 allowed employers to deduct their child care contributions to centers and programs (Michel 1998). A 1978 change in the tax code created "flexible benefits" systems or "cafeteria plans" so that employees may choose among a variety of services. This system allows young parents to use child care services (e.g., vouchers subsidizing child care, information and referral services) while other employees take advantage of other services (e.g., fitness centers, eye care plans). The most common form of employers' child care assistance, the tax-free spending account, is a direct result of the 1981 *Economic Recovery Tax Act* that created *Dependent Care Assistance Plans* (DCAPs) (Vanderkolk and Young 1991).

The federal government has also helped define the idea of "family-friendly" policies and provided free publicity to organizations with extensive corporate family policies. Following President Carter's 1980 White House Conference on Families, a number of federal agencies sponsored workshops on corporate family policies (Friedman 1983; Kamerman and Kahn 1987, p. 8). The Reagan administration increasingly emphasized private sector programs in the 1980s, as part of the drive to minimize federal government activity. After the first family leave bill had been introduced to Congress in 1985, politicians and business leaders stressed their support for "voluntary" corporate family policies.[2] Many public figures claimed they were eager to see employers provide benefits that assisted families, but they did not want those programs to be mandated by the government. For example, Shirley Dennis, the director of the Women's Bureau in the second Reagan administration, spoke of the importance of balancing work and family responsibilities and of the need for employers' involvement. But she also urged Congress "to go slowly and to be careful not to saddle us with laws" because laws "lock you in" (*Personnel Administrator* 1987, pp. 51, 57). I suggest that corporate family policies—those chosen and administered by employers or their vendors—were increasingly promoted by some politicians in the late 1980s as part of the resistance to public family policies.

There have been numerous occasions where federal government officials celebrated "family-friendly" companies, thus legitimating and advocating corporate involvement in family issues. These events provide free publicity to the organizations involved, and may encourage other employers to develop corporate family policies and seek federal cheerleading of their own (e.g., *The New York Times* 1988). The Clinton administration has taken publicity for "family-friendly" companies to new heights, with an annual conference hosted by Vice President Al Gore and regular coverage of work and family issues in Presidential addresses (Shellenbarger 1997).

To summarize, the federal government has played an important role in promoting corporate family policies. The relatively meager federal social provisions for working families create a gap that corporations, as well as other institutions, might fill. The federal government has encouraged employers to fill that gap in many ways, including requiring certain benefits, creating tax incentives for other programs, and praising model employers.

PROFILING THE ADVOCATES' ARGUMENTS

Building the Business Case

Work-family specialists, corporate champions, and federal government officials have argued that corporate family policies are good for business. They claim that corporate family policies help organizations attract employees, manage their work forces, and increase productivity. I call these arguments "the business case." Early discussions of corporate family policies, in the 1960s and 1970s, focused on corporations' social responsibilities, but the business case became prominent in the early 1980s (Friedman 1993, pp. 9-10). The Reagan administration espoused privatization as a political goal at the same time that other advocates began to stress productivity issues related to changes in the labor force. Friedman attributes the focus on productivity to the 1987 appearance of *Workforce 2000*, a high-profile report on demographic changes. Advocates began arguing that work-family programs would help organizations get more out of a shrinking labor force, and this claim received extensive attention in the years after *Workforce 2000* (Friedman 1993; Galinsky et al. 1991). In the recession of the early 1990s, corporate family policies were also discussed as a way to appease the remaining workers after downsizing (Friedman 1993; Hochschild 1997; Martinez 1994).

Arguments that focus on recruitment, retention, and motivation assure executives that there are valid reasons for corporations to get involved with these programs. This type of argumentation translates the need for corporate family policies into familiar management rhetoric, giving advocates a script that managers and executives are willing to hear. These arguments dominate popular and management discussions of corporate family policies, even though the connections between corporate family policies and positive business outcomes have not been clearly demonstrated.

Motives for Corporate Action

The business case assumes that employers with corporate family policies have been motivated by business needs, which are broadly construed as a concern with productivity and a desire to attract and retain good workers. Since most organizations believe they have those concerns and needs, advocates suggest that other organizations should also respond with corporate family policies.

Executives sometimes explicitly say they are not motivated by "altruism," and instead try to make a hard-nosed argument for corporate family policies as a way to increase productivity or attract the right workforce. Ted Childs, Manager of Work/Life Programs for IBM described these programs as "a business expense, not a charitable contribution. . . and that's important. This is not altruistic. This is an investment in the long-term economic and competitive health of the company" (quoted in Morgan and Tucker 1991, p. 91). Childs points out that: "If you have a problem with an elderly relative or a child that's a care-giving problem, no matter what your commitment to work is, that problem will be your priority . . . And we ought to be trying to respond to your problems so that we can eliminate your distractions. It's not altruistic" (quoted in Morgan and Tucker 1991, p. 90). Another executive, Charles R. Romeo, director of employee benefits for Conagra Refrigerated Foods, reported that his organization "subsidized child care for business reasons, not as a form of philanthropy" (Pear 1997, p. 1). A human resources manager I interviewed explained her company's job-sharing and flex-time options this way: "We're in business to make money. And we're not a charity organization. We don't do this to be benevolent. You do it because you want to get and keep good people."

Other corporate champions combine altruistic or paternalistic motivations with the business case. Robert E. Allen, Chairman of the Board at AT&T, pointed to both company tradition and the business case in a December 1989 letter to employees. He noted that

> Providing benefits that are responsive to the needs of employees and their families is a tradition at AT&T. The Work and Family Program not only continues that tradition, but also recognizes the changes in American families that are affecting our lives. The way we address the family concern of AT&T's people is an important issue for all of us—a competitive issue . . . These initiatives will help us attract and keep the talented work force we need to win in the

marketplace. And they will help all of us maintain a healthy balance between our work and families, so we can concentrate on giving our customers the best we have to offer (quoted in Morgan and Tucker 1991, pp. 36-37).

Reuben Marks, CEO of Colgate-Palmolive, explicitly focused on social responsibility but also referred to the business case when he explained his firm's programs: "Developing a family-friendly workplace is the right thing to do and must be done from both a social and moral viewpoint. Beyond this, it is good business . . ." (quoted in Peters et al. 1990, p. 9).

In recent years, corporate identity as an "employer of choice," which can attract and retain the best workers, has led some firms to adopt corporate family policies. Business writers and work-family experts have repeatedly claimed that providing generous family benefits and flexible work arrangements will help an organization become an "employer of choice." As one work-family manager explained, "What we're really trying to do is respond to the needs of business, not just today but for five, ten, fifteen year from now—to become an employer of choice" (quoted in Johnson and Rose 1992, p. 12).

Consequences of Corporate Action

Both work-family experts and business writers proclaim that corporate family policies will lead to positive business outcomes. Over seventy percent of the sampled articles ($N = 139$) declared that there would be some beneficial economic result—better retention, better morale, easier recruitment, reduced absenteeism, lower costs, higher productivity, or all of these—to responding to work-family issues. The publicity that comes from being known as a "family-friendly" star is another important benefit for organizations. In particular, winning a place on *Working Mother* magazine's list of best companies (or on one of the newer lists in *Fortune, Business Week*, and other sources) leads to a great deal of free publicity. So companies try to get on, or return to, the increasingly prominent lists by adding new family programs (Joyce 1998; Shellenbarger 1998; Stewart 1997).

While positive business outcomes and good publicity are promised, work-family experts also predict dire consequences for organizations that do not change. Karol Rose, a work-family expert who has worked as an independent consultant, an internal work-family manager, and now as an executive at a benefits consulting company, emphasizes that corporate family policies are crucial to organizational success. She uses arguments such as "Our survival is at stake because the talent won't put up with it anymore . . . You have to do these things, or the workers will go somewhere else. At least, the ones that can, will; and the ones that can't aren't the ones you want leading the company anyway" (Rose 1997). The CEO of Aetna, Ronald Compton, offers the following perspective on the importance of changing the way work is managed: "What would I say to a CEO who resists greater employee flexibility because of concerns about loss of accountability and productivity? I'd hope he was a competitor and I'd keep my mouth shut. Companies that don't believe in this are going to be trapped by it in the end" (WFD 1998).

Advocates' Use of the Business Case

Work-family specialists, business leaders, and federal officials make the business case in their private conversations and their public proclamations. In the early 1980s, Friedman (1983, p. 7) claimed that "The lack of awareness of the potential value of family supports as a tool to achieve management objectives is a primary obstacle to their implementation by corporations." In the years following Friedman's observation, work-family experts articulated the link between corporate family policies and business goals, and then shared their arguments and evidence with corporations. The Conference Board published several reports on making the business case for corporate family policies, such as *Work and Family Policies: The New Strategic Plan* (Peters et al. 1990), *Linking Work-Family Issues to the Bottom Line* (Friedman 1991), and *Strategies for Promoting the Work-Family Agenda* (Friedman and Johnson 1991). These guides cover topics like "applying marketing principles to communicate work-family programs, anticipating and overcoming resistance, tailoring efforts to an organization's culture, and connecting work-family issues to business concerns" (Friedman and Johnson 1991, cover page). By the 1990s, in-house work-family managers reported that "defining and communicating the business case is the most important and pervasive part of the job. 'I market 99 percent of the time,' says one" (Johnson and Rose 1992, p. 16).

Besides claiming that businesses will benefit from adopting corporate family policies, work-family specialists provide tools to try to substantiate these claims. For example, *Dependent Care Connection*, a large information and referral service, offers a return-on-investment calculator on its web-site, so that managers can enter company data and immediately see specific figures on their organization's utilization and costs (*Dependent Care Connection* 1998). WFD, the consulting business that grew out of IBM's information and referral efforts, has developed a Commitment Index for "linking work-family initiatives with employee performance and organizational effectiveness" (WFD 1998). This index is suggested for use with "the most skeptical executives—those who are often unaffected by ROI [return on investment] data" (WFD 1998).

Work-family experts also encourage rank-and-file managers and employees to use business needs rhetoric when lobbying their employers. For example, in the introduction to their book of case studies of family-friendly organizations, Morgan and Tucker advise interested workers to: "Make the business case. Find out what the competition is doing. Cite the bottom-line return in lower turnover and recruitment costs, improved morale, and increased productivity" (Morgan and Tucker 1991, p. 31). When an AT&T employee sent a letter to the CEO, urging him to investigate corporate family policies, the employee argued that child care difficulties led to productivity problems such as absenteeism, reduced hours, and lost time while at work. With the letter, the employee sent John Fernandez's 1986 book, *Child Care and Corporate Productivity* (Morgan and Tucker 1991, pp. 41-42). This example illustrates how workers can use the business case, as developed by work-family experts, to lobby their executives for corporate family programs.[3]

Federal government officials emphasize the business case. President Clinton himself argues that federal agencies should expand their flexible work arrangements in order "to recruit and retain a work force that will provide the highest quality of service" (Shellenbarger 1994a). Treasury Secretary Robert E. Rubin makes most of the arguments associated with the business case, and explicates the federal government's role in promoting these programs, in his introduction to the report, *Investing in Child Care*. Rubin states:

> it makes good business sense to create a work environment that supports the needs of each individual, such as by providing access to child care. It not only benefits the individual, but it also benefits the company by enabling it to attract and retain the best people. With the changing nature of the workforce and a growing economy, this is more important to individual businesses now than ever before. And child care is also critically important to all businesses and our economy because today's children are tomorrow's workers.

> The report carries an important lesson: investments in child care can pay off in real dividends for employers and employees. I encourage businesses to draw lessons from the best practices presented here to help determine what best meets their needs going forward. By identifying and publicizing programs such as the ones contained in this report, we hope to replicate these successes around the country in large and small businesses (U.S. Department of Treasury 1998).

Government regulations have also incorporated elements of these arguments. In 1973, the Internal Revenue Service ruled that employers could write off their child care contributions if the purpose of the center or vouchers was to increase productivity, reduce absenteeism, and minimize labor costs associated with turnover (Michel 1998; cf. *Internal Revenue Cumulative Bulletin* 1973, p. 31). The IRS rule encouraged employers to conceptualize and discuss child care programs as business initiatives, rather than as programs that advance women's employment opportunities or improve child well-being.

Implicit in the Business Case

The business case relies on a certain view of work-family issues as private problems that sometimes affect employees' performance. This perspective is found in most recent mainstream and business press articles, which present work and family issues as personal troubles, family problems, or business conflicts. In the two hundred sampled articles, difficulties balancing work and family responsibilities and employers' problems with workers (due to their family responsibilities) were the most common diagnoses of the issue at hand.

The idea that workers need to "balance" or "juggle" work and family demonstrates the assumption, found in many popular press articles, that work-family problems are private difficulties. When balancing or juggling are the challenges, we focus on individuals who negotiate their particular situations, constantly readjusting and reassessing their needs in order to avoid tipping the scale or losing control. Under this frame, we are less likely to focus on the (perhaps unreasonable) demands of work or on the unresponsiveness of community and state institutions as the critical problems. In addition to the idea of "juggling" or "balancing," the academic concepts of "work-family conflict" or "role conflict" also keep attention focused on individuals' difficulties. These concepts focus attention on individuals' dual roles and identities or on their inability to meet two sets of practical demands.

Although work-family problems are often defined as private issues, advocates and authors in the mainstream and business press regularly suggest that corporations and government bodies should respond to these problems. Corporate family policies are the most commonly proposed solutions, suggested in almost a third of the sampled articles. Following corporate family policies, state mandates for organizational policies, state services, and individual adjustments are common resolutions suggested in these articles.

Organizational solutions make sense because many advocates and managers link individuals' work-family problems to poor work performance. From this perspective, family needs are private problems that businesses need to manage in order to get all they can out of workers. Businesses respond by "accommodating" workers' needs. Accommodation involves making small adjustments for individual workers and instituting relatively narrow family programs; it does not usually involve examining the work systems and work culture in a critical way (Rapoport and Bailyn 1996, p. 15).

ALTERNATIVES TO THE BUSINESS CASE

The business case is by far the most prominent argument for corporate family policies found in the popular, business, and advocacy discourse surveyed here, but alternative perspectives on organizational involvement in family life can be found in some of the discourse and in the history of corporate family policies themselves. Business case arguments are so common and seem so plausible that it is easy to forget that they represent a strategy employed by advocates, rather than a simple statement of facts. Looking at the less familiar arguments highlights the choices advocates have made in their theorization. Here I introduce some of the alternatives to the business case and the following sections discuss some of the consequences of these choices.

Several corporate family programs have emerged from, or been linked to, social policies not directly related to family needs. Anti-discrimination efforts prompted the spread of maternity leave in the 1970s (Vogel 1993; Kelly and Dobbin 1999).

Changes in sex discrimination law led many employers to offer short leaves for new mothers. Corporate child care programs appeared as part of anti-poverty programs sponsored by the federal government and a few progressive companies in the late 1960s and early 1970s (Friedman 1987; Michel 1998). These programs focused on helping poor workers find and keep employment, rather than claiming to meet family needs or address work-family conflicts. Flextime, developed in Germany and imported to the United States, was heralded as a way to reduce traffic congestion (Ferber and Farrell 1991, p. 167; Kamerman and Kahn 1987, p. 235; Bohen and Viveros-Long 1981). Environmental concerns have also been tied to telecommuting or work-at-home arrangements. The Clean Air Act of 1990 and related state laws directed employers to cut the ratio of cars to employees at their work sites. These provisions led some organizations to develop or expand work-at-home arrangements (McNerney 1994, p. 22).

In short, several corporate family policies began as social policies and their history could have shaped how they are discussed and promoted now. But these connections to other policy domains are not emphasized in discourse about corporate family policies. Instead, advocates have stressed the business case while ignoring the different backgrounds and purposes of these programs.

In stressing the business case, advocates and writers have also neglected the role that corporate family policies might play in advancing gender equity. Some advocates worry about marginalizing their programs as "women's issues" or fear creating a "mommy track" which actually limits women's advancement and income. For example, Friedman and Johnson (1991, p. 15) advise: "Despite the fact that linking gender equity and work-family issues makes sense, it remains problematic." They quote a human resources executive who claims "We see work-family as a gender issue only in the respect that it affects both genders" (Friedman and Johnson 1991, p. 16). Only seven articles, of 130 articles sampled from the business press, argued that public or corporate family policies might have a role in advancing women's employment opportunities. Most articles did not discuss gender equity as a central part of the need for or the potential effects of corporate family policies. Some of the notable exceptions to this finding were two early *Personnel Administrator* articles that promoted part-time work and flexible working arrangements as elements of equal opportunity programs (Copperman 1979; Barrett 1983). Also, some articles linked maternity leave to equal opportunity law in the 1970s, when the EEOC and courts were dealing with pregnancy discrimination as a new issue. In general, though, gender issues are conspicuously absent from public discussions of corporate family policies.

Besides discussing particular corporate family policies as anti-poverty, environmental, or gender equity initiatives, advocates might have stressed the freedom and self-determination involved in setting one's own schedule or working from home. Cole (1989) found that these concerns were prominent in the advocacy of quality circles and other small group activities. In fact, he concluded that "it is difficult to mobilize managers and employees in response to abstraction such as the labor shortage, so broader ideologies, involving the virtues of partici-pation as leading to self-actualization, democratization, dignity, improved qual-ity of work life, and so on, are often brought into play." In the discourse on corporate family policies, though, self-actualization and dignity are relatively underdeveloped themes, while labor concerns have been emphasized by a variety of advocates and observers.

While the business case implicitly conceptualizes work-family conflicts as per-sonal problems that affect the workplace, these alternative perspectives present work-family conflicts as social issues, tied to structural causes and collective solu-tions. If corporate family policies were discussed as social policies that improve the quality of work life as efforts to promote gender equity, individuals and fami-lies would continue to experience these conflicts. But they might be encouraged to think of their experiences as part of broader structural changes and social condi-tions. The structural conditions leading to work-family conflict include the increased hours worked by many employees, and by most family units as more women join the labor force; the stagnating wages of many workers, which encour-age long hours; and the lack of high-quality, inexpensive care for children, teens, and elders. Under the business needs frame, these broader discussions of the causes of work-family conflicts are largely absent.

DISCUSSION

The previous sections lay out the cultural work done by advocates of corporate family policies, showing how these actors have characterized certain policies and programs as "family-friendly" and as good for business. Now I turn to three more evaluative questions. First, how successful have advocates been in institutionaliz-ing corporate family policies? Second, what factors explain the limited diffusion of corporate family policies? Third, what are the implications of focusing on cor-porate family policies instead of other collective responses to changing work and family experiences?

Incomplete Institutionalization

Has advocates' theorization of corporate family policies led to the institutional-ization of these new practices in organizations? Corporate family policies have become legitimate and fairly common. This marks an important change, since these policies did not exist or were extremely rare twenty or thirty years ago. How-ever, organizational commitment does not seem to be very deep, whether mea-sured by the number of programs adopted or the managerial changes made as part of implementing these programs.

Two recent surveys suggest that "family-friendly" firms with multi-faceted fam-ily programs are still unusual. An early 1990s study limited to very large firms found that the majority of these companies either had no formal response to family needs or had recently adopted a program or two (Galinsky et al. 1991, p. 3). About twenty percent of these firms had multiple programs, dedicated work-family staff, and vocal executive support. Only the second group of organizations would match the profile of the "family-friendly" companies that are so lauded in public discourse and in the work-family field. My 1997 survey, used for Table 1, finds that most organizations have now taken at least one step (in addition to the leaves legally required of some employers) towards recognizing the family needs of their workers (cf. Osterman 1995; Knoke 1996). Over two-thirds of organizations in this survey have at least one non-mandated corporate family policy. But many organizations have only responded in a shallow way, with one or two practices. In fact, only one-third of these organizations have three or more non-mandated corporate family policies in place.

Furthermore, many observers report frustration with the actual changes in work experiences or family life, even when a host of corporate family policies are adopted. Policies and programs may be in place, but workers may believe that using these new programs will have long-term negative consequences for their careers (Fried 1998; Hochschild 1997; Rapoport and Bailyn 1996). Also, formal policies to increase workers' flexibility may be offset by particular supervisors' rigidity or inability to manage workers in non-traditional arrangements (Galinsky et al. 1991; Hochschild 1997; Rapoport and Bailyn 1996). In sum, corporate family policies are now common, but organizations often adopt only one or two programs and implement them in uneven ways.

In more theoretical terms, advocates' cultural work has helped legitimate corporate family policies but it has not led to their institutionalization. Institutionalization involves at least two elements: the sense that a practice is taken-for-granted and the sense that a practice is embedded in other practices and discourses. While corporate family policies have moved from a novelty to a common and legitimate option for employers to take, these programs are not a self-evident part of what all (or all good) employers should do. Rather than being taken-for-granted, corporate family policies are still the subject of explicit argumentation by fairly marginalized advocates. Institutionalized practices or structures also seem to be built into the very system of which they are a part. This embeddedness helps keep the practice or structure from being questioned, by creating the sense that the new practice works and indeed fits naturally into a larger context. Corporate family policies are not yet firmly embedded in other corporate practices.

In fact, many elements of work systems and management practices conflict with the intention of increasing flexibility and reducing work-family conflict. For instance, many organizations evaluate departments (in terms of budget, performance, etc.) on the basis of their size. When "head counts" are used in organizational decision making, allowing workers to shift to a reduced-hours schedule will feel dangerous to supervisors whose budget and performance evaluations depend on the number of employees and the total output from those employees. Simple solutions, such as shifting to "full-time equivalents" as the unit of analysis, are available. Unless those changes are made, though, corporate family policies will be out of sync with other organizational practices and structures. These disjunctures between current practices and new programs will prevent corporate family policies from being fully utilized or fully accepted.

EXPLAINING INCOMPLETE INSTITUTIONALIZATION

Why might corporate family policies be so broadly touted but so shallowly adopted and implemented? One could argue that organizations are making independent, rational decisions not to adopt these programs because they are too costly or unnecessary. Alternatively, one could argue that organizations are influenced by advocates' cultural work, but that theorization of corporate family policies has been inadequate thus far. After reviewing the first possibility briefly, I discuss how the current theorization of corporate family policies may have limited the diffusion of these programs. In particular, the status of the advocates and the choice of arguments may help explain the moderate success of advocates' theorization.

Organizations may decide not to adopt these new practices because they are too costly or because they do not perceive a clear need for the programs. Some corporate family policies are relatively inexpensive, including unpaid leaves, tax-free spending accounts, and flex-time. Other corporate family policies can be costly, especially employer-sponsored child care, paid family leaves, and flexible working arrangements that add benefits costs, equipment costs, or liability costs. The costs of these corporate family policies may discourage employers from adopting these programs, even when corporate involvement has been accepted and praised by advocates and executives. Because the evidence for corporate family policies' effectiveness at recruiting, retaining, and motivating workers is limited (Miller 1984; Googins 1997; Glass and Estes 1997), organizations may decide that the costs outweigh the potential benefits of adopting these new programs. Furthermore, some researchers claim that workers are not demanding new corporate family policies or using available programs (e.g., Hochschild 1997). Workers may be wary of using these policies and programs, for fear that they will be sidelined on a "mommy track" or considered less committed and therefore expendable. Workers may also find other solutions to the challenges of combining work and family responsibilities, such as increasing investment in their work lives (Hochschild 1997), limiting the demands of work life (Becker and Moen 1998), or working less than full-time, full-year (Bianchi and Cohen 1998).

In addition to these practical concerns with costs, efficiency, and demand from workers, it may be that advocates' theorization has been less effective than it could be. Next I discuss how theorization by powerful actors could further boost the popularity of corporate family policies. Then I consider some ingrained assumptions that the business case—advocates' primary argument thus far—has failed to expose and challenge.

The Role of Powerful Actors

Theorization may not lead to the diffusion of new practices unless powerful actors push for change. In the case of corporate family policies, powerful actors such as the state and some unions have won corporate family policies. But these actors' involvement has been limited to certain policies or periods and the most active advocates—work-family specialists—have had limited power and prestige.

Scholars point to the importance of the coercive pressures of the state as a critical element for organizational change (Dobbin and Sutton 1998; Edelman and Suchman 1997). The American state often presents broad and vague requirements for employers. Professionals, state agencies, and courts then iteratively work to define compliance and create specific organizational practices and structures that will demonstrate compliance. The state sets new standards for employer conduct, criticizes old practices, presents threats (often of legal liability or loss of contract) to those employers who do not change, and rewards employers who adopt new practices with free publicity, government contracts, or protection from lawsuits.

The state has had an important role in promoting corporate family policy as well. Where the federal government has developed mandates or incentives (i.e., regarding family leaves and tax-free spending accounts), a majority of the sampled organizations have programs in place. In the areas of child care provision and alternative working arrangements, there has been little coercive pressure from the state and the prevalence of these policies is quite low.

In addition to the state, unions are potentially powerful actors who have sometimes promoted corporate family policies. The labor movement has historically been about corporate family programs, favoring national programs for child care, federal legislation for family leave, and contract agreements that uphold the eight-hour standard day. After years of focusing on lobbying for public policies, unions have turned attention to family programs in recent years (Cornfield and Kane 1998; Cowell 1993). Unions have worked hard to win corporate family policies in some contract negotiations, but their success at winning extensive child care programs or paid leaves has been fairly limited (York 1991). In theory, unions could be important advocates for corporate family policies; but their commitment to employer-based family programs has been low, at least until recently, and their power is increasingly limited as membership shrinks and capital mobility increases.

Diffusion may also be aided when professionals and professional organizations promote new practices. In particular, when well-established or elite professionals decree that a new practice is reasonable and necessary, organizational decision-makers may be more likely to adopt these practices. In other studies of institutional pressures for organizational change, personnel professionals, lawyers, and accountants have pushed the new practices (e.g., Edelman et al. 1992; Mezias 1990). While human resources managers and top executives have promoted corporate family policies in some settings, work-family experts have been the main advocates of these practices. These specialists work outside the organization, except in the case of new work-family managers, and they do not have a history as an established profession. Many specialists came out of child care services or child development research, and almost all work-family experts are women (Hochschild 1997; Johnson and Rose 1992, pp. 20-21). These attributes may signal "business outsider," since women concerned with child care have historically been located outside the business world rather than lobbying inside the corporation. Without an entrenched or prestigious professional group to promote corporate family policies, theorization may not be effective in achieving widespread changes.

Also, advocates have not established a "national infrastructure" to guide companies in choosing, evaluating, and implementing family policies. Comparative research suggests that new organizational practices spread widely and have broader effects on work experiences when there is a national association of employers who commit to the practice (Cole 1989). A national association can routinize organizations' decisions to adopt new practices and regularize their implementation of those practices. Other ways of dealing with the inherent uncertainty involved in new practices include the use of consultants and the creation of professional networking organizations for advocates. Cole's (1989) work on quality circles suggests that these developments, which describe the work-family field, produce fewer changes than corporate coalitions.

Resistance from Existing Institutions

Assumptions and Practices

Diffusion of corporate family policies may be limited because the new practices challenge firmly institutionalized practices, beliefs, and rationales. Some of these entrenched assumptions are that organizations should not be involved in family life, that the worlds of work and family are largely separate, and that work-family conflict arises from personal choices (usually women's "choice" to work while parenting) so difficulties should be handled by individuals and families (Bailyn 1993; Useem and Kochan 1992). In American culture, employment is conceptualized as a contract between an organization and an unencumbered individual; families are not relevant and a worker's focus on family needs signals a lack of commitment. Real change in work, to allow for family and personal life, "creates resistance because it touches core beliefs about society, success, gender roles, and the place of work and family in our lives" (Rapoport and Bailyn 1996, p. 36).

Resistance to corporate family policies is often not explicit. In my sample of two hundred work and family articles, only eight explicitly argued against corporate family policies or gave them a negative review. However, the almost-complete absence of public arguments against corporate family policies does not necessarily mean that these practices are universally accepted. It may show that advocates have successfully defined the issue as support for families, making it tricky to voice clear opposition to corporate family policies without seeming to be a cold-hearted ogre. For example, major business organizations and politicians argued against the family leave law by focusing on the costs of the leave mandate and claiming that employers were already providing leaves (Kelly and Dobbin 1999). After the leave law was passed, a Bell Atlantic human resources manager argued for changing the law by saying, "I want to make the record clear. Bell-Atlantic is for family-friendly, but the act has some unintended consequences . . ." (quoted in Martinez 1995, p. 86).

Furthermore, the case against corporate family policies can be left implicit because it is embodied in organizational structures, practices, and expectations. These institutionalized structures, practices, and expectations subtly stymie the range and effectiveness of the new practices. The privacy of family caregiving and the primacy of work commitments are two important and well-institutionalized assumptions that may be blocking institutional change in work and family arrangements. Their institutionalization is firm in both senses; these arrangements are "taken-for-granted" as the way things are and they are reinforced by a variety of institutional arrangements.

The assumed privacy of family life creates many of the conflicts experienced by employed caregivers. For example, school days and school years do not match working parents' schedules, but parents accept that they must find substitute care on their own. In contrast to many European states, the federal government has neither provided child care services for most young children nor set up public supports (e.g., family allowances, reduced hours legislation) for those who want to devote more of their own time to dependent care. Constitutional protections of "the right to privacy" and political calls for "freedom of choice" are embedded in administrative regulations, case law, and legal debates on such topics as reproductive decisions, schooling, and parental rights. All of these conditions support the belief that family responsibilities are private matters.

This focus on private choices reappears in individuals' assessments of work-family issues.[4] Many workers accept the idea that family responsibilities are solely private matters, and so they do not even imagine collective or corporate ways of providing dependent care (Becker and Moen 1998). Others accept that work and family duties naturally conflict. For instance, a young woman who passed up a promotion said that it was "unreasonable" for her to consider the new position because "I chose to have these kids, and now I have to take care of them" (quoted in Rapoport and Bailyn 1996, p. 18). Although work patterns and family structures have changed significantly in recent decades, families (especially mothers, but also involved fathers and elder caregivers) still have sole responsibility for dependent care or for arranging that care.

Despite their private responsibility for family caregiving, employers expect that workers will give work duties and work identities the central place in their daily lives. Many organizations still push workers to "act as though you have no other loyalties, no other life" (Bailyn 1993; Shellenbarger 1993, 1994b; Swiss and Walker 1993; quoted phrase from Kanter 1977, p. 15) and they reward those who demonstrate this focus on work. Professional, managerial, and administrative workers may be judged by whether they place any limits on their time or effort at work, such as leaving at a regular time or refusing to travel for business. These expectations persist as the length of work weeks has increased among many high-level workers and as work days have been lengthened by early morning meetings, planning sessions at the dinner hour, and training at remote sites (Jacobs and Gerson 1997; Rapoport and Bailyn 1996, p. 16). Often, "facetime" seems more important in demonstrating commitment than actual performance does (Bailyn 1993; Shellenbarger 1994b). In non-managerial and non-professional settings, production and service workers are labeled as "trouble-makers" or as "unreliable" workers when they request flexibility in regimented schedules or when they miss work because of family emergencies.

In addition to these organizational pressures, both national policies and personal decisions reinforce the primacy of work. *The Fair Labor and Standards Act* exempts supervisory, managerial, and professional workers from its requirements for overtime pay. This exemption rule encourages employers to accept and even demand very long hours from their exempt employees (Jacobs and Gerson 1997). The growing costs of employer benefits provide a further incentive to get the most work possible out of current employees, rather than hiring new workers or allowing workers to shift to part-time work. Of course, the primacy of work is not just located "out there" in the organization of work and the policies of the federal government. Many workers accept and enjoy their focus on work responsibilities and work identities (Barnett and Rivers 1996; Hochschild 1997; cf. Becker and Moen 1998; McKenna 1997).

Gender as Subtext

There is a gendered subtext to the institutionalized privacy of family life and the institutionalized primacy of work. Families and work organizations are embedded in a system of gender relations that is itself a social fact, even though there is some flexibility in how individuals enact their gender identities (Connell 1987; Lorber 1994; West and Zimmerman 1987). Neither the implicit expectations about work commitment nor the new corporate family programs explicitly deal with gender. In fact, most articles discussed work and family issues in carefully gender-neutral terms, even though they relied primarily on evidence about mothers' and wives' experiences.

Gendered roles and identities affect who is likely to meet the expectations about work commitment (i.e., many men and women who are not mothers) and who feels comfortable using the corporate family benefits (i.e., mostly mothers). Since women have historically performed most family caregiving work and most women still do the majority of domestic work and dependent care, the privatization of family life disproportionately burdens women and may limit their opportunities at work. Men have historically been seen as the "breadwinner," whose prioritization of work supported their families financially and who were supported by their wives in many practical ways. Recently, feminist scholars have argued that seemingly gender-neutral facets of work—from the identification of skills, to the career paths required to reach top positions, to the requirements of pension systems—assume a worker whose primary attention is devoted to work and whose daily needs are met by another person, working behind the scenes in the home (e.g., Acker 1990). These work structures were built around the male breadwinner/female homemaker pattern, and so they are less and less consonant with the experiences and expectations of many of today's workers.

Corporate Family Policies as Challenges to these Institutions

Corporate family policies potentially challenge these institutionalized assumptions about family life, work life, and men's and women's place in each sphere. Corporations with dependent care programs buck the cultural and institutional expectations that child-rearing and care of elderly relatives belong entirely in the private sphere. Similarly, corporations that develop extensive flexible working arrangements challenge the reigning assumption that good workers will give their all—in terms of time and focus—to the work organization. Corporations that create a variety of career paths minimize the costs of many women's temporary focus on family needs. Those organizations that encourage men's use of family programs legitimate the choice of some men to prioritize family responsibilities. Yet this kind of challenge seems to be relatively rare even among organizations that adopt several corporate family policies (Galinsky et al. 1991; Rapoport and Bailyn 1996).

Generally, advocates have not helped organizations explore these assumptions (but see Rapoport and Bailyn 1996 for a model of more reflective change efforts). Advocates sometimes voice frustration with the shallow implementation of these new programs and they call for "culture change" in addition to formal policies (e.g., Galinsky et al. 1991; Miranda and Murphy 1993). But few have explored exactly what assumptions, expectations, and management practices must be changed—and what resistance might be encountered in trying to promote cultural and structural changes in the way family caregiving and work systems are organized.

To summarize, corporate family policies are not well-institutionalized in American organizations. Many organizations have made only token acknowledgments of family needs and corporate family programs may be contradicted, in practical and symbolic ways, by a variety of existing assumptions, expectations, and practices. These institutionalized assumptions include the sense that caring for children and elderly relatives is strictly a private responsibility and the sense that full commitment to one's work means being willing to take on any task, at any time. Gender roles and gendered identities mean that these assumptions often have different effects for men's and women's family experiences and work lives. The current theorization of corporate family policies ignores these entrenched assumptions and the gendered underpinnings of the current work-family system.

CORPORATE FAMILY POLICIES AS SOCIAL POLICY

In the past decade, corporate family policies have received more attention from advocates, opinion-makers, and public officials than have public policies for working families.[5] Yet when we consider these programs as social policy, that is, as part of a private-public welfare state, corporate family policies are problematic in several ways. These problems point to the importance of other collective responses to work and family issues, as well as workplace reforms.

What are some of the limitations of corporate family policies as social policy? First, access to corporate family policies is limited to those individuals who are employed by particularly generous firms or organizations. Some corporate family policies, such as family leaves, have been pushed by the federal government and are now available to a broad range of workers. Other policies and programs, though, are available at only a small percentage of firms, leaving many employees without access to these services or benefits. Second, corporate family policies can tie workers to firms in ways that are not helpful to workers in the long run. Like health insurance provided by employers, some benefits—perhaps especially on-site child care—are so attractive that workers may refuse other job opportunities in order to keep their benefits. In short, corporate family policies can extend the stratified and potentially coercive system of employer-based benefits.[6]

Additionally, corporate family policies may limit the development of other policies to aid working families. The political consequences of corporate family policies may include increased loyalty to employers rather than to unions (Cornfield 1990) and reduced calls for universal, federal programs when middle-class and professional workers are served by their employers (Michel 1998; Stevens 1988).

Coupling public policies for working families and corporate involvement would address these limitations. Because leaves and flexible working arrangements involve the employment contract and the way work is organized, employers will have to remain intimately involved in these arrangements. Since employers must be involved, advocates may want to work for improved access to leaves and flexible work arrangements. Family leave is one successful example of a new work-family right established through public policy. Advocates might work for laws providing paid leaves (funded through unemployment insurance programs) and establishing reduced hours options with pro-rated benefits. These changes would make leaves and reduced-hours schedules real possibilities for a variety of workers. Also, reforming the federal wages and hours laws to include managers and professionals would make it more costly for organizations to ask these workers to put in extremely long hours.

While employers must remain involved in leaves and flexible schedules, community-based services for children and elderly people would provide broader access than employer-based child care services. Like other employee benefits, child care benefits tend to be distributed unevenly and employees lose the benefits when they lose their jobs. Alternatives to employer-sponsored dependent care services include public day care available to all families using a sliding-scale fee system, extended-day programs tied to schools, resource and referral services located in community service organizations, child care for mildly ill children located in hospitals or community service organizations, paid leaves, and family allowances which would provide some financial support to parents who wanted to reduce their work hours or take extended breaks from employment.

CONCLUSION

Popular discussions of corporate family policies focus on employers' desire to recruit, retain, and motivate their workers. Work-family specialists, business allies, and federal officials have developed and repeated these accounts over the past twenty years. Despite the prevalence of the business case, corporate family policies are not well-institutionalized in American organizations. Many practices are still rare, the programs conflict with other structures and practices, and many organizations see corporate family policies as legitimate but optional actions.

Corporate family policies potentially challenge some deeply held assumptions about the privacy of caregiving responsibilities and the primacy of career commitment. Yet by focusing on the business case for corporate family policies, advocates have avoided critically examining these assumptions and the way they play out in family caregiving and work practices. Advocates have often tried to push these new practices without exposing and indicting the current gendered system. This leads to shallow changes in employers' practices and unequal access to family benefits. In order to achieve real institutional change, whether through corporate family policies or other collective responses, advocates will have to confront and attempt to delegitimate the existing assumptions about work, family, and gender.

APPENDIX

For this analysis, I rely on three types of discourse: a sample of mainstream and business press articles, reports from work-family experts employed in research, advocacy, and service-provision organizations, and interviews with human resources managers. I also refer to preliminary results from a new survey of American employers.

Press Sample

The press sample is drawn from three sources: *The New York Times*, chosen because of its status as an influential general news source; *The Wall Street Journal*, chosen because of its status as an influential business news source; and *HRMagazine* (formerly *Personnel Administrator*), chosen because it is the official journal of the primary national association of human resource professionals. The target audiences of these sources do not necessarily include the typical workers trying to combine work and family responsibilities. Instead, I have focused on sources that may influence those who think about and make decisions about public and corporate policies.

I first created population lists that catalogue all articles dealing with work and family issues. The aggregate population list includes 3,332 articles from these three sources. The search criteria were designed to find articles related to work and family issues (not only corporate family policies) in order to see what problems were defined and what solutions were suggested. I used Lexis/Nexis HLEAD searches to create population lists for the *New York Times* and *Wall Street Journal*. HLEAD searches examine the headlines and lead paragraphs of all sub-sections in an article, checking for specified key words. The key words searched included specific family policies (e.g., "family leave") and general terms describing new work and family situations that might lead to a variety of public or corporate family policies (e.g., "working parents"). These searches produced a population list of relevant *New York Times* articles from 1969 to February 1998 and a population list of relevant *Wall Street Journal* articles from 1974 to February 1998. I then searched the annual print indices for the *Wall Street Journal* from 1965 to 1973, checking all titles under the headings of families, labor—general, labor—legislation, labor—state labor laws, and labor—women workers. I added all articles that covered family policies or discussed combining work and family roles and responsibilities to the population list for the *Wall Street Journal*. To create the population list for *Personnel Administrator/HRMagazine*, I searched the ABI Inform database for keywords covering families and family policies. This search produced a population list for 1972 through 1997, but the coverage in the early-1970s seemed questionable. I completed the population list by searching the *Business Periodical Index*, a printed source, for relevant *Personnel Administrator* articles from 1965 to 1980, checking relevant headings. I also scanned the table of contents for all available issues of *Personnel Administrator* from 1970 to 1975.

I sampled articles randomly from each source and read and coded the full text of the sampled articles. I read and coded 197 articles, 67 from the *New York Times*, 69 from the *Wall Street Journal*, and 61 from *Personnel Administrator/HRMagazine*. I considered several questions when coding each article, following the methodology and themes of previous work on the social construction of problems in public discourse (e.g., Gusfield 1981; Gamson and Modigliani 1989; Burstein, Bricher and Einwohner 1995; Burstein and Bricher 1997). How was the problem or situation described? What causes were identified? Who should respond to the problem (or who has responded)? What solutions are discussed and what solution is emphasized? What motives are described for action, and who has those motives? What consequences are expected from or attributed to implementing the solution? I also coded information on how the argument was made, including what family policies (public and corporate) were mentioned, what the author's stance was toward corporate family policies, what sources were relied upon, what experts were named, and what type of evidence was used. In addition to these questions about the basic argument and rhetoric, I coded the articles' descriptions and assumptions (when clear) about family life, women's and men's work statuses, equal opportunity, and the relationship between work and family.

Reports From Work-Family Organizations

My analysis of reports from work-family organizations was less formal than the press analysis, and it is not an exhaustive examination of all materials, or even all formal reports, created by these specialist organizations. However, I analyzed over thirty reports published by work-family organizations over the past twenty years. These included research reports from Catalyst, the Conference Board, Families and Work Institute, and New Ways to Work. All these organizations try to reach business leaders, as well as other work-family experts, with their research. The research varies in purpose, rigor, and representativeness, with Families and Work Institute research generally following methods very similar to academic work, Catalyst research generally focusing on implementation and case studies, and Conference Board research often reporting the "best practices" of large firms. I have also collected some materials from WFD (Work/Family Directions), Dependent Care Connection, and other work-family consulting and resource services.

Interviews with Human Resources Managers

I conducted eighteen interviews with human resources managers working at organizations in the New York City and central New Jersey areas. I used the *Hoover's Directory of Human Resources Executives* (1996) to randomly sample companies located in these two areas that reported at least fifty employees at the firm. Smaller organizations were excluded because they would be unlikely to have formal policies or to have a manager whose job focused on keeping up with these issues. I wrote letters to the sampled managers and conducted interviews with all those who agreed to see me (about 45% of the managers contacted). In the letter and initial contacts, I described my research in general terms (i.e., "how companies meet the needs of today's changing workforce"), so that I would be able to speak to managers at organizations with few family policies as well as with those who were proud of their organization's responses to family needs. The respondents included managers at firms of varying sizes (from about one hundred to several thousand employees) and in a variety of industries (including durable and nondurable manufacturing firms, advertising agencies, a hospital, a publishing company, a retail company, a non-profit organization, a university, and a government agency). Interviews lasted one to two hours and covered a variety of topics. Interviews focused on work and family issues, how the organization handled family issues and why they had responded in that way, what family programs had been discussed or why no programs had been discussed, how managers learned about family policy options, who they discussed these topics with, and management support or resistance for corporate responses to family needs. Interviews were tape recorded and transcribed.

Survey of Employers

I report some results from a new survey of American work establishments with fifty or more employees, which was funded by the Alfred P. Sloan Foundation, designed by Frank Dobbin and myself, and conducted by the University of Maryland Survey Research Center in 1997. The respondents were 389 managers—human resources managers where possible, general managers otherwise—from these establishments. The sample was a national, stratified random sample of work establishments with fifty or more employees, drawn from Dun & Bradstreet sources. The sample was stratified by size and industry, with the following industries included: food manufacturing, chemicals manufacturing, transportation equipment manufacturing, computer equipment manufacturing, trucking and transport service, wholesale trade, banks, business services, non-profit social services, and local government agencies. The cooperation rate (i.e., percentage of contacted establishments that completed the survey) was 72 percent.

ACKNOWLEDGMENTS

I want to express my gratitude to the Alfred P. Sloan, Jr. Foundation, the University Center for Human Values (Princeton University), and the Bendheim-Thoman Center for Research on Child Well-being (Princeton University) for their support of this research. Thanks also go to Paul DiMaggio, Frank Dobbin, Jackie Gordon, Sara McLanahan, Toby Parcel, and the members of the Dissertation Writing Group for their helpful comments.

NOTES

1. Of course, corporations have long provided for "family needs" such as good wages, safe conditions, health insurance and other benefits. A previous incarnation of welfare capitalism also provided

workers in some organizations with company-owned or subsidized homes, libraries, and schools. Employer-sponsored child care has a long history, dating back to the early days of the United States, but there were only a handful of firms involved for most of the time (Michel 1998; Morgan and Tucker 1991, pp. 19-25). The largest early initiative occurred during World War II when industry set up, and the federal government subsidized, child care centers for mothers doing essential war-time work.

2. Politicians and business leaders pointed to "voluntary" maternity leave programs as evidence that organizations responded to market pressures to create any benefits that were needed. They argued that government intervention was not necessary. They seemingly forgot that many of these maternity leave programs were initiated in the 1970s in response to changing definitions of sex discrimination, not in response to changes in the labor market (Kelly and Dobbin 1999).

3. Alternative accounts of AT&T's extensive involvement in work-family issues point to the importance of labor bargaining and demands emerging from unionized workers (Friedman and Johnson 1991, p. 8; York 1993, pp. 138-140).

4. Interestingly, the theme of forced choices was prominent in debates about the Family and Medical Leave Act. Supportive politicians and other advocates of a leave law argued that workers faced an impossible or unjust choice "between the jobs they need and the children they love" (Michael Dukakis, quoted in Googins 1990, p. 269; similar language is used by child advocates, *New York Times* 1987; by the bill's first sponsor, Representative Patricia Schroeder, Vogel 1993, pp. 106-107; and by union activists, York 1990, p. 177).

5. This may be changing, as broader childcare initiatives develop. For example, President Clinton and especially Hillary Clinton have tried to bring childcare back to the public agenda. Also, work-family organizations, such as the Families and Work Institute, are beginning public awareness programs that deal with multiple childcare issues, not just employer involvement in childcare.

6. The business case acknowledges these two situations, but presents them as positive conditions for employers. The business case relies on the uneven distribution of family programs, claiming that these programs will give the employer a competitive advantage in attracting and retaining workers. The promised competitive advantage only appears if other firms are not offering the same benefits. Advocates and executives claim that corporate family policies help organizations retain workers; from the point of view of the worker, this can feel coercive or limiting.

REFERENCES

Acker, J. 1990. "Hierarchies, Jobs, Bodies: A Theory of Gendered Organizations." *Gender and Society* 4(2): 139-158.

Bailyn, L. 1993. *Breaking the Mold: Women, Men, and Time in the New Corporate World*. New York: Free Press.

Barnett, R. C., and C. Rivers. 1996. *She Works/He Works: How Two-Income Families and Happier, Healthier, and Better Off*. New York: Harper Collins.

Barrett, N. 1983. "Part-Time Work Will Increase, Bringing Change to Social Mores and Standards of Compensation." *Personnel Administrator* 94-98: 104.

Becker, P. E., and P. Moen. 1998. "Scaling Back: Dual-Career Couples' Work-Family Strategies." Working Paper, Cornell Careers Institute.

Bianchi, S. M., and P. Cohen. 1998. "Marriage, Children, and Women's Employment: Do We Know What We Think We Know?" Paper presented at the Eastern Sociological Society meetings, Philadelphia, PA, March 1998.

Bohen, H., and A. Viveros-Long. 1981. *Balancing Jobs and Family Life: Do Flexible Work Schedules Help?* Philadelphia, PA: Temple University Press.

Burstein, P., R. M. Bricher, and R. L. Einwohner. 1995. "Policy Alternatives and Political Change: Work, Family, and Gender on the Congressional Agenda, 1945-1990." *American Sociological Review* 60: 67-83.

Burstein, P., and M. Bricher. 1997. "Problem Definition and Public Policy: Congressional Committees Confront Work, Family, and Gender, 1945-1990." *Social Forces* 75(4): 135-169.

Colomy, P. 1998. "Neofunctionalism and Neoinstitutionalism: Human Agency and Interest in Institutional Change." *Sociological Forum* 13(2): 265-300.

Connell, R.W. 1987. *Gender and Power.* Cambridge, UK: Polity Press.

Copperman, L. 1979. "Alternative Work Policies in Private Firms." *Personnel Administrator* 40-44.

Cornfield, D. B. 1990. "Labor Unions, Corporations, and Families: Institutional Competition in the Provision of Social Welfare." *Marriage and Family Review* 15(3/4): 37-57.

Cornfield, D. B., and M. D. Kane. 1998. "Gender Segmentation, Union Decline, and Women Workers: Changes in the AFL-CIO Policy Agenda, 1955-1993." Paper presented at the annual meeting of the American Sociological Association, San Francisco, CA.

Cowell, S. 1993. "Family Policy: A Union Approach." Pg. 115-128 in *Women and Unions: Forging a Partnership,* edited by D. S. Cobble. Ithaca, NY: ILR Press.

Dependent Care Connection. 1998. Http://www.dcclifecare.com/main.html

Devroy, A. 1990. "President Vetoes Bill on Unpaid Family Leave." *Washington Post* p. A4.

DiMaggio, P. J. 1988. "Interest and Agency in Institutional Theory" Pp. 3-22 in *Institutional Patterns and Organizations,* edited by L. G. Zucker. Cambridge, MA: Ballinger.

DiMaggio, P.J., and W. W. Powell. 1983. "The Iron Cage Revisited: Institutional Isomorphism and Collective Rationality in Organizational Fields." *American Sociological Review* 35: 147-160.

_____. 1991. "Introduction." Pp. 1-40 in *The New Institutionalism in Organizational Analysis,* edited by W. W. Powell and P. J. DiMaggio. Chicago: University of Chicago Press.

Dobbin, F. 1994. "Cultural Models of Organization: The Social Construction of Rational Organizing Principles." Pp. 117-153 in *The Sociology of Culture: Emerging Theoretical Perspectives,* edited by D. Crane. Cambridge, MA: Blackwell.

Dobbin, F., J. R. Sutton, J. W. Meyer, and W. R. Scott. 1993. "Equal Opportunity Law and the Construction of Internnal Labor Markets." *American Journal of Sociology* 99(2): 396-427.

Dobbin, F., and J. R. Sutton. 1998. "The Strength of a Weak State: The Employment Rights Revolution and the Rise of Human Resources Management Divisions" *American Journal of Sociology.*

Edelman, L. B. 1992. "Legal Ambiguity and Symbolic Structures: Organizational Mediation of Civil Rights Law." *American Journal of Sociology* 97(6): 1531-1576.

Edelman, L. B., S. E. Abraham, and H. S. Erlanger. 1992. "Professional Construction of Law: The Inflated Threat of Wrongful Discharge." *Law and Society* 26(1): 47-83.

Edelman, L. B., and M. C. Suchman. 1997. "The Legal Environment of Organizations." *Annual Review of Sociology* 23: 479-515.

Ferber, M. A., and B. O'Farrell. 1991. *Work and Family: Policies for a Changing Work Force.* Washington, DC: National Academy Press.

Fernandez, J. P. 1986. *Child Care and Corporate Productivity: Resolving Family/Work Conflicts.* Lexington Books.

Fligstein, N. 1990. *The Transformation of Corporate Control.* Cambridge, MA: Harvard University Press.

Frank, M., and R. Lipner. 1988. "History of Maternity Leave in Europe and the United States." Pp. 3-22 in *The Parental Leave Crisis,* edited by E. F. Zigler and M. Frank. New Haven: Yale University Press.

Freeman, C. A., and S. T. Etzkorn. 1987. "Parental/Pregnancy Leave: Added Burdens in a Changing Work Force." *Personnel Administrator* 30-32.

Fried, M. 1998. *Taking Time: Parental Leave Policy and Corporate Culture.* Philadelphia: Temple University Press.

Friedman, D. 1983. *Encourging Employer Supports to Parents: Community Strategies for Change.* New York: Center for Public Advocacy Research/Carnegie Corporation of New York.

_____. 1987. *Family-Supportive Policies: The Corporate Decision-Making Process.* New York: Conference Board.

_____. 1991. *Linking Work-Family Issues to the Bottom Line*. New York: Conference Board.

_____. 1993. "Evolving the Case." Pp. 9-10 in *Work-Family: Redefining the Business Case*, edited by E. J. Miranda and B. E. Murphy. New York: Conference Board.

Friedman, D. E., and A. A. Johnson. 1991. *Strategies for Promoting a Work-Family Agenda*. New York: Conference Board.

Galinksy, E., D. E. Friedman, and C. A. Hernandez. 1991. *The Corporate Reference Guide to Work-Family Programs*. New York: Families and Work Institute.

Gamson, W. A., and A. Modigliani. 1989. "Media Discourse and Public Opinion on Nuclear Power: A Constructionist Approach." *American Journal of Sociology* 95: 1-37.

Glass, J., and S. B. Estes. 1997. "The Family Responsive Workplace." *Annual Review of Sociology* 23: 289-313.

Googins, B. K. 1997. "Shared Responsibility for Managing Work and Family Relationships: A Community Perspective." Pp. 220-231 in *Integrating Work and Family*, edited by S. Parasuraman and J. H. Greenhaus. Westport, CT: Quorum Books.

Gusfield, J. 1981. *The Culture of Public Problems: Drunk Driving and the Symbolic Order*. Chicago: University of Chicago Press.

Hochschild, A. R. 1997. *The Time Bind: When Work Becomes Home and Home Becomes Work*. New York: Metropolitan Books.

Hoover's Directory of Human Resources Executives. 1996. Austin, TX: The Reference Press.

Internal Revenue Cumulative Bulletin. 1973. "Section 162, Rev. Rul. 73-348." Washington, DC: Department of Treasury, Internal Revenue Service.

Jacobs, J. A., and K. Gerson. 1997. "The Endless Day or the Flexible Office: Work-Family Conflicts and Gender Equity in the Professional Workplace." A Report for the Alfred P. Sloan Foundation.

Jepperson, R. L. 1991. "Institutions, Institutional Effects, and Institutionalism." Pp. 143-162 in *The New Institutionalism in Organizational Analysis*, edited by W. W. Powell and P. J. DiMaggio. Chicago: University of Chicago Press.

Johnson, A. A., and K. L. Rose. 1992. *The Emerging Role of the Work-Family Manager*. New York: Conference Board.

Jordano, R., and M. Oates. 1998. "Invest in Workers for Best Child Care." *New York Times* p. 13.

Joyce, A. 1998. "Companies Making Strides to Be Working Mother-Friendly." *Washington Post* p. H6.

Kamerman, S. B., and A. J. Kahn. 1987. *The Responsive Workplace: Employers and a Changing Labor Force*. New York: Columbia University Press.

Kamerman, S. B., and A. J. Kahn. 1991. *Child Care, Parental Leave and the Under 3s: Policy Innovation in Europe*. New York: Auburn House Publishing.

Kanter, R. M. 1977. *Work and Family in the United States: A Critical Review and Agenda for Research and Policy*. New York: Russell Sage Foundation.

Kelly, E., and F. Dobbin. 1999. "Civil Rights Law at Work: Sex Discrimination and the Rise of Maternity Leave Policies." *American Journal of Sociology*. Forthcoming, September.

Knoke, D. 1996. "Cui Bono? Employee Benefit Packages." Pp. 232-253 in *Organizations in America*, edited by A. L. Kalleberg, D. Knoke, P. V. Marsden, and J. L. Spaeth. Thousand Oaks, CA: Sage Publications.

Lawson, C. 1991. "Making Child Care America's Business." *New York Times* Section C, p. 1.

Lorber, J. 1994. *Paradoxes of Gender*. New Haven: Yale University Press.

Martinez, M. N. 1994. "FMLA: Headache or Opportunity?" *HRMagazine* February, pp. 42-45.

_____. 1995. "Employers Question FMLA Provisions." *HRMagazine* December, pp. 86-91.

McKenna, E. P. 1997. *When Work Doesn't Work Anymore: Women, Work, and Identity*. New York: Delacorte Press.

McNerney, D. J. 1994. "A strategic partnership: Clean Air Act and Work-Family." *HR Focus* November, pp. 22-23.

Meyer, J. W., and B. Rowan. 1977. "Institutionalized Organizations: Formal Structure as Myth and Ceremony." *American Journal of Sociology* 83: 340-363.

Mezias, S. 1990. "An Institutional Model of Organizational Practice: Financial Reporting at the Fortune 200." *Administrative Science Quarterly* 35: 431-457.

Michel, S. 1998. "The Corporate Cradle." In *The Modern Worlds of Business and Industry: Cultures, Technology, Labor,* edited by K. Merrill. Brepols Publishing.

Miller, T. I. 1984. "The Effects of Employer-Sponsored Child Care on Employee Absenteeism, Turnover, Productivity, Recruitment or Job Satisfaction: What is Claimed and What is Known." *Personnel Psychology* 37: 277-289.

Miranda, E. J., and B. E. Murphy. 1993. *Work-Family: Redefining the Business Case.* New York: Conference Board.

Morgan, H., and K. Tucker. 1991. *Companies that Care: The Most Family-Friendly Companies in America—What They Offer and How They Got That Way.* New York: Fireside/Simon and Schuster.

New York Times. 1988 (May 6). "43 Employers Are Honored by Congress over Child Care." Section A, p. 17.

Osterman, P. 1995. "Work/family programs and the employment relationship." *Administrative Science Quarterly* 40: 681-700.

Overman, S. 1989. "Government Steers HR's Future: More Federal Regulation Likely in the 1990s." *Personnel Administrator* 61-63.

Pear, R. 1997. "Clinton to Offer a Child Care Plan, White House Says." *New York Times* Section 1, p. 1.

Personnel Administrator. 1987. "Is Work a Family Affair?" (Interview with Shirley Dennis) August: 50-57.

Peters, J. L., B. H. Peters, and F. Caroposo. 1990. *Work and Family Policies: The New Strategic Plan.* New York: Conference Board.

Pleck, J. H. 1992. "Work-Family Policies in the United States." Pp. 248-276 in *Women's Work and Women's Lives,* edited by H. Kahne and J. Z. Giele. Boulder: Westview Press.

Rapoport, R., and L. Bailyn. 1996. *Relinking Life and Work: Toward a Better Future.* New York: Ford Foundation.

Rose, K. L. 1997. Personal Interview.

Shellenbarger, S. 1993 (June 21). "So Much Talk, So Little Action." *Wall Street Journal* p. B1.

_____. 1994a (August 3). "Workers Get Better at Balancing Act." *Wall Street Journal* p. B1.

_____. 1994b (December 28). "How to Look Like a Workaholic While Still Having a Life." *Wall Street Journal* p. B1.

_____. 1997 (February 19). "Karen Nussbaum Plans to Focus Unions on Family Issues." *Wall Street Journal* p. B1.

_____. 1998 (August 26). "Those Lists Ranking Best Places to Work are Rising in Influence." *Wall Street Journal* p. B1.

Stevens, B. 1988. "Blurring the Boundaries: How the Federal Government Has Influenced Welfare Benefits in the Private Sector." Pp. 123-148 in *The Politics of Social Policy in the U.S.,* edited by M. Weir, A. Orloff, and T. Skocpol. Princeton, NJ: Princeton University Press.

Stewart, J. K. 1997. "The Lure of the Lists: How Valuable Is the Family-Friendly Label?" *Chicago Tribune* p. 7.

Strang, D., and J. W. Meyer. 1993. "Institutional conditions for diffusion." *Theory and Society* 22: 487-511.

United States Department of the Treasury. 1998. *Investing in Child Care: Challenges Facing Working Parents and Private Sector Response.* Washington, DC: GPO. (http://www.treas.gov/press/releases/chcare.pdf)

Useem, M., and T. A. Kochan. 1992. "Creating the Learning Organization." Pp. 391-406 in *Transforming Organizations,* edited by T. A. Kochan and M. Useem. New York: Oxford University Press.

Vanderkolk, B. S., and A. A. Young. 1991. *The Work and Family Revolution: How Companies Can Keep Employees Happy and Business Profitable.* New York: Facts on File.

Vogel, L. 1993. *Mothers on the Job: Maternity Policy in the U.S. Workplace.* New Brunswick, NJ: Rutgers University Press.

West, C., and D. H. Zimmerman. 1987. "Doing Gender." *Gender and Society* 1(2): 125-151.

WFD. 1998. http:// www.wfd.com/spotlight.htm viewed August 1998.

York, C. 1991. "The Labor Movement's Role in Parental Leave and Child Care." Pp. 176-188 in *Parental Leave and Child Care: Setting a Research and Policy Agenda,* edited by J. S. Hyde and M. J. Essex. Philadelphia: Temple University Press.

BECOMING FAMILY-FRIENDLY:
WORK-FAMILY PROGRAM INNOVATION AMONG THE LARGEST U.S. CORPORATIONS

Kristine M. Witkowski

ABSTRACT

Examining innovation among the largest corporations in the United States, this analysis investigates how: (1) boundary-spanning units, (2) organizational approaches to problem-solving, and (3) the organizational life-cycle affect the institutionalization of work-family programs. Using data collected from a sample of 188 of the top ranking Fortune 1,000 companies, discrete-time event history analysis assesses how exogenous organizational characteristics shape family program innovation between 1974 and 1995. Information from existing archives and a recent mail survey supplements data collected from *The Corporate Reference Guide to Work-Family Programs survey* (Galinsky, Friedman and Hernandez 1991) is used. Analyses reveal that the innovative effects of integrative problem-solving consistently influence various dimensions of work-family programs. Female-representation on governing boards and reliance on industrial labor markets dominated by women in management and human resource occupations

Research in the Sociology of Work, Volume 7, pages 203-232.
Copyright © 1999 by JAI Press Inc.
All rights of reproduction in any form reserved.
ISBN: 0-7623-0605-X

consistently increase family program institutionalization. Likewise, total quality management, communication programs, and matrix structures promote innovation.

INTRODUCTION

Since the early twentieth century, the percentage of U.S. women participating in the labor force has dramatically increased to the point that 60 percent of women now work (U.S. Department of Labor 1998). This increase was greatest among women with young children (U.S. Census Bureau 1997). Because of long term role conflicts, working mothers have consistently higher rates of absenteeism and labor force inactivity than women with no children and married men (Spilerman and Schrank 1991; Klein 1986).

In hopes of reducing labor costs by increasing employee productivity and reducing turnover, some employers have responded to their workers' family needs by offering a variety of programs that help alleviate the conflicts between family and work roles. While the availability of these family programs is rising (Wiatrowski 1995), a majority of companies still do not offer such supports. Furthermore, we know little about the conditions that facilitate and impede family program innovation.

I examine the family-work innovation process by assessing how exogenous organizational and environmental characteristics influence the institutionalization of family programs. "Family programs" are organized efforts by employers to ease the role conflicts that can potentially affect employee performance. The characteristic of family-work innovations I analyze is the likelihood of having (i.e., institutionalizing) different types of family programs over time. Specifically, I study the institutionalization of cafeteria plans, dependent care assistance packages, child care resource and referrals, elder care resource and referrals, family leave programs, flextime, flexplace or telecommuting, part-time work schedules, and job-sharing programs.

LITERATURE REVIEW

Early studies of family program adoption conducted cross-sectional surveys of firms and produced descriptive data (McNeely and Fogarty 1988; Auerbach 1990; Christensen and Staines 1990; Galinsky and Stein 1990; Friedman 1990; Miller, Stead and Pereira 1991). While empirically insightful, this research fails to inform theory. However, more recent studies have incorporated organizational theory to explain employer responsiveness to work-family issues (Goodstein 1994, 1995; Osterman 1995).

Goodstein (1994, 1995) brings together institutional and strategic choice theories in his analyses of employer responsiveness to work-family conflicts. When encountering institutional pressures from human resource offices, employees, or special-interests groups, organizations can interpret and choose which issues they will address. Goodstein (1995) investigates how an organization's recognition and interpretation of its environment influences its response to workers' elder care needs. The visibility of and an organization's exposure to elder care issues are associated with recognition of family issues. Once brought to its attention, an organization's response to employee needs depends on whether it interprets elder care as an important issue. Factors influencing interpretation stem from employee-needs assessments, organizational values, workforce characteristics, and the productivity impact of elder care concerns.

Besides recognizing and interpreting their environments, organizations can choose their reaction to these pressures. The way an organization strategically responds varies by the characteristics of institutional pressures. Consequently, the number and types of family programs an organization adopts reflect its strategic manner of adapting to its institutional environment (Goodstein 1994).

Finally, Osterman (1995) studied the adoption of family programs in relation to broader employment strategies. He found that formalized employment relations increase the introduction of new formal programs (i.e., family programs). Besides internal labor markets, total quality management and quality circles are other employment strategies used to increase employee commitment to the firm. Companies that use these high-commitment programs to attract and retain productive workers are more likely to have family programs.

While recent studies have provided theoretical insight, they have virtually ignored the literature on organizational innovation. They also do not adequately address or analyze the dynamic and innovative processes that underlie organizational adoption of family programs. For purposes of this analysis, I focus on the innovation process within firms rather than diffusion of innovations among organizations as it relates to the institutionalization of administrative innovations, namely family programs. These programs may be either internally or externally institutionalized. I investigate the complexity of the innovation process by examining the effects of: (1) boundary-spanning units, (2) organizational approaches to problem-solving, and (3) the organizational life-cycle to explain the institutionalization of family programs.

THEORY AND HYPOTHESES

Drawing on the complex organization literature, I view the institutionalization of family programs as an outcome of organizational decision making mechanisms that allocate slack resources to innovations. Innovative behavior is influenced by organizational structures that determine the flow of information into a firm and within it, and the complexity of decision making processes (Fennell 1984; Mintzberg 1979). This approach takes both an organizational and an institutional/environmental slant in explaining how a firm's boundary-spanning units and problem-solving approach influence innovation.

Boundary-Spanning Units

One boundary-spanning unit influencing innovative behavior in organizations is the governing board. This group represents a powerful constituency that: (1) monitors the organization's environment, (2) affects information flows into and within the organization, and (3) directly shapes innovative policies (Fennell and Alexander 1987; Alexander and Scott 1984; Mintzberg 1979). Diversity in board membership is paramount to diversity in boundary-spanning functions; in turn, I expect greater diversity in boundary-spanning units to facilitate the recognition of and response to work-family conflicts. Under these conditions, governing board size and leadership turnover may increase the institutionalization of family programs by increasing the flow of innovative information.

Hypothesis 1a.   Governing board size increases the likelihood of institutionalizing family programs.

Hypothesis 1b.   High governing board turnover increases the likelihood of institutionalizing family programs.

Human resource departments are another organizational feature that increase the availability of family program information into and throughout organizations. Furthermore, human resource professionals may directly or indirectly influence companies through their presence in innovative institutional environments. In an industrial environment characterized by a high number of human resource employees, these employees comprise a constituency that shares professional values supportive of innovative human resource programs (i.e., a normative isomorphic constituency). This group can exert a concerted effort to promote family programs when companies in which its members are embedded rely on this professional labor market. Companies sharing a common industrial labor market also face pressures to behave similarly (i.e., mimetic forces). Consequently, companies interacting within the same human resource environment—or drawing from a labor market comprised largely of human resource professionals—may mimic one another by adopting family programs (Zucker 1987). Hypothesis 1c addresses the effect of human resource departments and employees as a reflection of boundary-spanning processes:

Hypothesis 1c.   Human resource environment size—or higher proportions of human resource workers in a firm's labor market—increases the likelihood of institutionalizing family programs.

Organizational Approaches to Problem-Solving

Previous research has related innovative behavior to: (1) organizational structures, (2) institutional environments, and (3) the personal characteristics of organizational leaders/authorities (Fennell 1984). Kanter (1983) brings together these approaches to innovative behavior in her conceptualizations of integrative action and segmentalism. Conducting case studies of ten core companies and more than 115 innovations, Kanter reveals various conditions that either facilitate or impede innovative behavior. Fundamental to these conditions' existence and their ability to promote innovation was the firm's orientation to problem-solving. Integrative action and segmentalism represent organizational orientations to problem-solving. As defined by Kanter (1983), integrative action and its approach to problem-solving consist of the "willingness to move beyond received wisdom, to combine ideas from unconnected sources, to embrace change as an opportunity to tests limits" (Kanter 1983, p. 27). This approach sees problems as organizationally interrelated (i.e., contextually integrative) and inherently challenges established practices while fostering innovative behavior. Segmentalist approaches "see problems as narrowly as possible, independently of their context, independently of their connections to any other problems" (Kanter 1983, p. 28). This approach upholds traditional practices and restricts innovative behavior. Following Kanter's (1983) discussion, I expect that integrative approaches to problem-solving favor the institutionalization of family programs:

Hypothesis 2. Integrative approaches to problem-solving increase the likelihood of institutionalizing family programs.

Gender and Organizational Cultures

A company's method of solving problems pervades its culture and structure, both of which influence an organization's innovative behavior. Integrative problem-solving cultures and innovative behavior are associated with organizational structures that: (1) decrease conflict/isolation between organizational units, (2) increase flows of information and new ideas across organizational boundaries, (3) ensure multiple perspectives will be taken into account in decisions, and (4) maintain collaboration and direction to the whole organization. By contrast, segmentalist problem-solving cultures and stagnant (i.e., non-innovative) behaviors are associated with organizational structures that isolate segments from each other. Segmentalist organizational structures reduce horizontal and vertical linkages, constrict their information flows, and segregate labor from management and women from men.

Gender diversity in organizational structures and environments promotes the integration of multiple perspectives in decision making processes. When companies also use project teams, total quality management, quality circles, and matrix organizational designs, they further enhance their integrative problem-solving with reduced organizational boundaries, increased information flows, and heightened collaboration. A decision making environment that includes female employees may lead to greater innovation because this inclusiveness may reflect both the firm's dependance on female labor, and thus its need to provide programs that will retain female workers, and the fact that women may bring fresh perspectives to the decision making process. Given the preceding descriptions of organizational structures and environments that reflect and shape a firm's problem-solving approach, hypotheses 2a-2g concern integrative problem-solving structures and their innovative effects.

> **Hypotheses 2a, 2b, and 2c.** High proportions of women (2a) on governing boards, (2b) in managerial environments, and (2c) in human resource environments increase the likelihood of institutionalizing family programs.

> **Hypotheses 2d, 2e, 2f, and 2g.** The presence of (2d) project teams, (2e) total quality management, (2f) quality circles, and (2g) matrix structures increase the likelihood of institutionalizing family programs.

In addition to the innovative effects of boundary-spanning units and problem-solving approaches, I also draw upon the organizational life-cycle literature to explain the institutionalization of family programs.

Organizational Life-Course: Foundation Year, Profound Organizational Change, and Organizational Life-Cycle

From its roots in biological analogy, the traditional approach to the organizational life-cycle is primarily conceptualized in terms of birth, growth, maturation, and decline. This theory sees the life-cycle of an organization as progressive and sequential. Furthermore, the amount and types of social resources available at the time of an organization's foundation shape its social system (Kimberly and Miles 1981). An organization often retains structures instituted at its birth through its maturation (Stinchcombe 1965).

As Kanter (1983) argues, a major transformation of factors affecting organizational design has occurred within the last century (Kanter 1983, pp. 42-43). These design factors influence how an organization is constructed at its birth and how it subsequently operates. Design factors that existed in the early twentieth century reflect a traditional production process characterized by simple and physical tasks, mechanical technology, and the reliance on uneducated, unskilled career employees. In contrast, design factors emerging within the last 30 years reflect a production process that demands more complex and intellectual tasks, electronic and biological technologies, and an educated, sophisticated, and temporary workforce.

Organizations founded between 1890 and 1930 faced very different circumstances than those firms created after the 1960s. Stemming from their traditional design factors, those firms founded between 1890 and 1930 have been imprinted with segmentalist structures that may decrease its innovative behavior. On the other hand, organizations created after 1960 are influenced by factors that are more conducive to integrative action. Current organizational characteristics should not alter these effects:

> **Hypotheses 3a and 3b.** (3a) Those organizations founded between 1890 and 1930 are less likely to institutionalize family programs and (3b) those organizations founded between 1960 and the 1990s are more likely to institutionalize family programs.

An alternative conceptualization of the organizational life course views the stages of the life-cycle as reflecting various issues and problems of a subsystem. Rather than evolutionary or developmental, major organizational reconstructions do not necessarily have to follow a sequential pattern. Therefore, an organization may return to earlier stages. Finally, the pathways an organization may take toward certain transitions may differ over time due to changes in organizational and environmental characteristics (Whetten 1987).

In turn, various types of organizational restructuring have been associated with the implementation of high quality family policies (Galinsky, Friedman and Hernandez 1991). Previous work focuses on several profound organizational changes that should be especially salient for the adoption of family programs. If such changes reflect a lack of fit between an organization and its environment, the organization may be directing too many of its resources to other challenges to be able to address work-family programs. I expect that profound organizational changes will generally decrease the institutionalization of family programs:

> **Hypotheses 4a, 4b, 4c, and 4d.** (4a) Headquarter relocation, (4b) mergers, (4c) acquisitional behavior, and (4d) workforce change (i.e., expansion, downsizing) will decrease the likelihood of institutionalizing family programs, compared with conditions of no organizational restructuring.

As Cameron, Kim, and Whetten (1987) discuss, we can also conceptualize the organizational life-cycle by four stages: (1) growth, (2) decline, (3) stability, and (4) instability. Organizational growth and decline are related to conditions that appreciably increase or decrease a system's resource base over a specified time period. Instability (i.e., turbulence) is further defined as the presence of a nontrivial, rapid, and fluctuating resource base. On the other hand, either insignificant change or the lack of change empirically represents stability. Prior research has found that an organization experiencing an unstable or declining resource base is less likely to be innovative (see Cameron, Kim and Whetten 1987 for literature summary).

In turn, I hypothesize that a firm bases its innovative behavior on recent trends in its economic condition. In deciding whether to institutionalize a family program, a corporation compares its current financial circumstances with previous organizational experiences. However, a firm may also look to its institutional environment to gauge how well it is doing. While a company may be experiencing a period of organizational decline, the firm may—at the same time—be faring much better compared with other organizations in its institutional environment. Therefore, a company may also base its innovative behaviors on institutional comparisons.

I hypothesize that life-cycle stages determine organizational adoption of family programs. Generally, firms experiencing instability or decline will be less innovative than firms that are growing or stable:

Hypothesis 5.   Conditions of organizational decline or instability decrease the likelihood of institutionalizing family programs.

To analyze the innovative effects of boundary-spanning units, problem-solving approaches, and the organizational life-course, this study takes a dynamic approach by using longitudinal data and event history methods to study family program institutionalization.

DATA AND METHODS

Sample and Data Sources

To study the institutionalization of family programs, I use data collected from *The Corporate Reference Guide to Work-Family Programs* survey (Galinsky, Friedman and Hernandez 1991). In 1988 and 1989, the Families and Work Institute (FWI) conducted a survey of the ten largest companies from 30 industry groups of the *Fortune* 500 Industrial and 500 Service list (1988). These companies represent some of the most profitable firms in the United States as compiled by *Fortune* magazine. Since they are the most successful, these organizations tend to be highly visible and innovative. This sample is most likely to capture organizational innovative behavior.

With a response rate of 63 percent, the FWI survey collected detailed information from 188 firms. These 188 of the largest *Fortune* 1,000 firms represent this study's sample. The FWI data provides adequate event history information for five family program types (cafeteria plans, dependent care assistance packages, child care resource and referral, elder care resource and referral, and family leaves). This information was updated in late 1989 and early 1990.

Supplementing the FWI survey, I conducted a mail survey to collect additional information on organizational characteristics and family program adoption. I contacted human resource representatives from each firm in the sample to solicit information about executives who could answer questions concerning their company's family programs. I then mailed a questionnaire to these executives in early October of 1995. With 52 companies completing their questionnaires, this survey had a response rate of 28 percent. (A copy of the survey is available from the author.)

In the questionnaire, I ask human resource executives whether their firm has adopted such horizontal networking structures as project teams, quality circles, or total quality management. If such structures have been used, I request the year of adoption. Providing illustrations and definitions of pyramidal and matrix organizational designs, I ask that the respondent describe their previous and current organizational design. While the FWI survey compiled extensive family program information, data for year of program adoption is limited. Therefore, my supplemental survey collected additional event history information for four program types: flexplace, flextime, job-sharing, and part-time work schedules.

Besides this survey, I extract supplementary measures from existing archives. In choosing the years from which longitudinal archival data are compiled, it was necessary to get an indication of when the adoption of family programs first started. Constituting the first observation year, FWI survey data reveal that the earliest year of program adoption was 1974. Consequently, I gathered annual longitudinal information from archival sources for 1974 to 1993. While data up to 1995 (when I fielded this study's supplemental survey) would have been ideal, the last two years were not readily available. The sources of this archival information are the *Reference Book of Corporate Managements* (Dun and Bradstreet 1974, 1978, 1981, 1985, 1989, 1993), the *Million Dollar Directory* (Dun and Bradstreet, Inc. 1974, 1978, 1981, 1985, 1989, 1993), the *Fortune Double Directory* (Fortune 1974-1993), the *Second Fortune Double Directory* (Fortune 1974-1993), the March edition of the *Current Population Survey* (U.S. Census Bureau 1974-1993), and *Mergers and Acquisitions* (Mergers and Acquisitions 1974-1993).

While providing a wealth of longitudinal information, this data set has limitations. Reflecting the Family and Work Institutes' sampling technique that collects information from top-ranking companies from 30 industry groups of the *Fortune* Industrial 500 and *Fortune* Service 500, sample comparisons between the 1991 *Fortune* 1,000 population and FWI sample reveal the elite nature of the FWI sample. Average sales, profits, assets, stockholders' equity, and number of employees are consistently higher for the FWI sample, in comparison to the *Fortune* 1,000 sample.

A low response rate to the supplemental survey is another data set limitation (28% response rate). Those companies responding to the supplemental survey have lower average sales. However, respondents and non-respondents do not differ in their average net worth. Respondents have higher average number of employees in 1993. At the same time, they are less likely to be in a period of organizational decline. Finally, lower proportions of respondents have family leaves (73%) and flextime programs (60%) in 1991, compared with non-respondents (100% and 77%, respectively).

Given the selective sampling framework, the results of this study may not be indicative of the innovative processes found within companies that are smaller and less economically successful as those ranked among the *Fortune* 1,000. Further caution should be used when interpreting analyses that use the supplemental survey data given its small sample size.[1]

Measurement

In this analysis, I model three fundamental concepts that affect family program innovation: (1) boundary-spanning units, (2) problem-solving approaches, and (3) the organizational life-course. I also incorporate several control variables into my models. Appendix A summarizes the proposed measures, the observation years, and data sources.

Family Program Adoption

This study focuses on the adoption of the following family program types: (1) cafeteria plans (CAFE), (2) dependent care assistance packages (DCAP), (3) child care resource and referrals (CCRR), (4) elder care resource and referrals (ECRR), (5) family leave programs (LEAVE), (6) flextime (FLXT), (7) flexplace or telecommuting (FLXP), (8) part-time work schedules (PTWK), and (9) job-sharing programs (JOBS). I measure each of the family innovations as a discrete event in the year in which the program was available. I also construct an indicator of the first year (FIRST) in which any of five family programs (i.e., CAFE, DCAP, CCRR, ECRR, and LEAVE) were adopted (years were unavailable for the other indicators). This measurement approach captures the innovation (i.e., event) histories for each organization through information about: (1) timing, (2) type, and (3) multiple/tied occurrences of family program adoptions during the study period.

Boundary-Spanning Units and Problem-Solving Approaches

To measure the innovative influences of boundary-spanning units and organizational problem-solving approaches, I create several variables across the 1974 to 1993 time period. Analyzing boundary-spanning determinants of family program institutionalization, I measure two dimensions of governing boards: size and turnover. The total number of top and secondary governing board members represents governing board size. Change in the name of the chief executive officer or president between time (t) and time (t-5) is the first measure of leadership turnover. The second measure of leadership turnover consists of the proportion of top governing board members at time (t) who were not listed five years earlier (t-5). Controlling for changes in governing board size, this measure captures turnover rates of remaining governing board positions.

Another aspect of boundary-spanning I study is human resource environments. Using the *Current Population Survey* (March edition), I derive the prevalence of human resource personnel in the institutional environment from industry aggregates (30 collapsed categories of 3-digit census industry codes). This variable indicates the proportion of employees in human resource occupations within the industrial labor market.

Representing Kanter's (1983) conceptualizations of segmentalist and integrative approaches to problem-solving, several aspects of a company's structure are considered: the proportion of governing board members who are women, whether a company has a female governing board member (= 1), the presence of projects teams (= 1), total quality management (= 1), quality circles (= 1), other communication programs (= 1), and matrix organizational design (= 1). Besides these organizational characteristics, the industrial workforce—from which a company traditionally relies on for labor—may also shape and reflect a company's approach to problem-solving. Derived from industry aggregates using the CPS, two measures consist of the proportion of women in managerial and human resource occupations.

Organizational Life-Course: Foundation Year, Profound Organizational Change, and Organizational Life-Cycle

Three dimensions of the organizational life-course are incorporated into this study: foundation period, profound organizational change, and life-cycle stage. The age of a company is inextricably linked to its period of foundation. Thus, my analysis focuses on period effects while controlling for a firm's age. Ownership date is used as a proxy for the year in which a company was founded. Ten percent of the companies had archival data collected for years preceding their ownership date. To account for this foundation year discrepancy, the value "1974" (i.e., year of first observation) was assigned as the year a company was founded if there was pre-ownership data. A dummy variable (FYPRBLM) is created to control for errors resulting from ownership date and foundation year mismatch (= 1).

Indicators of headquarter relocation, merger and acquisition behavior, and workforce change are also constructed. Headquarter relocation indicates that a company experienced a change in address (= 1). This study's measures of acquisition behaviors consist of the total number of incidents in which (1) a sample company acquired any interest in another firm and (2) another firm acquired any interest in a sample company. Whether a company has experienced a merger (= 1) is another measure of profound organizational change. Finally, the measure of workforce change consists of the proportional change in the number of employees between time (t) and time (t-1).

I construct two sets of life-cycle stage indicators that capture fluctuations in a company's net worth relative to the organization itself and to the Fortune 1,000 institutional environment (see notes for details on the classification system.)[2] Following work by Alexander, Fennell and Halpern (1993) and Cameron, Kim and Whetten (1987), each firm's resource base is characterized along two dimensions of change: (1) growth, decline, or stationary (a set of dummy variables where stationary is the omitted category) and (2) stable or unstable (unstable is the omitted category). To estimate a firm's resource base, net worth is calculated as the sum of four monetary measures: sales, profits, assets and equity.

Controls

Previous research has suggested additional variables that influence innovative behavior. Reflecting increased employee demand or a firm's desire to reduce absentee and quit rates of those most likely to experience work-family conflicts (Auerbach 1990; McNeely and Fogarty 1988), high proportions of female employees are likely to increase the adoption of all family programs. Using the CPS, I construct an industry-level measure of female representation in labor markets from which a company traditionally relies. Using *Fortune* data, I measure organizational size as the number of employees (logged). A positive association between organizational size and the adoption of family programs generally indicates the firm's greater demand for programs and returns-to-scale. However, a negative association between organizational size and innovation adoption reflects the firm's higher dependence on formalization and bureaucracy; both of which decrease innovative behavior (Scott 1987; Kimberly and Evanisko 1981). Additional controls include measures of: (1) slack resource base (log of net worth), (2) regional location (northeast, midwest, west, and south as omitted category), (3) service industry, and (4) subsidiary company status.

Discrete-Time Event History Analysis

Since event histories of family program adoption are measured in yearly intervals, the most appropriate analytical technique is discrete-time analysis (Allison 1984). Documentation of this study's event history file construction is available from the author.

To test hypotheses 1a-1c, 2, 2a-2g, 3a-3b, 4a-4d, and 5, the general logit regression model takes the following form:

$$\log \frac{P_{ij}(t)}{1 - P_{ij}(t)} = a_t + \begin{matrix} B_1\,V + B_2\,W + B_3 X \\ + B_4 (\text{Controls}) \end{matrix}$$

Where V =   vector of boundary-spanning variables;
            W =   vector of problem-solving approach variables;
            X =   vector of organization life-course variables; and
            Pij =   hazard rate specified as a conditional probability that a
                             program is institutionalized at time t.

In this model, B_1, B_2, B_3, and B_4 represent the coefficients of lagged independent variables that more adequately capture their causal relationships with family program institutionalization. These coefficients indicate the effects of the explanatory variables on the instantaneous probability of an event. A one-unit increase in an independent variable changes the logit (i.e., log-odds) of having a program by the value of its parameter. Further, a_t indicates that the unparameterized (i.e., unknown) baseline hazard rate is allowed to vary over time. The number of years without a family program is modeled to determine the actual shape of this underlying hazard function of innovation (Allison 1984).

To maximize the number of models that would converge, I analyze each vector of variables separately along with the set of controls. Appendix B provides event history sample size information for each model.

ANALYSIS PRESENTATION

Family Program Descriptive Statistics

Table 1 shows that most family programs have been adopted after 1985. Yet these programs vary significantly as to when they entered the institutional realm of innovation choices. For instance, the earliest any company in this sample first started adopting elder care resource and referrals was in 1985. On the other hand, these corporations have institutionalized work scheduling programs and family leaves as early as 1974.

Figures 1 and 2 also present trends in the institutionalization of these innovations.[3] Looking at the cumulative proportions of companies having a given program (Figures 1 and 2), we see that family program innovation has quickly spread across this sample of elite companies. In 1974, only 1 percent of this sample had either cafeteria plans, dependent care assistance packages, child care and elder care resources and referrals, or family leave programs. After 1984, companies rapidly increased their repertoire of family support. In fact, nearly every company in 1991 (99%) had at least one family program. Family leave and part-time work schedules are the most popular programs with, respectively, 90 percent and 71 percent of the sample providing these supports in 1991. Following in popularity, 53 percent of this sample offered flextime programs while 51 percent provided dependent care assistance packages in 1991.

Table 1.   Distribution of Family Program Year of Adoption

Program Type	Mean	SD	Range
FWI Data			
FIRST	1986.0	3.3	1974-1991
CAFE	1987.3	2.4	1980-1991
DCAP	1987.5	2.1	1981-1991
CCRR	1986.6	2.3	1982-1991
ECRR	1988.4	1.8	1985-1991
LEAVE	1985.4	4.7	1974-1989
Survey Data			
FLXT	1987.5	5.2	1974-1995
FLXP	1991.0	4.6	1974-1995
JOBS	1989.3	4.9	1974-1995
PTWK	1982.0	7.7	1974-1995

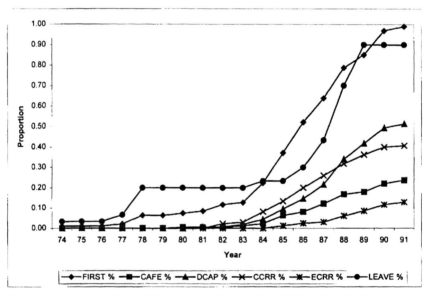

Figure 1.   Proportion of Companies Institutionalizing Family Programs
by Innovation Type, 1974-1991 (FWI Survey, $N = 188$)

Independent Variables Descriptive Statistics

Cross-sectional comparisons (Table 2) show significant changes in the characteristics of this sample of *Fortune* 1,000 companies between 1978 and 1993. As of
1978, the *Fortune* 1,000 workforce was expanding at an annual rate of 5 percent.

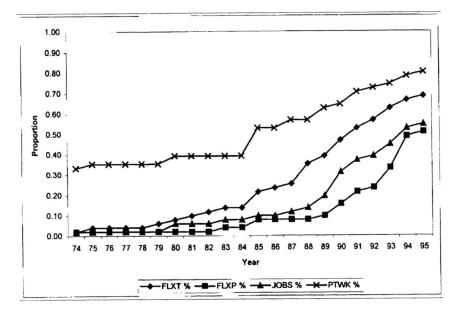

Figure 2. Proportion of Companies Institutionalizing Family Programs by Innovation Type, 1974-1995 (Supplemental Survey, $N = 52$)

In contrast, companies in this sample were downsizing their workforce at a rate of 6 percent in 1993. Trends in downsizing parallel changes in boundary-spanning units. The number of governing board members has dropped from an average of 39 to 30 members. The proportion of employees who are in human resource occupations has also decreased from .7 percent to .3 percent.

During this period of fluctuating employment opportunities, women's representation in the workforce steadily increased by 7 percentage points. Women also made inroads into managerial occupations. In 1993, 83 percent of *Fortune* 1,000 companies had at least one woman on their governing board, compared with 53 percent in 1978. Reflecting the token nature of female governing board representation, the proportion of governing board members who are women has slightly increased from 2 to 7 percent. However, low- and middle-management occupations have experienced a 23-percentage point increase in female representation. Finally, human resource occupations have become female-dominated with 86 percent female human resource workers in 1993 versus 25 percent in 1978.

Besides the rise in female representation in managerial and human resource environments, increased adoption of communication programs and matrix structures further suggests changes in problem-solving approaches. As of 1993, 81 percent and 68 percent of this sample used project teams and total quality management, respectively. While pyramid designs are still used by 80 percent of

Table 2. Descriptive Statistics of Independent Variables

Label	1978 Cross-Section Mean	1993 Cross-Section Mean	1993-1978 Difference
NEAST	0.45	0.39	−0.08
MIDW	0.32	0.31	−0.01
WEST	0.12	0.11	−0.01
SOUTH	0.12	0.20	0.08*
SALES (million$)	14510	16208	1698
PROFIT (million$)	761	498	−263
ASSET (million$)	16604	24813	8209*
EQUITY (million$)	452	4101	3649*
NET (million$)	34898	43892	8994
EMP	68291	63854	−4437*
%EMP-F	0.32	0.39	0.07
SUBSID	0.02	0.14	0.12*
SERVIND	0.21	0.27	0.06
GVB	38.97	29.90	−9.07*
NEWCEO	0.45	0.50	0.05
%GVB-N	0.37	0.37	0.00
%EMP-HR	0.0067	0.0031	−0.0036*
%GVB-F	0.02	0.07	0.05*
FGVB	0.53	0.83	0.30*
%MNG-F	0.13	0.36	0.23*
%HR-F	0.25	0.86	0.61*
NEWHQ	0.15	0.22	0.07
NEWSTATE	0.03	0.07	0.04
ACQ	0.41	1.23	0.82*
BACQ	0.02	1.09	1.07*
MERGER	0.05	0.01	−0.05*
DOWNSIZE	0.05	−0.06	−0.11*
O-GROW	0.19	0.08	−0.11*
O-DECLINE	0.00	0.05	0.05*
O-NOCHING	0.81	0.88	0.07
O-STABLE	0.39	0.25	−0.14*
O-UNSTABLE	0.61	0.75	0.14*
I-GROW	0.09	0.11	0.02
I-DECLINE	0.04	0.01	−0.03
I-NOCHING	0.87	0.88	0.01
I-STABLE	0.25	0.24	−0.01
I-UNSTABLE	0.75	0.76	0.01

(continued)

Table 2   (Continued)

Label	1978 Cross-Section Mean	1993 Cross-Section Mean	1993-1978 Difference
PJTM	0.20	0.81	0.61*
TQM	0.11	0.68	0.57*
QC	0.05	0.54	0.49*
OTHCOM	0.05	0.40	0.35*
MATRIX	0.08	0.20	0.12*
FYPRBLM	—	0.09	—
COAGE	—	78.35	—
FY-30	—	0.65	—
FY-3159	—	0.13	—
FY-60	—	0.21	—

Note: Significant differences between 1993 and 1974 cross-sectional means are designated with an asterick ($p < .05$).

this sample (in 1993), the implementation of matrix designs has increased by 12 percentage points since 1974.

Possibly constraining innovative behaviors, this sample of firms has experienced a rise in profound organizational changes and resource base instability and decline. On average, a sample firm acquired interest in another company approximately 1.23 times in 1993. Furthermore, these sample companies had interest acquired by another firm 1.09 times that year. These acquisitional behaviors have dramatically increased since 1978. At the same time, the number of mergers has fallen from .05 occurrences to .01 per firm, on average.

Along with these profound organizational changes, this sample is 11 percentage points less likely to be in a period of organizational growth in 1993 than it was 15 years prior. Organizational decline and instability have become more prevalent with, respectively, 5 percent and 75 percent of these firms experiencing declining and unstable resource bases in 1993.

Event History Analyses

Table 3 presents the results of my series of event history analyses. The first model illustrates the effects of control variables on the institutionalization of family programs. Over time, companies increasingly institutionalize a host of family programs. The longer a company is without a program, the more likely the firm is to adopt and institutionalize cafeteria plans (CAFE), dependent care assistance packages (DCAP), child and elder care resource and referral systems (CCRR and ECRR), family leave programs (LEAVE), flextime (FLXT), flexplace (FLXP), and job-sharing programs (JOBS). However, companies are not likely to institutionalize part-time work schedules (PTWK) as time passes. One explanation may

Table 3. Parameter Estimates of Family Program Institutionalization

	FIRST	CAFE	DCAP	CCRR	LEAVE	FLXT	FLXP	JOBS	PTWK
MODEL 1: CONTROLS									
INTERCEPT	-17.29*	-2.33	-10.80*	-23.18*	-10.01	-26.18*	-19.08*	-15.79*	-7.45*
	(2.99)	(2.70)	(2.04)	(2.92)	(4.56)	(4.22)	(4.30)	(4.00)	(3.32)
YWO	0.44*	0.14*	0.25*	0.07+	0.31*	0.14*	0.22*	0.15*	0.00
	(0.04)	(0.04)	(0.03)	(0.04)	(0.05)	(0.03)	(0.05)	(0.04)	(0.02)
NEAST	0.43	0.50	0.56*	0.65*	2.28*	-0.14	-0.66	-0.59	-0.40
	(0.32)	(0.48)	(0.29)	(0.32)	(1.06)	(0.40)	(0.46)	(0.41)	(0.35)
MIDW	1.37*	0.97*	0.56+	0.28	3.00*	-0.78+	-0.27	-0.63	-0.27
	(0.37)	(0.46)	(0.30)	(0.35)	(1.23)	(0.42)	(0.45)	(0.41)	(0.38)
WEST	-1.26*	1.26*	0.50	-1.02+	1.87	-0.13	-1.18+	-2.89*	-0.77
	(0.55)	(0.53)	(0.38)	(0.58)	(1.19)	(0.60)	(0.69)	(0.78)	(0.67)
LNET	0.75*	-0.02	0.33*	1.08*	0.23	1.22*	1.05*	1.11*	0.26
	(0.18)	(0.16)	(0.12)	(0.16)	(0.36)	(0.25)	(0.25)	(0.25)	(0.22)
LEMP	-0.64*	-0.17	-0.05	-0.45*	-0.23	-0.51*	-0.89*	-1.25*	0.03
	(0.18)	(0.17)	(0.13)	(0.16)	(0.44)	(0.23)	(0.23)	(0.24)	(0.22)
%EMP-F	2.70*	0.95	1.18*	2.37*	3.02*	1.85+	1.95+	3.27*	1.14
	(0.79)	(0.77)	(0.60)	(0.78)	(1.42)	(0.96)	(1.17)	(1.06)	(0.82)
SUBSID	0.50	-1.01	-1.11	-0.10	-0.98	-0.51	-1.30	-1.42+	-0.45
	(0.79)	(1.04)	(0.76)	(0.68)	(1.55)	(0.81)	(1.09)	(0.82)	(1.12)
SERVI	-0.92*	-0.21	-0.49+	-2.69*	-0.62	-1.59*	-0.84	-1.60*	-0.25
	(0.37)	(0.39)	(0.29)	(0.44)	(0.81)	(0.51)	(0.57)	(0.56)	(0.48)
MODEL 2: BOUNDARY-SPANNING[a]									
GVB	0.00	0.03*	0.00	0.02*		0.00	-0.01	0.02	
	(0.01)	(0.01)	(0.01)	(0.01)		(0.01)	(0.01)	(0.00)	
%EMP-HR	-21.95	59.83*	28.19	-39.75		36.39	21.97	1.03	
	(23.75)	(25.35)	(20.43)	(25.43)		(35.91)	(48.33)	(40.20)	
NEWCEO	0.48*	-0.21	-0.04	0.12		0.66*	-1.10*	-0.09	
	(0.24)	(0.26)	(0.19)	(0.22)		(0.29)	(0.38)	(0.30)	
%GVB-N	0.67	-1.28*	0.26	0.72		-1.58*	0.35	-1.47+	
	(0.57)	(0.63)	(0.45)	(0.52)		(0.76)	(0.93)	(0.86)	
MODEL 3: INTEGRATIVE PROBLEM-SOLVING AND FEMALE REPRESENTATION[a]									
FGVB	0.43	0.59+	-0.31	-0.36	1.28*	1.30*	1.78*	1.00*	1.16*
	(0.29)	(0.34)	(0.24)	(0.31)	(0.60)	(0.39)	(0.58)	(0.41)	(0.36)
%MNG-F	4.82*	0.68	3.59*	6.01*	6.52*	0.25	-4.22*	-0.51	2.21
	(1.45)	(1.69)	(1.34)	(1.83)	(2.11)	(1.43)	(1.87)	(1.46)	(1.43)
%HR-F	0.34	0.31	0.30	-0.30	1.07+	0.76+	0.87	0.56	0.13
	(0.36)	(0.36)	(0.28)	(0.36)	(0.55)	(0.43)	(0.56)	(0.44)	(0.46)

(continued)

Table 3 (Continued)

	FIRST	CAFE	DCAP	CCRR	LEAVE	FLXT	FLXP	JOBS	PTWK
MODEL 4: INTEGRATIVE PROBLEM-SOLVING, COMMUNICATION PROGRAMS, AND MATRIX DESIGN[a]									
PJTM	2.10+		-0.14			-0.58	0.52	-0.31	
	(1.11)		(0.68)			(0.49)	(0.57)	(0.48)	
TQM	-2.61		2.55*			2.23*	0.14	1.30*	
	(1.95)		(1.05)			(0.66)	(0.67)	(0.63)	
QC	1.48		-1.31			0.10	0.73	1.05+	
	(1.59)		(0.87)			(0.61)	(0.61)	(0.60)	
OTHCOM	-1.95+		0.59			0.03	1.88*	1.65*	
	(1.07)		(0.65)			(0.50)	(0.54)	(0.50)	
MATRIX	-3.65+		-2.49*			2.19*	0.94	1.26+	
	(2.20)		(1.08)			(0.76)	(0.66)	(0.67)	
MODEL 5: FOUNDATION YEAR AND PROFOUND ORGANIZATIONAL CHANGE[a]									
FYPRBLM	0.79			2.78*				0.61	-1.05
	(0.75)			(1.10)				(1.35)	(1.19)
COAGE	0.01			0.00				0.00	0.00
	(0.01)			(0.00)				(0.01)	(0.01)
FY-3159	-0.01			0.51				0.52	-0.82
	(0.44)			(0.44)				(0.85)	(0.68)
FY-60	-1.13			-2.32*				-0.34	-0.40
	(0.75)			(1.13)				(0.97)	(0.70)
NEWHQ	0.02			0.08				-0.41	0.46
	(0.35)			(0.31)				(0.43)	(0.34)
ACQ	0.01			0.07				0.13	-0.17+
	(0.06)			(0.06)				(0.08)	(0.10)
BACQ	-0.21			-0.15				0.36*	0.16
	(0.17)			(0.18)				(0.17)	(0.15)
MERGER	-0.38			0.39				1.41	-0.09
	(0.78)			(0.85)				(0.92)	(0.92)
DOWNSIZE	0.90			0.51				-0.25	0.97
	(0.67)			(0.41)				(0.31)	(1.00)
MODEL 6: ORGANIZATIONAL LIFE-CYCLE[a]									
O-GROW	1.09*			1.27*					
	(0.46)			(0.48)					
O-DECLINE	0.35			0.99					
	(0.79)			(0.72)					
O-UNSTABLE	-0.38			0.36					
	(0.40)			(0.43)					

(continued)

Table 3   (Continued)

	FIRST	CAFE	DCAP	CCRR	LEAVE	FLXT	FLXP	JOBS	PTWK
MODEL 7: INSTITUTIONAL LIFE-CYCLE[a]									
I-GROW	1.07[+]		1.35[*]	0.56		0.05			
	(0.58)		(0.67)	(0.61)		(0.66)			
I-DECLINE	1.13		1.09	1.32[+]		−0.71			
	(0.83)		(0.85)	(0.79)		(1.20)			
I-UNSTABLE	0.38		1.08[+]	0.17		−0.14			
	(0.49)		(0.63)	(0.53)		(0.55)			

Notes: $^*p < .05$
$^+p < .10$
Numbers in parenthesis are standard errors. Estimates are unstandardized regression coefficients.
Event history sample sizes for each model are reported in Appendix B.
[a]Controls used in analysis but not shown consist of years without program, region, log of net worth, log of number of employees, percent of industrial workforce that are female, subsidiary status, and service industry.

be the long tradition of using part-time work to manage slack labor demands and to reduce labor costs. Given this long institutional tradition, corporations may implement part-time work early only when it benefits their production process and reduces labor costs. While similar concerns motivate the institutionalization of other innovations, most family programs have not been within the institutional nexus of innovation choices until recently.

Indicated by the composite measure of net worth, wealthier companies are more likely to institutionalize family programs. Ability to pay (i.e., large slack resource base) increases innovativeness in family programs. Companies facing an industrial workforce characterized by high proportions of female employees are also more likely to institutionalize programs. This innovative effect reflects a firm's desire to recruit and retain workers from a labor pool that is most likely to experience high levels of work-family conflict. However, large numbers of workers employed at a firm decreases the chances that it has family programs. Controlling for resource base size, the negative effect of workforce size indicates innovative barriers due to a company's reliance on formalization and bureaucracy.

Controlling for company subsidiary status, slack resource base, size and labor force gender composition, being in a service industry generally reduces the likelihood of having a family program. The effects of service industry on family program adoption indicate location-specific processes that influence innovativeness. Large manufacturing companies have relatively few establishments, each of which employs large numbers of workers. In contrast, service companies operate within industries that have a larger number of work sites with relatively fewer employees per establishment. For instance, hotels, banks, fast-food, and health care industries are characterized by geographically dispersed work sites with relatively small numbers of employees. Therefore, lower economies of scale associated with smaller service establishments reduce the institutionalization of family programs (Osterman 1995).

Event History Analyses of Boundary-Spanning Units

The second section in Table 3 presents the results of the boundary-spanning unit model (control variable coefficients do not significantly change across models; thus they are not shown). Through increased information flows and the reduction of organizational inertia, a new chief executive officer is an advocate for the adoption of a company's first family program. However, CEO turnover reduces the likelihood of adopting flexplace programs. High turnover of other governing board members also generally reduces the adoption of family programs. One explanation for these findings is that high leadership turnover fosters decision making instability and lowers innovative risk taking. Overall, little support has been found for Hypothesis 1b.

In contrast, analyses show that size of governing boards and reliance on human resource labor markets generally increase the likelihood of having family programs. Interpreting these effects, a company's large governing board and its ties to human resource environments seem to expand the flow of innovative information into an organization and subsequently increase its family program institutionalization. Hence, there is some support for Hypotheses 1a and 1c.

Event History Analyses of Integrative Problem-solving Approaches

Model 3 shows analyses focusing on the integrative role of women in organizations. Having a woman on the governing board generally increases the likelihood of having family programs. High proportions of women in managerial and human resource environments also generally increase the institutionalization of family programs. Employers have an institutional incentive to adopt family programs. "Family-friendly" companies that recruit employees from industrial labor markets characterized by high female-representation in managerial and human resource occupations may find it easier to attract and retain these women.

Reducing segmentalism in problem-solving, communication programs generally increase the likelihood of having family programs (Model 4). Analyses also indicate that matrix designs promote the institutionalization of family programs. Matrix structures increase the chances of having flextime and job-sharing programs through reductions in administration problems associated with complex work scheduling within and among organizational units. However, pyramid structures are more conducive to the institutionalization of dependent care assistance programs. While matrix designs provide a communicatively integrative structure that support the institutionalization of DCAPs, pyramidal designs best serve in their implementation (analyses not shown). In sum, analyses support Hypotheses 2a-2g but with qualifications as to the integrative nature of matrix structures.

Event History Analyses of Foundation Year and Profound Organizational Change

Controlling for systematic errors in the measure for foundation year, the variable FYPRBLM is also a proxy for changes in ownership (see discussion on variable construction). Presenting Model 5 results, it follows that ownership change increases the chances that a company has a child care resource referral system. Loss of control over one's holdings (i.e., BACQ) also increases the institutionalization of the flexplace programs. However, inconsistent or insignificant effects of foundation period were found. Hence, these results provide little insight into how a company's period of foundation affects innovative behaviors (Hypotheses 3a and 3b). Furthermore, limited support is found for the argument that profound organizational change reduces innovation (Hypotheses 4a-4d). In fact, there is some indication that organizational change actually creates the opportunity to innovate.

Event History Analyses of Organizational and Industrial Life-Cycle

Looking at Models 6 and 7 analyses, firms undergoing a period of organizational growth are more likely to institutionalize family programs (especially child care resource and referral programs), compared to those who are experiencing no change or decline in their slack resource base. Furthermore, companies that are growing at a faster rate than other *Fortune* 1,000 firms are more likely to institutionalize dependent care assistance packages (DCAPs). In turn, analyses show some support for Hypothesis 5, indicating that organizational growth increases the chances of an organization adopting these innovations.

CONCLUSIONS

With the rising labor force participation of women and the accompanying escalation of work-family conflict, investigating organizational attempts to reduce such conflict is important. This analysis addresses basic questions about the declining boundary between work and the family. Specifically, what organizational characteristics help integrate the workplace and the family? Furthermore, we gain insight into how organizations can be innovative in facing an ever-changing labor force environment. Consequently, this study informs both private and public policy efforts.

Despite their wealth, companies that employ a large workforce typically have difficulty institutionalizing family programs. High costs in providing family supports to a large number of employees are a hindrance to innovation. However, firms face additional barriers when integrating a large number of employees into production processes, whereby they typically rely more heavily on formalization and bureaucracy. Established practices and bureaucratic systems constrain innovation when companies are unable to maneuver within or modify their own subsystems (i.e., organizational inertia).

Large corporations can promote innovation by reducing organizational inertia in different ways. While I have analyzed a variety of determinants, the most important of this study's findings is the consistent support for the innovative effects of integrative problem-solving. Female representation on governing boards and reliance on industrial labor markets dominated by women in managerial and human resource occupations generally increase family program institutionalization. Given the low proportion of female governing board members, it is hard to believe that so few have so much power. Rather, this positive effect indicates an organizational shift toward a more integrative problem-solving approach. This cultural change supports both the desirability of having at least one woman on the governing board member as well as family programs. Likewise, total quality management, communication programs, and matrix organizational design promote innovation. Hence, a cultural shift towards integrative problem-solving is an important first step in the innovation process that increases the types and amounts of information flowing into and within an organization.

An alternative interpretation of these findings assumes that my industry-level measure of female managerial representation serves as a proxy for internal structures. With this in mind, lower- and middle-management actually represent a key information channel from production workers to higher authorities. High female representation in this information flow is conducive to integrative problem-solving and innovative behaviors. Since professionals and management may also play the role of advocate of their own interests, women in lower- and middle-management may actually reduce innovation if a family program undermines their authority or power, as indicated by the negative relationship between flexplace adoption and female-representation in management.

Large governing boards and human resource environments also increase the chances that a company has family programs. By fostering boundary-spanning activities of governing boards and human resource departments, firms can promote innovation by more effectively monitoring their institutional environment. Low governing board membership turnover coupled with the arrival of a new chief executive officer further maximizes innovation opportunities. These effects of leadership turnover reflect the delicate innovative process by which companies reduce organizational inertia while increasing decision making capabilities.

Besides the innovative effects of integrative problem-solving and boundary-spanning activities, there is also some indication that organizational life-cycle stage affects innovation. Companies experiencing growth in net worth are the most innovative. The same is true for those firms growing at a faster rate than the rest of the *Fortune* 1,000 population.

While this study provides insight into innovation processes found within America's most successful corporations, additional research on a broad array of organizations needs to be conducted. Analyses investigating innovative "thresholds" as they relate to program cost, company wealth, and workforce size would be especially useful. Helping us to further understand how companies come to invest into comprehensive and high quality family programs, studies focusing on the parallel and synergistic innovation processes would also be beneficial.

Companies are primarily motivated to instititutionalize family programs when they increase productivity and reduce labor costs from absenteeism and turnover. Likewise, individuals who are seeking employment may find it beneficial to work in firms with family programs. Reduction in work-family conflict is one obvious benefit from working in corporations that provide family programs. However, an organization's institutionalization of a family program does not necessarily benefit all workers. Specific characteristics (i.e., quality and convenience) and programmatic guidelines of a family program may constrain employee utilization of these supports.

Appendix A. Variables, Measures, Data Sources, and Observation Years

Variables	Label	Measures	Data Source[a]	Observation Years
Family Program Innovation				
1. First Family Program	FIRST	Presence of First Family Program	FWI	1974 to 1991
2. Cafeteria Plan	CAFE	Presence of Cafeteria Plan	FWI	1974 to 1991
3. Dependent Care Assistance Package	DCAP	Presence of Dependent Care Assistance Package	FWI	1974 to 1991
4. Child Care Resource and Referral	CCRR	Presence of Child Care Resource and Referral	FWI	1974 to 1991
5. Elder Care Resource and Referral	ECRR	Presence of Elder Care Resource and Referral	FWI	1974 to 1991
6. Family Leave Beyond Maternity Disability Leave	LEAVE	Presence of Family Leave Beyond Maternity Disability Leave	FWI	1974 to 1991
7. Flextime	FLXT	Presence of Flextime	Survey	1974 to 1995
8. Flexplace (Telecommuting)	FLXP	Presence of Flexplace (Telecommuting)	Survey	1974 to 1995
9. Job Sharing	JOBS	Presence of Job Sharing	Survey	1974 to 1995
10. Part-Time Work Schedules	PTWK	Presence of Part-Time Work Schedules	Survey	1974 to 1995
Boundary-Spanning Unites				
1. Governing Board Size	GVB	# of Top and Secondary Governing Board Members	RBCM/MDD	1974, 1978, 1981, 1985, 1989, 1993
2. Governing Board Leader Turnover	NEWCEO	CEO Name Change between Time (1) and Time (2)	RBCM/MDD	1974, 1978, 1981, 1985, 1989, 1993
3. Governing Board Membership Turnover	%GVB-N	% of Top Governing Board Members at Time (2) Not Listed at Time (1)	RBCM/MDD	1974, 1978, 1981, 1985, 1989, 1993
4. Human Resource Environment Size	%EMP-HR	% of Industrial Labor Market Environment in Human Resource Occupation	CPS	1974 to 1993

(continued)

227

Appendix A (Continued)

Variables	Label	Measures	Data Source[a]	Observation Years
Problem-Solution Approach				
1. Female Governing Board Representation	%GVB-F	% of Governing Board Members that are Female	RBCM/MDD	1974, 1978, 1981, 1985, 1989, 1993
2. Female Governing Board Member	FGVB	Female Governing Board Member	RBCM/MDD	1974, 1978, 1981, 1985, 1989, 1993
3. Female Management Environment	%MNG-F	% of Industrial Labor Market Environment in Managerial Occupations that are Female	CPS	1974 to 1993
4. Female Human Resource Environment	%HR-F	% of Industrial Labor Market Environment in Human Resource Occupations that are Female	CPS	1974 to 1993
5. Project Teams	PJTM	Presence of Project Teams	Survey	1974 to 1995
6. Total Quality Management	TQM	Presence of Total Quality Management	Survey	1974 to 1995
7. Quality Circles	QC	Presence of Quality Circles	Survey	1974 to 1995
8. Other Communication Programs	OTHCOM	Presence of Other Communication Programs	Survey	1974 to 1995
9. Matrix Structure	MATRIX	Presence of Matrix Structure	Survey	1974 to 1995
Organizational Life-Course				
1. Company Age	COAGE	Foundation Year-Survey Year	MDD	1993
2. Foundation Period	FY-30 FY-3159 FY-60	1890 to 1930; 1930 to 1960; 1960 to Survey Year	MDD	1993
3. Headquarter Relocation	NEWHQ	Change in Company Address	RBCM/MDD	1974, 1978, 1981, 1985, 1989, 1993
4. Acquisition and Mergers	ACQ	# of Incidents that Sample Company Acquired Any Interest in Another Firm	M&A	1974 to 1993
	BACQ	# of Incidents that Sample Company had Any Holdings Acquired by Another Firm	M&A	1974 to 1993
	MERGER	Sample Company Merged with Another Firm	M&A	1974 to 1993

Organizational Life-Course (continued)

	Code	Description	Source	Years
5. Downsizing	DOWNSIZE	Proportional Change in # of Employees	Fortune	1974 to 1993
6. Organizational Relative Change in Resource Base (3%) Over Last 5 Years	O-GROW O-DECLINE O-NOCHG O-UNSTABLE O-STABLE	Proportional Change in Net Worth; Organizational Comparison	Fortune	1974 to 1993
7. Industrial Relative Charge in Resource Base (3%) Over Last 5 Years	I-GROW I-DECLINE I-NOCHG I-UNSTABLE I-STABLE	Proportional Change in Net Worth; Industrial Comparison	Fortune	1974 to 1993

Control Variables

	Code	Description	Source	Years
1. Years without Family Program	YWO	# of Years without Family Program	FWI/Survey	1974 to 1995
2. Regional Location	NEAST MIDW WEST SOUTH	Regional Location	RBCM/MDD	1974, 1978, 1981, 1985, 1989, 1993
3. Resource Base	LNET SALES PROFIT ASSET EQUITY	Net Worth = Sales + Profits + Asset + Equity (1993 Dollars) (Logged)	Fortune	1974 to 1993
4. Size	LEMP	# of Employees (Logged)	Fortune	1974 to 1993
5. Female Employee Environment	%EMP-F	% of Industrial Labor Market that are Female	CPS	1974 to 1993
6. Subsidiary Company	SUBSID	Subsidiary Company Status	RBCM/MDD	1974, 1978, 1981, 1985, 1989, 1993
7. Service Industry	SERVIND	Collapsed to Reflect 3-Digit Census Codes	Fortune	1974 to 1993

Notes: [a]FWI = Family Work Institute Survey; = Supplemental Survey, RBCM = Reference Book of Corporate Managements; MDD = Million Dollar Directory, Fortune = Fortune Double 500 Directory and Second Fortune Double 500 Directory; M&A = Mergers and Acquisitions; CPS = Current Population Survey

Appendix B.   Event History Sample Size by Model

MODEL	FIRST	CAFE	DCAP	CCRR	LEAVE	FLXT	FLXP	JOBS	PTWK
1	809	1271	1075	794	286	499	398	481	365
2	578	1206	1016	742	—	415	369	453	—
3	595	915	742	545	218	361	276	358	295
4	217	—	272	—	—	409	323	388	—
5	556	—	—	697	—	—	349	427	—
6	565	—	—	722	—	—	—	—	—
7	565	—	991	722	—	405	—	—	—

ACKNOWLEDGMENT

The author thanks Kevin Leicht, Mary Fennell, Dennis Hogan, Daniel Lichter, David Ribar, and David Eggebeen for their helpful comments. Grants from the National Science Foundation and the Pennsylvania State University supported this research. An earlier version of this paper was presented at the 1997 American Sociological Association Meetings. Findings of this paper do not reflect the opinion of the Institute for Women's Policy Research.

NOTES

1.   I conduct preliminary analyses to see whether response bias to my supplemental survey was significant. A sample selection variable was constructed using 1993 cross-sectional information. I derived this selection variable from the following logistic function:

$$\text{survey respondent} = f(\text{subsid, neast, midw, west, lnet, lemp, servind, \%emp-}f)$$

Representing the set of controls, I chose these predictors to construct the selection variable because they have the least missing information. Including this sample selection variable in model 4 did not allow for the convergence of many of my innovation logistic models. However, none of the predictors of survey response was significant. Hence, I dropped this selection variable from my analyses believing that response bias to the supplemental survey was minimal.

2. Key to the construction of organizational life-cycle classification system is the proportional change in a company's net worth as derived from four monetary measures (standardized to 1993 dollars):

$$\text{net proportional change } (t) = \frac{[\text{net}(t) - \text{net}(t\text{-}1)]}{\text{net}(t)}$$

where: $\text{net} = \text{sales} + \text{profits} + \text{assets} + \text{equity}$

I use the same classification scheme for the organizational life-cycle measures to create institutional life-cycle variables. However, I assume that the institutional environment which this sample of firms compares itself is the *Fortune* 1,000. Hence, the *Fortune* 1,000 average net worth (Inet) is incorporated into the proportional change measure:

$$\text{net proportional change } (t) = \frac{[\text{net}(t) - \text{Inet}(t) - [\text{net}(t\text{-}1) - \text{Inet } (t)]}{[\text{net}(t) - \text{Inet}(t)]}$$

where: net = net worth for a sample company
                 Inet = average net worth for the *Fortune* 1,000 environment

To categorize trends in resource base, proportional change measures are calculated by four juxtaposed pairs of years: $t_1 - t_2$, $t_2 - t_3$, $t_3 - t_4$, and $t_4 - t_5$. For 1978, only four years of data (1974-1977) and three pairs are used. A firm is said to be a grower if the proportional increase in resource base exceeds 3 percent for all four pairs of years. On the other hand, a decliner is indicated by a proportional decrease in resource base that is greater than 3 percent for all four periods.

No real change in the rates of growth or decline is denoted by a proportional increase/decrease that does not exceed 3 percent for a pair of years. A stable firm is one which has only one pair of either growth or decline years, or no real change across all four time periods. On the other hand, instability is defined by a combination of growth, decline, and stable experiences during a 5-year period. An unstable company has undergone either two periods of growth, or two periods of decline, or one period of each.

3. As the titles of Figures 1 and 2 indicate, the two base samples consist of 188 and 52 companies, respectively. Given variation within each of the 188 companies in missing information on the adoption dates of different types of family programs, the denominators used to calculate cumulative proportions fluctuate across program types: cafeteria plans ($N = 174$), dependent care assistance packages ($N = 159$), child care resource and referrals ($N = 136$), elder care resource referrals ($N = 164$), family leave programs ($N = 30$), and first program of the previous five adopted ($N = 94$). Likewise, each of the 52 companies with supplemental survey data also had missing adoption information which resulted in different denominators used in my calculations: flextime ($N = 45$), flexplace ($N = 45$), jobsharing ($N = 43$), and part-time schedules ($N = 27$).

REFERENCES

Alexander, J. A., M. L. Fennell, and M. T. Halpern. 1993. "Leadership Instability in Hospitals: The Influence of Board-CEO Relations and Organizational Growth and Decline." *Administrative Science Quarterly* 38: 74-99.

Alexander, J. A., and W. R. Scott. 1984. "The Impact of Regulation on the Administrative Structure of Hospitals: Toward an Analytic Framework." *Hospital and Health Services Administration* 29(3): 71-85.

Allison, P. 1984. *Event History Analysis: Regression for Longitudinal Event Data. Series: Quantitative Applications in the Social Sciences.* Beverly Hills, CA: Sage Publications, Inc.

Auerbach, J. D. 1990. "Employer-Supported Child Care as a Women- Responsive Policy." *Journal of Family Issues* 11: 384-400.

Bureau of Labor Statistics. 1998. Labor Force Statistics from the Current Population Survey. "Series Title: Labor Force Participation Rate—Civilian Population Female (Series ID : LFS600002)." <http://stats.bls.gov/> or <http://146.142.4.24/cgi-bin/surveymost?lf>

Cameron, K. S., M. U. Kim, and D. A. Whetten. 1987. "Organizational Effects of Decline and Turbulence." *Administrative Science Quarterly* 32: 222-240.

Christensen, K. E., and G. L. Staines. 1990. "Flextime: A Viable Solution to Work/Family Conflict?" *Journal of Family Issues* 11: 455-476.

Downs, G.W., Jr., and L.B. Mohr. 1976. "Conceptual Issues in the Study of Innovation." *Administrative Science Quarterly* 21:700-714.

Dun and Bradstreet, Inc. 1974, 1978, 1981, 1985, 1989, 1993. *Million Dollar Directory: America's Leading Public and Private Companies.* Parsippany, NJ: Dun and Bradstreet, Inc.

————. 1974, 1978, 1981, 1985, 1989, 1993. *Reference Book of Corporate Managements.* Parsippany, NJ: Dun and Bradstreet, Inc.

Fennell, M. L. 1984. "Synergy, Influence, and Information in the Adoption of Administrative Innovations." *Academy of Management Journal* 27(1): 113-29.

Fennell, M. L., and J. A. Alexander. 1987. "Organizational Boundary Spanning in Institutional Environments." *Academy of Management Journal* 30(3): 456-76.

Fortune. 1974-1993. *Fortune Double 500 Directory.* Trenton, NJ: Fortune Directories.

_____. 1974-1993. *Second Fortune Double Directory.* Trenton, NJ: Fortune Directories.

Friedman, D. E. 1990. "Corporate Responses to Family Needs." *Marriage and Family Review* 15(1-2): 77-98.

Galinsky, E., and P. J. Stein. 1990. "The Impact of Human Resource Policy on Employees: Balancing Work/Family Life." *Journal of Family Issues* 11: 368-383.

Galinsky, E., D. E. Friedman, and C. A. Hernandez. 1991. *The Corporate Reference Guide to Work-Family Programs.* New York: Families and Work Institute.

Goodstein, J. D. 1994. "Institutional Pressures and Strategic Responsiveness: Employer Involvement in Work-Family Issues." *The Academy of Management Journal* 37(2): 350-382.

Goodstein, J. D. 1995. "Employer Involvement in Eldercare: An Organizational Adaption Perspective." *The Academy of Management Journal* 38(6): 1657-1671.

Kanter, R. M. 1983. *The Change Masters.* New York: Simon and Schuster.

Kimberly, J.R., and M.J. Evanisko. 1981. "Organizational Innovation: The Influence of Individual, Organizational, and Contextual Factors on Hospital Adoption of Technological and Administrative Innovations." *Academy of Management Journal* 24(4): 689-713.

Kimberly, J.R., and R.H. Miles (Eds.). 1981. *The Organizational Life Cycle.* San Francisco: Jossey-Bass.

Klein, B. W. 1986. "Missed Work and Lost Hours, May 1985." *Monthly Labor Review* 109(11): 26-30.

McNeely, R.L., and B. A. Fogarty. 1988. "Balancing Parenthood and Employment: Factors Affecting Company Receptiveness to Family-Related Innovations in the Workplace." *Family Relations* 37: 189-195.

Mergers and Acquisitions. 1974-1993. *Mergers and Acquisitions.* Washington, DC: Mergers and Acquisitions Inc.

Miller, J. J., B. A. Stead, and A. Pereira. 1991. "Dependent Care and the Workplace: An Analysis of Management and Employee Perceptions." *Journal of Business Ethics* 10: 863-869.

Mintzberg, H. 1979. *The Structuring of Organizations.* Englewood Cliffs, NJ: Prentice Hall.

Osterman, P. 1995. "Work/Family Programs and the Employment Relationship." *Administrative Science Quarterly* 40(4): 681-700.

Scott, W. R. 1987. *Organizations: Rational, Natural, and Open Systems.* Englewood Cliffs, NJ: Prentice-Hall, Inc.

Spilerman, S., and H. Schrank. 1991. "Responses to the Intrusion of Family Responsibilities in the Workplace." *Research in Social Stratification and Mobility* 10: 27-61.

Stinchcombe, A. L. 1965. "Social Structure and Organizations." Pp. 142-193 in *Handbook of Organizations,* edited by J.G. March. Chicago, IL: Rand McNally.

U.S Census Bureau. 1974-1993. *Current Population Survey* (March edition). Washington, DC: U.S. Department of Commerce.

_____. 1997. "Table H4. Women 15 to 44 Years Old Who Have Had a Child in the Last Year and Their Percentage in the Labor Force: Selected Years, June 1976 to Present." Published November 25, 1997. <http://www.census.gov/population/socdemo/fertility/fert95/tabH4.txt>

Whetten, D. A. 1987. "Organizational Growth and Decline Processes." *Annual Review of Sociology* 13: 335-358.

Wiatrowski, W. 1995. "Methods of Providing Child-Care Benefits to Employees." Washington, DC: Bureau of Labor Statistics. <http://stats.bls.gov/ebs2/cwc3.txt>

Zucker, L.G. 1987. "Institutional Theories of Organizations." *Annual Review of Sociology* 13: 443-464.

MATERNAL EMPLOYMENT AND MEASURES OF CHILDREN'S HEALTH AND DEVELOPMENT AMONG FAMILIES WITH SOME HISTORY OF WELFARE RECEIPT

Martha Zaslow, Sharon McGroder, George Cave, and Carrie Mariner

ABSTRACT

The present study focuses on the association between maternal employment and measures of young children's developmental outcomes in a sample of families with some history of welfare receipt. Findings point to more positive child outcomes across multiple measures of development for children of employed mothers. However, analyses also indicate that pre-existing differences between employed and non-employed mothers in this sample accounted for all but one of the bivariate associations between maternal employment and the measures of development, including

Research in the Sociology of Work, Volume 7, pages 233-259.
Copyright © 1999 by JAI Press Inc.
All rights of reproduction in any form reserved.
ISBN: 0-7623-0605-X

an assessment of children's school readiness, and maternal report measures of children's positive social behaviors and internalizing behavior problems. With respect to mothers' ratings of the children's health, efforts to control for pre-existing differences between employed and non-employed mothers resulted in a model that failed to reach statistical significance, precluding an examination of the degree to which maternal employment remains predictive of children's health ratings, net of selection factors.

INTRODUCTION

Welfare policies in the United States have historically had, as a goal, the protection of the well-being of children in poor families. Yet the primary strategy for achieving this goal has changed markedly as welfare policies have evolved. The earliest welfare legislation, part of the *Social Security Act* of 1935, viewed it as essential that mothers stay home to care for their children, and it focused particularly on the needs of widows. In sharp contrast, the *Personal Responsibility and Work Opportunity Reconciliation Act* of 1996 requires that welfare recipients become employed and, reflecting changing demographics, focuses especially on unwed (including very young) mothers (Blank and Blum 1997; Chase-Lansdale and Vinovskis 1995; Zaslow, Tout, Smith and Moore 1998).

Multiple provisions of the 1996 legislation are designed to move recipients of public assistance to employment. For example, under this legislation, work or work-related activities must be undertaken within 24 months of receiving benefits, and sooner at state option. There is a lifetime limit on the receipt of benefits of 60 months. States must meet participation goals for engagement in work activities, reaching 50 percent of their single-parent caseloads by 2002 (although states can receive a reduction in this target if their overall caseload diminishes). The work requirement applies to mothers with infants and toddlers, though states may opt to exempt mothers with children younger than 12 months. It has been estimated that approximately 800,000 individuals will enter the labor force through 2002 as a result of the legislation (McMurrer, Sawhill and Lerman 1997).

A fundamental question, given the strong emphasis placed on employment in the new legislation, is whether moving recipients of public assistance into the workforce will indeed continue to protect the development and well-being of their children. In this paper we focus on the developmental outcomes of young children in a sample of families, followed longitudinally, that had applied for or were receiving welfare benefits at the start of the study ("baseline"). In particular, we ask whether measures of the children's health, behavioral adjustment, and cognitive development differ in light of their mothers' employment status at the time of follow-up, two years after baseline. In addition, we examine the background characteristics of the families that are antecedent to and predictive of maternal employment, and consider the extent to which these predictors of employment help to explain any differences in child outcomes found in light of employment status.

Previous Research on Maternal Employment and Child Outcomes in Low-income Families

Research on maternal employment and child outcomes has focused disproportionately on middle-class samples. Only a small set of studies focuses specifically on outcomes for children when low-income mothers work, and a yet smaller set of studies focuses specifically on families receiving public assistance (Zaslow and Emig 1997; Moore and Driscoll 1997). Thus, there is little evidence to draw upon in anticipating the implications for children of the new legislation.

As a whole, the body of research on maternal employment and children has concluded that, rather than a single uniform pattern of outcomes occurring for children (e.g., a pattern that would suggest that maternal employment either benefits or harms children overall), findings instead differ for particular subgroups. The implications of maternal employment appear to be moderated by child characteristics (e.g., gender, age), maternal attitudes (e.g., attitudes about maternal work and home roles), family characteristics (e.g., socioeconomic status, racial/ethnic and cultural background), and characteristics of the mother's job (e.g., part time/ full time; job complexity, wages) (see series of landmark reviews, including Hoffman 1974, 1979, 1984, 1989, in press; chapters in Kamerman and Hayes 1982; Menaghan and Parcel 1995; Parcel and Menaghan 1994).

Given this complex patterning of results, it is not surprising that researchers have hypothesized that maternal employment will have differing implications for children according to key background characteristics of the family, such as socioeconomic status (Belsky and Eggebeen 1991; Bronfenbrenner and Crouter 1983; Desai, Chase-Lansdale and Michael 1989). Researchers have suggested that the implications of maternal employment will reflect the balance of specific positive and negative influences on such factors as parent-child time together, family income, and the quality of child care relative to the quality of parent-child interactions (Desai et al. 1989). For children in low-income families, on average, benefits are hypothesized to outweigh negative influences.

For example, Desai and colleagues (1989) note that while children of all backgrounds stand to lose time and attention from their mothers when they are employed, the relative importance of the additional income from maternal employment is greater in low-income than in higher-income families. Further, they hypothesize that the educational background of parents and substitute caregivers is likely to be more similar in low-income than higher-income families and, thus, the care more comparable. By contrast, these researchers hypothesize that substitute care may involve less stimulation than by parents in the home environment for children from middle class families, and thus serve as a negative factor in the overall balance of cumulative influences associated with maternal employment for middle income families. Thus, according to this hypothesis, on balance maternal employment yields favorable influences for children in low-income families.

In general, studies that contrast the development and well-being of children in low-income families in which the mother is or is not employed have been fairly consistent in pointing either to no differences in outcomes or to more favorable outcomes among children of employed mothers.[1] Whereas further studies have carried out *within group* analyses looking only at families with employed mothers, for example, considering outcomes for children in low-income families when their mothers are employed in jobs with higher or lower wages, full or part time, with sporadic or overtime hours (Parcel and Menaghan 1990; Piotrkowski and Katz 1982; Woods 1972), we focus here on the *between group* studies, or those that contrast outcomes for children when the mother is or is not employed.

Cherry and Eaton (1977), for example, found a pattern of primarily favorable outcomes among children of employed mothers in a sample of low-income families, with analyses focusing on developmental outcomes for children in particular subgroups of families (e.g., families in which the father was or was not employed, and families that were or were not experiencing residential overcrowding). For example, in families with the father present, at particular ages, children with employed mothers showed better language development, weighed more, were taller and had larger head circumferences. In keeping with the hypothesis of Desai and colleagues, these findings suggest that the income available through employment may be of particular importance in low-income families, helping to provide for such basic resources as food.

Allesandri (1992) found more positive outcomes for children (particularly for daughters) whose mothers were employed in a sample of 10-to-12 year old children, all from families headed by single mothers and living in inner-cities. Children of mothers employed both full- and part-time had higher self-esteem and perceived their families as showing greater cohesion than children of nonemployed mothers. In addition, daughters of mothers employed full time had higher grade point averages and described their families as stressing achievement and independence more than other children in employed and non-employed families.

Vandell and Ramanan (1992), also focusing on low-income families, examined second graders' cognitive and behavioral outcomes in light of mothers' "early" (first three years of life) and "recent" (most recent three years) employment, using data from the *National Longitudinal Survey of Youth-Child Supplement*. Even taking into account child and family background characteristics, factors predictive of maternal employment, and current family circumstances, early maternal employment in this sample predicted higher math achievement in second grade, while recent employment predicted higher reading achievement and receptive vocabulary. No differences were found with respect to behavioral adjustment. In no case did early or recent employment predict *poorer* developmental outcomes.

Focusing on a later developmental period, McLoyd and colleagues (1994) found that maternal *unemployment* was associated with greater stress for both mothers and adolescents in a sample of low-income single-parent African-American families. In this sample, compared to unemployed mothers, employed mothers were less depressed, perceived less financial strain, and felt greater instrumental social support; and their seventh and eighth grade children perceived the relationship with the mother more favorably, had lower anxiety levels, and perceived less economic hardship in the family. In addition, a sequence was found in which greater depression among currently unemployed mothers was associated with heightened maternal punishment of the adolescent, which was in turn predictive of greater depression and cognitive distress in the adolescents.

Moore and colleagues (Moore, Zaslow and Driscoll 1996; Moore and Driscoll 1997) carried out one of the few studies of child outcomes and maternal employment specifically in a sample with some history of welfare receipt. They identified families in the 1992 wave of the *National Longitudinal Survey of Youth-Child Supplement* who reported having received Aid to Families with Dependent Children for at least one month during the years 1986 to 1990. They then examined measures of development for 5- to 14-year-old children in light of mothers' employment status and wages (<$5.00/hour; $5.00-$7.50/hour; >$7.50/hour) in 1991. Analyses controlled for a range of background characteristics hypothesized to be predictive of both maternal employment and children's outcomes. In this sample, maternal employment was predictive of fewer behavior problems (assessed using the total score of the Behavior Problems Index) but only when the mother earned relatively higher wages.

For other outcomes, there were effects of employment but only for specific race/ethnicity and gender subgroups and at specific wage levels (Moore et al. 1996). Reading comprehension (the PIAT reading comprehension assessment) differed for children of employed and nonemployed mothers only at the lowest wage level, and here findings differed by race/ethnicity. Compared to no employment, low-wage maternal employment was associated with higher scores for minority (especially Hispanic) children, but lower scores for non-minority children. (This latter result represents one of the isolated findings of an unfavorable outcome associated with maternal employment in a subgroup of families). For the math assessment (PIAT math), findings differed especially according to gender. Compared to children with non-employed mothers, girls had higher scores when their mothers were employed at (relatively) higher wages, but boys had lower math scores when their mothers were employed at higher wages. In addition, boys of mothers who were employed in the lowest wage jobs had the lowest math scores of any children. This study, then, generally found maternal employment associated with better behavioral outcomes at relatively higher wage levels, but mixed findings regarding cognitive outcomes for children in certain subgroups, especially for those whose mothers were employed at low wage levels.

The Issue of Selection Into Employment

Research has documented that mothers with certain characteristics and from certain backgrounds are more likely to become employed. Employed mothers tend, on average, to have greater cognitive skills and more education (Vandell and Ramanan 1992; Moore and Driscoll 1997), better psychological well-being (Coiro 1997; Parcel and Menaghan 1990; Vandell and Ramanan 1992), and less traditional attitudes toward women's roles (Moore and Driscoll 1997; Parcel and Menaghan 1990; Vandell and Ramanan 1992) than non-employed mothers. In addition, studies examining the barriers to employment faced by low-income mothers indicate the critical roles of access to child care and transportation (Siegal and Loman 1991; GAO 1994) in facilitating their employment. The factors that predispose certain mothers to employment may also be important predictors of children's development. For example, both educational attainment and maternal cognitive test scores are among the strongest predictors of children's developmental outcomes (D'Amico, Haurin and Mott 1983; Duncan, Brooks-Gunn and Klebanov 1994; Moore and Snyder 1991).

In sum, child characteristics, maternal attitudinal and psychological variables, basic family sociodemographic characteristics, and external contextual factors may *all* serve as predictors of both maternal employment and child outcomes, and these "selection" factors may be partly responsible for the apparent "effect" of maternal employment on children. Indeed, because of these "selection effects," some researchers have even cautioned against using the term "effect" to describe statistical associations between maternal employment and children's developmental outcomes (Zaslow, Rabinovich and Suwalsky 1991).

Studies vary substantially in the extent to which they seek to identify predictors of employment and examine their role in predicting child outcomes. In some studies, differences in the characteristics of the families according to mothers' employment status are noted, yet no attempt is made to take these into account as possibly helping to explain differences in child outcomes (e.g., Alessandri 1992). On the other hand, further studies are careful to examine whether differences in child outcomes persist when a wide range of background characteristics of the families are controlled (e.g., Vandell and Ramanan 1992; Moore et al. 1996; Moore and Driscoll 1997).

Controlling for selection factors may be especially important in a sample of families receiving public assistance. In such families, barriers to employment—such as maternal depression, limited literacy, and residence in an area with limited public transportation—may be more prevalent than in other population groups (Moore, Zaslow, Coiro, Miller and Magenheim 1995). Those who receive welfare who eventually go on to become employed may differ in terms of the number or severity of barriers and/or the motivation and support to overcome them. That is, differences between families in which the mother does and does not become employed may be particularly marked in families with some history of welfare receipt; therefore, it is particularly important to attempt to account for such factors in order to isolate the role of employment per se in shaping child outcomes.

The Present Study

The present study makes use of a longitudinal dataset with detailed information about family characteristics and circumstances, mothers' employment, and children's development, to examine: (1) whether there are bivariate associations between maternal employment and measures of five- to seven-year-old children's cognitive development, behavioral and emotional adjustment, and health; (2) the extent to which baseline variables are significant predictors of maternal employment in a sample of families that, at baseline, all had applied for or were receiving welfare benefits; and (3) whether associations between maternal employment and child outcomes remain when antecedent child characteristics, maternal attitudinal and psychological variables, family sociodemographic characteristics, and variables reflecting the external contextual circumstances of the family are taken into account.

METHODS

The Child Outcomes Study of the National Evaluation of Welfare-to-Work Strategies (NEWWS)

The current analyses use data from the *Child Outcomes Study* of the National Evaluation of Welfare-to-Work Strategies. This study examines the effects on children of mothers' assignment to a welfare-to-work program implemented as part of JOBS (the Job Opportunities and Basic Skills Training program), the set of programs put in place following passage of the Family Support Act of 1988.

The Family Support Act legislation called for an experimental evaluation of the economic impacts of JOBS programs. This study, the *National Evaluation of Welfare-to-Work Strategies*, which is being carried out by the Manpower Demonstration Research Corporation, involves 55,000 families in seven research sites around the country. Families that had applied for or were receiving Aid to Families With Dependent Children and that were not exempt from participation in a JOBS program were enrolled in the evaluation. Families were randomly assigned to a control group (free of the requirements of participation in a JOBS program, but eligible for all AFDC benefits) or to an experimental group (mandated to participate in a JOBS program or face a reduction in benefits, but simultaneously eligible for the augmented case management and access to the program services of a JOBS program). Through administrative records and surveys, program impacts are being tracked over time on such outcomes as welfare receipt, employment, earnings, and total household income (Hamilton, Brock, Farrell, Friedlander and Harknett 1997).

Following passage of the *Family Support Act*, the U.S. Department of Health and Human Services recommended that a further study be carried out focusing on the effects of JOBS programs on children, in recognition of the fact that the well-being of children is a primary goal of welfare policies and that children are influenced when their mothers' lives are changed. This *Child Outcomes Study* is being conducted by Child Trends under subcontract to the Manpower Demonstration Research Corporation. It focuses on a subset of about 3,000 families in the full evaluation, each with a child of preschool-age (between about three- and five-years-old) at the time of enrollment in the evaluation. The *Child Outcomes Study* is being carried out in three of the seven research sites of the full evaluation: Atlanta, Georgia; Grand Rapids, Michigan; and Riverside, California. The children's development in multiple domains—cognitive development and academic achievement, emotional and behavioral adjustment, and physical health and safety—is being followed over time through direct developmental assessments, maternal report measures and, in the final follow-up, through teacher report and child self-report measures.[2]

Data for the families in the *Child Outcomes Study* have thus far been collected at two points in time: at *baseline*, just prior to random assignment, and as part of a *Two-year Follow-up*, an interview and developmental assessment carried out in the families' homes.[3] A further survey, the *Five-year Follow-up*, is currently in the field. In addition, the information collected on economic outcomes in the full evaluation is also available for the subset of *Child Outcomes Study* families.

Data collected at baseline include basic sociodemographic information, information on maternal attitudes and psychological well-being (e.g., presence of depressive symptoms, preferences regarding working, feelings about leaving the child in child care), and information on the families' circumstances (e.g., whether the family resides in public housing, whether transportation is a problem, availability of social support). As part of the Two-year Follow-up, measures of the focal children's well-being and development were collected, including a direct assessment of the child's school readiness (the *Bracken Basic Concept Scale/School Readiness Composite*), and maternal report measures of the children's health, behavior problems, and positive social behaviors. The Two-year Follow-up also inquired about the mother's employment, including whether she was employed in the month prior to the interview.

Delineation of the Sample for the Present Analyses

We viewed it as crucial to examine, as a first step, the association between maternal employment and child outcomes among families previously receiving welfare, specifically, *when mothers chose employment at their own volition*. Participation in a mandatory welfare-to-work program (as in the experimental groups of the NEWWS *Child Outcomes Study*) may alter both the process of selection into employment, and the association between employment and child outcomes. Accordingly, the present analyses focus on families in the control group, for whom participation in a welfare-to-work program was not required. Subsequent work is planned that will build on these analyses by looking at child outcomes when maternal employment comes about in the context of a mandatory program. These further analyses will be critical to help ascertain the potential implications of the current policies, yet should build on an understanding of the transition to employment as it occurs without an imperative from policy.

Preliminary analyses indicated that family characteristics and child outcome measures differed substantially for families in the three *Child Outcomes Study* sites (McGroder, Zaslow, Moore and LeMenestrel, forthcoming). We thus focus on a single study site—Atlanta, Georgia—in the present analyses, selecting this site on the grounds of its relatively large sample size (from among the three sites) and its relative homogeneity with respect to racial/ethnic characteristics of sample families.[4] Given the racial/ethnic composition of families in this research site (95% of families are African-American), well-documented differences in the rates of maternal employment by race/ethnicity, and the possibility that patterns of associations with child outcomes might differ by race/ethnicity (Heyns 1982), we further chose to restrict the sample to African-American families. As a final restriction, the present sample includes only families for which there were data on maternal employment and child outcome measures in the Two-Year Follow-up.[5]

Measures

Table 1 provides a description of each of the measures included in the analyses, and notes the source of the data. The child outcome measures collected during the Two-Year Follow-up, when the children were approximately five-to seven-years of age, include the proportion of children rated by their mothers as in very good or excellent health (Coiro and Zill 1994), maternal report of the frequency of positive social behaviors (on the *Positive Child Behavior Scale/Social Competence Subscale*; Polit 1995), maternal report of the frequency of internalizing and externalizing behavior problems (subscale scores on the *Behavior Problems Index*; see Peterson and Zill 1986; Zill 1985), and age-adjusted raw scores on the Bracken *Basic Concept Scale/ School Readiness Composite* (Bracken 1984). Mothers also reported whether or not they had been employed at any point in the month prior to the Two-Year Follow-up survey.[6]

The variables hypothesized to reflect selection into employment—namely, measures of child characteristics, maternal attitudinal and psychological variables, maternal and family sociodemographic characteristics, and variables that reflect contextual circumstances external to the family—are all derived from information collected as part of enrollment in the evaluation, just prior to random assignment (i.e., at baseline).

Table 1.   Description of Measures

Category/Variable	Source	Description
	Baseline 2-Year	

I. Hypothesized Predictors of Maternal Employment

A. Child Characteristics

Focal child age	√	Age, in months, at baseline
Focal child gender	√	Focal child is male or female (1 = male)

B. Maternal Attitudes and Psychological Well-being

Multiple depressive symptoms	√	Mother reports she felt sad, depressed, lonely, and unable to shake off the blues either a moderate amount or most or all days in the previous week.
External locus of control	√	Agreed or agreed a lot with *each* of the following statements: "I have little control over things that happen to me. " "I often feel angry that people like me never get a fair chance to succeed. " "Sometimes I feel I am being pushed around in life. " "There is little that I can do to change many of the important things in my life"
Would accept a job that paid less than welfare	√	Responded "probably yes" vs. "probably no"to question: "Would you take a FULL-TIME job right now if the job paid a little *less* than welfare?"
Prefer home to work	√	Agreed or agreed a lot with the statement: "Right now, I would prefer not to work so I can take care of my family full-time. "
Afraid to leave child(ren) in child care	√	Agreed or agreed a lot with the statement: "I cannot go to a school or job training program right now because I am afraid to leave my children in day care or with a baby sitter. "

C. Other Maternal and Family Characteristics

Three or more children	√	Mother is primary caregiver to three or more children under age 19 living in the household
Mother ever married as of baseline	√	As of baseline, mother was either married and living with her spouse, separated, divorced, or widowed.
Low score on test of literacy	√	Scored in the lowest two of four levels (indicating, for instance, that the mother would have difficulty reading a bus schedule)
Duration receiving welfare as of baseline	√	Categorized into two dummy variables: "less than two years," and "five or more years" ("two up to five years" is the omitted category)
Never worked full time for six months or more for same employer	√	Caseworker noted whether the mother ever worked full-time for six months or more for one employer. Coded "1" if mother *never* had such an employment history as of baseline.

(continued)

Table 1   (Continued)

Category	Source	Description
	Baseline 2-Year	
Ill family member	√	Agreed or agreed a lot with either of the following statements: "I cannot go to a school or job training program right now because I: "have a health or emotional problem" "have a child or family member with a health or emotional problem"

D. "External" Contextual Circumstances

Reside in public housing	√	Caseworker noted whether the client resided in public housing.
No transportation	√	Agreed or agreed a lot with the statement: "I cannot go to a school or job training program right now because I have no way to get there every day"
Have someone trustworthy to care for child	√	Agreed or agreed a lot with the statement: "If I got a job, I could find someone I trust to take care of my children. "
Cannot afford child care	√	Agreed or agreed a lot with the statement: "I cannot go to a school or job training program right now because I cannot afford child care. "
Have someone to talk to	√	Agreed or agreed a lot with the statement: "When I have troubles or need help, I have someone I can really talk to. "
Have friends to loan cash if needed	√	Agreed or agreed a lot with the statement: "When I have an emergency and need cash, friends and family will loan it to me. "

II. Current Maternal Employment

Mother's employment status during month prior to interview	√	Mothers answered "yes" to the question: "In (PRIOR MONTH), did you or anyone you lived with, have a job or do any work for pay?" Subsequent items were used to identity only the mothers who were employed.

III. Child Outcome Measures

Bracken Basic Concept Scale/School Readiness Composite (Bracken 1984)	√	This direct assesment of school readiness administered to the focal child uses the 5 subtests comprising the School Readiness Composite and assessed the focal child's knowledge of colors, letters, numbers/counting, comparisons, shapes.

(continued)

Table 1   (Continued)

Category/Variable	Source		Description
	Baseline	2-Year	
Positive child Behavior Scale/Social Competence Subscale (Polit 1995)		√	Mothers reported on how well the following statements described the focal child's behavior in the previous three months [with 1 = not true, 2 = sometimes true, 3 = often true]: "is warm, loving" "gets along well with other children" "is admired and well-liked by other children" "shows concern for other people's feelings" "is helpful and cooperative" "is considerate and thoughtful of other children" "tends to give, lend, share"
Externalizing Behavior Problems Subscale of the Behavior Problems Index (see Peterson and Zill 1986; Zill 1985)		√	Mothers reported on how well the following statements described the focal child's behavior in the previous three months [with 1=not true, 2= sometimes true, 3=often true]: "bullies or is cruel or mean to others" "cheats or tells lies" "is disobedient at home" "is disobedient at school" "does not seem to feel sorry after she or he misbehaves"
Internalizing Behavior Problems Subscale of the Behavior Problems Index (see Peterson and Zill 1986; Zill 1985)		√	Mothers reported on how well the following statements described the focal child's behavior in the previous three months [with 1=not true, 2=sometimes true, 3=often true]: "is unhappy, sad, or depressed" "feels or complains that no one loves him or her" "feels worthless or inferior" "is not liked by other children" "is withdrawn, does not get involved with others"
Child Health Rating (Coiro and Zill 1994)		√	Mothers rated the focal child's overall health in response to the single interview question: "Would you say that your child's health in general is excellent, very good , good, fair, or poor?" This dichotomous measure indicates ratings of "very good" or "excellent"

Note: Through a design oversight, the focal child's gender was not obtained at baseline nor in the Two-Year Follow-up survey, but only for the subsample of Atlanta families who also participated in the Descriptive Study, about half of which are also in the present study's sample. Thus, for the remaining half for whom focal child's gender was not available, we "imputed" focal child's gender based on children's names. Coders, matched according to race/ethnicity with the respondents, were asked to judge, based on the name of the child, whether the child was a boy or a girl. As a check on the accuracy of this procedure, we compared actual and imputed child gender for the 790 Atlanta families for whom actual gender was available. There was agreement as to child gender for 92 percent of the cases in the full Atlanta sample. Fortunately for future analyses, the Five-Year Follow-up survey obtains information on focal child's gender.

Sample Characteristics

The final sample for the present analyses included 386 families. As we have noted, at baseline, all of these families had applied for or were receiving Aid to Families with Dependent Children. Table 2 provides descriptive information on baseline characteristics of these sample families.

Child Characteristics

Children in the sample averaged about 4 1/3 years of age at baseline, and just over half of the children in the sample (51%) were boys.

Table 2.   Baseline Characteristics of the Study Sample (*N*=386)

Sample Characteristic	Percent or Mean	(Standard Deviation)
Child Characteristics		
Age of child (in months)	52. 13	(8.91)
Gender of child (1= male)	0. 51	(0.50)
Maternal Attitudes and Psychological Well-being		
"Many" depressive symptoms	0. 19	(0.39)
External locus of control	0. 15	(0.35)
Would accept a low paying job	0. 37	(0.48)
Prefer not to work in order to care for family full-time	0. 17	(0.37)
Afraid to leave child(ren) in child care	0. 15	(0.36)
Other Maternal and Family Characteristics		
Three or more children	0. 34	(0.47)
Ever married	0. 30	(0.46)
Low levels of literacy	0. 45	(0.50)
As of baseline, received welfare less than two years	0. 28	(0.45)
As of baseline, received welfare five or more years	0. 38	(0.49)
Never worked FT for 6 + months for same employer	0. 30	(0.46)
Ill family member	0. 22	(0.41)
"External," Contextual Circumstances		
Reside in public housing	0. 30	(0.46)
No transportation	0. 28	(0.45)
Have someone trustworthy to care for child	0. 77	(0.42)
Cannot afford child care	0. 71	(0.46)
Have someone to talk to	0. 76	(0.43)
Have friends to loan cash if needed	0. 51	(0.50)

Maternal Attitudes and Psychological Well-Being

Nearly one in five mothers (19%) in the present sample reported, at baseline, feeling sad, depressed, lonely, and unable to "shake off the blues" either a moderate amount or on most or all days in the previous week—suggesting symptoms of depression. Fifteen percent agreed with each of four statements (such as "There is little that I can do to change many of the important things in my life") indicating a more external locus of control at baseline. In addition, three measures of work-related attitudes were included. About one-third of the mothers in the sample indicated at baseline that they would be willing to accept a full-time job even if it paid a little less than welfare. A minority of the mothers, yet a non-trivial proportion, indicated that they would prefer not to work so that they could take care of their family full-time (17%), and 15 percent reported that they were afraid to leave their children in child care.

Maternal and Family Sociodemographic Characteristics

A majority of the mothers in the sample (70%) had never been married (as of baseline). Baseline characteristics indicated the presence of a number of factors that could serve as impediments to employment. About a third of the mothers (34%) had three or more children at baseline. The assessment of literacy revealed that 45 percent of the mothers in the sample scored at the lowest two levels, indicating for instance that the mother would have difficulty reading a bus schedule. As of baseline, about a quarter of the mothers in the sample (28%) had received welfare for less than two years, 34 percent had received welfare for two to five years, and 38 percent had received welfare for five or more years. A third of the mothers had never worked full-time for the same employer for six months or more, which we use as an indicator of even a minimal history of stable, full-time employment. A little more than one in five mothers (22%) indicated they could not engage in work preparation activities because they or another family member had a health or emotional problem.

External Contextual Circumstances

Looking outside of the family at contextual factors that might hypothetically foster or hinder employment, at baseline, 30 percent of the mothers reported living in public housing, areas known for scant employment opportunities. Also, 28 percent indicated that they could not engage in work preparation activities because they lacked transportation. In addition, whereas more than three-quarters reported at baseline that they had someone trustworthy to care for the focal child should they find a job, 71 percent indicated concerns about paying for child care. Most of the mothers in the study indicated, at baseline, that they had social support available to them in terms of accessibility of someone to talk to (76%), and of a friend or family member who could loan them cash if they needed it (51%)—both of which are expected to facilitate employment.

Strategy of Analysis

In the present analyses, we began by examining the bivariate relationship between mothers' employment status and each of the measures of children's developmental outcomes at the Two-Year Follow-up. A one-way ANOVA indicated whether there was a main effect of concurrent maternal employment for each child outcome. We then examined the extent to which mothers who were and were not employed at the Two-year Follow-up differed on a range of baseline variables. Antecedent variables that predicted mothers' employment status two years later were considered "selection" factors for this sample and were, thus, controlled in subsequent multivariate analyses predicting children's developmental outcomes from mothers' employment status. In reporting results, we note the extent to which a previously statistically significant bivariate association between maternal employment and child outcomes disappears once selection factors are considered, and we identify which selection factors are responsible for the apparent "effect" of maternal employment on children.

FINDINGS

Current Employment in This Sample

Almost 40 percent of the mothers in the sample (150 out of 386) reported some employment in the month prior to the Two-Year Follow-up. Twenty-nine percent of these employed mothers were also receiving AFDC, whereas 92 percent of the non-employed mothers were receiving AFDC in the month prior to the Two-Year Follow-up. These employment rates are comparable to those for the population of U.S. welfare recipients; for example, almost one in three families who received welfare in 1996 were employed in the following year (Storrs 1998).[7]

Bivariate Relationship Between Maternal Employment and Child Outcomes

Table 3 shows unadjusted means for the five child outcome measures according to mothers' employment status. Significant differences according to mother's employment status occurred for four of the five child outcome measures considered: the assessment of school readiness, the frequency of positive child behaviors, the frequency of internalizing behavior problems, and the rating of child health. As can be seen in Table 3, unadjusted means indicate that, in each instance, children of employed mothers had more favorable scores on these child outcomes.

Table 3.   Unadjusted Means (SDs) on Child Outcome Measures, by
              Mothers' Current Employment Status ($N = 386$)

Child Outcome	No Employment in Prior Month ($n = 236$)	Employment in Prior Month ($n=150$)	$F(1,385)$
Adjusted[1] Raw Score on Bracken Basic Concepts Scale/School Readiness Composite (mean)	45.96	49.26	49.22***
Frequency of Positive Social Behaviors (mean)	2.50	2.59	4.21*
Frequency of Externalizing Behavior Problems (mean)	1.47	1.40	2.65
Frequency of Internalizing Behavior Problems (mean)	1.24	1.13	12.40***
Child's Health Rating (proportion in very good or excellent health)	0.72	0.84	6. 98**

Notes: Child health measure indicates the proportion of focal children in very good or excellent
          health. Child behavioral outcomes rated on the scale: 1 (never), 2 (sometimes), 3 (often). Raw
          Bracken scores can range from 0 to 61 and indicate the number of correct responses.
          $+p \leq .10$
          $*p \leq .05$
          $**p \leq .01$
          $***p \leq .001$
          [1]Raw Bracken scores adjusted for child's age. $d.f. = 2,384$

On the assessment of the children's school readiness, children with employed mothers had scores about three points higher than those of nonemployed mothers, indicating that children with employed mothers understood 49 (of a possible 61) concepts important for school readiness, whereas children with non-employed mothers understood only 46 concepts, on average.

On the ratings of the children's behavior, employed mothers noted positive social behaviors as occurring more frequently, and internalizing behavior problems less frequently, than nonemployed mothers. Whereas the means for externalizing behavior problems fell in the same direction as the means for the other behavioral measures (i.e., children of employed mothers showing fewer externalizing behavior problems), the difference did not reach statistical significance, and hence will not be examined in subsequent analyses.

Mothers who were employed were more likely to rate their children's health as excellent with no limiting conditions. Whereas 81 percent of employed mothers gave their children this health rating, only 68 percent of the non-employed mothers did so.

Selection into Maternal Employment

As suggested by previous research (see review in Zaslow and Emig 1997), there were pre-existing differences between employed and non-employed mothers in this sample. Differences occurred in each of the categories considered, namely, child characteristics, maternal attitudinal and psychological variables, basic family sociodemographic characteristics, and external contextual factors (see Table 4).

Table 4. Unadjusted Means (SDs) on Hypothesized Selection Factors, by Mothers' Current Employment Status ($N = 386$)

Baseline Variable	No Employment in Prior Month ($n=236$)	Employment in Prior Month ($n=150$)	$F(1,384)$
Child Characteristics			
Gender of child (1= male)	0.49 (.50)	0.53 (.50)	0.78
Age of child (in months)	51.4 (8.4)	53.3 (9.6)	4.59*
Maternal Attitudes and Psychological Well-being			
"Many" depressive symptoms	0.20 (.40)	0.16 (.37)	1.14
External locus of control	0.17 (.38)	0.11 (.31)	2.93+
Would accept a full-time job paying less than welfare	0.37 (.48)	0.37 (.49)	0.00
Prefer not to work so can care for family full-time	0.21 (.41)	0.10 (.30)	7.80**
Afraid to leave child(ren) in child care	0.19 (.40)	0.08 (.27)	9.67**
Other Maternal and Family Characteristics			
Three or more children	0.36 (.48)	0.30 (.46)	1.48
Ever married	0.28 (.45)	0.34 (.48)	1.58
Low levels of literacy	0. 53 (.50)	0.31 (.46)	20.07***
Received welfare less than two years	0.19 (.39)	0.42 (.50)	26.65***
Received welfare five or more years	0.46 (.50)	0.26 (.44)	15.73***
Never worked FT for 6+ months for same employer	0.36 (.48)	0.21 (.41)	9.97**
Ill family member	0.28 (.45)	0.13 (.33)	12.24***
"External," Contextual Circumstances			
Reside in public housing	0.33 (.47)	0.25 (.43)	3.40+
No transportation	0.34 (.47)	0.18 (.39)	11.86***
Have someone trustworthy to care for child	0.74 (.44)	0.83 (.38)	4.19*
Cannot afford child care	0.75 (.43)	0.63 (.48)	6.44*
Have someone to talk to	0.73 (.45)	0.80 (.40)	2.53
Have friends to loan cash if needed	0.48 (.50)	0.55 (.50)	1.81

Notes: $^+p \le .10$
$^*p \le .05$
$^{**}p \le .01$
$^{***}p \le .001$

From among the child characteristics, mothers who were employed at the time of the Two-Year Follow-up were more likely to have had a child who was somewhat older (within the age span considered here of approximately three-to five-years) at baseline. Although some research indicates that employment is less likely among mothers of boys, in the present analyses, maternal employment was not associated with child gender.

Among the variables reflecting maternal attitudes and psychological well-being, three baseline variables were significant predictors of two-year employment: locus of control, a preference not to work in order to care for their family full-time, and the expression of concern about leaving child(ren) in child care. Mothers who were employed at the Two-Year Follow-up were less likely, at baseline, to have indicated a more external locus of control; less likely, at baseline, to note a preference not to work in order to care for their family full-time; and less likely, at baseline, to express concerns about child care. It is interesting to note that neither the report of multiple symptoms of depression nor the willingness to accept a low paying job at baseline served as significant predictors of subsequent employment.

Among the maternal and family sociodemographic characteristics, findings indicate that mothers who were employed at the Two-Year Follow-up were less likely to have had low literacy scores on the baseline literacy assessment, and had, as of baseline, received welfare benefits for a shorter period of time (i.e., they were more likely to have received welfare for less than two years, and less likely to have received welfare for five or more years). In addition, mothers who went on to become employed were less likely to indicate that they had never worked full-time for the same employer for six months or more, and they were also less likely to indicate that there was an ill family member at baseline. Among the variables considered in this category, only two (presence, at baseline, of three or more children, and whether or not the mother had ever been married as of baseline) were not found to be significant predictors of employment.

The majority of baseline variables reflecting external contextual circumstances considered here also predicted employment at the Two-Year Follow-up. Mothers employed at the Two-Year Follow-up were less likely to have been living in public housing at baseline, to have indicated a lack of transportation at baseline, and to indicate that they could not afford child care. Mothers employed at the Two-Year Follow-up were more likely to indicate that there was someone that they trusted who could care for the child if they found a job.

Maternal Employment and Child Outcomes, Controlling for Selection

We turn now to the question of whether maternal employment continued to act as a significant predictor of the child outcomes after controlling for differences between employed and non-employed mothers at baseline.

Bracken Basic Concept Scale/School Readiness Composite

The first column on Table 5 indicates that maternal employment no longer predicts more favorable school readiness scores, once baseline factors that predicted two-year employment are controlled. That is, the positive bivariate association between maternal employment and children's Bracken scores can be attributed to the fact that employed mothers in this sample tended, at baseline, to have somewhat older children, better literacy, a shorter time on welfare, a stable work history, and they had not expressed fears about leaving their child in child care nor indicated that they or another family member's illness prevented them from working—and that these factors are also predictive of higher Bracken scores.

Positive Social Behaviors

Maternal employment also no longer predicts more frequent positive behaviors, once selection factors are controlled (column 2 of Table 5). The previous "main effect" for maternal employment on positive child behaviors can be explained by the fact that employed mothers tended, at baseline, to have better literacy and were less likely to have identified transportation as a barrier to employment. Mothers' literacy and their access to transportation are predictive of more frequent positive child behaviors.

Internalizing Behavior Problems

Similarly, maternal employment is no longer predictive of less frequent internalizing behavior problems, once selection factors are controlled (column 3 of Table 5). The apparent effect of mothers' employment status on children's internalizing behavior problems is actually a reflection of the less external locus of control, greater literacy, a stable work history, and better access to transportation, at baseline, among employed than non-employed mothers in this sample. These factors were also predictive of less frequent internalizing behavior problems in focal children.

Health Rating

In contrast to the multivariate findings thus far, the model predicting children's health rating from mothers' employment status and from antecedent selection variables was not statistically significant (see column 4 of Table 5). This indicates a poorly specified model and precludes an examination of the degree to which maternal employment remains predictive of children's health ratings after controlling for any pre-existing differences between employed and non-employed mothers in this sample.

Table 5.   Multiple Regression Coefficients for Maternal Employment
Status and Antecedent Selection Factors Predicting
Children's Outcomes ($n = 386$)

	Unstandardized Regression Coefficient			
Predictor	Bracken School Readiness	Positive Social Behaviors	Internalizing Behavior Problems	Health Rating
Employed in Prior Month	1.03	0.01	−0.04	0.09[+]
Child Characteristics				
Age of child (in months)	0.50[***]	0.00	0.00	0.00
Maternal Attitudes and Psychological Well-being				
External locus of control	1.64	0.04	0.08[+]	0.01
Prefer not to work so can care for family full-time	−2.05	−0.01	0.05	0.08
Afraid to leave child(ren) in child care	−3.40[*]	0.01	0.01	−0.05
Other Maternal and Family Characteristics				
Low levels of literacy	−3.10[**]	−0.16[***]	0.12[***]	0.00
Received welfare less than two years	2.62[*]	0.08	−0.02	0.01
Received welfare five or more years	0.78	0.00	0.02	−0.04
Never worked FT for 6+ months for same employer	−3.65[***]	0.00	0.07[*]	−0.06
Ill family member	−2.41[+]	−0.05	0.01	−0.03
"External," Contextual Circumstances				
Reside in public housing	−0.47	0.03	−0.01	0.02
No transportation	0.28	−0.15[**]	0.08	−0.10[+]
Have someone trustworthy to care for child	−1.07	−0.06	0.04	−0.01
Cannot afford child care	1. 59	0. 06	−0. 01	0. 01
F(14,371).	12.02[***]	3.01[***]	4.52[***]	1.13
Adj R-sq	0.29	0.07	0.11	0.01

Notes: [+]$p \leq .10$
  [*]$p \leq .05$
  [**]$p \leq .01$
  [***]$p \leq .001$

SUMMARY

In this sample of families who, at baseline, all had applied for or were receiving
Aid to Families with Dependent Children, an examination of the bivariate association between mother's employment status and child outcome measures pointed to

more favorable scores for children of employed mothers on four of five outcomes considered. Children of employed mothers appeared to be faring better in terms of school readiness, on two of three measures of behavioral adjustment, and in terms of health.

However, for three of the four child outcomes on which a difference by employment status had been found, when selection factors were taken into account, maternal employment at the Two-Year Follow-up no longer predicted the child outcome. Moreover, it proved important to consider possible selection factors in each of the broad categories identified here: child characteristics, mothers' attitudes and psychological well-being, maternal and family sociodemographics, and external contextual circumstances. Most often, pre-existing differences between employed and non-employed mothers on *sociodemographic characteristics of the mothers and/or family* were responsible for the apparent effect of maternal employment on children. In particular, the most consistent predictor of both maternal employment and the three child outcomes was mothers' literacy. This is in accord with previous research (Vandell and Ramanan 1992; Moore and Driscoll 1997). Also important for understanding the apparently favorable "effect" of maternal employment on children's school readiness and internalizing behavior problems was the greater likelihood of previous, minimally stable employment among employed mothers.

DISCUSSION

We have noted the importance in the present policy context of having a basic understanding of how maternal employment affects children among families with some history of welfare receipt. As in previous studies of low-income families, we see little basis for concern that maternal employment is associated with unfavorable outcomes, in general.[8] The present findings caution against excessive optimism that employment in low-income families will benefit children, however. The more favorable picture that emerged for children of employed mothers disappeared when antecedent characteristics of the mothers, families, or the context surrounding the families were taken into account. That is, our findings indicate that in this sample of African-American families in Atlanta, Georgia—all of whom had applied for or were receiving welfare at baseline—the bivariate associations between maternal employment and measures of children's cognitive and behavioral outcomes reflect *who* becomes employed and are not indicative of the *consequences* of maternal employment.

At the same time, questions remain as to whether pre-existing differences between employed and non-employed mothers in this sample underlie the positive bivariate association between maternal employment and the rating of the focal child's overall health. The fact that the multivariate model predicting reports of children's health from mothers' employment status (and controlling for selection into employment) was not statistically significant, despite a statistically significant bivariate model, suggests that: (1) we did a poor job identifying pre-existing differences between employed and non-employed mothers in this sample that are also germane to ratings of children's health, and/or (2) there truly is a favorable main effect of maternal employment on children's health ratings that was obscured in the multivariate model containing a large number of irrelevant predictors. With respect to this first possibility, our future work will conduct a yet more exhaustive study of the role of "observable" child, maternal, family, and external variables in explaining the linkages between maternal employment and child outcomes, as well as model "unobserved" selection factors through an "instrumental variables" approach—in which a variable (the "instrument") that is predictive of maternal employment but not directly of a given child outcome is used to control for all unobserved selection factors.

Regarding the second possibility—that is, that there truly is a main effect of maternal employment on children's health ratings—a plausible hypothesis may be that maternal employment provides a source of health insurance not otherwise available in these low-income, predominantly single-parent families. However, not only were families who received AFDC categorically eligible for Medicaid (including up to 12 months of "transitional" Medicaid after becoming employed), but the jobs attained by these employed low-income mothers are not likely to offer health benefits. Our future research will examine the role of health benefits and access to health care more closely.

It is clear from the present findings that a wide range of antecedent factors—both internal and external to the family, across a number of different domains—can help to explain the association between maternal employment and child outcomes. In the context of previous research, it is particularly important to note the role documented here for factors outside of the family, particularly the issues of lack of transportation. That is, it is important to take into account in explaining differences in child outcomes in light of maternal employment, not only variables reflecting what goes on within the mother and the family, but also factors reflecting the external environment. Such factors may simultaneously function as obstacles to employment and to the children's positive development.

It is important to note that the present findings diverge from previous research with samples defined more broadly as "low-income." In such previous work (e.g., Vandell and Ramanan 1992), antecedent characteristics of the employed mothers did not completely explain the more favorable outcomes identified for children of employed mothers. An important implication of the present study is that for mothers who have received public assistance, for whom there may be more intrafamilial and extrafamilial obstacles to becoming employed, the process of self-selection may be more marked. It may also play a larger role in explaining child outcomes.

Further work is needed examining the associations between maternal employment and child outcomes when mothers are mandated by policies to make a transition to employment. In theory, and by design, such policies should diminish or even eliminate the role played by selection factors. However, this prediction should be directly and carefully assessed. The possibility exists that, in reality, despite the requirement that they find employment, mothers will only become employed if they: (1) have skills for which employers are willing to pay or find employers willing to invest in the development of such skills; (2) have access to necessary support services to facilitate their employment; and (3) prefer employment to staying home with their children (and facing possible financial sanctions for non-compliance with the mandate). It is possible that mandatory welfare-to-work programs will diminish or eliminate selection effects only to the extent that they adequately address the reasons that welfare mothers are not employed in the first place, for example, by improving literacy through basic skills education and by providing transportation and child care. Further, because it may be more difficult to increase mothers' feelings of control over their lives, alter their preferences regarding caring for their family full-time, and alleviate fears about child care—all of which predicted non-employment in the present sample—pre-existing differences on these and related attitudinal variables between employed and non-employed mothers may quite possibly remain salient selection factors when examining maternal employment in a mandatory context. Thus, there are reasonable bases for two contrasting hypotheses: one predicting that selection effects will be diminished, and another predicting that selection will continue to play an important role. It will be important to ask whether, when mothers with a history of welfare receipt make a transition to employment in a mandatory context, their children continue to show outcomes that are similar to or more favorable than those of children with nonemployed mothers.

   A strength of the present study is its focus on a population that, while of great importance from a policy perspective, has received little attention in the previous research on maternal employment. A further strength is the consideration of a wide range of antecedent characteristics in explaining the linkages between maternal employment and child outcomes. Yet there are limitations of the present study that should also be taken into account in interpreting the findings. First, most of the child outcome measures rely on maternal report. The problem of common measurement error is thus a factor. In the Five-Year Follow-up of the *Child Outcomes Study*, measures of the children's behavioral adjustment and academic progress will be available from further respondents, and thus this problem can be addressed in the future. In addition, the findings of the present study pertain to one study site, and to one racial/ethnic group. The extent to which the results generalize to other social and economic contexts, and to families of other backgrounds remains open. Further work is needed to examine the generalizability of the findings reported here.

ACKNOWLEDGMENT

This paper was written with funding from the National Institute of Child Health and Human Development Family and Child Well-being Research Network (NICHD Grant No. 1 U01 HD30930-01). This study uses data from the *Child Outcomes Study of the National Evaluation of Welfare-to-Work Strategies* (NEWWS), which is funded by the Offices of the Assistant Secretary for Planning and Evaluation (ASPE) and the Administration for Children and Families in the U.S. Department of Health and Human Services (DHHS), as well as the U.S. Department of Education. The *Child Outcomes Study* of the NEWWS is being conducted by Child Trends under subcontract to the Manpower Demonstration Research Corporation. We gratefully acknowledge the permission and encouragement to pursue these analyses with the NEWWS *Child Outcomes Study* data by Audrey Mirsky-Ashby, Martha Moorehouse, and Ann Segal of ASPE, and Howard Rolston of ACF. We thank Kristin Moore and Toby Parcel for their thoughtful feedback on drafts of this manuscript. Finally, we thank Jennifer Sargent for her much appreciated assistance in summarizing analyses in table format. Although data come from the *Child Outcomes Study* of the NEWWS, these analyses do not reflect the experimental impacts of the welfare-to-work strategies implemented under the Job Opportunities and Basic Skills (JOBS) Training Program. Results pertaining to the impact of these programs on children and families are contained in the upcoming report, "The National Evaluation of Welfare-to-Work Strategies: Impacts on Children and Families Two Years After Enrollment: Findings from the *Child Outcomes Study*" (McGroder, Zaslow, Moore and LeMenestrel 1999).

NOTES

1. There are occasional reports of unfavorable outcomes for certain subgroups of children with employed mothers in low-income families; see Moore, Zaslow, and Driscoll (1996), as in this paper summarized it's no longer below.

2. A report documenting the experimental impacts of these three sites' JOBS programs on children of enrollees (McGroder, Zaslow, Moore and LeMenestrel forthcoming) will be released in 1999.

3. In one of the study sites, Atlanta, Georgia, a further survey wave was carried out close to the start of the evaluation in order to provide a descriptive portrayal of family circumstances and the children's developmental status soon after baseline (see Moore et al. 1995).

4. Future work will replicate the present analyses in the other research sites. Such work will help establish, for example, if the predictors of employment differ or are similar for families with a history of some welfare receipt residing in different economic and social contexts, and with differing background characteristics (e.g., racial/ethnic background).

5. Complete data on maternal employment and child outcome measures were available for 386 of the 453 African-American families in the control group of the Atlanta site.

6. Preliminary analyses examined the longitudinal pattern of employment (i.e., if any employment since random assignment and if any in the month prior to the survey). Results indicated a main effect for current employment; there was little information added by examining those who had been employed at some point since random assignment but not in the previous month. Consequently, this paper focuses on mothers' "current" employment status (i.e., in the month before the survey).

7. The comparable rates of employment in this sample and in the nation as a whole provides further evidence that mothers' employment status at a given point in time (i.e., in the month prior to the

two-year survey) may be reflective of more stable employment and is not a spurious indicator of employment.

8. However, we have not examined the implications of maternal employment for children in subgroups of families—for example, in non-minority families in which the mother is employed in a low-wage job (see Moore et al. 1996). Consideration of such subgroups will be examined in future work.

9. Raw Bracken scores adjusted for child's age. d.f. = 2,384.

REFERENCES

Alessandri, S. M. 1992. "Effects of Maternal Work Status in Single-Parent Families on Children's Perception of Self and Family and School Achievement. *"Journal of Experimental Child Psychology* 54: 417-433.

Blank, S. W. , and B. Blum. 1997. "A Brief History of Work Expectations for Welfare Mothers." *Future of Children* 71: 28-39.

Bracken, B. A. 1984. *Bracken Basic Concept Scale: Examiner's Manual.* The Psychological Corporation. Harcourt Brace Jovanovich, Inc.

Bronfenbrenner, U., and A. C. Crouter. 1982. "Work and Family Through Time and Space." Pp. 39-83 in *Families that Work: Children in a Changing World.* Washington, DC: National Academy Press.

Chase-Lansdale, P. L., and M. A. Vinovskis. 1995. "Whose Responsibility? An Historical Analysis of the Changing Roles of Mothers, Fathers, and Society." Pp. 11-37 in *Escape from Poverty: What Makes a Difference for Children?* Cambridge, UK: Cambridge University Press.

Cherry, F. F., and E. L. Eaton. 1977. "Physical and Cognitive Development in Children of Low-Income Mothers Working in the Child's Early Years." *Child Development* 48: 158-166.

Coiro, M. J. 1997. "Maternal Depressive Symptomatology as a Risk Factor for the Development of Children in Poverty." Paper presented at the 1997 Biennial Meeting of the Society for Research in Child Development, Washington, DC.

Coiro, M. J., and N. Zill. 1994. *The Health of United States Children: 1988.* Washington, DC: National Center for Health Statistics, Vital Health Statistics.

D'Amico, R. J., R. J. Haurin, and F. L. Mott. 1983. "The Effects of Mothers' Employment on Adolescent and Early Adult Outcomes of Young Men and Women." Pp. 130-219 *Children of Working Parents: Experiences and Outcomes.* Washington, DC: National Academy Press.

Desai, S. , P. L. Chase-Lansdale, and R. T. Michael. 1989. "Mother or Market? Effects of Maternal Employment on the Intellectual Ability of 4-year-old Children. " *Demography* 26: 545-561.

Duncan, G. J., J. Brooks-Gunn, and P. K. Klebanov. 1994. "Economic Deprivation and Early Childhood Development." *Child Development* 65: 296-318.

U. S. General Accounting Office. 1994. *Child Care Subsidies Increase the Likelihood that Low-income Mothers will Work.* GAO/HEHS95-20. Washington, DC: GAO.

Hamilton, G., T. Brock, M. Farrell, D. Friedlander, and K. Harknett. 1997. *Evaluating Two Welfare-to-Work Program Approaches: Two-Year Findings on the Labor Force Attachment and Human Capital Development Programs in Three Sites.* Washington, DC: U. S. Department of Health and Human Services, Administration for Children and Families and Office of the Assistant Secretary for Planning and Evaluation.

Hoffman, L. W. 1974. "Effects on Child." Pp. 126-166 in *Working Mothers.* San Francisco: Jossey-Bass.

_____. 1979. "Maternal Employment: 1979. " *American Psychologist* 34: 859-865.

_____. 1984. "Maternal Employment and the Young Child." Pp. 101-128 in *Minnesota Symposium in Child Psychology,* Vol. 17. Hillsdale, NJ: Erlbaum.

_____. 1989. "Effects of Maternal Employment in the Two-Parent Family." *American Psychologist* 44: 283-292.

_____. In press. *Maternal Employment and Children's Well-Being: A Study of Families in Middle America.* Cambridge, UK: Cambridge University Press.

Kamerman, S. B., and Hayes, C. D. Eds. 1982. *Families that Work: Children in a Changing World.* Washington, DC: National Academy Press.

McGroder, S. M., M. J. Zaslow, K. A. Moore, and S. M. LeMenestrel. forthcoming. *The National Evaluation of Welfare-to-Work Strategies: Impacts on Children and Families Two Years After Enrollment: Findings from the Child Outcomes Study.* Washington, DC: U. S. Department of Health and Human Services.

McLoyd, V. C., T. E. Jayaratne, R. Ceballo, and J. Borquez. 1994. "Unemployment and Work Interruption Among African American Single Mothers: Effects on Parenting and Adolescent Socioemotional Functioning." *Child Development* 65: 562-589.

McMurrer, D. P., I. V. Sawhill, and R. I. Lerman. 1997. "Welfare Reform and Opportunity in the Low-Wage Labor Market. " *Opportunity in America 5.* Washington, DC: Urban Institute.

Menaghan, E. G., and T. L. Parcel. 1995. "Social Sources of Change in Children's Home Environments: The Effects of Parental Occupational Experiences and Family Conditions." *Journal of Marriage and the Family* 57(2): 69-84.

Moore, K. A., and A. K. Driscoll. 1997. "Low-Wage Maternal Employment and Outcomes for Children: A Study. " *Future of Children* 7(1): 122-127.

Moore, K. A., and N. O. Snyder. 1991. "Cognitive Attainment Among Firstborn Children of Adolescent Mothers." *American Sociological Review* 56: 612-624.

Moore, K. A., M. J. Zaslow, M. J. Coiro, S. M. Miller, and E. B. Magenheim. 1995. *How Well Are They Faring? AFDC Families with Preschool-Aged Children in Atlanta at the Outset of the JOBS Evaluation.* Washington, DC: Department of Health and Human Services and U. S. Department of Education.

Moore, K. A., M. J. Zaslow, and A. K. Driscoll. 1996. "Maternal Employment in Low-Income Families: Implications for Children's Development. " Paper presented at meeting From Welfare to Work: Effects on Parents and Children, sponsored by the Packard Foundation and the American Academy of Arts and Sciences. Airlie Center, Virginia.

Parcel, T. L., and E. G. Menaghan. 1994. *Parents' Work and Children's Lives.* New York: Aldine de Gruyter.

_____. 1990. "Maternal Working Conditions and Children's Verbal Facility: Studying the Intergenerational Transmission of Inequality From Mothers to Young Children." *Social Psychology Quarterly* 53(2): 132-147.

Peterson, J., and N. Zill. 1986. "Marital Disruption and Behavior Problems in Children." *Journal of Marriage and Family* 48: 295-307.

Piotrkowski, C. S., and M. H. Katz. 1982. "Indirect Socialization of Children: The Effects of Mothers' Jobs on Academic Behaviors." *Child Development* 53: 1520-1529.

Polit, D. 1995. *Parenting Measures in the New Chance 18-Month Survey.* New York: Manpower Demonstration Research Corporation.

Siegal, G. L., and L. A. Loman. 1991. *Child Care and AFDC Recipients in Illinois: Patterns, Problems, and Needs.* St Louis, MO: Institute of Applied Research.

Storrs, M. 1998. "Working Together to Help Families." *Child Support Report,* XX(10). Washington, DC: Office of Child Support Enforcement, Administration for Children and Families, U. S. Department of Health and Human Services.

Vandell, D. L., and J. Ramanan. 1992. "Effects of Early and Recent Maternal Employment on Children From Low-Income Families." *Child Development* 63: 938-949.

Woods, M. B. 1972. "The Unsupervised Child of the Working Mother." *Developmental Psychology* 6: 14-25.

Zaslow, M., B. Rabinovich, and J. Suwalsky. 1991. "From Maternal Employment to Child Outcomes: Pre-Existing Group Differences and Moderating Variables." Pp. 237-282 in *Employed Mothers and Their Children*. New York: Garland Publishing, Inc.

Zaslow, M., K. Tout, S. Smith, and K. Moore. 1998. "Implications of the 1996 Welfare Legislation for Children: A Research Perspective." *Social Policy Report of the Society for Research in Child Development*, XII(3).

Zaslow, M. J., and C. A. Emig. 1997. "When Low-Income Mothers Go to Work: Implications for Children." *Future of Children* 7(1): 110-115.

Zill, N. 1985. *Behavior Problems Index*. Washington, DC: Child Trends.

THE EFFECTS OF FAMILY OBLIGATIONS AND WORKPLACE RESOURCES ON MEN'S AND WOMEN'S USE OF FAMILY LEAVES

Joanne C. Sandberg

ABSTRACT

Growing numbers of employees must balance the demands of the workplace with caregiving obligations at home. One strategy used by some employees to meet the conflicting responsibilities is to take leaves from work. Although approximately half of the workforce is currently entitled to take family leaves under federal legislation, we still have relatively little information about the variables that influence leave-taking decisions. The paper draws upon the *Family and Medical Leave* Commission's 1995 national survey of employees (which oversamples leave-takers and leave-needers) to explore this issue. Multinomial logistic regression is used to analyze the effects that family obligations and workplace resources have on the odds of employees taking family leaves from work. The results indicate that family obligations have significant effects on both men's and women's use of family leaves. Workplace

Research in the Sociology of Work, Volume 7, pages 261-281.
Copyright © 1999 by JAI Press Inc.
ISBN: 0-7623-0605-X

resources, however, are better predictors of men's use of family leaves than women's use of family leaves.

INTRODUCTION

Increasing numbers of employees in the United States can expect to need time away from their paid work to care for newborns, ill family members, or aging parents. Despite the growing numbers of workers with significant caregiving responsibilities, information about women's and men's utilization of family leaves in this country is remarkably scant. Furthermore, knowledge about the effects of gender on employees' use of formal and informal family leaves is insufficient. This study will contribute to our knowledge about family leaves through a gendered analysis of the effects of workplace resources and family obligations on leave-taking behavior of U.S. workers.

COMBINING WORK AND FAMILY

At times the demands of work and family become difficult, if not impossible, to reconcile. Some employees have dealt with the conflicting demands by taking leaves from work. With the implementation of the *Family and Medical Leave Act* (FMLA) in 1993, approximately 55 percent of the workforce is federally guaranteed the right to take up to 12 weeks per year of unpaid family and medical leaves (Commission on Family and Medical Leave 1996). The provision of unpaid leaves enables covered employees to take leaves for their own "serious health conditions," those of members of their immediate families, or to care for newborns, newly adopted children, or newly placed foster children without risking their jobs or medical benefits. Despite the number of workers who have the federally protected right to take leaves and the number of workers who may reasonably expect to be in the position of needing to take leaves during their work-life, we know very little about women's and men's leave-taking behavior.

The potential for conflict between work and family demands is immediately apparent when one views recent changes in employment and demographic patterns. Between 1960 and 1995 in the United States, the labor force participation rate of married women with children under the age of six rose from 18.6 percent to 63.5 percent. Married women with older, minor children and single, divorced, and widowed mothers substantially increased their participation in the paid labor force as well. Men's labor force participation rates did not show a corresponding decrease during that period to offset changes in women's employment. In addition, more people are living longer. This increase is particularly noticeable among those 85 and older, those who tend to need the most care (U.S. Bureau of the Census 1996). The changes in women's patterns of labor force participation (and relative lack of change in men's) and increased life expectancy result in a labor force that has increased caretaking responsibilities. Many American employees may therefore need to take family leaves at some point during their years in the paid work force.

Many companies have experienced pressure to adapt their policies to meet the needs of the increasing number of employees with family responsibilities. Some changes in workplace benefits can be directly attributed to changes in state and federal legislation. In addition, employers are increasingly aware that situations at home affect employees at the worksite. Benefits to employers, such as reduced absenteeism, decreased turnover (particularly among women), and increased productivity have also encouraged the expansion of "family-friendly" benefits. These benefits include an array of services available to employees, such as referral services for child care and elder care, and seminars on issues faced by workers with dependent care responsibilities. Employers may also provide on-site child care, flexi-time, part-time work, "family days," and lengthy paid or unpaid family leaves (Hyland 1995; Hewitt Associates 1991; Pitt-Catsouphes, Mirvis and Litchfield 1995).

Despite the fact that many employees in the United States may need to take family leaves, information about leave taking remains limited. Knowledge about men's and women's use of family leaves is restricted, in part, due to the data. Many studies focus on particular organizations or geographic regions. These studies may be limited by the small number of people included in the study, the lack of information about the frequency of leaves among the employee population as a whole, and/or the potential uniqueness of the particular regions or worksites (Bond et al. 1991; Fried 1996; Hochschild 1997; Hyde, Essex and Horton 1993). Some data sets have very few work or family variables, limiting the complexity of analysis (Hyde, Essex and Horton 1993). Others explore only men's or women's use of family leaves, restricting the opportunity to directly compare the gendered effects of work and family variables (Hyde, Essex and Horton 1993; Joesch 1994; Hofferth 1996).

Studies that explore specific types of family leaves face unique limitations as well. Research that examines women's behavior following childbirth frequently do not have data that allow one to discern whether women quit their jobs and later reentered to the paid labor force or took leaves from work following the birth of their children (see Joesch's 1994 study, for example).[1] Others do not explore leave-taking as a dependent variable (e.g., Hofferth 1996).

Between 75 and 91 percent of men take some time off following the birth of a child, often drawing upon vacation days and personal days that employees and employers often do not regard as parental leaves (Bond et al. 1991; Hyde, Essex and Horton 1993; Pleck 1993). This highlights the fact that informal leaves (those that do not explicitly draw upon formal company policy or state or federal legislation) as well as formal leaves (those taken formally under federal or state legislation or company policy) need to be included in analyses. However, formal leaves often remain the primary focus of the analyses of men's and women's use of family leaves (Fried 1996; Hochschild 1997). In a similar vein, although there are quite a few studies that examine women's and, to some degree, men's absences from work due to child care and elder care (sometimes including spousal care) responsibilities, they often do not distinguish between time away from work to care for seriously ill family members and other family concerns (Gewirtz 1995; Neal, Ingersoll-Dayton and Starrels 1997; Scharlack and Boyd 1989; Stone, Caffarata and Sangl 1987). This limits our ability to understand how employees deal with their families' serious health conditions or newborn care.

The reports issued by the Commission on Family and Medical Leaves (1996) and University of Michigan's Survey Research Center (McGonagle et al. 1995) draw from the same national data set of male and female employees that is used in this analysis. Although their studies explore a range of variables that influence leave-taking behavior, the omission of sophisticated multivariate analyses limits our understanding of the complex interplay of the effects of different work and family variables. Sandberg and Cornfield (forthcoming) also draw upon the FMLA data set to explore leave-taking behavior using multivariate analyses. That study, however, examines the gendered effects of workplace and family constraints and resources on decisions to return from both family and medical leaves, not the likelihood of taking family leaves.

Current research has not adequately addressed employees' family leave decisions. Geographic limitations, lack of distinction between leaves and withdrawal from the paid labor market, and the virtual absence of multivariate analyses based on a national sample of male and female employees that includes questions about use of family leaves limits our understanding of leave-taking behavior. In addition, research has not explored the likelihood of employees taking family leaves versus (a) taking medical leaves, (b) needing but not taking leaves, and (c) neither needing nor taking leaves. This study is a multivariate analysis that explores the gendered effects of family responsibilities and workplace resources on the likelihood of taking family leaves versus falling into the three other categories listed above. It is based on a national probability sample of male and female employees, and should therefore provide a significant contribution to our understanding of the gendered use of family leaves.

Gendered Nature Of Caregiving And Breadwinning

Decisions about whether to take family leaves occur at the intersection of workplace and caretaking obligations. Although women have entered the workplace in increasing numbers, caregiving and breadwinning continue to be gendered. Women, in general, have more responsibility for the day to day care of family members, including those who are sick or newborns, than men. Men, in contrast, often emphasize their financial contributions to their households.

Caregiving remains disproportionately associated with women, and is reflected in attitudes and practices associated with the care of children and ill adults.

Although many studies have suggested that men provide more child care than a generation ago, most women still provide the majority of actual care and hold more responsibility for the care of their children. This is true for single mothers as well as employed women in dual-income households (Coltrane 1996; Coverman 1985; Gerson 1993; Hertz 1986; Hochschild 1989, 1997). Women also tend to spend more time providing care for aging parents than men (Galinsky, Bond and Friedman 1993; Ingersoll-Dayton, Starrels and Dowler 1996; Stone, Caffarata and Sangl 1987). Although there is some conflicting evidence (Neal, Ingersoll-Dayton and Starrels 1997), research indicates that men generally provide care that fits into their schedules more easily while women are more likely to provide personal care and perform daily chores that have a greater potential to conflict with employment obligations (Matthews 1995; Stoller 1990).

The impact of gender may be less strong for spousal care than for other types of care. There is conflicting evidence regarding whether wives provide more care for ailing partners than husbands (Allen 1994; Enright 1991; Stone, Caffarata and Sangl 1987). However, husbands generally receive more assistance caring for their spouses than wives do. This holds true for employed caretakers as well as those not in the paid labor market (Allen 1994; Enright 1991).

Breadwinning has been associated with the normative role for men in their families. It entails a sense of responsibility for the financial needs of their households, and identification of their income as providing for basic needs, as opposed to items that are optional or extra. Furthermore, their contributions as wage earners form an important and central component of their self-understanding. Even when men are unable to fulfill their expectations of what constitutes a "good" breadwinner, the cultural ideal still provides a yardstick against which they often judge themselves (Gerson 1993; Potuchek 1997).

Economic concerns may influence leave-taking decisions as well. Women, on average, earn less than men, even in dual-income households (Bond, Galinsky and Swanberg 1998). Couples may therefore decide that it is rational for wives to bear primary responsibility for family caregiving, while husbands focus on paid employment (Becker 1991). Furthermore, the gendered nature of caregiving and breadwinning roles makes many men reluctant to take formal or unpaid family leaves. Men therefore often draw upon informal paid options, such as vacation days, when they take leaves (Fried 1996; Pleck 1993). Nor is it surprising that fathers who are able to take paid time off from work to care for sick children without sacrificing vacation days or having to make excuses about their absences are more likely to take leaves than fathers without similar options (Bond, Galinsky and Swanberg 1998). Finally, after childbirth, women need leaves to physically recuperate. Taking leaves after children are born therefore becomes a necessity for mothers, while being optional for fathers.

Gender may influence leave-taking decisions through the norms workers experience at the workplace. Employers and coworkers often have greater acceptance of women's dual obligations as caregivers and employees than of men's dual obligations (Gewirtz 1996; Hochschild 1997). Since the attitudes of supervisors are more predictive of reduction in work-family conflict than the presence of "family-friendly" policies and programs, gendered expectations at the workplace may strongly influence leave-taking decisions (Galinsky Bond and Friedman 1996).

Family Obligations and Workplace Resources

This study focuses on the effects of family obligations and workplace resources on the use of family leaves. Family obligations represent the potential caretaking responsibilities that employees may have for family members. Workplace resources are used in this study to indicate the availability of conditions at work that enable employees to take leaves more easily than they could otherwise. They reflect conditions and benefits available to workers that may reduce the actual or perceived negative ramifications of taking family leaves.

Employees' families represent potential obligations. Minor children in the household may become seriously ill and need parental care. Furthermore, the presence of infants reflects that newborn care would have been needed during the previous year. The number of potential caregiving recipients would be expected to influence the likelihood that workers need family leaves.

Being married may increase potential obligations, although the situation is complex. The key effect of marriage may be the presence of an additional person, the spouse, who may need care. Since husbands and wives both appear to provide significant amounts of care for their ailing partners, this effect could be significant for both men and women.

Since it is true that more men than women have a partner who is not in the paid labor market (Galinsky, Bond and Friedman 1993), a greater percentage of men than women have partners who are potentially available to provide care to family members during work hours. However, the presence and employment status of the spouse do not appear to have a significant effect on the number of days that employees miss paid work to care for their children, suggesting that marital status would have a limited effect on the use of leaves to care for sick children (Galinsky, Bond and Friedman 1993; Hofferth et al. 1991). Marriage does appear to have at least one benefit for women: among women who are primary caretakers of their parents, married women receive more assistance than their non-married counterparts, primarily from their husbands and children (Brody et al. 1994). As a whole, it therefore appears that being married may function more as an obligation than a resource in the context of family leave decisions.

Working at larger worksites can provide a resource for workers through a variety of mechanisms. Worksites that have at least 50 employees at one site are covered under the FMLA. Also, larger companies generally provide better benefits than smaller organizations, although findings are mixed regarding the effect of size on leave benefits (Galinsky, Bond and Friedman 1993; Glass and Fujimoto 1995).

However, workplace size may reflect the availability of benefits such as having access to paid vacation days or sick days, that may influence workers' ability to take informal family leaves. In addition, in some organizations availability of multiple formal family benefits may signal that upper management is concerned about work-family issues, be it out of concern for employees, employee retention, or increased productivity.

Workplace size may also indicate that the workload of an individual can be more easily absorbed by others or temporarily reassigned. At large workplaces there may be numerous employees who possess comparable skills, and the organizations may have sufficient resources to hire temporary help. These factors may influence employees' likelihood of taking leaves (Commission on Family and Medical Leave 1996). Since larger worksites may have more ways to cover the work of leave-takers, the pressure on workers to forgo leaves may be reduced.

Having worked for the same employer for an extended period of time may also make it easier for employees to take family leaves. Employees must have worked for the same employer for at least one year to be eligible to take leaves under the FMLA. Since employees often accrue vacation days and sick days over time (U.S. Dept. of Labor and Labor Statistics 1996), employees who have worked for an employer for an extended period of time often have more formal and informal options (such as vacation and personal sick days) than recently hired workers. Finally, employees who have had sufficient time to demonstrate their capabilities and commitment to their jobs may be more likely to ask for, and receive, time away from work to care for their families.

The expected effects of full-time (versus part-time employment) are not as clear. Employees must have worked at least 1,250 hours for the same employer during the previous year to be eligible to take leaves under the FMLA. In addition, part-time employees are less likely to have paid vacation time or paid sick time to use for family leaves (Bond, Galinsky and Swanberg 1998). Research on shift work and child care suggests that some women who work part-time appear to limit their work hours due to difficulty finding adequate child care (Presser 1988); other findings suggest that many women choose part-time work because it enables them to meet the demands of their families more easily (Rothstein 1996). Female part-time workers may therefore be more willing to take leaves from their work to care for family members. Although the effects may be mixed, working more hours may be conceptualized best as a resource since it is associated with better access to benefits.

Salaried employees generally have better benefits than nonsalaried workers. As Bond, Galinky, and Swanberg's 1998 study indicated, a greater percentage of salaried than hourly employees have paid vacation and paid personal sick days. They also found that parents who hold management and professional jobs (and therefore most likely to be salaried) are more likely to be able to take paid time away from work to care for ill children and not lose vacation days than parents who hold other types of jobs. However, women in upper management often experience the same degree of pressure as that often felt by men at all levels to not take family leaves

(Fried 1996). Gender and status in the workplace may therefore influence leave-taking decisions.

Prior to the implementation of the FMLA, being a union member increased workers' likelihood of having formal access to unpaid maternity and paternity leaves. It did not, however, increase the likelihood of having paid parental leaves, a situation particularly detrimental to those with lower household incomes. Nor were union members more likely to have paid vacations or paid sick days than employees not covered by union contracts (Glass and Fujimoto 1995; Wiatrowski 1995). However, the emphasis on workers' rights may enable unionized employees to take family leaves more easily than those not covered by union contracts.

The gendered effects of workplace resources and family obligations on employees' leave-taking decisions remains understudied. Since increasing numbers of men and women can expect to face caretaking responsibilities during their work lives, this is an important area for research. Current literature suggests that work and family resources and obligations, as well as widely held norms, may influence employees' leave-taking decisions. However, men and women may not be similarly influenced by these factors. It is therefore important to determine how gender interacts with workplace opportunities and family obligations.

DECISION TO TAKE FAMILY LEAVES

Men and women face different expectations, responsibilities, and opportunities that have the potential to influence the decisions they make regarding families and work. Caregiving is generally associated with women, breadwinning with men. Although men's participation is substantial in some households, women generally perform more caretaking for family members than men, even when part of two-income households. Furthermore, women need to physically recuperate following the birth of children, due to labor and delivery. Given these conditions, I posit:

Hypothesis A1.   female employees will take leaves to care for ill or newborn family members more frequently than male employees, even when they have comparable family obligations.

Women spend more time than men on caretaking tasks, even among couples or siblings who share. Furthermore, women's caretaking tasks tend to be chores that cannot be easily postponed or reserved for weekends. It therefore appears that family demands will have a greater effect on women's use of time than men's. I therefore posit:

Hypothesis A2.   women's family obligations will have a greater effect on their likelihood of taking family leaves than men's family obligations have on their likelihood of taking family leaves.

Workplace resources may influence the opportunities that employees have to take leaves, both formal and informal. However, as discussed above, the norms, including those in the workplace, support women's role as caregiver more strongly than men's role as caregiver. Therefore, regardless of resources at the workplace, women may be more likely than men to feel as if they have no choice but to take family leaves (formal or informal) when the need arises. Since men may perceive that taking family leaves is optional for them, workplace resources may have a greater effect on their leave-taking decisions. I therefore posit:

Hypothesis A3.   controlling for family responsibilities, workplace resources will have a greater impact on men's likelihood of taking family leaves than women's.

Methods

In order to test my hypotheses listed above, I use the FMLA data set. The University of Michigan Survey Research Center conducted a national telephone survey to gather the data for the U.S. Commission on Family and Medical Leave. The data set has the advantage of being the first national probability sample designed to explore both men's and women's decisions and experiences regarding taking family and medical leaves. Since leave-takers and leave-needers were oversampled, the sample size is large enough to enable me to conduct multivariate analyses.

The sample was restricted to adults who were in the paid work force at some point between January 1994 and the summer of 1995, when the survey was conducted. Since the researchers wanted to oversample leave-takers and leave-needers, they first conducted an initial screening of 8,492 households. This enabled them to determine the percentage of workers who fell in each and to select an appropriate number from each category for the detailed survey (McGonagle et al. 1995). The following question was used during the initial screening to determine the leave-taking status of all adult household members who were or had been in the paid labor force during the specified period:

> Since January 1, 1994, (have you, has RELATIONSHIP) taken a leave from work to care for a newborn, newly adopted or new foster child or for (your/their) own serious health condition, the serious health condition of (you/their) child, spouse, or parent that lasted more than 3 days or required an overnight hospital stay? (McGonagle et al. 1995, Appendix III, p. 2).

The wording of the question corresponds to the basic restrictions of the FMLA. Since the respondents were told that leaves refer to both unpaid and paid time off from work, including vacation days or personal sick days, formal as well as informal leaves are included in the data. However, approximately nine percent of family leave-takers took leave to care for family members not covered under the FMLA. Based on the information gained from the initial screening, the researchers selected individuals to include in the detailed survey, resulting in

2254 completed surveys, with a large oversampling of leave-takers ($n = 1218$) and leave-needers (those who needed a leave but did not take one; $n = 206$). I excluded cases with missing independent variables (other than income, for which values were imputed), reducing the effective number of cases to 2186.[2] Of these, 1033 are men, and 1153 are women.

Likelihood of Taking Family Leave

I use multinomial logistic regression to examine the effects of family obligations and workplace resources on the likelihood of taking family leaves. The full sample includes both males and females, and gender is controlled through use of an independent variable. I then split the full sample used in the first model to explore interaction effects, with separate analyses run for women and men.

Multinomial logistic regression is particularly well-suited for the data and questions posed in this analysis. Since multinomial logistic regression is a form of logistic regression, it allows for the inclusion of continuous as well as dichotomous independent variables. This method has the additional advantage of allowing the dependent variable to reflect a discrete set of choices (Agresti 1990). This enables me to compare the odds of respondents taking family leaves to the odds of falling into one of several other categories. The response variable indicates that between January 1, 1994 and the time of the survey, approximately 18 months later, the respondents (1) took leaves to care for family members with serious health conditions, or to care for newborns, or newly adopted or placed children, (2) took leaves for their own serious health conditions (including maternity-related illnesses), (3) needed, but did not take leaves, or (4) neither needed nor took leaves. Respondents who had multiple leaves were instructed to think only of their longest leave when completing the survey. The advantage of using multinomial logistic regression, as opposed to logistic regression, is that it does not force me to assume that all non-family leave-takers are alike, and therefore allows for a more nuanced examination of leave-taking behavior.

The results of the multinomial logistic regressions examine the effects of the covariates on the odds of taking family leaves versus neither needing nor taking leaves, the odds to taking family leaves versus needing, but not taking, family leaves, and the odds of taking family leaves versus medical leaves.

Predictor Variables

In order to test the hypotheses listed above that explore the effects of family obligations and workplace resources on employee's leave-taking behavior, three sets of variables, other than gender (female = 1), are used.

Family Obligations

The first set of variables reflects family obligations and therefore family care-giving demands that employees may experience. The number of minor children in the household indicates the potential need to take family leaves to care for off-spring. It is reflected by a set of dummy variables, 1 child, 2 children, and > 2 children. Having no minor children in the household is the omitted category. The set of dummy variables was used since the preliminary analysis indicated that the number of children has a nonlinear effect.[3] Two family variables indicate employees' participation in ongoing obligations: whether the respondents care for an ill person (yes = 1; only three are non-family members) or a baby, newly adopted child or newly placed foster child on a daily basis at the time of the survey (yes = 1; only three were newly adopted or placed). Being married (yes = 1) can reflect the presence of an additional person who may need care. Marriage may also represent the availability of an additional person to share caregiving tasks, and, particularly for women, the availability of another income in the household. On balance, however, it may have its greatest effect in terms of increasing the possibility that employees may need leaves to care for their spouses.

Workplace Resources

Workplace resources reflect workplace conditions that minimize the costs (both monetary and nonmonetary) and perceptions of the costs of taking family leaves. Being covered by a union contract (yes = 1), being salaried (yes = 1), having worked for the same employer for at least 12 months during the previous 18-month period (yes = 1) and having worked at a worksite with at least 50 employees within a 75-mile radius (yes = 1) all appear to reflect resources that may enable employees to take needed family leaves more easily. Similarly, working at least 25 hours a week (yes = 1) may signify a resource since full-time employment is associated with access to benefits that may reduce the negative effects of taking family leaves.

Socioeconomic and Demographic Variables

Finally, variables that control for the socioeconomic and demographic background of the respondents are included since they often influence opportunities and constraints experienced by employees. The race of the respondents is reflected by a set of dichotomous variables that reflects whether the workers are African American (yes = 1), Latino/a (yes = 1), or belonged to another nonwhite group (yes = 1). Nonhispanic whites is the omitted category. Age is reflected in a dichotomous measure that indicates whether the respondent is as old as or older than the median age of 38 years (yes = 1). The dichotomous measure is used since it appears to have the best fit in the preliminary analysis, possibly a reflection of a cohort effect.

Education reflects a six-point scale, from not being a high school graduate to having had some graduate work.[4] Since preliminary analysis indicated that income has a nonlinear effect in the full sample, I use a set of three dummy income variables for the full sample.[5] In the gender-specific models, the logarithmic value of household income is used, and is logged to reduce skewness. Since the model fit for the set of three dichotomous household income variables is not significantly better than with the continuous measure of the income variable for either of the subsamples (male or female), as it is in the full sample, the more parsimonious variable for income is included in the gender-specific models. Finally, missing income[6] is a dummy variable that reflects whether an imputed value is used.

The mean values of the dependent and independent variables are compared by gender. I computed weighted means since the comparison would vastly overrepresent the effect of leave-takers and leave-needers otherwise. Unweighted values are used for the multinomial logistic regressions since the weights primarily reflect the oversampling of leave-takers and leave-needers, which is taken into account in the response variable.

Results

The weighted means, as shown in Table 1, reflect that there are significant differences between women's and men's leave-taking behavior. More women than men take both family leaves and medical leaves. Men and women are equally likely to be leave-needers, however. Men are more likely than women to have neither taken nor needed leaves than women.

There are gender differences in family obligations as well. Employed women in this sample are more likely than men to care for newborn children, newly adopted children or newly placed foster children on a daily basis. Although more women than men care for family members, this difference is not significant. Furthermore, we do not know the relative amount of time that men and women caretakers spend on tasks or the types of tasks performed. More women than men have two children. Finally, more employed men than women are married.

Among workplace variables, there are two significant differences. Women work in larger establishments than men and are therefore more likely to be employed at workplaces covered under the FMLA. Men are, however, more likely than women to work at least 25 hours a week.

Results from the multinomial logistic regression full sample indicate that gender has a significant and substantial effect on leave-taking behavior. Gender does not appear to affect the likelihood of taking family versus medical leaves. However, women employees have a 75 percent greater likelihood (odds ratio of 1.754) of taking family leaves versus neither needing nor taking leaves than men. This is significant at $p < .001$. Women are also 43 percent more likely than men to take family leaves than to need leaves but not take them ($p < .05$). (Full results are available upon request.) Hypothesis 1 is therefore supported. It

Table 1. Weighted Means and Standard Deviations of Variables by Gender

	Women n = 1153		Men n = 1033	
	Mean	*S.D.*	*Mean*	*S.D.*
Leave-taker status				
Took family leave	0.080***	0.254	0.046	0.223
Needed leave	0.036	0.174	0.033	0.189
Took medical leave	0.130***	0.316	0.087	0.298
No leave	0.755***	0.404	0.834	0.395
Family Variables				
Care-ill	0.041	0.186	0.030	0.182
Care-baby	0.040**	0.184	0.019	0.143
1 child	0.188	0.366	0.166	0.394
2 children	0.189*	0.367	0.157	0.386
> 2 children	0.085	0.261	0.087	0.299
Married	0.595***	0.461	0.693	0.489
Work Variables				
50 employees	0.702**	0.429	0.643	0.508
Same employer	0.882	0.302	0.867	0.360
≥ 25 hours	0.889***	0.295	0.972	0.175
Salaried	0.368	0.452	0.394	0.518
Union Contract	0.149	0.334	0.173	0.401
Controls				
White	0.783***	0.387	0.840	0.388
African American	0.103**	0.285	0.070	0.271
Latino/a	0.072	0.242	0.056	0.243
Other Race/Ethnicity	0.042	0.189	0.034	0.191
Age	39.156	11.430	39.770	13.488
Education	4.030	1.128	3.951	1.315
Household Income	46,375	57,761	48,598	65,056
Missing Income	0.218*	0.387	0.257	0.463

Notes: *$p < .05$
**$p < .01$
***$p < .001$
Men's and women's means significantly different

appears that women take family leaves more frequently than men, even when work resources and family responsibilities are controlled. This finding is consistent with other research that indicates that, even among couples and siblings who share in the care of their children and parents, women usually bear the primary responsibility for coordinating and providing care (Coltrane 1996; Gerson 1993; Hertz 1986; Matthews 1995).

The results do not support Hypothesis 2, which posits that women's family responsibilities will have a greater effect on their likelihood of taking family leaves than men's family responsibilities have on their likelihood of taking family leaves. As Table 2 indicates, caring for ill family members on a daily basis has a significant and positive effect on both men's and women's likelihood of taking family leaves versus no leaves, and taking family leaves versus medical leaves. Furthermore, the coefficients do not vary significantly by gender. Some family variables do, however, affect men and women employees' likelihood of taking family leaves differently. The presence of minor children in the household has a strong and positive effect on men's likelihood of taking family leaves versus not taking needed leaves, an effect that is not present for women. Furthermore, the *t*-tests of the coefficients indicate that the effects of having one child on the likelihood of taking family leaves versus no leaves or medical leaves are significantly greater for men than women. It is not clear why this is so. It may be that the presence of children may compel men to take needed leaves more than non-children family demands or their own medical conditions, or they may feel fewer sanctions for taking leaves to care for children than other family members.

In addition, caring for infants on a daily basis significantly increases women's likelihood of taking family leaves versus needing, but not taking family leaves. This effect is not present among men. This effect of caring for infants among women may reflect the necessity that women take leaves after the labor and delivery. Since women need at least some period of physical recovery after childbirth, they have very little choice but to take leaves, although the lengths vary significantly.

Although marital status does not affect men's leave-taking decisions, being married does increase the likelihood that employed women will take family leaves rather than remain at work when family leaves are needed. The effect of marriage on women's leave-taking decisions may be due, in part, to the availability of another income in married women's households, which could reduce the negative impact of taking leaves. Access to a second income could be particularly important if the needed leaves would be unpaid. This suggests that marriage might best be considered a leave-taking resource for women. The lack of significance for men's leave-taking decisions may reflect that breadwinning norms reinforce men's ties to paid work regardless of the presence of a second income in the household.

There is some support for Hypothesis 3 which posits that, controlling for family responsibilities and socioeconomic characteristics, workplace resources will have a greater effect on men's leave-taking decisions than women's leave-taking decisions. As Table 2 indicates, the only workplace variable examined that affects women's decisions to take family leaves is the number of hours worked. Women who work at least 25 hours per week are more likely than those who work fewer hours to take family leaves versus neither needing nor taking leaves. No other workplace condition has a significant effect on women's leave-taking decisions.

Table 2. Multinomial Logistic Regression of Leave-Taking Behavior on Gender, Family, and Control Variables, Split Sample Odds Ratio Regression Coefficient

	Women N = 1153			Men N = 1033		
	Family Leave vs. No Leave	*Family Leave vs. Need Leave*	*Family Leave vs. Medical Leave*	*Family Leave vs. No Leave*	*Family Leave vs. Need Leave*	*Family Leave vs. Medical Leave*
Intercept	(−2.063)*	(0.552)	(−2.041)**	(−2.870)**	(0.205)	(−1.313)
Family						
Care-ill	7.691***	1.341	1.875*	5.988***	2.404	3.246**
	(2.040)	(0.293)	(0.629)	(1.790)	(0.877)	(1.178)
Care-baby	14.527***	28.115***	2.461***	8.530***	1.547	3.680**
	(2.676)	(3.336)	(0.901)	(2.144)	(0.436)	(1.303)
1 child	1.855**	1.079	1.756**	4.366***	3.637***	3.906***
	(0.618)	(0.076)	(0.563)	(1.474)	(1.291)	(1.363)
2 children	2.627***	1.447	2.142***	4.276***	3.077**	4.343***
	(0.961)	(0.369)	(0.762)	(1.453)	(1.124)	(1.469)
> 2 children	2.296**	2.258	4.354***	4.446***	3.681**	5.108***
	(0.831)	(0.815)	(1.471)	(1.429)	(1.303)	(1.631)
Married	1.295	1.963**	1.239	0.871	1.008	1.188
	(0.259)	(0.675)	(0.215)	(−0.139)	(0.008)	(0.172)
Work Var.						
50 employees	1.158	1.138	1.001	1.668*	1.858*	1.364
	(0.147)	(0.130)	(0.001)	(0.512)	(0.620)	(0.310)
Same employer	1.082	1.050	1.169	0.860	0.502	0.646
	(0.079)	(0.049)	(0.156)	(−0.151)	(−0.690)	(−0.437)
≥ 25 hours	1.826*	0.375	0.766	0.678	0.214	0.372
	(0.602)	(−0.981)	(−0.266)	(−0.389)	(−1.543)	(−0.990)
Salaried	0.872	1.473	1.087	1.339	2.072*	1.918**
	(−0.137)	(0.387)	(0.084)	(0.292)	(0.729)	(0.651)
Union Contract	0.923	1.048	0.797	0.845	0.933	0.600
	(−0.080)	(0.047)	(−0.227)	(−0.168)	(−0.070)	(−0.511)
Controls						
African American	0.613	0.315***	0.568*	1.408	0.779	1.219
	(−0.490)	(−1.155)	(−0.566)	(0.342)	(−0.250)	(0.198)
Latino/a	0.824	0.842	0.792	2.223*	1.220	1.670
	(−0.193)	(−0.173)	(−0.233)	(0.799)	(0.199)	(0.513)

(continued)

Table 2   (Continued)

	Women (N = 1153)			Men (N = 1033)		
	Family Leave vs. No Leave	Family Leave vs. Need Leave	Family Leave vs. Medical Leave	Family Leave vs. No Leave	Family Leave vs. Need Leave	Family Leave vs. Medical Leave
Other race/ethnicity	0.810 (−0.211)	0.970 (−0.030)	0.778 (−0.250)	1.079 (0.076)	0.551 (−0.597)	0.896 (−0.109)
≥ 38 years	0.785 (−0.242)	0.646 (−0.436)	0.932 (−0.070)	0.506** (−0.681)	0.491** (−0.711)	0.342*** (-1.073)
Education	1.177 (0.163)	1.123 (0.116)	1.226* (0.204)	1.180 (0.166)	1.099 (0.094)	1.178 (0.164)
Household Incomelog	0.969 (−0.032)	1.002 (0.002)	1.010 (0.010)	1.051 (0.049)	1.066 (0.064)	1.024 (0.024)
Missing income	0.927 (−0.076)	1.503 (0.408)	1.191 (0.175)	0.748 (−0.291)	2.205* (0.791)	1.132 (0.124)

Notes: *$p \leq .05$
          **$p \leq .01$
          ***$p \leq .001$

Size of workplace and being a salaried employee both affect men's leave-taking behavior. Being employed at a worksite having at least 50 employees increases men's likelihood both of taking family leaves, compared to neither taking nor needing leaves, and of taking family leaves versus needing, but not taking leaves. This does not appear to be a direct result of coverage under the FMLA. Substituting a single variable that reflects eligibility to take leaves under the FMLA (as determined by working at a covered worksite for one year and averaging at 25 least hours a week) for the three components in the model indicates that eligibility does not have a significant effect on leave-taking behavior (not shown). It may therefore be that better benefits, such as lengthier paid vacations and sick days, that are often associated with larger organizations, may influence men's leave-taking decisions. The availability of a greater number of coworkers at large worksites who may be able to perform some of the leave-takers tasks may reduce pressure on men to not take family leaves.

In addition, the findings reveal that salaried men are more likely than nonsalaried men to take family leaves versus needing leaves, and are more likely to take family leaves versus medical leaves. Salaried employees may have more job flexibility that could enable them to take family leaves, particularly short leaves, more easily. The importance of this job condition is highlighted by Neal, Ingersoll-Dayton and Starrels' (1997) finding that job flexibility does influence the number of days employees take off to care for non-child family members. The effect of being salaried on leave-taking behavior may also be a result of better benefit packages often associated with being salaried employees.

It is also interesting to note that being African American decreases women's likelihood of taking family leaves versus needing, but not taking, family leaves or taking medical leaves (as reflected in odds ratio values of less than one). This effect is not present for men. The findings may reflect that African Americans generally have poorer benefits and less job flexibility than many non-minority workers (Galinsky, Bond and Friedman 1993). Latino men are more likely to take family leaves than not take leaves. Finally, it is notable that there seems to be a cohort effect for men but not women. Age does not seem to influence women's leave-taking behavior, while younger men are more likely than older men to take family leaves. Younger men may therefore be more open to taking time off from work to care for family members than older men.

DISCUSSION

The results of this study confirm that employees' decisions to take family leaves are influenced by gender, thus supporting Hypothesis 1. This remains true even when family responsibilities and workplace resources are controlled. Since two of the family variables reflect ongoing participation in caretaking activities, as opposed to merely having family members who may need someone's assistance, these findings are particularly interesting. Even when provision of daily care for ill family members or infants is held constant (although the amount of time spent on caretaking tasks is not), being female continues to increase workers' likelihood of taking family leaves. This is consistent with previous research that has found that even when caretaking tasks are shared, women tend to perform the majority of the work, especially among tasks that cannot be easily postponed (Mathews 1995; Stoller 1990).

Hypothesis 2, that caregiving responsibilities will have a greater effect on the leave-taking behavior of women than men, is not supported. Both male and female workers appear to be strongly influenced by their obligations. Children, who may potentially need extended care, increase both men's and women's likelihood of taking family leaves. Furthermore, actual provision of daily care affects employees' use of family leaves. Leave-taking decisions therefore appear to be influenced by ongoing patterns of care. Although marriage has a significant effect on women's but not men's leave-taking decisions, it is also true that the presence of children influences men's, but not women's, likelihood of taking family leaves versus needing leaves.

The final hypothesis receives moderate support. Workplace resources appear to influence men's decisions to take family leaves more than they do women's. Although the number of workplace resources that influences men's leave-taking behavior is limited, it does appear that men' leave-taking decisions may be more readily affected by opportunities at the workplace than women's. Men may perceive that taking family leaves is somewhat discretionary and therefore their decisions are more easily influenced by workplace opportunities than women's.

CONCLUSION

The results of this study highlight the importance of conducting gendered analyses of U.S. employees' leave-taking behavior. Although women take family leaves more frequently than men, family demands have significant and substantial effects on both men's and women's leave-taking decisions. It therefore appears that many men, as well as women, experience pressure to manage the demands of paid employment with the need to provide care for family members. However, the effects of family obligations and workplace resources on leave-taking decisions are not identical for women and men employees. This suggests that it would be useful to integrate a gendered analysis into additional research on employees' family leave behavior.

As noted, the findings of this study suggest that workplace conditions influence men's likelihood of taking family leaves. This is consistent with research that finds that men who can care for sick children without losing pay, vacation days, or who must present more "legitimate" reasons for their absences are more likely to take time away for work to care for ill children than fathers without similar options (Bond, Galinsky and Swanberg 1998). Hochschild (1997), on the other hand, highlights the degree to which men rarely limit their time at the workplace in order to attend to their families. Even men who initially attempt to hold their employers' demands in check seem unable to sustain their resolve over time, given the gendered norms at the workplace and the approval given to men who demonstrate whole-hearted commitment to their jobs. However, her study was limited to one worksite. In contrast, the findings from the FMLA data indicate that men's use of informal and formal leaves are affected by workplace opportunities. It would therefore be fruitful to explore more fully how conditions of employment, workplace policies, and company culture can increase men's opportunities to care for the needs of their ill and newly added family members when necessary.

Finally, the significant effects of family obligations and workplace opportunities on men's and women's use of family leaves suggest that further research is needed to examine how family obligations may interact with workplace conditions to influence leave-taking behavior. This area of inquiry could enable us to better understand the experiences of caregivers who juggle employers' and families' needs and how workplaces can enable workers to manage their dual obligations more easily.

NOTES

1.   We know much more about the leave-taking behavior of European men and women following the birth of a child. Haas (1992, 1993) provides a particularly helpful examination of variables that influence men's and women's experiences following the birth of a child.

2.   Most of the independent variables in the model are dichotomous. Education, which is ordinal, accounts for only four of the cases that were deleted due to missing values. When missing education values were repalced with the mean, the results are virtually identical to those presented in this paper.

3.   In order to determine the best-fit model, I tested whether the number of children has a linear relationships to the dependent variable. Due to the small number of households with more than three children, I created a set of dummy variables reflecting whether a respondent had one, two, or more than two children less than the age of 18 in the household (none being the omitted category). In addition, the number of children was made into a dichotomous variable which simply reflected whether one or more children were present in the household. The models with the set of dummy variables and the single dichotomous variables were run separately. The results of each new model were then compared to the baseline model. The coefficients for the set of dummy variables were examined to determine whether age has a nonlinear effect. Since it appeared to be nonlinear, the chi square of the set of dummy variables were compared to the ordinal and dichotomous variables. The set of dummy variables provided significantly more explantory power, and was therefore incorporated into the final model.

4.   A set of five dummy variables corresponding to the five highest levels of education, as determined by the survey instrument, were also included in the preliminary analysis. The lowest level of education was the comparison. Education was also recorded into a dichotomous variable reflecting whether the respondent was a college graduate. This variable was created since credentials, as opposed to simply years of education, may have a significant effect. Comparisons of these reconfigured models to the baseline model which included the ordinal measure for the full sample, indicated that the ordinal measure should be retained.

5.   Respondents with an income of $24,005 to $37,986 fall within the second quartile. Those with household incomes that extend from $37,987 to $54,994 are in the third quartile, and those with incomes over $54,994 fall within the fourth quartile. The lowest quartile is the omitted category (Demaris 1992).

6.   If the respondent refused to give an exact figured for income, several additional questions were asked. These questions were designed to enable researches to identify the range within which the respondent's income fell. For each possible range, the median income was computed, based on the values given by respondents who gave exact figures within each particular range. The appropriate median values were then used in the cases in which the respondents refused to giver precise, or any, income values.

REFERENCES

Agresti, A. 1990. *Catagorical Data Analysis*. New York: Wiley.

Allen, S. M. 1994. "Gender Differences in Spousal Caregiving and Unmet Need for Care." *Journal of Gerontology* 49(4): S187-S195.

Becker, G. S. 1991. *A Treatise on the Family: Enlarged Edition*. Cambridge, MA: Harvard University Press.

Bond, J. T. E. Galinsky, M. Lord, G. L. Staines, and K. R. Brown. 1991. *Beyond the Parental Leave Debate: The Impact of Laws in Four States*. New York: Families and Work Institute.

Bond, J. T., E. Galinsky, and J. E. Swanberg. 1998. *The 1998 National Study of the Changing Workforce*. New York: Families and Work Institute

Brody, E. M., S. J. Vitvin, S. M. Albert, and C. J. Hoffman. 1994. "Marital Status of Daughters and Patterns of Parent Care." *Journal of Gerenotology* 49(2): S95-S103.

Catalyst. 1986. *Report on a National Study of Parental Leaves.* New York: Catalyst.

Coltrane, S. 1996. *Family Man: Fatherhood, Housework and Gender Equity.* New York: Oxford University Press.

Commission on Family and Medical Leave. 1996. *A Workable Balance: Report to Congress on Family and Medical Leave Policies.* Washington, DC: Women's Bureau, U.S. Department of Labor.

Coverman, S. 1985. "Explaining Husband's Domestic Labor." *The Sociological Quarterly* 26(1) 81-97.

Demaris, Alfred.1992. *Logit Modeling: Practical Applications.* Newbury Park, CA: Sage Publications.

Enright, R. B., Jr. 1991. "Time Spent Caregiving and Help Received by Spouses and Adult Children of Brain-Impaired Adults." *The Gerontologist* 3(3): 375-383.

Fried, M. 1996. *Caregiving Choices, Company Voices: Workplace Cultures and Parental Leave at Premium, Inc.* Unpublished Dissertation. Brandeis University.

Galinsky, E., J. T. Bond, and D. E. Friedman. 1993. *The Changing Workforce: Highlights of The National Study.* New York: Families and Work Institute.

Gerson, K. 1993. *No Man' Land: Men's Changing Commitments to Family and Work.* New York: Basic Books.

Gewirtz, M. L. 1995. *Employers' Perspectives Regarding Eldercare Initiatives: The Experience at Travelers.* Unpublished Dissertation. Boston University.

Glass, J., and T. Fujimoto. 1995. "Employer Characteristics and The Provision of Family Responsive Policies." *Work and Occupations* 22(4): 380-411.

Haas, L. 1993. "Nurturing Fathers and Working Mothers: Changing Gender Roles in Sweden." In *Men, Work and Family.* Newbury Park, CA: Sage Publications Inc.

_____. 1992. *Equal Parenthood and Social Policy: A Study of Parental Leave in Sweden.* Albany, NY: State University of New York Press.

Hertz, R. 1986. *More Equal than Others: Women and Men in Dual-Career Marriages.* Berkeley, CA: University of California Press.

Hewitt Associates. 1991. *Work and Family Benefits Provided by Major U.S. Employers in 1991: Based on Practices of 1,026 Employers.* Spec Summary. Lincolnshire, IL: Hewitt Associates.

Hochschild, A. R. 1997. *The Time Bind: When Work Becomes Home and Home Becomes Work.* New York: Henry Holt and Co., Inc.

Hochschild, A. with A. Machung. 1989. *The Second Shift.* New York: Avon Books.

Hofferth, S. A. 1996. "Effects of Public and Private Policies on Working After Childbirth." *Work and Occupations* 23(4): 378-404.

Hofferth, S. A., A. Brayfield, S. Deich, and P. Holcomb. 1991. *National Child Care Survey, 1990.* Urban Institute Report 91-5. Washington, DC: The Urban Institute Press.

Hyde, J. S., M. J. Essex, and F. Horton. 1993. "Fathers and Parental Leave: Attitudes and Experiences." *Journal of Family Issues* 14(4): 616-641.

Hyland, S. 1995. *Helping Employees with Family Care. Employee Benefits Survey: A BLS Reader.* Bulletin 2459.

Ingersoll-Dayton, B., M. E. Starrels, and D. Dowler. 1996. "Caregiving for Parents and Parents-In-Law: Is Gender Important?" *The Gerontologist* 36(4): 483-491.

Joesch, J. M. 1994. "Children and The Timing of Women's Paid Work after Childbirth: A Further Specification of The Relationship." *Journal of Marriage and the Family* 56: 429-440.

Long, J. S. 1997. *Regression Models for Categorical and Limited Dependent Variables.* Thousand Oaks, CA: Sage Publications.

McGonagle, K. A., J. Connor, S. Heeringa, P. Veerkamp, and R. M. Groves. 1995. *Commission Leave Survey of Employees on the Impact of the Family and Medical Leave Act.* Institute for Social Research, Survey Research Center, The University of Michigan.

Matthews, S. H. 1995. "Gender and the Division of Filial Responsibility between Lone Sisters and their Brothers." *Journal of Gerontology* 50B(5): S312-S320.

Neal, M. B., B. Ingersoll-Dayton, and M. Starrels. 1997. "Gender and Relationship Differences in Caregiving Patterns and Consequences among Employed Caregivers." *The Gerontologist* 37(6): 804-816.

Pitt-Catsouphes, M., P. K. Mirvis, and L. C. Litchfield. 1995. *Behind the Scenes: Corporate Environment and Work-Family Initiatives.* Boston, MA: Center on Work and Family at Boston University.

Pleck, J. H. 1993. Are 'Family Supportive' Employer Policies Relevant to Men? In *Men, Work and Family.* Newbury Park, CA: Sage Publications Inc.

Potuchek, J. L. 1997. *Who Supports the Family? Gender and Breadwinning in Dual-Earner Marriages.* Stanford, CA: Stanford University Press.

Presser, H. B. 1988. "Shift Work and Child Care among Young, Dual-Earner American Parents." *Journal of Marriage and the Family* 50(1): 133-148.

Rothstein, D. S. 1996. "Entry into and Consequences of Nonstandard Work Arrangements." *Monthly Labor Review,* 119(10): 75-82.

Scharlach, A. E., and S. L. Boyd. 1989. "Caregiving and Employment: Results of an Employer Survey." *The Gerontologist* 29: 382-387.

Stoller, E. P. 1990. "Males as Helpers: The Role of Sons, Relatives and Friends." *The Gerontologist* 30(2): 228-235.

Stone, R., G. L. Caffarata, and J. Sangl. 1987. "Caregivers of the Frail Elderly: A National Profile." *The Gerontologist* 27: 616-626.

Trzcinski, E., and M. Finn-Stevenson. 1991. "A Response to Arguments Against Mandated Parental Leave: Findings from the Connecticut Survey of Parental Leave Policies." *Journal of Marriage and the Family* 53(2): 445-460.

U.S. Bureau of the Census. 1996. *Statistical Abstract of the United States.* 116th Edition. Washington, DC.

U.S. Dept. of Labor and Bureau of Labor Statistics. *Employee Benefits in Small Private Establishments, 1994, Bulletin 2475.* 1996. Washington, DC: U.S. Department of Labor and Bureau of Labor Statistics.

Wiatrowski, W. J. 1995 "Employee Benefits for Union and Nonunion Workers." In *Employee Benefits Survey: A BLS Reader, Bulletin 2459.* Washington, DC: Bureau of Labor Statistics.

Printed in the United States
84994LV00001B/13/A